The Unwilling and The Reluctant

The Unwilling and
The Reluctant:
Theoretical Perspectives on Disobedience in the Military

Edited by
Craig Leslie Mantle

Copyright © 2006 Her Majesty the Queen, as represented by the Minister of National Defence.

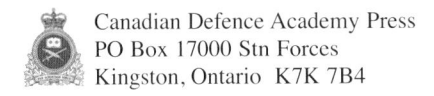

Canadian Defence Academy Press
PO Box 17000 Stn Forces
Kingston, Ontario K7K 7B4

Produced for the Canadian Defence Academy Press
by 17 Wing Publishing Office.
WPO 30160

Front Cover Image: Anne S.K. Brown Military Collection, Brown University Library
Back Cover Image: Library and Archives Canada, C-037591, "Scenes at La Prairie, 1812-1813"

Library and Archives Canada Cataloguing in Publication

The unwilling and the reluctant : theoretical perspectives on disobedience in the military / Craig Leslie Mantle (editor).

Issued by Canadian Defence Academy
Includes bibliographical references.

Soft Cover
ISBN 0-662-43251-7
Cat. no.: D4-5/1-2006E

Hard Cover
ISBN 0-662-43273-8
Cat. no.: D4-5/1-2006-1E

1. Military discipline—Canada. 2. Military offenses—Canada. 3. Canada. Canadian Armed Forces—Discipline. 4. Military discipline. 5. Command of troops. I. Mantle, Craig Leslie, 1977- II. Canadian Defence Academy

UB26.U58   2006 355.1'30971   C2006-980117-7

Printed in Canada

1 3 5 7 9 10 8 6 4 2

ACKNOWLEDGEMENTS

Winston Churchill once said, "Writing a book is an adventure. To begin with, it is a toy and an amusement; then it becomes a mistress, and then it becomes a master, and then a tyrant. The last phase is that just as you are about to be reconciled to your servitude, you kill the monster, and fling him out to the public." I think Sir Winston would be genuinely pleased to know that my experience here differed little from his own!

Despite having but a single editor, this volume was the product of a collective effort, or in other words, many have helped me to slay the proverbial monster. From the outset, numerous individuals, both military and civilian alike, offered their encouragement and assistance to this project. Without their support, this book could not have been realized. First and foremost, I would like to thank Colonel, Dr. Bernd Horn, the Director of the Canadian Forces Leadership Institute, for his confidence in the editor, his wise counsel, his direction, and most of all, his patience. His experience in both military and academic settings proved exceptionally beneficial, not only during the formulation and subsequent expansion of this project, but also during the editing and publishing phases. Such support is indeed rare and I am grateful for his efforts. In much the same vein, Howard Coombs aptly played the roles of colleague, champion and friend. His unwavering enthusiasm and passion are truly commendable.

Joanne Simms and Carol Jackson, the administrative staff of CFLI, deserve special mention for their service over the past year. They ensured that every organizational need of this project – and there were a great many – were met in a timely, professional and cheerful manner. Their assistance was nothing short of invaluable and they made my responsibilities lighter by degrees. Other members of CFLI gave freely of their time and knowledge as well. Lieutenant-Colonel, Dr. Allister MacIntyre and Dr. Robert Walker served as my links to the world of psychology, while Dr. Daniel Lagacé-Roy and Mélanie Denis offered their expertise *en français*. Commander Bob Edwards, as usual, was a source of constant support. Although providing technical assistance to the Canadian Defence Academy as a whole, Erik Hormann was always available to answer my information-age questions and to fix my broken information-age machines.

To the many members of today's Canadian Forces who provided their insight into the issues that are discussed herein, I must offer my sincere gratitude. Whether through formal interviews, a story told in the halls or a quick chat over a "coffee" in the mess, their candour and eagerness to help a civilian understand the cultural nuances and dynamics of the military is deeply appreciated and I am all the better for their efforts. They are indeed professionals in every sense of the word. Specifically, I would like to thank Corporal Al Hennessey, Sergeant Kurt Grant, Chief Warrant Officer Mike Boland, Chief Warrant Officer Robert Lamothe, Chief Warrant Officer Jules Moreau, Major

ACKNOWLEDGEMENTS

Tony Balasevicius, Major Brent Beardsley, Major Dave Lambert and Lieutenant-Colonel Mike Goodspeed.

I would be remiss if I did not acknowledge the efforts of the many contributors whose work appears in this book. It has been a pleasure to work with them all. Their cheerful readiness to endure my many inquiries for clarification speaks volumes about their character, as does their willingness to allow their work to be critiqued and edited by a relative newcomer to the world of academe. If I was a burden in any way, I apologize, but I think that the final product more than justifies these intrusions and I hope that they will agree.

And finally, but no less important, I should like to thank my wife, Angela, who has endured the demands of this volume with her typical grace and understanding. She has sacrificed much and received little in return, and for that I am truly thankful. My only hope is that she will be willing to endure this process yet again.

TABLE OF CONTENTS

Foreword	....	v
Preface	....	vii
Introduction	....	1
Chapter 1	....	13
	Obedience to Military Authority: A Psychological Perspective *Peter Bradley*	
Chapter 2	....	43
	Loyal Mutineers: An Examination of the Connection between Leadership and Disobedience in the Canadian Army since 1885 *Craig Leslie Mantle*	
Chapter 3	....	87
	Mutiny and the Royal Canadian Navy *Christopher M. Bell*	
Chapter 4	....	113
	Beyond Mutiny? – Instrumental and Expressive Understandings of Contemporary "Collective Indiscipline" *Christopher Ankersen*	
Chapter 5	....	127
	A Law Unto Themselves? – Elitism as a Catalyst for Disobedience *Bernd Horn*	
Chapter 6	....	145
	Combat Stress Reaction and the Act of Disobedience: Does the Significance of Acts of Disobedience Diminish Under the Pressure of Combat Stress? *Gordon (Joe) Sharpe and George Dowler*	
Chapter 7	....	169
	"But … It's Not My Fault!" – Disobedience as a Function of Fear *Bernd Horn*	
Chapter 8	....	193
	Disobedience of Professional Norms: Ethos, Responsibility Orientation and Somalia *George Shorey*	
Chapter 9	....	213
	"We Don't Like You, Sir!" – Informal Revenge as a Mode of Military Resistance in the British Army *Charles Kirke*	
Contributors	....	235
Glossary	....	237
Index	....	241

FOREWORD

I am pleased to introduce *The Unwilling and The Reluctant: Theoretical Perspectives on Disobedience in the Military*. As part of the Canadian Forces Leadership Institute's Strategic Leadership Writing Project, this volume is yet another effort by the Canadian Defence Academy to provide service members with both innovative and practical knowledge that they can apply on a daily basis, whether serving in garrison or while deployed on operations. This seminal volume is truly groundbreaking. Never before has so much attention and effort been directed toward the issue of disobedience in the specific context of the Canadian Forces. As a result, this book represents a significant milestone in our collective professional development.

Admittedly, this topic is controversial and may be unsettling to some. Above all, disobedience is anathema to what is expected of all Canadian Forces members. In the end, though, disobedience has been a constant throughout history. Nonetheless, it is only through candid discourse and discussion that the origins and parameters of this type of behaviour can be fully understood and reconciled. By being fully informed, leaders at all levels can strive to prevent its occurrence. This volume, therefore, is both timely and relevant. I trust that it will effectively serve to educate and inform the military and academic communities, as well as the public at large. Moreover, the Canadian Defence Academy looks forward to the discussion that this book will generate.

P.R. Hussey
Major-General
Commander
Canadian Defence Academy

PREFACE

The Canadian Forces Leadership Institute (CFLI) is proud to release the latest addition to its Strategic Leadership Writing Project, which is designed to create a distinct body of Canadian operational leadership knowledge to assist with the professional development of military personnel, as well as to educate the public in regards to the Canadian Forces' contribution to the nation. This volume, *The Unwilling and The Reluctant: Theoretical Perspectives on Disobedience in the Military*, is especially noteworthy since it breaks ground that has not previously been examined in detail. Specifically, this book, the first of a seminal series of three volumes, examines the theory and practice of disobedience in the military.

This subject is often taboo. After all, disobedience often indicates a lack of professionalism, control and / or poor leadership. Therefore, it is always easier, if not prudent, for those who are career minded to let such matters fade quietly into history and encourage a focus on the more dramatic and inspiring aspects of military art and science, such as heroic leadership and great battles. However, disobedience is a reality that has always, and will always, be present in military affairs. Its impact can be insidious, as well as cataclysmic. It can determine the fate of leaders and battles, if not the survival of nations. As such, it is essential that the issue of disobedience be examined, analyzed and discussed in detail. The better leaders understand the root causes and contributing factors to disobedience, the more empowered they will be to prevent its occurrence. As the cliché goes – knowledge is power.

I believe you will find this volume, which focuses on the theory and practical aspects of disobedience, both interesting and enlightening. Importantly, it provides the background and context for the next two volumes, which examine specific case studies of military disobedience throughout Canadian history. I encourage all to participate in the discussion of this very important topic. We at CFLI welcome your comments.

Bernd Horn
Colonel
Director
Canadian Forces Leadership Institute

INTRODUCTION

Disobedience has been a constant throughout the Canadian military experience. The many conflicts and operations in which Canadians have participated have all been marked, to one extent or another, by inappropriate conduct. The 20th century certainly witnessed its fair share of such behaviour: the loss of discipline that accompanied the refusal of Canadian soldiers to continue their engagement in South Africa in 1900; the demobilization riots at Kinmel Park in 1919; the disturbances that accompanied Victory in Europe Day celebrations in Halifax in 1945; the abuse, attempted rape and murder of Korean civilians in 1951; and the torture-killing of a Somali youth and the misconduct at Bacovici and elsewhere in the Former Yugoslavia in the early- to mid-1990s, during the so-called "Decade of Darkness," are but a few of the more notable and disturbing examples.[1] Many more instances, surely, have escaped the public's eye and the historian's pen. At all times, therefore, disobedience has been the unwanted and constant companion of honourable and praiseworthy conduct, conduct that has brought great credit to Canada and the nation's military and which has exemplified the "highest standards of military professionalism."[2] This reality is unlikely ever to change, the reasons for which, this volume will make clear.

All in all, large-scale mutinies and serious breaches of discipline are generally absent from the Canadian record, but the smaller, less dramatic and sometimes barely noticeable acts of disobedience most certainly are not. Much debate has surrounded the causes of both. An early work on mutiny, written by T.H. Wintringham in the mid-1930s, viewed such conduct as singular "…battles in the struggle between classes, a struggle that runs through all the events of history; the cause underlying all mutinies is the refusal of subject classes to remain in subjection, to accept the limits allotted to them."[3] More recently, Elihu Rose argued that mutinies sometimes stemmed:

> … from the belief by the troops that an aspect of their service is unacceptable for ethical, moral, intellectual, or political reasons. Unwilling to participate in a particular military undertaking, they protest the essential nature of their duty rather than its material condition. The troops are, in effect, concerned with the 'why' rather than the 'how' of their employment.[4]

Drawing on the writings of the intellectual historian and philosopher Michel Foucault, Leonard Smith claimed that mutinies, especially those witnessed in the French Army in 1917, were an outgrowth of a "power relationship" in which the protagonists – the leaders and the led – constantly negotiated the parameters of authority. Disobedient "confrontations," according to this theory, erased "…the rules of the old power relationship and put in place new ones" that guided conduct from that point onward until another confrontation redefined the prevailing boundaries yet again.[5]

INTRODUCTION

But the debate does not end there. Leonard Guttridge contended that a "gross personal failure of officership" contributed to the outbreak of such instances.[6] Another historian, Lawrence James, believed that disobedience resulted primarily from the conditions of service to which personnel were exposed. Such instances of misconduct:

> ...were protests by servicemen who felt that their sufferings had become so unbearable that only the last resort of collective action could achieve relief. Such mutineers believed that they were justified by natural justice and that this, coupled with the seriousness of their complaints, outweighed all the forms of naval and military law which they were breaking. Complaints were invariably confined to injuries which had their causes in the everyday routine of service life. Overwork, unpalatable or inadequate rations, the removal of privileges, the imposition of new burdens, uncomfortable accommodation, heartless officers and NCOs, vindictive and excessive punishments, low wages and, in earlier periods, slowness in their payment, were the commonest sources of discontent and mutiny. Behind mutinies for such causes was the implication that officers had broken their word or else had been indifferent towards their men's well-being.[7]

James also believed that many of the disturbances that occurred within the military forces of Great Britain and the Commonwealth were due to the unchangeable civilian proclivities of the participants. Once in the military, so it was assumed, many "...continued to think that in some ways they could continue to behave as if they were still civilians," and this behaviour oftentimes consisted of questioning authority and relying on strikes as a means of expressing their dissatisfaction.[8] And finally, Jane Hathaway warned that mutinies rarely "...stem solely from the mundane material grievances that have become cliché." Instead, "...revolts typically draw on much wider-ranging, long-term social and political ills."[9]

Many scholars have put forth many reasons that, in their estimation, account for the outbreak of disobedience. Following in this tradition, this volume also seeks to uncover the underlying causes of disobedient conduct. Admittedly, some of the explanatory factors raised herein are not particularly novel, for they oftentimes echo and expand upon some of the aforementioned points. Conversely, several causes are indeed fresh and innovative and provide a different perspective altogether. This volume differs from those that have come before in that the issue of disobedience has been approached from a multi-disciplinary perspective. History, psychology, sociology and anthropology are all well represented and therefore each chapter provides a different analysis of a common issue. What is revealed in one is frequently expounded upon, or indeed confirmed, in another. It is heartening to see so many disciplines arriving at similar conclusions and for similar

INTRODUCTION

reasons. The strength of this work also lies in the fact that both academics and serving officers, who are often established academics in their own right, have contributed to this volume. This mix, which offers academic rigour combined with the perspective of experienced practitioners, again allows for the exploration of this issue from different, yet complementary, perspectives. It is therefore hoped that the following chapters will allow for a greater understanding of disobedience, not only in a Canadian context, but in an international setting as well.

This volume also continues the recent trend of focussing on disobedience from a purely academic, rather than a popular, perspective.[10] This emphasis, perhaps, is a result of the general willingness of the historical community at large to devote greater attention and effort to the more "social" side of military history. While some still study campaigns and the individuals who led them, others have started to devote considerable attention to topics that, until recently, would barely have mustered any notice at all. Now, the role, life and experiences of the individual, usually as they relate *to* specific campaigns and *to* specific leaders, are of great interest. Topics that were once relegated to the lonely solitude of a footnote, or not mentioned at all, have now become article- or book-length explorations.[11]

Unlike nearly every other work on the subject, this volume will neither argue about nor dwell on the definitions and nuances of such terms as "disobedience" and "mutiny." Other researchers have discussed the development and usage of these terms in the context of many Western nations, most notably Great Britain and the United States, and interested readers are encouraged to consult these works.[12] No concerted effort has been made here to synthesize these many arguments into a coherent whole, although some contributing authors do explain these terms as general preludes to their chapters. For the purposes of this volume, disobedience will be understood as the failure of military personnel to follow the orders of their superiors to the best of their ability. Being broad and general, this definition is one that will probably resonate with the majority of readers, and as such, it suits the following discussion. According to this definition, disobedience need not be confined to the outright refusal of orders. Executing the letter but not the spirit of a directive and exacting revenge to "even the score" for a past wrong are but two examples of disobedient conduct. As will become clear, those under arms resorted to other forms of protest as well. Disobedience consequently encompasses a wide spectrum of behaviours that range from the serious and grave, like "fragging" [13] and mutiny, to the relatively benign and mundane, such as malingering. All of these behaviours, regardless of their nature, negatively impact the good order, discipline and overall efficiency of the military unit in which they occur, however large or small.

When beginning to examine the issue of disobedience in the military, the Canadian Forces Leadership Institute (CFLI) thought that a single volume

INTRODUCTION

that included theoretical discussions supported by relevant historical examples drawn from the Canadian experience was indeed best and most practical. Faced with an overwhelming willingness of both the academic and military communities to discuss and debate this issue, CFLI soon realized that a much larger undertaking was not only required, but in fact justified. For this reason, what was originally intended as a single tome blossomed into three. As the first in this "series," this volume discusses some of the more theoretical aspects of disobedience; the second provides historical examples from 1812 to 1919; and the third offers a number of interesting case studies from 1920 to the present. When dealing with instances of disobedience that have occurred in recent memory, the reader will appreciate the requirement to purposely omit those details that could potentially lead to the identification of the individuals involved. Taken together, these volumes explore the relationship between superior and subordinate in the context of the Canadian military over the last two centuries.

The theoretical grounding provided in this volume will hopefully offer additional insights into the case studies that will follow. On the other hand, issues that come to light in the historical case studies will undoubtedly add colour and a touch of realism to the more technical elements that are captured here. Although this "set" is comprised of three volumes, each can be used separately for none is so dependent on another that it cannot stand on its own merit. By design, each volume is intellectually separate and thus can be read as such. In the end, these three volumes will hopefully provide a more profound, comprehensive and in-depth look at the issues surrounding disobedience than would otherwise have been possible with one.

This volume is roughly divided into three parts. The first offers broad discussions of disobedience; the second raises some issues that might be considered in mitigation of such behaviour; and the third expands upon particular issues that were raised in earlier chapters. In sum, this volume offers a collection of learned studies that seek to describe, at its most fundamental level, the causes for, the manifestations of, and the means to prevent, disobedience. The following material is presented in the hope that it will spur additional research into these and other related areas. Additionally, it is also intended that these discussions will be of some use to our friends and allies as they too grapple with the realities of these behaviours within their own military forces.

Written by Lieutenant-Colonel (ret'd), Dr. Peter Bradley, Chapter 1 offers a psychological perspective on both obedience to and disobedience of military authority. Being a book that is principally concerned with the latter, it seemed logical to start with a discussion of what is expected, rather than what is feared. After describing a number of psychological theories that seek to explain how both obedience and disobedience occur, which are later put to good use in exploring a number of recent examples of misconduct,

INTRODUCTION

Bradley refers to the famous conformity experiments of Stanley Milgram and vividly demonstrates just how powerful the will to obey can be. He then proceeds to describe those circumstances in which disobedience is appropriate, such as when one is confronted with a "manifestly unlawful" order, and how disobedience sometimes results when the motivations of leaders and followers diverge. His chapter concludes with a number of suggestions that leaders might consider employing in order to encourage and reaffirm follower obedience.

Chapter 2 belongs to the editor and traces the intimate connection between leadership and disobedience over time in the context of the Canadian Army. Put simply, those leaders who exercised common sense and who respected and cared for their subordinates tended to encourage, on the whole, fewer acts of disobedience than those who were less conscientious and concerned. Certain themes that are raised in this particular discussion, such as the exacting of revenge by the disaffected, are explored in much greater detail in later chapters. Since leadership provides one of the overarching themes of this volume, it is introduced early so that the context of many of the following chapters can be established.

Authored by Dr. Christopher Bell, Chapter 3 again approaches the issue of disobedience, or more specifically, mutiny, from an historical perspective. Beginning with a general discussion of the various classes of mutiny in evidence during the first half of the 20th century – from those intended merely to correct local grievances to those that were attempts at social and political revolution – he shows that the Royal Canadian Navy (RCN) has a very long and well established tradition of mutiny that derived, in large measure, from the influence exerted by Great Britain's Royal Navy. He ably demonstrates that the spate of mutinies that racked the RCN during 1949 were not isolated incidents, to be understood on their own, but were rather manifestations of this tradition. Through the use of mess-deck lock-ins, which were non-violent and easily resolved, Canadian sailors attempted to inform their leaders that all was not well and that their ship was not "happy." Their grievances sometimes revolved around shipboard conditions, but more often than not, ratings took issue with the manner in which their leaders were treating them. In this respect, distinct parallels with the second chapter are evident.

Written by Christopher Ankersen, Chapter 4 underscores the fact that today's CF is not immune to large-scale mutiny. He begins his discussion by noting that mutinies still occur on the modern battlefield and that the likelihood that they will occur again is very real, especially amongst those individuals who question the validity of the dictum, "mission, troops, self." He continues by outlining the various mechanisms that Canadian service personnel can utilize to air their complaints and argues that the sheer number of such avenues has lulled some into believing that mutiny is all but impossible in this age of

INTRODUCTION

empowerment and voice since seeking redress for grievances has never been easier. He warns against viewing mutinies solely as a consequence of materialistic concerns, such as poor working conditions, and suggests that many acts of disobedience resulted from individuals who questioned the reason behind, rather than the manner of, their employment on the battlefield. In his estimation, the "why" has been a more powerful factor in encouraging misconduct than the "how." Complacency and arrogance, he cautions, must not cloud the fact that mass disobedience, because of the success that it has enjoyed in the past, will always be a viable option for those who choose not to avail themselves of the many sanctioned methods for voicing their displeasure.

The next few chapters move away from a general discussion of disobedience and focus primarily on the idea of mitigation. These studies challenge the reader to decide just how much weight, if any, such factors like stress and fear should really be given when faced with understanding or resolving an act of indiscipline. To be certain, there are no easy answers. In Chapter 5, Colonel, Dr. Bernd Horn examines the relationship between elitism and disobedience. He observes that a rigorous selection process, a special and differentiated role and a reputation for excellence all foster a "cult of the elite" in which members, acting as a "law unto themselves," define their own behavioural norms and standards of conduct. In this context, disobedience is not so much a reaction to local conditions, such as inadequate leadership, but is rather an outcome of the inherent culture of elite formations. Because leaders within elite units undergo the same rites of passage as those whom they command, they too belong to this "cult" and some ultimately permit, or in extreme cases commit, acts that run counter to conventional military behaviour and expectations.

Chapter 6, a joint effort of Brigadier-General (ret'd) Gordon Sharpe and Chief Petty Officer 1st Class (ret'd) George Dowler, employs the Command and Control model developed by Dr. Ross Pigeau and Carol McCann to explain the alleged 1993 poisoning of Warrant Officer (ret'd) Matt Stopford by a number of his subordinates in Croatia. After analyzing the difficult and stressful situation in which members of Stopford's platoon found themselves, the authors conclude that the poisoning resulted not from leadership failings, as is commonly believed, but rather occurred due to the composition of the platoon itself, in which members did not have a sufficient amount of time to bond with one another and to create the connections of trust and confidence that would probably have seen them through such an environment. Sharpe and Dowler ultimately question whether or not the adverse manifestations of combat stress, such as the poisoning of one's superiors, should be considered in the same vein as more traditional forms of mutiny in which the participants object to working conditions or failings in leadership. Like other contributors to this volume, they reinforce the notion that acts of disobedience usually have a deeper cause, rather than that which appears most plain and obvious.

INTRODUCTION

Chapter 7 continues the theme of mitigation with another chapter by Bernd Horn that exposes the link between fear and disobedience. Rather than viewing disobedience as a deliberate act taken by the disaffected in response to prevailing circumstances, he argues that a *de facto* disobedience – breaking and retreating, failing to fire one's weapon, becoming overly cautious or inactive, etc. – sometimes occurs amongst even the most loyal troops who are wrapped, even paralyzed, by fear. The causes of fear are clearly illustrated, as are its effects. Despite the potential for fear to erode military discipline and overall effectiveness, a number of remedies are provided to allay its pervasive nature, the majority of which relate to leadership and training. The remedies for fear are also, in part, the remedies for disobedience.

Lieutenant-Commander George Shorey concludes the discussion of mitigating circumstances in Chapter 8. Set against the backdrop of the Canadian deployment to Somalia in the early-1990s, he devotes considerable attention to the manner in which certain psychological factors, such as the bystander effect and the diffusion of responsibility, reduced the likelihood that soldiers who were aware of the beating being inflicted on the captured Somali youth, Shidane Arone, would come to his aid. While certainly not offering an excuse for the conduct of those who committed this heinous crime, he describes some of the factors that, at least in part, account for the unwillingness and reluctance of others to help someone who was clearly in distress. Lieutenant-Commander Shorey argues that in terms of preventative measures, Canada's military ethos must be continually espoused, practiced and internalized if disobedience toward lawful authority is to be minimized. Professional leadership, in which the ethos is reflected in all that the leader does, is put forward as a means to reduce undesirable conduct.

The focus of the volume shifts once again in Chapter 9 where Lieutenant-Colonel (ret'd), Dr. Charles Kirke examines "informal revenge" in the context of the British Army. He asserts that those acts that transgress the bounds of acceptable military conduct, but which fall short of the dramatic measures that are more characteristic of mutiny, are intended to inform leaders in no uncertain terms that their subordinates are dissatisfied with their leadership. By developing a model that explores organizational culture at the unit level, he convincingly demonstrates that manifestations of disobedience usually have deep cultural roots and these nuances must be examined and understood if the cause of "everyday resistance" is to be fully appreciated. He contends that such acts are very much a form of dialogue that disaffected soldiers frequently employ when regular channels of contact, either formal or informal, are not fully used or fail altogether. All in all, this chapter reinforces the themes of communication and leadership that earlier discussions raise. Dr. Kirke concludes his chapter by drawing parallels between the British and Canadian experiences, thus making his model all the more relevant to the study of similar events in the context of the Canadian military.

INTRODUCTION

The belief that disobedience, common as it is, has the potential to seriously impact the efficiency and effectiveness of units that are deployed on operations or garrisoned across the country gave impetus to this work. It must be made clear from the very outset that this volume was not written in response to any widespread disciplinary problem within today's Canadian Forces (CF). Although some argue that the CF *is* poorly disciplined – they cite, for instance, the sloppy dress amongst some personnel and the habitual failure of others to properly acknowledge the rank of their superior – there are many more who are just as convinced that discipline, as evidenced by the success that the CF has enjoyed in recent years in rebuilding its once-tarnished reputation, is on a relatively sure and stable footing. This volume, perhaps to the disappointment of some, will not come to any substantiated conclusion regarding the state of discipline within the CF today. Such an investigation must wait for another time and is perhaps best left to those who are better acquainted with such matters at the macro-level rather than the micro-level. This volume endeavours, first and foremost, to illustrate some of the many causes of disobedience and, by so doing, offers a few insights that might prevent such acts from occurring in the future. In peacetime and in wartime, disobedience of one sort or another has been, is, and will continue to be, a constant of military life. While increased opportunities for training and professional development will certainly help minimize the frequency and severity of disobedience, there will always be poor leaders, for instance, and stress and fear will always be present on operations.

The mission of the Canadian Defence Academy, and therefore that of CFLI as well, "…is to champion lifelong learning and Canadian Forces professional development thereby helping the men and women of the CF to deal with [the] complexities of current and future security environments through education."[14] It is hoped, therefore, that this volume, along with those that follow, will in some small measure contribute to realizing this all-important goal. If these works provide even one leader with additional insight into the problems of disobedience, then we shall all be satisfied with that singular result and our efforts will be more than amply justified and rewarded.

C.L.M.
Kingston

ENDNOTES

[1] Carman Miller, *Painting the Map Red: Canada and the South African War, 1899-1902* (Montreal and Kingston: McGill-Queen's University Press [MQUP], 1993), 141-47; Desmond Morton, "'Kicking and Complaining': Demobilization Riots in the Canadian Expeditionary Force, 1918-19," *Canadian Historical Review*, LXI, No. 3 (1980), 334-60; R.H. Caldwell, "The VE Day Riots in Halifax, 7-8 May 1945," *The*

Northern Mariner, Vol. 10, No. 1 (2000), 3-20; regarding Korea, see Chris Madsen, *Another Kind of Justice: Canadian Military Law from Confederation to Somalia* (Vancouver: University of British Columbia [UBC] Press, 1999), 109-10; *Dishonoured Legacy: The Lessons of the Somalia Affair: Report of the Commission of Inquiry into the Deployment of Canadian Forces to Somalia* (Ottawa: Public Works and Government Services Canada, 1997); Donna Winslow, "Misplaced Loyalties: The Role of Military Culture in the Breakdown of Discipline in Two Peace Operations," Ross Ellis Memorial Lecture in Military and Strategic Studies, University of Calgary, 21 January 1999; and Donna Winslow, *Bacovici: A Report on the Breakdown of Discipline in CANBAT II: A Report Prepared for the Chief of the Defence Staff* (1998). In Yugoslavia, Canadian soldiers were accused of committing such crimes as "misuse of alcohol, sexual misconduct, insubordination, violence and black market activities." See Winslow, "Misplaced Loyalties." And certainly, inappropriate conduct has not been confined to those units that have been deployed overseas; disobedience occurred in Canada as well. See, for instance, P. Whitney Lackenbauer, "The Military and 'Mob Rule:' The CEF Riots in Calgary, February 1916," *Canadian Military History*, Vol. 10, No. 1 (2001), 31-43, and P. Whitney Lackenbauer, "Under Siege: The CEF Attack on the RNWMP Barracks in Calgary, October 1916," *Alberta History*, Vol. 49, No. 3 (2001), 2-12. Official histories offer some evidence concerning disobedient conduct, but their treatment is minimal at best. Regarding the Canadian Army, see G.W.L. Nicholson, *Official History of the Canadian Army in the First World War: Canadian Expeditionary Force, 1914-1919* (Ottawa: Queen's Printer, 1962), 530-33, and C.P. Stacey, *Official History of the Canadian Army in the Second World War - Six Years of War: The Army in Canada, Britain and the Pacific* (Ottawa: Queen's Printer, 1966), 433, for a brief description of the troubles surrounding demobilization. Regarding the Royal Canadian Air Force (RCAF) and its antecedents, see S.F. Wise, *Canadian Airmen and the First World War: The Official History of the Royal Canadian Air Force*, Vol. I (Toronto: University of Toronto Press [UTP], 1980), 432-34, for evidence of a possible mutiny in 1917 by pilots who apparently refused to participate in a bombing and strafing run because "they did not consider that the probable results were worth the risk to machines and pilots." See also, W.A.B. Douglas, *The Creation of a National Air Force: The Official History of the Royal Canadian Air Force*, Vol. II (Toronto: UTP, 1986), 398, for evidence of the involvement of RCAF personnel in the Victory in Europe Day riots. More comprehensively, see Allan English, *The Cream of the Crop: Canadian Aircrew, 1939-1945* (Montreal and Kingston: MQUP, 1996), 82 and 93, for a discussion of those individuals who committed acts that could be regarded as disobedient, such as returning early from a mission without having flown over the target, flying at the edges of a target to avoid German flak, flying on only the safest of missions, etc. Concerning the RCN, the endnotes to Chapter 3 provide a detailed listing of the most significant works in the field that refer to disobedience.

INTRODUCTION

2   Canada, Department of National Defence, *Duty with Honour: The Profession of Arms in Canada* (Kingston: Canadian Defence Academy – Canadian Forces Leadership Institute, 2003), 2.

3   T.H. Wintringham, *Mutiny: Being a Survey of Mutinies From Spartacus To Invergordon* (London: Stanley Nott, 1936), 338.

4   Elihu Rose, "The Anatomy of Mutiny," *Armed Forces and Society*, Vol. 8, No. 4 (Summer 1982), 566.

5   Leonard V. Smith, *Between Mutiny and Obedience: The Case of the French Fifth Infantry Division During World War I* (New Jersey: Princeton University Press, 1994), 11-7. Another commentator has also raised the possibility of mutiny and disobedience as being "...simply another routine tactic in the negotiating repertoire..." of the troops; such action did not, therefore, constitute an "absolute challenge" to authority. See Rose, "Anatomy of Mutiny," 573. The notion of a reciprocal relationship has also been noted elsewhere. See, for instance, Herbert C. Kelman and V. Lee Hamilton, *Crimes of Obedience: Toward A Social Psychology of Authority and Responsibility* (New Haven: Yale University Press, 1989), 55.

6   Leonard F. Guttridge, *Mutiny: A History of Naval Insurrection* (Annapolis: Naval Institute Press, 1992), 2.

7   Lawrence James, *Mutiny in the British and Commonwealth Forces, 1797 – 1956* (London: Buchan & Enright, 1987), 13. Edmund Fuller would agree with this assessment for he observes, "Mutinies often are the work of men with just grievances, men under the utmost provocation." See Edmund Fuller, *Mutiny! Being Accounts of Insurrections, Famous and Infamous, on Land and Sea, from the Days of the Caesars to Modern Times* (New York: Crown Publishers, 1953), xii. He further contends, "Complaints, really a form of strike, over questions of pay, length of service, or food, are a frequent basis of mutiny." Fuller, *Mutiny!*, 250. Arrears in pay were certainly a cause of some mutinies in the ancient world. See Stefan Chrissanthos, "Caesar and the Mutiny of 47 B.C.," *Journal of Roman Studies*, Vol. XCI (2001), 63-75. Misconduct is further discussed from a classical perspective in Elizabeth Carney, "Macedonians and Mutiny: Discipline and Indiscipline in the Army of Philip and Alexander," *Classical Philology*, Vol. XCI (January 1996), 19-44.

8   James, *Mutiny in the British and Commonwealth Forces*, 9. To this end, "Since the adjustment to a world of compliance and quietism [never speaking up] was never easy for the masses of civilians unwillingly conscripted during periods of national crisis, mutinies became more frequent during world wars." Ibid., 12.

9   Jane Hathaway, ed. *Rebellion, Repression, Reinvention: Mutiny in Comparative Perspective* (Westport: Praeger, 2001), xv.

10   For example, held in Toronto, Ontario, in October 2004, the Inter-University Seminar on Armed Forces and Society (IUS) included a full panel on mutiny and disobedience. The work of many of the panellists is represented in either this volume or in the volumes of historical case studies that follow. Many of the works listed in endnote 3 of Chapter 3, which concern

INTRODUCTION

discipline in the RCN from its inception in 1910 to 1949, might also be seen to be part of this trend.

11   Only a representative selection of titles follow: Desmond Morton, *Fight or Pay: Soldiers' Families in the Great War* (Vancouver: UBC Press, 2004); Paul Jackson, *One of the Boys: Homosexuality in the Military during World War II* (Montreal and Kingston: MQUP, 2004); Tim Cook, "'More a medicine than a beverage': 'Demon Rum' and the Canadian Trench Soldier of the First World War," *Canadian Military History*, Vol. 9, No.1 (Winter 2000), 6-22; and Andrew B. Godefroy, *For Freedom and Honour? The Story of the 25 Canadian Volunteers Executed in the Great War* (Nepean: CEF Books, 1998). From the British perspective, see G.D. Sheffield, *Leadership in the Trenches: Officer-Man Relations, Morale and Discipline in the British Army in the Era of the First World War* (London: Macmillan, 2000).

12   Such discussions, for instance, can be found in Fuller, *Mutiny!*, ix-x; Rose, "Anatomy of Mutiny," 561-65; Hathaway, *Rebellion, Repression, Reinvention*, xii; Guttridge, *A History of Naval Insurrection*, 1-4; and, Christopher M. Bell and Bruce A. Elleman, *Naval Mutinies of the Twentieth Century: An International Perspective* (London: Frank Cass, 2003), 1-3.

13   The term "fragging" is used to describe the assassination or attempted assassination of leaders, be they commissioned or non-commissioned, who were perceived by their subordinates to be acting recklessly. See Richard Gabriel and Paul Savage, *Crisis in Command: Mismanagement in the Army* (New York: Hill & Wang, 1978).

14   Major-General P.R. Hussey, *Canadian Defence Academy Commander's Intent*, 2005, 1.

CHAPTER 1

Obedience to Military Authority: A Psychological Perspective

Peter Bradley

> *If the orders had always been obeyed, to the letter, the entire French army would have been massacred before August 1915.*[1]

The importance of obedience becomes clear in the first few hours of a military recruit's career. Typically, it begins with someone in authority, an officer or a squad instructor perhaps, making a request or giving a direction. It very quickly becomes apparent to everyone present that a compliant response is expected, and the quicker the better. Basic training is essentially an exercise in socialization and indoctrination into military culture, and obedience is one of the core values that are emphasized. Even though obedience is highly valued in the military profession, disobedience does occur, and this is not always a bad thing according to Jean Norton Cru, who is quoted above. Soldiers occasionally disobey orders, ignore certain rules and regulations, or fail to live up to the professional standards of military behaviour. (The word "soldier" is used here in a generic sense to refer to all military men and women, whether they be in the Army, Navy or Air Force, commissioned or non-commissioned.) Because disobedience is contrary to espoused military values, it is an issue that is worth examining.

This chapter presents theory and research from the field of psychology in an attempt to explain the factors that lead military personnel to obey or disobey. This chapter has eight sections. First, I establish the importance of obedience in the military, for the military is a unique organization in which the requirement for obedience is paramount. Second, I describe a number of psychological processes and theories that provide a conceptual framework for understanding how obedience and disobedience occur. Third, I introduce the conformity research of Stanley Milgram, a remarkable series of studies that illustrate just how far people will go to obey those in authority. Fourth, I present some thoughts on disobedience in the military with an emphasis on the tendency to display outward compliance toward military authority while privately rebelling. Fifth, I describe some circumstances in which disobedience is appropriate. Sixth, I show how the motivations of leaders and followers differ and how this may contribute to disobedience. Seventh, I provide several "real life" cases of disobedience in the military and explain how these cases may have been influenced by some of the psychological processes discussed earlier. Eighth, I complete the chapter with some suggestions that leaders might consider for encouraging follower obedience.

The Central Role of Obedience in the Military

Military personnel have a duty to obey those above them in the chain of command and, at the same time, have the right to demand obedience from those

CHAPTER 1

below them. Documents like the *National Defence Act*, the *Queen's Regulations and Orders* (*QR&Os*) and others, instruct all military personnel to obey lawful authority. These same documents also give legitimate authority to military leaders and prescribe when, where and how they can expect others to obey them. While the duty to obey appears relatively straightforward, the duties of leaders with respect to their followers are more complex, more loosely defined and typically revolve around the obligation to provide discipline and competent leadership.

But why is obedience important in the military? In the introduction to his study of obedience and mutiny in the French Army during the First World War, Leonard Smith points out that military operations are hierarchical activities, "thought out and organized from above, and executed (however imperfectly) from below."[2] Thus, obedience is essential if military operations are to be effective. According to Samuel Huntington, obedience and loyalty are "the highest military virtues."[3] Field-Marshal Wilhelm Kietel describes obedience as a "cardinal virtue."[4] Huntington contends that the military exists to serve the state and is organized in a hierarchy of obedience wherein orders come down from senior political authorities through the chain of command. When it comes to obedience, he leaves no room for equivocation:

> When the military man receives a legal order from an authorized superior, he does not argue, he does not hesitate, he does not substitute his own views; he obeys instantly. He is judged not by the policies he implements, but rather by the promptness and efficacy with which he carries them out. His goal is to perfect an instrument of obedience...."[5]

In a thoughtful article on obedience, Lieutenant-Colonel Kenneth Wenker contends that military personnel should obey for three reasons. First, soldiers make a promise to obey the orders of their superiors (i.e., the oath of allegiance made on enrolment) when they join the military. Promises are supposed to be kept, particularly this one, and its importance is underscored by the solemn, if brief, ceremony in which the oath is made. Second, this promise is actually more than a simple promise. It is a contract and thus entails an obligation of justice that is stronger than the obligation of fidelity linked with promise keeping. Wenker's third point is one of functionality. The military's goals are the nation's goals and must therefore be obeyed. According to Wenker, authorities higher in the chain of command should be obeyed because: 1) they have more experience and a better appreciation of the situation; 2) they are legitimate authorities; and 3) most of the time, they are right. As a result, the soldier's duty is to follow the orders of the nation as expressed by his or her chain of command.[6]

Another writer on the subject of obedience in the military, Michael Wheeler, makes an important distinction between blind, unquestioning obedience and reflective obedience. While some in the military might applaud blind obedience, pointing to combat situations as evidence that the military requires immediate, unquestioning obedience, Wheeler suggests that, even in combat, there is often time for a more reflective obedience. The problem with blind obedience is that "when soldiers have in fact wrapped themselves up in their jobs and obeyed orders unthinkingly, they have aided in perpetrating some of the gravest crimes in human history."[7] Wheeler goes on to cite a number of great American military leaders who have inspired extraordinary levels of obedience from their subordinates. From these examples, Wheeler suggests a causal chain in which obedience is derived from the loyalty that subordinates have for their leader, and that loyalty follows from trust that, in turn, is derived from the leader's integrity. Thus, in Wheeler's view, obedience is essentially a product of leader integrity.

Theoretical Concepts

The objective of the discipline of psychology is to determine why people behave as they do. As a psychologist, Herbert Kelman has spent many years studying obedience. In his three-process model of social influence, Kelman proposes that individuals can be influenced through *compliance*, *identification* and *internalization*.[8] These processes are qualitatively distinct, but not mutually exclusive. He notes:

> Compliance, identification, and internalization therefore mix and overlap in a given person, a given situation, a given relationship, and even a given influence attempt. Yet the distinction among these processes is analytically useful, particularly since at different times, in different contexts, and for different individuals, one or another of them predominates.[9]

Compliance occurs when followers accept the leader's influence to achieve a favourable response (e.g., to receive a reward or a positive response from the leader) or to avoid an unfavourable response (e.g., to avoid the displeasure of the leader or punishment). A subordinate who works hard for a superior in the hope of receiving a "plum" posting for his or her hard work is an example of the compliance influence process in operation. Kelman and his colleague, V. Lee Hamilton, contend that followers operating on compliance are less reliable, more difficult to control and need to be watched to ensure a positive response to the leader's influence attempts.[10]

Identification occurs when followers adopt the attitudes and behaviours that are associated with a particular role that they find self-defining. An important element in the identification process of social influence is the presence of formal and informal leaders who are strong role models. Imagine an "average soldier" serving in a small unit of "strong soldiers" and excellent

CHAPTER 1

leaders. The average soldier acting in a courageous manner to emulate his unit mates and leaders is a strong example of the identification process because belonging to this unit is self-defining. Kelman and Hamilton also suggest that guilt and shame can also be activated in the identification process making it "most conducive to social control."[11]

Internalization occurs when the followers obey because the demanded behaviour is consistent with their own values. According to Kelman and Hamilton:

> In the case of internalization, in contrast to compliance and identification, the content of the induced behaviour [e.g., the order or request] is intrinsically rewarding. The person adopts it because it appears useful for solving a problem, or is congenial to his worldview, or is demanded by his moral convictions – in short, because he perceives it as inherently conducive to the maximization of his values.[12]

Internalization is the type of influence relationship that we might see with transformational leaders since an important aspect of transformational leadership is the encouraging of followers to accept unit values and objectives as their own. However, followers operating on internalization are more likely to question influence demands according to Kelman and Hamilton. "Internalized" followers tend to continue to make their own value judgments just as they have decided that they accept the organization's values because they are compatible with their own values. Consequently, they will question the organization's values just as they would examine their own values. In Kelman's three-process model of social influence, the influencing agent (i.e., the leader or anyone else who is trying to influence the behaviour, attitudes or beliefs of others) will be successful to the extent that their demands will achieve the goals of these "others." The changes produced by the influencing agent can be positive or negative, overt or covert. Furthermore, Kelman contends that resistance is an important, if implicit, aspect of the model.

As suggested above, some influence attempts will be more successful than others. Gary Yukl distinguishes among three possible responses to influence attempts – *commitment*, *compliance* and *resistance*.[13] As with Kelman's model of influence processes, these outcomes are qualitatively different, but may overlap as well. Yukl's framework of influence outcomes has been included in the recently published Canadian Forces (CF) doctrine manual, *Leadership in the Canadian Forces: Conceptual Foundations*. When responding with commitment, followers behave as directed by their leader and maintain a positive attitude toward the leader's direction. This response is similar to Kelman's internalization. In *Conceptual Foundations*, compliance is much like Kelman's compliance in that followers need to be closely supervised. When responding with resistance, followers engage in "delaying, avoidant and non-complying behaviour coupled with attitudinal opposition."[14] Leaders might witness some blurring of these response types as the actual responses of their followers may contain elements of more than one response type; perhaps, some of these response types will be stronger than others. For example, a junior non-commissioned officer (NCO) who is slated for an upcoming mission may be generally committed to the goals of the mission (commitment), but somewhat resentful at being sent on the mission (resistance) because he recently returned from another. At the same time, though, he may welcome the potential rewards that the mission has to offer as it presents an opportunity to receive a good assessment which, in turn, might lead to promotion (compliance). In situations such as this, leaders are likely to witness multiple responses to their influence attempts.

Another theoretical model that is relevant to our discussion of the psychological processes underlying the decision to obey or not is Icek Ajzen's theory of planned behaviour, as shown below in Figure 1.1.[15] Designed as a model to explain how people choose among several behavioural options, this model can also inform our understanding of the factors that lead to obedience or disobedience. In this model, the actions that people take, when they have a choice, are determined by their *attitudes* toward the target behaviour, the *normative influences* (and pressures) from significant others and the amount of *personal control* that they have at the time. The model conceptualizes attitudes as all the beliefs that the individual has about the consequences of the action under consideration and the importance (or value) that he places on these consequences. Normative influences are conceptualized as the beliefs that significant others (i.e., family members, friends, work mates) have about the action that the individual is considering and the extent to which the individual is motivated to comply with the opinions of these significant others. Personal control refers to the extent to which the actor feels that he has the freedom to act as he wants. If the individual feels that there are significant restraints on him, he is said to have low levels of personal control. In situations where an individual has plenty of personal control and few social pressures from significant others, he will act in accordance with his attitudes toward the target behaviour. When normative pressures are strong and levels of personal control are low, the attitudes of an individual contemplating a decision will have less influence on the action chosen.

For example, an individual who believes that volunteering for a particular assignment will give him recognition, which might lead to promotion and give him the opportunity to learn important new skills, will have a positive attitude toward volunteering for this assignment if he values recognition, promotion and the opportunity to develop new skills. On the other hand, if someone important to him – a spouse, close family member or influential work mate – has a more negative attitude toward the idea of volunteering for the assignment, and if this individual is inclined to comply with the wishes

CHAPTER 1

of this significant other, the normative influences in this case could overpower the individual's positive attitude toward volunteering and lead him to avoid volunteering altogether. When individuals have little personal control, they are not able to act in accordance with their attitudes and are more inclined to conform to the most powerful normative influences present.

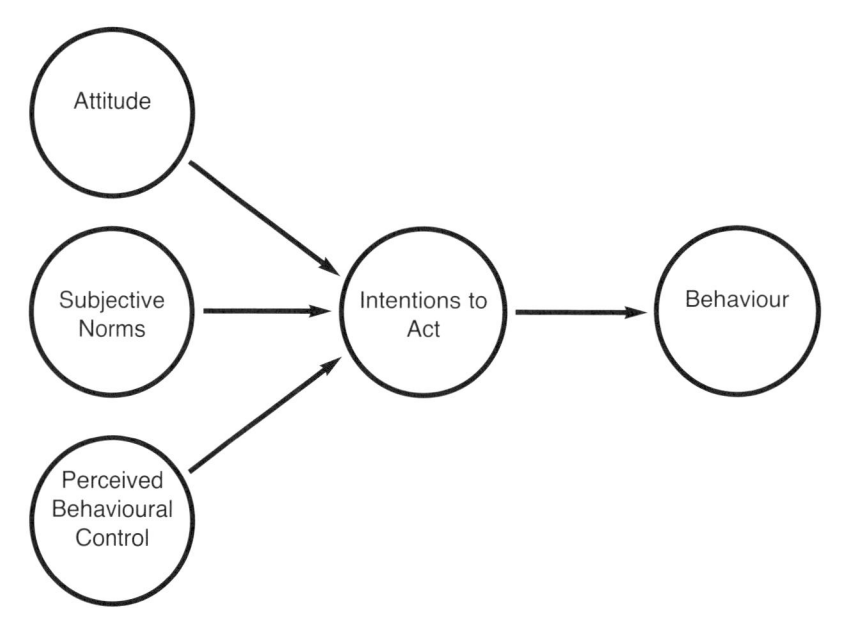

Figure 1.1: The Theory of Planned Behaviour.[16]

While the social influence processes and outcome types presented above provide important insights into how leaders influence followers and how followers may respond, our understanding of obedience and disobedience can be further informed by considering the systems view of organizational effectiveness as presented in the CF doctrinal manual, *Leadership in the Canadian Forces: Conceptual Foundations*. This model describes behaviour in institutions (such as the CF) at three levels – the *individual*, the *group* and the *institution*.[17] At the individual level, factors that can influence a soldier's decision to obey or disobey include personal characteristics like their personality, values, attitudes, ability, perception and motivation. For example, a soldier may perceive that he is not able to do a particular task, may become afraid and then may look for ways to avoid the task.

All members of organizations belong to one or more groups within the organization and these groups also have the ability to influence behaviour in powerful ways. People will do things while in a group that they would not do on their own. An otherwise law-abiding citizen might throw a rock through a store window during a demonstration, but would never consider doing such a thing while on his own. Group-level factors that can influence follower obedience include group cohesion, leadership influences in the group, the group's structure and communication processes within the group itself. For example, a soldier may be willing to comply with the orders of his superiors, but may also be influenced by powerful members of his group who do not accept the superior's orders. One might speculate, perhaps, that this is what happened with some of the "loyal soldiers" of the now disbanded Canadian Airborne Regiment in the months leading up to the regiment's deployment to Somalia in late-1992. Describing some of the misplaced loyalties in that unit, Donna Winslow reported, "Just before the regiment was deployed to Somalia, in-group loyalty was so strong that authorities were unable to find out who had participated in the burning of an officer's car. Investigations encountered only a wall of silence concerning this serious breach of discipline."[18]

Institutional-level influences also impact on the individual. To this end, the systems view depicts the culture of the organization, the organization's structure, leadership and technology, and its policies and practices in regards to human resources, as potential influences on the behaviour of organizational members. Major William Genert illustrates how such influences might lead to unprofessional behaviour in his article, *On Fostering Integrity*, in which he argues that some managerial processes were contributing to the erosion of integrity within the US Air Force officer corps. As examples, he cited the practice of: 1) encouraging Air Force applicants to lie about previous drug use (i.e., the applicants knew that they would not be enrolled if they admitted to prior drug use so they were forced to lie if they wanted to join the Air Force); 2) tacitly forcing officers to inflate the performance appraisals of their subordinates because everybody else was inflating performance ratings and officers would therefore be passed over for promotion if their assessments were not also inflated; and 3) forcing officers to sign reports for which it would be practically impossible for them to honestly certify (e.g., unit phone call records, unit immunization records, etc.).[19]

Propensity to Obey

Humans are social creatures. They are therefore inherently motivated to get along with others. There is a powerful urge within us all, called conformity by social psychologists, which predisposes us to accept the direction of authority figures. Just how powerful this drive is can be seen in a series of studies conducted by Stanley Milgram in the 1960s and 1970s. Milgram describes his first experiment as follows:

> Two people come to a psychology laboratory to take part in a study of memory and learning. One of them is designated as a 'teacher' and the other as a 'learner'. The experimenter explains that the study

is concerned with the effects of punishment on learning. The learner is conducted into a room, seated in a chair, his arms strapped to prevent excessive movement, and an electrode attached to his wrist. He is told that he is to learn a list of word pairs; whenever he makes an error, he will receive electric shocks of increasing intensity.

The real focus of the experiment is the teacher. After watching the learner being strapped into place, he is taken into the main experimental room and seated before an impressive shock generator. Its main feature is a horizontal line of 30 switches, ranging from 15 volts to 450 volts, in 15-volt increments. There are also verbal designations which range from SLIGHT SHOCK to DANGER – SEVERE SHOCK. The teacher is told that he is to administer the learning test to the man in the other room. When the learner responds correctly, the teacher moves on to the next item; when the other man gives an incorrect answer, the teacher is to give him an electric shock. He is to start at the lowest shock level (15 volts) and to increase the level each time the man makes an error, going through 30 volts, 45 volts, and so on.

The 'teacher' is a genuinely naïve subject who has come to the laboratory to participate in an experiment. The learner, or victim, is an actor who actually receives no shock at all. The point of the experiment is to see how far a person will proceed in a concrete and measurable situation in which he is ordered to inflict increasing pain on a protesting victim. At what point will the subject refuse to obey the experimenter?

Conflict arises when the man receiving the shock begins to indicate that he is experiencing discomfort. At 75 volts, the 'learner' grunts. At 120 volts he complains verbally; at 150 he demands to be released from the experiment. His protests continue as the shocks escalate, growing increasingly vehement and emotional. At 285 volts his response can only be described as an agonized scream.[20]

Most who have read about these experiments find the results unbelievable. In Milgram's first experiment with 40 men varying in age from 20 to 50, 25 teachers (i.e., 63 percent of the sample) kept increasing the shocks up to 450 volts. In a follow-on experiment with 40 new participants, Milgram had the learner state that he had a slight heart condition as he was being strapped into the chair. The experimenter responded by explaining that the shocks would not cause permanent damage and, in the end, the results of this study were virtually identical to the first, in that 26 teachers obeyed the experimenter up to 450 volts. Obedience to the experimenter's commands was strongest when the authority figure, the experimenter, was near the teacher. When the experimenter gave his commands by telephone, full obedience dropped to 21 percent. In the phone study, some teachers stopped applying the shocks and then lied to the experimenter by stating that they were continuing to shock the learner. In a different variation of this experiment, the experimenter was called away from the site; another staff member then assumed command. Full obedience in this condition dropped to 20 percent. In yet another version of the study, two confederates were included in the study to object to the experimenter's commands. The result was that 90 percent of the teachers sided with the dissenting confederates and refused to carry on.

So what do the Milgram studies tell us about obedience that we can apply to a military setting? There are four important generalizations that are relevant for military leaders who wish to increase the chances of being obeyed by their subordinates. First, people have a strong compulsion to conform to the orders of their leaders, even those orders that are distasteful (in the Milgram studies, the orders were more than distasteful, they were morally repugnant!). Second, individuals are less likely to comply with difficult orders if the leader is not present. Third, people are less likely to comply with leaders whom they do not accept as legitimate authorities. Fourth, when someone expresses resistance to distasteful orders, other followers will be influenced and obedience levels will diminish.

Is There a Military Tradition of Disobedience?

In his book, *Combat Motivation*, Anthony Kellett states that soldiers have long been able to display outward compliance to orders while actually doing much less than their orders require. He observes:

> ... outright disobedience is a relatively rare occurrence in combat because it too obviously invites sanctions. Yet in modern warfare soldiers have found ways of reducing the risks implicit in their orders without inviting retribution. That is, they may comply with the letter of their instructions, but not necessarily with the spirit.[21]

Kellett goes on to describe the outward compliance systems of the live-and-let-live activities of soldiers in the First World War. He also draws on more recent wars to give other examples of outward compliance and private rebellion, like patrolling activities that deliberately avoided enemy contact and voluminous, yet inaccurate, firing on the enemy.

While visiting a CF training unit recently, a senior instructor suggested to me that possibly one of the reasons why disobedience occurs so frequently is because of an "institutionalized" propensity to disregard orders in the CF. The officer then gave several examples of orders that he had seen broken from time to time. Later, I discussed this observation with officers in other

CHAPTER 1

units and heard of other situations in which orders, rules and regulations were customarily broken or disregarded. Some examples include:

Violating safety regulations. Examples include failing to follow safety procedures (e.g., conducting water operations training without sufficient life jackets or life guards) and the improper use of vehicles and tools.

Hazardous material handling. Examples include failing to use drip pans to control leakage in the field and failing to use correct fuelling procedures to ensure proper handling of hazardous material.

Mishandling of classified material. Examples include storing classified material in unauthorized cabinets, not using proper locks and transporting classified material in improper packaging.

Performance appraisal. The performance development report (PDR) is an important element of the CF performance appraisal system, but is not always completed properly in the actual personnel evaluation reporting (PER) process.[22]

The above list is but a portion of the broken rules that I heard about while speaking with only a few officers. There are likely many others. What these examples have in common is that there was a rule that was not followed, perhaps because it was inconvenient, time consuming or the proper equipment was not readily available.

If there is a tendency to break rules in the CF, the logical follow-on question is: How does this contribute to disobedience in greater matters? There is no way to answer this question with certainty. On the one hand, we could take the view that most CF personnel are capable of knowing when it is permissible to break a rule and that breaking "smaller" rules and regulations will not lead to more widespread disobedience. On the other hand, we could say that breaking minor rules might lead to a more generalized disregard of rules and regulations and perhaps develop into a habit of defying authority. Similarly, we could consider the power and subtlety of social influence and suggest that junior personnel who observe their seniors break certain rules in certain instances, without knowing the full range of considerations that went into the leader's decision to break the rule in the first place, might interpret this example as tacit authorization to disobey at other times in the future.

When Disobedience is Acceptable

A fact that is perhaps not well known outside military circles, or even in the junior ranks of the military for that matter, is that there are times when mili-

CHAPTER 1

tary personnel *may* disobey. To begin with, soldiers are *required* to disobey orders that are "manifestly unlawful." According to the *QR&Os*, there is usually no doubt when an order is manifestly unlawful because such orders typically direct subordinates to commit illegal acts. According to this document:

> A manifestly unlawful command or order is one that would appear to a person of ordinary sense and understanding to be clearly illegal; for example a command by an officer or man to shoot another officer or man for only having used disrespectful words; or a command to shoot an unarmed child.[23]

With varying degrees of clarity, different writers have tackled the idea of when disobedience is acceptable in the military. Huntington lists four conditions in which military personnel can disobey their superiors. The first is when the orders are illegal. The second is when they are immoral. Certainly, illegal orders meet the manifestly unlawful criterion mentioned above, but immoral orders might be more difficult to identify because morality is a subjective concept. In some of the examples presented later in this chapter, Canadian military personnel disobeyed certain orders which were lawful, but which might have resulted in immoral actions if the orders were followed at that time. Does this make them immoral orders? Perhaps not. There is a difference between orders that are clearly immoral (most orders which are clearly immoral are also illegal) and orders which, if followed in the here and now, would likely lead to outcomes most of us would find immoral.

The third condition in which Huntington permits disobedience is in operations where disobedience is necessary "to further the objective of the superior." Such an example might be a junior commander ranging outside his assigned area of operations to exploit an unforeseen tactical advantage because complying with the original orders would result in a military disaster. The fourth condition in which Huntington also permits a degree of disobedience is in "doctrinal matters" where the junior military member is aware of a tactical or technological innovation which would contribute to military effectiveness, but which is not yet accepted by higher military authorities. However, Huntington cautions, "the subordinate officer must tread judiciously in pushing doctrines which seem to him to be manifestly superior to those embodied in manuals."[24]

Michael Walzer and Nicholas Rescher examine the matter of obedience and disobedience in the military from the perspective of conflicting obligations. Unfortunately, neither of these writers offers a clear answer for soldiers who are presented with moral dilemmas involving orders which conflict with professional (or moral) obligations. Walzer categorizes the obligations that soldiers have as being either hierarchical, as in obligations to those above them and below them in the chain of command, or non-hierarchical, as in the obligations that soldiers have to people who are not within the chain of

CHAPTER 1

command, but who may nevertheless be affected by a soldier's actions (e.g., refugees).[25] Rescher presents a hierarchy of obligations, ranging from the soldier's chain of command, up through their service and nation, and ending with civilization and humanity as a whole. By presenting these obligations in a hierarchy, Rescher implies that obligations to the chain of command are less important than obligations to service, nation, etc., but he does not state this in explicit terms.[26]

As for deciding which obligation should be satisfied when there are competing obligations, Walzer and Rescher refer individuals to ethical reasoning models like utilitarianism (e.g., comparing the consequences of pursuing one option over another), virtue based ethics (e.g., comparing the motives involved in each option) and deontological ethics (e.g., evaluating the underlying principles and ethical obligations that are reflected in each option). Unfortunately, such analytical models are complex and many military personnel have not been trained to employ them effectively. Moreover, our background and our place in the military hierarchy often shape our professional perspective and this can lead to different points of view on professional dilemmas.

Differences in Rank and Motivation

A number of writers have examined how the motivational differences of leaders and followers have led to disobedience in combat. Mark Osiel observes that some of the best-known examples are:

> … the small-scale mutinies [which] occurred with some frequency among combat units in the French trenches during the First World War. These mutinies arose in response to orders requiring troops to risk near-certain death when, in the soldiers' view, the objective of the assault either had become clearly unobtainable or had lost its strategic value.[27]

Two other commentators on this topic, J.A. Blake and S. Butler, suggest that:

> Men and officers have a fundamentally different orientation or appraisal of the battle situation. The primary loyalty and identification of the enlisted men is with their peers – their buddies – while that of the officers is with the organization. The implication is that men will act first and foremost to help their peers; while officers, to support the organization.[28]

A recent study of 2,470 Canadian Army personnel (called the *Army Culture-Climate Survey*) shows just how divergent professional perspectives can be.[29] Researchers measured the opinions of officers and non-commissioned personnel on the relative importance of mission success and troop safety

CHAPTER 1

(sometimes referred to as force protection) in combat operations to defend Canadian territory. Mission success in operations is often achieved at the cost of troop safety and vice versa. These two professional "imperatives" are always in conflict in combat operations and they are often in conflict in "near combat" as well. Table 1.1 clearly illustrates that those at the higher ranks placed more importance on mission success than those at the lower ranks. These results are perhaps not surprising. One might expect that those who anticipate having to endure most of the personal risk (i.e., the lower ranks) would place more importance on troop safety. The question (for which there is no ready answer) is to what extent will these differences in the relative importance of mission success and troop safety influence how energetically subordinates follow difficult or dangerous orders?

Rank	Sample Size	% for Mission Success	% for Troop Safety
Private	415	84.3	15.7
Corporal	704	81.4	18.6
Master-Corporal	335	74.0	26.0
Sergeant	355	83.3	16.7
Warrant Officer	170	78.6	21.4
Master Warrant Officer	46	86.7	15.2
Chief Warrant Officer	14	29.0	71.0
Second-Lieutenant	17	94.1	5.9
Lieutenant	66	98.5	1.5
Captain	189	93.1	6.9
Major	71	91.6	8.4
Lieutenant-Colonel	15	93.3	6.7

Table 1.1: Mission Accomplishment and Troop Safety (By Rank). Respondents were asked: "When engaging in combat operations to defend Canadian territory which is more important?"

The story of Delta Company, 2nd Battalion, Princess Patricia's Canadian Light Infantry (2 PPCLI) is perhaps a dramatic example of what can happen when leaders and subordinates differ greatly on mission importance. In September 1993, soldiers in 2 PPCLI found themselves participating in what seemed to be an impossible mission in Croatia. Ostensibly on a peacekeeping mission, they were actually in the middle of a war of ethnic cleansing. Spread thinly over an area much too large for the Canadian contingent to easily manage, they were outnumbered and outgunned. Many of the soldiers feared for their lives, were not sure why they were there and hoped that the mission would end soon. Many of the soldiers also thought that caution and

CHAPTER 1

security were the answer. A number of the leaders, in contrast, thought that aggressive action was the way to go. According to Carol Off in her book, *The Ghosts of Medak Pocket*, some of the soldiers conspired to poison some of their company leaders, those being the company commander, the company sergeant-major and one of the platoon warrant officers. Off reports that the unit medical officer had heard from one of his medics that:

> There were people within Delta Company trying to poison the command structure ... Brown [the Medical Officer] learned from his sources ... that men were putting substances such as Visine in [Warrant Officer] Matt Stopford's coffee, digging graves for their commanders and "carrying an extra bullet", an old military expression for preparing to take out one of your own. ... Brown took the mutiny up with Jim Calvin [the Commanding Officer].[30]

Let us now consider Off's description of Delta Company in the Medak Pocket against what we know from Milgram's conformity research about the origins of resistance to leaders. In order for Brown to have heard of this conspiracy, there had to have been soldiers talking about Delta Company leaders in a rebellious manner, and we know that this is where resistance and disobedience begin. It sometimes takes only a few resisters to spawn disobedience. The Milgram studies showed that the presence of two individuals who resisted the experimenter's exhortations was enough to build resistance in the teacher. Such influence can lead to a positive outcome when the orders are immoral, as in the case of the Milgram experiments, or in the example described by Osiel in which an Israeli soldier "selectively resisted orders to deport the families of suspected Palestinian militants when there was no reason to suspect family members of terrorism." His commander agreed with him and senior authorities cancelled the order.[31] But what about those situations where the orders are simply dangerous, the sort that may put the lives of soldiers at risk? Perhaps this is what happened with 2 PPCLI in the Medak Pocket in September 1993.

Examples of Disobedience

To this point, my discussion of obedience and disobedience has been theoretical and prescriptive. I would now like to turn to a few concrete examples of the latter.[32] Taken from Terence Robertson's book on Dieppe, the first example is from the Second World War. When Canadian and British soldiers assaulted the German defences of Dieppe, France, on the morning of 19 August 1942, many men stormed the beaches with all the gallantry expected of highly motivated soldiers. Others had to be prodded out of the landing craft by their officers and NCOs. Unfortunately for the Canadians, the assault did not go well against the strong German defences and many of those in the first wave of the assault were either killed or wounded.

Believing that the first wave was having some success, the commander of the force, Canadian Major-General J.H. Roberts, ordered the second wave of soldiers (a commando of the Royal Marines) ashore. When the first landing craft hit the beach, the commander of the Royal Marines, Colonel Phillips, could see that the first wave had not broken through the enemy's defences and that there was no initial success to be exploited on the beach; he duly ordered the landing craft to return his troops to their ships.[33]

During the Somalia operation in 1993, Canadians were forbidden to transport Somalis in Canadian vehicles. A Canadian NCO, accompanied by a soldier-driver, was tasked to escort a foreign military convoy. During this assignment, the convoy met a truck carrying a number of Somalis and a load of humanitarian aid on a rural road quite far from any built up areas. The aid truck went off the road and overturned. Several of the Somalis were hurt, seriously enough that they required medical care beyond the first aid treatment that was possible at the accident site. Despite being "under orders" not to transport Somalis in Canadian vehicles, the soldiers took the injured to a medical clinic.

A similar incident occurred several years later in the Former Yugoslavia. Again, Canadian soldiers were forbidden to transport local residents in Canadian vehicles. A Canadian officer, accompanied by a senior NCO and a soldier-driver, came across a severely wounded combatant from one of the warring factions. Unfortunately for the wounded soldier, he had been left alone some distance from the safety of his own territory. Despite being "under orders" not to transport locals, the Canadians hid the injured soldier in their vehicle and brought him through several checkpoints that were manned by belligerent factions in order to deliver him to the care of his comrades.

During a conference on military ethics in 1996, Canadian Major-General Guy Tousignant described an ethical dilemma that he had experienced the year before as commander of the United Nations Assistance Mission for Rwanda (UNAMIR). At the time, the Rwandan government was closing refugee camps that had been established to house those people who had been displaced during the ethnic cleansing of the previous years. A large number of people were not going home however, and had instead collected at a camp in Kibeho. Tousignant anticipated that the Rwandan government might use force to disperse the refugees and reported his concerns to UN Headquarters (UNHQ) in New York. In response, UNHQ forbade him from using his UNAMIR troops to intervene. He ultimately disobeyed and kept a Zambian battalion in the area. He believes that he saved a large number of refugees by doing so.[34]

Another episode from the Former Yugoslavia involves a junior officer who displayed more self-serving motives. Dispatched by his major to investigate a report of shots having been fired in a particular area, the junior officer returned soon after to report that he was unable to determine the target and

CHAPTER 1

source of the shooting. Later, the major who had sent the junior officer on the shot report investigation learned that the reason he had returned so quickly was that he had encountered an armed para-military "soldier" in an abandoned village and had decided to abort his investigation. When questioned about the incident later, the junior officer told the major that with only a week-and-a-half left in his tour, he was not prepared to accept the personal risk attached to this assignment.

Journalist Adam Day writes of a Canadian patrol that he accompanied during one of the early rotations of Operation ATHENA in Afghanistan. Led by a senior NCO, the mission was planned as an eight-hour patrol. After about five or six hours, the group parked in a courtyard and remained there for the balance. Day recounts, "During our conversation the soldiers made it clear this was what they considered a pointless patrol and that they could accomplish as much sitting here as they would driving around in circles for the rest of the night." After several hours in the courtyard, the patrol returned to Camp Julien.[35]

My last example of disobedience is actually a hybrid of several similar stories that I have been told or have read about in recent years. In this example, a senior leader, while on an operational deployment in which alcohol consumption was prohibited or strictly controlled, appeared intoxicated in the company of junior unit members in clear violation of the alcohol policy in effect at that time.

Each of the above examples involves some sort of disobedience. Some can be categorized as examples of breaking rules, while several others can be seen as outright disobedience of orders. Under normal circumstances, disobedience is wrong. But sometimes, it is not. Let us now consider each of the above scenarios against some of the criteria that permit disobedience.

The Dieppe example is complex and its analysis is made all the more difficult by the fact that Colonel Phillips was killed shortly after giving the order to return to the ships. We therefore have no account of his motives or reasons for abandoning the attack. It is possible that his actions were consistent with Huntington's condition that disobedience is acceptable when it coincides with the "spirit" of the commander's intent. After all, Dieppe was a raid to harass German defences, not to establish a beachhead, and so when he saw no potential to harass the defences further, he perhaps thought it acceptable to order the retreat. It is also possible that Phillips' action was consistent with the commander's intent, for Major-General Roberts had dispatched the second wave based on the understanding that there was some success to be exploited on the beach. Unfortunately, Roberston's account of this battle does not discuss this aspect.

In terms of the ethical reasoning conventions recommended by Walzer and Rescher, this case is an example of the familiar wartime conflict between the leader's obligation to complete his mission and the competing obligation not to waste his soldiers' lives on lost causes. While a complete ethical analysis of this action using the utilitarian, deontological and virtue-based approaches is beyond the scope of this chapter, I will nevertheless offer a few observations to illustrate how such analyses might proceed. A utilitarian analysis would compare the consequences of continuing the attack with the consequences of aborting the attack, taking into account the anticipated consequences for all stakeholders (i.e., the assaulting soldiers in the second wave, the soldiers already on the shore from the first wave, the command elements, etc.). The option that presented the greatest good for the greatest number would be determined to be the most ethical option, although it might not be the most legal option. A deontological analysis would focus on the competing imperatives of supporting the commander's intent and not wasting soldiers' lives on lost causes. A virtue-based analysis is difficult in this instance without knowing the motives of Phillips and the intent of Roberts.

The two cases involving Canadian soldiers who disobeyed regulations against transporting locals (in both Somalia and Yugoslavia) are examples of a moral conflict that frequently occurs on military operations – the conflict between the professional imperative to obey orders and the moral imperative to do what one thinks is "the right thing." In these cases, the individuals likely considered the consequences of their options as best they could evaluate them, considered their obligation to obey the "no transporting locals in Canadian vehicles" regulation and thought about their obligation to relieve the suffering of the casualties who had no other help available to them. In the end, they ultimately decided to satisfy the moral obligation and helped the injured.

Major-General Tousignant's case is similar to the above examples from Yugoslavia and Somalia in that it involves a conflict between orders and morality, but his experience was certainly larger in scope as the potential threat to life was much greater; his decisions would ultimately impact some 125,000 refugees. Tousignant's dilemma was almost identical to the one experienced several years earlier by then Brigadier-General Romeo Dallaire who had been directed to abandon several thousand refugees who were under UN protection in a sports stadium in Kigali. In both cases, the generals defied orders and tried to fulfil their moral obligations as they saw them. Both saved many lives. Perhaps the fact that neither of these officers was ever publicly reprimanded or charged for their disobedience implies tacit approval for the actions that they took.

The junior officer who conducted the hasty investigation of the shot report in Bosnia initially responded to this unwanted tasking with outward compliance by physically going through the motions of conducting the investigation and then submitting a report. When challenged by his major, however, he admitted that he had not conducted a thorough investigation and stated that performing the task thoroughly was not worth the personal risk that would be incurred. This situation is very similar to the "psychic dissonance" reported by Paul Bartone in his research on US Army soldiers in Bosnia.[36] Dissonance resulted from the fact that Bartone's subjects believed that there was an imbalance between the personal costs to themselves and the value of the mission that they were engaged in. This assessment is likely common amongst soldiers sent to foreign lands on peacekeeping missions. Such missions have a certain value to soldiers, but not the same value as those in which they are defending national interests more directly. Soldier motivation in such missions will likely be lower than in missions where national interests are more visible.

What can be said about the case of the Canadian patrol in Afghanistan? Applying Yukl's range of responses described earlier (i.e., *compliance*, *commitment* and *resistance*), this situation reflects no commitment, some compliance and plenty of resistance. Events like this probably happen in operations more often than we would like to think. Is this example not similar to the live-and-let-live system of outward compliance, but internal rebellion, that First World War historians have reported? Likewise, is it not similar to Kellett's example, mentioned earlier, of patrolling with the aim of avoiding the enemy? Perhaps events unfolded like this: the soldiers did not understand the importance of the mission or did not agree that it was important; resistance developed à la Milgram studies; formal or informal leaders in the group arrived at a consensus that the orders were "stupid;" and a decision was made to disobey some of the intent of the order that sent them on the patrol.

The example of intoxication is perhaps the easiest to evaluate. There is nothing positive to say about the senior leader who was under the influence of alcohol. He was in clear violation of the very rules that he would be expected to enforce with the junior members of his unit. His behaviour reflected a lack of self-discipline and trustworthiness and, in all likelihood, probably eroded his credibility and legitimacy in the eyes of his subordinates, peers and superiors.

Increasing the Probability of Being Obeyed

The remainder of this chapter describes those actions that leaders can take to increase the chances that their followers will obey them. These suggestions evolve from Kelman's theory of influence processes and Yukl's framework of influence outcomes, both of which were explained earlier. Considering Kelman's theory, most leaders would prefer leader-follower relationships that are built on identification and internalization, rather than on compliance. With respect to Yukl's taxonomy, most leaders would likely agree that the preferred follower response is commitment, followed by compliance if commitment cannot be solicited. To be certain, leaders do not want resistance, except in those instances where the leadership thrust is misguided and the leader needs to be alerted to the error. The paragraphs below offer some suggestions in the following areas:

1. Developing your social power;
2. Lessons from the theory of planned behaviour;
3. Lessons from the Milgram studies;
4. Communications;
5. Knowing your subordinates; and
6. Strengthening your character (particularly building trust).

1. *Developing Social Power*. Increasing the likelihood that you will be obeyed is really about enhancing your leadership qualities. At its core, leadership is about influencing the behaviour, values and attitudes of others. Influence is the by-product of power, so to influence others, leaders must have social power. Chapter 5 of *Conceptual Foundations* describes two classes of social power: *position power* and *person power*. A leader's position power is derived from the authority that the individual has as a function of his or her role, or position, in the military. Person power, on the other hand, comes from the individual's character, personality, effort, competence, and so on. *Conceptual Foundations* cautions that power can be transitory and therefore needs to be maintained:

> Because power is an attribution made by others, and because leaders cannot control how others perceive and interpret their behaviour, leaders have to be mindful of the fact that they are always 'on parade' and that their conduct and performance will add to, or detract from, their power credits (this is one of the reasons military professionals emphasize the notions of military service as a way of life and the 24/7 applicability of the military ethos and *Code of Service Discipline*). To the extent that leaders demonstrate personal competence, good conduct, consideration of others, character, and other valued qualities, and to the extent that they use their authority appropriately and fairly, they will accrue power and enhance their capacity to influence others. Conversely, professional lapses or failings will erode their power, perceived legitimacy, and capacity to lead.[37]

The more power that leaders have, the greater is the chance that their followers will obey them. Strengthening position and person power is therefore the proper way for leaders to enhance their ability to inspire obedience and reduce follower resistance. In his textbook, *Leadership in Organizations*, Gary Yukl offers some suggestions for increasing and maintaining leader power; these are reprinted below in Table 1.2. Using this table as an *aide-memoire*, leaders can review their own leadership qualities, determine where their power bases may be weak and then apply some of Yukl's tips to increase their ability to influence others.

CHAPTER 1

Position Power	Person Power
Legitimate Power • Gain more formal authority • Use symbols of authority • Get people to acknowledge your authority • Exercise authority regularly • Follow proper channels in giving orders • Back up authority with reward and coercive power **Reward Power** • Discover what people need and want • Gain more control over rewards • Ensure people know you control the rewards • Don't promise more than you can deliver • Don't use rewards in a manipulative way • Avoid complex, mechanical incentives • Don't use rewards for personal benefit **Coercive Power** • Identify credible penalties to deter unacceptable behaviour • Gain authority to use punishments • Don't make rash threats • Don't use coercion in a manipulative way • Use only punishments that are legitimate • Fit punishments to the infraction • Don't use coercion for personal benefit	**Expert Power** • Gain more relevant knowledge • Keep informed about technical matters • Develop exclusive sources of info • Use symbols to verify your expertise • Demonstrate competence by solving difficult problems • Don't make rash, careless statements • Don't lie or misrepresent the facts • Don't keep changing your position **Referent Power** • Show acceptance and positive regard • Act supportive and helpful • Don't manipulate or exploit people for personal advantage • Defend subordinates' interests and back them up when appropriate • Keep promises • Make self-sacrifices to show concern • Use sincere forms of ingratiation

Table 1.2: Yukl's Hints for Increasing and Maintaining Social Power.[38]

2. *Lessons from Planned Behaviour*. Ajzen's theory of planned behaviour suggests three potential lessons for leaders. First, leaders may be able to influence the attitudes of subordinates by presenting the actions that he or she wants them to take in positive terms and by encouraging followers to place positive value on the consequences of these actions. Second, leaders will do well to

understand the normative influences on followers. Except for significant others within the military (e.g., unit mates, informal leaders, etc.), the chances of military leaders influencing the beliefs and attitudes of other significant others is minimal. The attitudes of unit mates can be influenced as described above (e.g., enhancing person and position power), but it is much more difficult to influence significant others who are not in the military. That said, the attitudes of significant others outside of the unit can possibly be influenced in subtle ways by the competence, knowledge and caring that the leader projects when interacting with these significant others. Third, lowering the amount of control subordinates have to choose one action over another can reduce the impact of followers' attitudes on the actions that they ultimately take. Close supervision and other constraints on the autonomy of followers will reduce their ability to act in accordance with their own attitudes and normative influences.

3. *Lessons from Milgram*. Leaders who want to increase the likelihood that they will be obeyed by their subordinates can consider the lessons from the Milgram studies: 1) be present when subordinates are carrying out your orders; 2) ensure that you have done everything in your power to be a legitimate leader to your subordinates; and 3) neutralize any resistance to your authority and your orders. Each of these actions is further described below.

Be present. Once leaders issue their orders to their subordinates, leaders trust (or hope, in some cases) that their directives will be carried out. However, difficult orders and dangerous tasks might not be carried out if the leader is not present. Or, perhaps they will be carried out, but not to the full extent that the leader has intended. The example presented earlier of the Canadian section in Afghanistan that completed only two-thirds of its assigned patrol shows what can happen when the leader is not present and the task has been assigned to someone who does not recognize its importance. Of course, leaders cannot be present for all of the duties that their subordinates undertake, but leaders should try to be present for the really difficult tasks and perhaps detail the more difficult ones which they cannot witness to a reliable subordinate leader, either one who has formal leadership authority by virtue of rank or one who has informal leadership authority because of their credibility with the rest of the team.

Be legitimate. Followers are less likely to comply with a leader whom they do not accept as a legitimate authority. Followers look for certain things from their leaders. In the life and death world of combat, followers are looking for competent leaders who will get the unit through the mission alive. In his article on combat stress, S. Noy refers to an Israeli study in which soldiers reported that the competence of their commanders was "the single factor which gave them the most security."[39] That said, being competent is not enough – it is also important that subordinates have the opportunity "to see and know their leader's talents."[40]

CHAPTER 1

Eliminate resistance. While the Milgram studies showed that individuals are generally prone to conformity and obedience, these same studies also demonstrated that the presence of a few rebels could strengthen the resistance of others. When followers are lukewarm to their leader's plan, resistance can spawn quickly in a group. Leaders might consider two approaches. First, give only orders that are reasonable and therefore more likely to be obeyed. "Wise leaders know that there is nothing so destructive of cooperation as the giving of orders that cannot or will not be obeyed."[41] The second approach is to eliminate resistance by knowing your followers well, knowing which ones support you and those who do not, and building trust accordingly. Strengthen the trust you have with those who already support you and establish trust with those who do not yet support you. More will be said on building trust later.

4. *Communication*. Communication is one area where many leaders fall down for they do not communicate enough with their subordinates. Brief speeches of command philosophy during a change of command ceremony are not enough. In the words of US Army General Dennis Reimer (a former Chief of Army Staff), "It's particularly important during this time of change that leaders communicate frequently and personally with their soldiers and civilian employees. Communicating means not only telling them what's going on, but listening to their concerns and doing something about them."[42] In a discussion on the topic of leader communication several years ago, a junior officer told me about his tour in Bosnia. I asked him if his soldiers knew why they were there at the time. He said "No" and added that he was not sure why they were there either. Clearly, unit leaders had not communicated well enough in this instance. Leaders have an important role in interpreting what their followers are doing and presenting it in terms which show followers how their actions are contributing to the commander's vision, the unit's mission and the nation's interests. Leaders must not leave this important role of interpreting the unit's work to informal leaders in the unit, lest these informal leaders introduce a cynical interpretation that might erode follower commitment to the mission.

Leaders need to communicate often and their communication needs to cover a wide array of topics such as unit mission, vision, national interests, military values, and so on. One way to look at this aspect of leader communication is as an important element of expressing "commander's intent." In their work on leadership theory development, Ross Pigeau and Carol McCann introduced the concepts of *explicit intent* and *implicit intent*.[43] These concepts are embedded in the framework of mission command, a leadership doctrine built around the central ideas that subordinates understand their higher commander's intent and that they execute this intent accordingly.[44] Pigeau and McCann describe explicit intent as that which is publicly communicated and therefore publicly known. Implicit intent is not vocalized and therefore less widely known. Leadership runs smoothly when there is plenty of implicit intent. When there is not an abundance of implicit intent, more explicit intent is required. The commander frequently talking and communicating with his or her subordinates allows for explicit intent to be relayed to all concerned.

Communicating organizational values to subordinates and aligning follower values with the values of the service (whether it be Army, Navy or Air Force) is an important leadership function that will promote obedience. It is very easy for leaders to take followership for granted. In his book, *Acts of War*, Richard Holmes states, "there is every chance that the group norms will conflict with the aims of the organization of which it forms a part."[45] We have seen many cases in which lower-level units (i.e., section-, platoon- and company-level) developed values and norms that were not consistent with higher (e.g., army-level) organizational norms. Most Canadian military personnel are well acquainted with two such examples, one American and one Canadian: 1) the US Army company that massacred several hundred non-combatants in My Lai, Vietnam, in 1968,[46] and 2) the Canadian Airborne Regiment (Cdn Ab Regt) that committed atrocities in Somalia in 1993.[47] According to David Bercuson and Donna Winslow, the Airborne Regiment harboured an ethic of ill-discipline and defiance toward authority in its junior ranks in garrison life in Canada before deploying to Somalia. This ethic of ill-discipline likely contributed to the atrocities that occurred later in Somalia. Military life naturally creates strong horizontal cohesion (i.e., the lateral bonds amongst peers and sometimes, immediate superiors) and this lateral loyalty can become so powerful that it leads to leadership failures like the two mentioned above. Vertical cohesion (i.e., the cohesive bonds that flow up and down the military hierarchy) is the glue that ensures that the values and norms of lower-level units are consistent with unit, service, and national interests. But vertical cohesion is difficult to achieve, hard to maintain and tactical level leaders may not appreciate its importance.

5. *Knowing your subordinates*. One of the keys to reducing resistance and increasing obedience is to know your troops. Unfortunately, knowing your followers well enough to establish trust is difficult in a hierarchical organization like the military where individuals have much more direct contact (i.e., face-to-face time) with their peers than with their superiors. People in the military spend a lot of time with their peers and informal peer-leaders can generate considerable influence on the attitudes and behaviour of others during these times. This means that officers and NCOs often have less time to influence their subordinates than do informal leaders in the soldier's peer group. Certainly, officers and NCOs have the legitimacy of their rank on their side, but the presence of unwilling followers with influence over reluctant followers is a recipe for resistance.

Many leaders take pride in knowing their people, but many of them do not have as good an understanding of their followers as they would like to think.

In his doctoral research on leadership, Lieutenant-Colonel Kelly Farley summarized a long line of research that demonstrates that military leaders often overestimate the attitudes of their subordinates. Farley describes the post-Second World War research of Samuel Stouffer who asked US Army soldiers how proud they were of their company; he then asked their company commanders how much pride their soldiers had in the company. The results are instructive for all military leaders who think that they know how their troops feel. Of the 53 company commanders surveyed, 83 percent overestimated the level of pride soldiers felt for the company.[48] More recent Canadian research by Farley and J.A. Veitch on units deployed in Bosnia (summarized in the recent Canadian Army publication, *Canada's Soldiers: Military Ethos and Canadian Values in the 21st Century*)[49] shows a similar tendency of platoon and company leaders to have a more positive impression of soldier attitudes than what the soldiers actually hold. In this study, leaders consistently overestimated the responses of their soldiers to questions measuring morale, cohesion and confidence in unit leaders.[50]

At a theoretical level, the potential for disobedience is apparent in Milgram's conformity research described earlier and in the Canadian research just described above on the tendency of leaders to overestimate the positive attitudes of their subordinates. Milgram showed how two resistant followers could lead to resistance in others and the Canadian research showed that leaders do not always know their followers as well as they think that they do. Consequently, disobedience can take root when followers who are discontent with a particular situation are combined with leaders who not only make overly positive assessments of their followers' commitment, but who also provide less supervision because they believe that their followers support the plan in the first place.

Perhaps the remedy is transformational leadership, particularly the transformational concepts of *idealized influence* and *inspirational motivation*. When engaged in idealized influence behaviours, the transformational leader presents a compelling vision to subordinates along with a high personal example for followers to emulate. Inspirational motivation is just what the words imply: the leader exhorts followers to transcend their own personal interests and accept the goals of the unit as their own (this is much like Kelman's internalization process mentioned earlier). Aspiring transformational leaders need to understand that idealized influence and inspirational motivation require a great deal of communication between leaders and followers.

6. *Character*. Leaders derive their power from followers' perceptions of the extent to which the leaders possess *expert power* and *referent power*. A large part of referent power comes from the leader's character, of which integrity should be present in large measure. Earlier, I summarized Wheeler's theory on obedience in which he contends that obedience begins with integrity. First, integrity leads to trust, which leads to loyalty, which then leads to

obedience.[51] Although there is no empirical evidence to support Wheeler's model, his causal chain of integrity, trust, loyalty and obedience is appealing. This model provides a clear linkage between integrity and obedience and suggests to all leaders that building, maintaining and demonstrating their integrity will increase the probability that their subordinates will obey them.

To better understand the importance of trust, leaders might spend some time reflecting on the follower's position, particularly the dependence of followers. On joining the military, soldiers forfeit much of their independence and become dependent on their leaders. The only way that soldiers can continue to give up their independence freely and obey their leaders is with the understanding that their leaders will take care of them. This is called trust and leaders need to nurture it. How do you develop trust? In his research on morale and cohesion, F.P. Manning cites a 1983 Israeli study by E. Kalay which "showed that soldiers' trust in their commanders depended on three qualities: professional capability (technical competence), credibility as a source of information, and the amount of care and attention he pays to the men."[52] *Leadership in the Canadian Forces: Conceptual Foundations*, reinforces this aspect of trust: "Three major personal qualities are critical to the development of trust in leaders: leader competence, the care and consideration of others displayed by the leader, and leader character (integrity, dependability and fairness)."[53] The manual then proceeds to suggest a number of actions that leaders can take to engender trust. These behaviours are reprinted below in Table 1.3.

- Be proficient and strive to enhance your proficiency
- Make good decisions, do not expose people to unnecessary risks
- Show trust and confidence in subordinates, give them authority and involve them in decision-making when you can
- Demonstrate concern for follower well-being, ensure the organization takes care of them
- Show consideration and respect for others, treat subordinates fairly
- Focus on the mission, maintain high standards, communicate openly and honestly
- Lead by example, share risks, do not accept special privileges
- Keep your word and honour your obligations

Table 1.3: How to Increase Your Trustworthiness.[54]

As a former member of the Royal Canadian Regiment (RCR), I would be guilty of neglecting my own professional upbringing if I did not show how the RCR motto of "Never pass a fault" can promote obedience in one's subordinates.[55] Correcting faults fits with the transactional style of leadership (it is called active management by exception in the transactional model) in which the leader establishes what standards are expected and then monitors performance to ensure that the required standard is met. The motto is also consistent with the transformational leadership practice of establishing high standards (called idealized influence in the transformational model). Therefore, applying the rule of never passing a fault is good leadership and can enhance follower obedience. General Reimer invokes a similar idea in his statement, "when leaders walk by a mistake they have just established a new standard."[56] By seeing leaders correct unsatisfactory performance, subordinates learn the standards expected in the unit, increase their understanding of "implicit intent" and have positive influences to reflect upon the next time that they are presented with a choice between obedience and disobedience.

The reference to Leonard Smith early in this chapter shows that military operations are hierarchical in nature, conceived by those at the top and executed by those at the bottom.[57] Consequently, obedience is required at all levels if military operations are to be effective. Fortunately, soldiers are conforming individuals who will generally comply with the leadership of military authorities; however, there are many influences, some personal (e.g., the soldier's courage and ability) and some environmental (e.g., the unit's leadership climate and organizational culture) that can generate follower resistance. Obedience or disobedience is the choice of the follower, but there are many things that the leader can do to ensure that the soldier makes the right choice. To this end, all leaders should be sensitive to the elements that contribute to their ability to influence others.

ENDNOTES

[1] Jean Norton Cru in *Témoins* (1929), as quoted in Leonard V. Smith, *Between Mutiny and Obedience: The Case of the French Fifth Infantry Division During World War I* (Princeton: Princeton University Press [PUP], 1994), 3.
[2] Smith, *Between Mutiny and Obedience*, 3.
[3] Samuel P. Huntington, *The Soldier and The State: The Theory and Politics of Civil-Military Relations* (Cambridge: Belknap, 1957), 48.
[4] Field-Marshal Wilhelm Kietel, *Memoirs of Field Marshall Kietel*, cited in Mark J. Osiel, *Obeying Orders: Atrocity, Military Discipline and the Law of War* (New Brunswick, NJ: Transaction Publishers, 2002), 1.
[5] Huntington, *The Soldier and The State*, 48.
[6] Lieutenant-Colonel Kenneth H. Wenker, "Morality and Military Obedience," *Air University Review*, Vol. 32, No. 5 (July-August 1982), 76-83.
[7] Michael O. Wheeler, "Loyalty, Honor, and the Modern Military," *Air University Review*, Vol. 24, No. 4 (May-June 1973), 173, as reprinted in M.M. Wakin, ed., *War, Morality and the Military Profession* (Boulder: Westview, 1986), 172.
[8] Herbert C. Kelman, "Further Thoughts on the Processes of Compliance,

Identification, and Internalization," in J.T. Tedeschi, ed., *Perspectives on Social Power* (Chicago: Aldine, 1974), 125.
[9] Herbert C. Kelman and V. Lee Hamilton, *Crimes of Obedience: Towards a Social Psychology of Authority and Responsibility* (New Haven: Yale University Press, 1989), 110.
[10] Kelman and Hamilton, *Crimes of Obedience*, 115.
[11] Ibid., 116.
[12] Ibid., 108.
[13] Gary Yukl, *Leadership in Organizations*, 4th Ed. (Upper Saddle River: Prentice Hall, 1998), 176.
[14] Canada, Department of National Defence [DND], *Leadership in the Canadian Forces: Conceptual Foundations* (Kingston: Canadian Defence Academy – Canadian Forces Leadership Institute, 2005), 72. Publication A-PA-005-000/AP-004.
[15] Icek Ajzen, "The Theory of Planned Behavior," *Organizational Behavior and Human Decision Processes*, Vol. 50 (1991), 179-211.
[16] Adapted from Ajzen, "The Theory of Planned Behavior."
[17] DND, *Conceptual Foundations*, Figure 1-1, "Systems View of Institutional Performance and Effectiveness," 3. See also, the "Basic OB Model" in Stephen P. Robbins and Nancy Langton, *Organizational Behaviour*, 3rd Ed. (Toronto: Pearson-Prentice Hall, 2003), 20.
[18] Donna Winslow, "Misplaced Loyalties: Military Culture and the Breakdown of Discipline in Two Peace Operations," in Carol McCann and Ross Pigeau, eds., *The Human in Command: Exploring the Modern Military Experience* (New York: Klwer Academic / Plenum Publishers, 2000), 306. See also, David Bercuson, *Significant Incident: Canada's Army, the Airborne, and the Murder in Somalia* (Toronto: McClelland and Stewart, 1996), Chapters 8 and 9, especially.
[19] William E. Genert, "On Fostering Integrity," *Air University Review*, Vol. 27, No. 6 (September-October, 1976), 62-7.
[20] Stanley Milgram, *Obedience to Authority: An Experimental View* (New York and Toronto: Harper and Row, 1969), 3.
[21] Anthony Kellett, *Combat Motivation* (Boston: Kluwer-Nijhoff Publishing, 1982), 147.
[22] The author would like to thank to Colonel Bernd Horn for suggesting these examples, 10 August 2005.
[23] *Queen's Regulations and Orders*. See notes to *QR & O* 19.015.
[24] Huntington, *The Soldier and The State*, 48.
[25] Michael Walzer, "Two Kinds of Military Responsibility," in L.J. Matthews and D.E. Brown, eds., *The Parameters of Military Ethics* (Toronto: Pergamon, 1989), 67-72.
[26] Nicholas Rescher, *In the Line of Duty: The Complexity of Military Obligation*, The Joseph A. Reich, Sr., Distinguished Lecture on War, Morality, and the Military Profession, presented at the United States Air Force Academy, Colorado, 15 November 1990.

CHAPTER 1

[27] Osiel, *Obeying Orders*, 225.
[28] J.A. Blake & S. Butler, "The Medal of Honor, Combat Orientations and Latent Role Structure in the United States Military," *The Sociological Quarterly*, Vol. 17 (1976), 561-67.
[29] Peter Bradley et al., *The Army Culture-Climate Survey* (Kingston: Royal Military College of Canada, 2004).
[30] Carol Off, *The Ghosts of Medak Pocket: The History of Canada's Secret War* (Toronto: Random House, 2004), 148.
[31] Osiel, *Obeying Orders*, 224.
[32] The examples of disobedience that were not taken from published sources were related to the author by the individuals who witnessed them.
[33] Terence Robertson, *The Shame and The Glory: Dieppe* (Toronto: McClelland and Stewart Ltd., 1962), 353.
[34] Major-General A.R. Forand, Major-General G. Tousignant, Colonel C. Lemieux and Colonel D. Matthews, "Ethical Dilemmas of Commanders on Operational Missions: Four Views," *The Many Faces of Ethics in Defence, Proceedings of the Conference on Ethics in Canadian Defence*, Ottawa, 24-25 October 1996, 30-42.
[35] Adam Day, "Somalia Redux? The Yahoo Defence, Terminal Bullshit Syndrome and the Myth of the Isolated Incident," in Colonel Bernd Horn, ed., *From the Outside Looking In: Media and Defence Analyst Perspectives on Canadian Military Leadership* (Kingston: Canadian Defence Academy Press, 2005), 149-151.
[36] Paul Bartone, "Stress in the Military Setting," in Christopher Cronin, ed., *Military Psychology: An Introduction*, 2nd Ed., (Boston: Pearson Custom Publishing, 2003), 130.
[37] DND, *Conceptual Foundations*, 59.
[38] Yukl, *Leadership in Organizations*, 97.
[39] E. Kallai, "Trust in the Commander," Academic paper delivered at the *Third International Convention of Psychological Stress and Coping in Times of War and Peace*, Tel Aviv, Israel, 1983, as cited in S. Noy, "Combat Stress Reactions," in R. Gal and A.D. Mangelsdorff, eds., *Handbook of Military Psychology* (Chichester: John Wiley and Sons, 1991), 513.
[40] Lieutenant-Colonel R. Riley, "The Darker Side of the Force: The Negative Influence of Cohesion," *Military Review*, Vol. LXXXI, No. 2 (March-April 2001), 66-72.
[41] Richard Holmes in *Acts of War*, as cited by Osiel, *Obeying Orders*, 226.
[42] Dennis J. Reimer, "Afterword," in J.G. Hunt, G.E. Dodge and L. Wong, eds., *Out-Of-The-Box Leadership: Transforming the Twenty-First-Century Army and Other Top-Performing Institutions* (Stamford: JAI Press, 1999), 290.
[43] Ross Pigeau and Carol McCann, "Redefining Command and Control," in McCann and Pigeau, *The Human in Command*, 165.
[44] William M. O'Connor, "Establishing Command Intent – A Case Study: The Encirclement of the Ruhr, March 1945," in McCann and Pigeau, *The Human in Command*, 95.

45 Richard Holmes in *Acts of War*, as cited by Osiel, *Obeying Orders*, 226.
46 Riley, "The Darker Side of the Force," 66.
47 Winslow, "Misplaced Loyalties," 306; Bercuson, *Significant Incident*, 214.
48 S. Stouffer et al., *The American Soldier – Adjustment During Army Life*, Vol. I., (Princeton: PUP, 1949), 393.
49 Canada, Department of National Defence, *Canada's Soldiers: Military Ethos and Canadian Values in the 21st Century* (Ottawa: Director General – Land Capability Development, 2005), 25-46.
50 Kelly Farley and J.A. Veitch, "Measuring Morale, Cohesion, and Confidence in Leadership: What are the Implications for Leaders?," *The Canadian Journal of Police and Security Services*, Vol. 1, No. 4 (2004), 353-64.
51 Wheeler, "Loyalty, Honor, and the Modern Military," 175.
52 E. Kalay, "The Commander in Stress Situations in IDF Combat Units During the Peace for Galilee Campaign," Academic paper delivered at the *Third International Convention of Psychological Stress and Coping in Times of War and Peace*, Tel Aviv, Israel, 1983, as cited in F.P. Manning, "Morale, Cohesion, and Esprit de Corps" in Gal and Mangelsdorff,
53 DND, *Conceptual Foundations*, 73.
54 Ibid., 72-3.
55 The Royal Canadian Regiment Charter, *RCR Regimental Standing Orders*, Chapter 1, Annex A.
56 Smith, *Between Mutiny and Obedience*, 3.
57 Reimer, "Afterword," 290.

CHAPTER 2

Loyal Mutineers: An Examination of the Connection between Leadership and Disobedience in the Canadian Army since 1885

Craig Leslie Mantle

> *To the extent that leaders demonstrate personal competence, good conduct, consideration of others, character, and other valued qualities, and to the extent that they use their authority appropriately and fairly, they will accrue power and enhance their capacity to influence others. Conversely, professional lapses or failings will erode their power, perceived legitimacy, and capacity to lead.*[1]

In June 1916, exactly one month before the Battle of the Somme commenced, Brigadier-General Reginald John Kentish authored a letter that outlined the state of discipline in the British brigade that he commanded. Being genuinely concerned that so much time, effort and resources were being wasted on courts-martial, especially "when we are all engaged in a life and death struggle for existence," he advocated giving Commanding Officers (CO) more power to deal with petty crime in their units, a change that he thought would ultimately lower the number of required trials. The methods currently in use, in his estimation, were simply too "old fashioned" and required immediate revision if they were to suit present circumstances. He further believed that poor morale, which in turn led to indiscipline, also contributed to the high number of courts-martial. From his perspective, dissatisfied soldiers tended to breach disciplinary norms more often than those who were relatively content. To support his claims, he listed a number of situations that quickly sapped the men's fighting spirit and impacted negatively on their discipline, all of which were perhaps drawn from his own experience as CO of the East Lancashire Regiment. Morale tended to suffer when:

1. The men, when resting from the trenches, are overstrained and overworked. This is a very common practice today, and is in my opinion, the chief destroyer of moral[e].
2. When men are not paid regularly.
3. When the men do not receive their bath and clean change of clothes regularly.
4. When the officers do not see that their [the soldiers'] amusements are not well catered for.
5. When the Commanding Officer fails to address and lecture weekly to his Battalion as a whole, and his Officers and N.C.Os [Non-Commissioned Officers] separately on every subject.
6. When the men are neglected.

Implicit in his argument was the contention that all leaders, be they commissioned or not, were obligated to pay close attention to the morale of their sol-

CHAPTER 2

diers. By meeting the needs of those beneath them, so he believed, individuals in positions of responsibility could significantly minimize the frequency of disobedience and thereby contribute greatly to military efficiency. "Our men are splendid…" he wrote, and they therefore "…require good leadership and direction." So convinced was he of the impact of a leader's behaviour on the frequency of disobedience that he asserted, "I have advocated certain methods of dealing with the soldier all my life, a certain form of treatment which has in some quarters been termed too progressive, but which none the less has always paid [off]…." Although he did not describe his "methods" in his letter, which was perhaps a little self-serving at times, he undoubtedly attempted to ensure that his soldiers, to the best of his ability, were properly cared for and well looked after in all that affected their welfare; he surely demanded the same from his subordinate commanders too.[2]

In his opinion, the excellent state of discipline that now existed in his brigade – he observed that between 6 April and 21 June 1916, no courts-martial had been convened [3] – resulted primarily from the competent and focussed leadership displayed by those in command and, in like manner, the soldiers' appreciation of such treatment. He concluded:

> This state of things is very creditable to the whole Brigade, and points to a whole hearted endeavor [sic] on the part of every Officer and N.C.O., to look after the interests of the men under them, and on the part of the latter to support their officers and N.C.Os in everything they call on them to undertake.[4]

His comments suggested that a reciprocal relationship between leader and follower was, in large measure, responsible for the envious position in which the brigade now found itself. Kentish believed, and his experiences probably supported him in this, that when soldiers were treated well and properly led, they were usually more willing to comply with their superiors' instructions since they knew that they were being well looked after. He contended that military effectiveness resulted from conscientious leaders who expressed a genuine concern for their subordinates. The converse of his argument was equally clear as well, although he did not explicitly state it as such. He implied throughout his letter that when soldiers were poorly treated or inadequately led, disciplinary problems were the predictable, if not the natural, result.[5]

Modern-day commentators have acknowledged this relationship as well. David Bercuson has observed, for instance, that history "…offers ample proof that soldiers who are not well led in both peace and war, cannot and in some cases will not, perform up to the Standards of professional behaviour and action in combat that is expected and required of them."[6] Major-General C.W. Hewson, while investigating the state of discipline within Canada's Special Service Force and the Canadian Airborne Regiment (Cdn AB Regt) during the mid-1980s, likewise concluded, "Some men vent their anger at being neglected by resorting to various forms of antisocial behaviour."[7] US Army officer Joel Hamby similarly conceded, "Mutiny is in essence a failure of morale."[8] A brief glance at the historical record, at least from the Canadian perspective, seems to support Kentish in his beliefs. As will become apparent, this simple dichotomy, in which the quality of leadership is directly related to the frequency and severity of indiscipline, serves to explain many of the disobedient acts that have occurred in the Canadian Army over the past century or so.

In such a restrictive climate as the Army, soldiers have always been discouraged through socialization and punishment from unilaterally transgressing the bounds of discipline in order to make their leaders aware of their grievances. Their complaints and concerns, however, could be brought to the attention of their superiors through the formal chain of command.[9] When time did not permit such channels to be used, or when these avenues failed altogether, soldiers, out of a sense of frustration and perhaps even desperation, frequently engaged in acts of protest in an attempt to immediately resolve a troublesome situation or to communicate to their leaders that, for whatever reason, all was not well.[10] Such acts assumed a variety of forms ranging from petty insubordination and wilful negligence to the exacting of revenge and outright mutiny.[11] Since strict obedience was demanded from all, *dis*obedience brought immediate attention to one's plight.

Soldiers were generally willing to use the established procedures for raising their concerns, but they also adopted more aggressive means, which were oftentimes illegal, when the circumstances so warranted. Every unfair situation, however, did not necessarily end in protest, for only when it exceeded their ability to cope and endure or was of such immediate import that it could be suffered no longer, did a demonstration of some sort become all the more likely. To this end, recent commentators on disobedience have noted, "Perceptions of what constitutes unacceptable treatment play a critical role in determining when men will feel that their grievances are serious enough to warrant mutiny." As will be seen, soldiers "…usually mutinied only when they believed they were being treated unfairly or with unusual severity."[12] Of course, "Discontent alone does not make a mutiny. Discontent is a mode of thought, mutiny a mode of action, and some kind of catalyst is necessary to convert the one to the other."[13] Yet, when soldiers are discontent, the possibility that an act of disobedience will occur becomes all the more likely as they become more unwilling to forgive additional lapses and errors.

In analyzing cases of indiscipline, whether perpetrated by single soldiers or by groups, the issue of motivation becomes particularly germane. The numerous examples offered by soldiers in their contemporary or postwar writings, or uncovered by historians of a particular period, naturally raises the question of whether or not the participants were in fact actuated by shortcomings in leadership or, on the other hand, by simple greed. In a force as diverse as the Canadian Army, comprised as it was of individuals from all socio-economic strata and from all regions of the country, although certainly not in equal or representative proportion, some undoubtedly acted out of pure selfishness. Other individuals surely desired to see how many concessions they could exact from their leaders and to what extent the Army could be manipulated for their ultimate benefit and gain.[14] There has always been present an element that, for whatever reason, did not conform to the encouraged modes of behaviour and whose disobedience served no other purpose than their own. The incorrigible and the irresponsible – "the professional misfits" as historian Desmond Morton has called them [15] – have always been a constant of military life and this reality seems unlikely to change in the future. As one modern-day soldier remarked, "There's going to be the odd soldier that won't respond to reason, discipline, punishment, retribution, corrective training...."[16] "The rebels" oftentimes tested the limits of discipline and went beyond the proscribed boundaries, yet the "smart ones watched and learned and survived."[17]

Few of the documents that soldiers left behind offer explicit and detailed explanations that account for their behaviour or that of a larger group about which they were writing, and as such, their actual motives are somewhat difficult to ascertain. Yet, the sheer frequency with which disobedience is described in the literature, perhaps with some embellishment for effect in specific cases, strongly suggests that acts of protest were much more than the deeds of individualistic or opportunistic soldiers. All in all, their disobedience seems to have been committed in the interest of improving their conditions of service.[18] Soldiers do not appear to have actively demonstrated against the legitimacy of the Army's purposes or goals, whatever their private opinions may have been at the time.[19] Bringing to an end the circumstances that induced a state of disaffection, or at least making their grievances known to those in command, usually necessitated no further activity on the part of the protestors for they now felt that, in some small measure, they had exercised a degree of control over their destiny in an organization that regulated all aspects of their daily lives. Certainly, soldiers "do want a say in decisions that affect them."[20] Large-scale mutinies were exceptionally rare within the Canadian experience, and yet, as will become apparent, relatively small, short-lived and non-violent acts of protest were not.[21] In either case, failings in leadership seem to have been the root cause.[22]

The Army, as opposed to either the Navy or the Air Force, or indeed the Canadian Forces (CF) as a whole, has been selected to provide the contextual setting for the following discussion for reasons of simplicity and ease. Simultaneously discussing instances of disobedience in all three environments, in all eras of Canadian history, and with an eye to the peculiarities of each service culture, would simply not be feasible within the confines of a single chapter. The major conclusions of this study, however, should not, and must not, be seen to apply to the Army exclusively. Many of the arguments offered herein to explain acts of protest in this single environment could, in all probability and perhaps with some minor modifications, be applied elsewhere. This chapter, moreover, does not pretend to offer a comprehensive analysis of these phenomena, complex and convoluted as they are, but rather introduces the singular notion that leadership and disobedience are profoundly connected.[23]

In the past, as today, leaders had to be competent in the execution of their duties and in the fulfilment of their responsibilities if they were to command effectively. Leaders encouraged their subordinates to trust in them by demonstrating that they understood their trade and possessed the requisite skills that would ensure both survival and success.[24] Trust, in turn, was essential for ensuring compliance, since soldiers were generally loath to follow with zeal a superior whom they believed was incompetent, reckless or dangerous. One modern-day soldier with years of experience both in Canada and abroad remarked, "If I trust somebody who is leading me, I am more likely to follow."[25] Another similarly noted, "First of all, the boss needs to be an example. He needs to be competent."[26] And yet another still observed that soldiers will "follow leaders who are competent, who aren't going to get them killed...."[27] All in all, "... soldiers asked only to be led bravely and decisively."[28] By creating commitment and trust, the two "essential pre-requisites for the willing acceptance of leader direction and influence,"[29] leaders minimized the frequency of those acts that hindered the smooth operation of the group over which they exercised control since their soldiers believed themselves well led and, in this regard specifically, had few reasons for concern.[30]

In Korea, for instance, a young Dan Loomis was advised by one of his sergeants that "'It helps to lead up front ... to show the troops you can do it....'"[31] One of Loomis' fellow officers, John Hayter, likewise encouraged his subordinates to trust him, despite his young age, by demonstrating his competence in battle. He recalled, "'Even as a nineteen-year-old patrol leader, I was required to set an example for others; that is, I was required to be cool, stand tall, be alert, be cautious, go about my business and let others do the same, and do all of the good things we had been taught about being professional.'"[32] The value of sharing in the dangers of one's subordinates cannot be underestimated. As historian Richard Holmes has observed, "It is a fundamental truth that a military leader will not succeed in battle unless he is prepared to lead from the front and to risk the penalties of doing so."[33] And again, "Perhaps the most signal reason for the ability of the officers to carry their men with them, even in the most dangerous activities, was their own acceptance of risk and sacrifice."[34] When soldiers believed that their leaders were competent and able to lead effectively, their commitment to the task at hand seems to have increased. Reflecting upon his service with the 1st Canadian Parachute Battalion during the Second World War, Private Sid Carignan recalled that for "Greenhorns like me ... What impressed me was

CHAPTER 2

the way Non-commissioned Officers checked and rechecked every man's gear, and went over the allotted tasks. Their calm confidant behaviour was very reassuring."[35] Such displays of competence encouraged Carignan and his mates to trust their leaders.

When saddled with an individual who was perceived to be lacking in ability, however, soldiers sometimes voiced their concerns, and not always in a manner that preserved the good order and discipline of the Army. In the words of one commentator, "Poor leadership at almost any level can foster and spark mutiny. Leaders who cannot identify with their troops, who cannot develop and maintain a bond of trust and faith with their men, contribute more than anything else to mutiny."[36] Trust and faith derived, in part, from being competent and, as will become evident, from caring for one's subordinates. In July 1916, for instance, after spending a considerable amount of time in the trenches, Donald Fraser of the 31st Battalion, Canadian Expeditionary Force (CEF), recorded in his journal that some reinforcements sent to replace earlier casualties "felt rather shaky trusting themselves to green non-commissioned officers, and gave vent to expression that they should be led by those who had experience of the line."[37] Months earlier, after two of his officers proved themselves completely incompetent in the face of enemy shelling, Fraser observed that "our estimation of our officers sank to zero and it was a lesson to us that in future it is best to rely on your own wits and do not expect too much from those senior to you."[38] Those "seniors" to which he referred would likewise have found it difficult to motivate Fraser and his pals, especially when trust was sorely lacking.

In more extreme cases, when a leader proved entirely hopeless and dangerous to others around him, some soldiers refused to follow at all. Agar Adamson, an officer who served with the Princess Patricia's Canadian Light Infantry (PPCLI) for the entire course of the First World War, offered some insight into how soldiers reacted when they encountered manifest incompetence. In a letter home to his wife after one of his first tours in the trenches, he related that certain NCOs had explicitly told their CO that if they were ever again ordered to go into the line with a certain officer, who had "'blew up' and hid himself in the only safe place in the trench for 48 hours," they would unilaterally "refuse and stand a Court Martial." The fact that their leader had left the front in order to have "imaginary wounds attended to" only furthered their defiant resolve.[39] Similarly, when in command of the 5th Canadian Armoured Division in Italy, Bert Hoffmeister was compelled to remove four officers from the Perth Regiment, which had recently suffered a bloody defeat at the Arieli River in January 1944, because "'the men had absolutely no confidence in them and were reluctant to go into battle with them.'"[40]

Just as they desired their leaders to be competent, especially in situations that were exceedingly dangerous, soldiers likewise expected that those placed over them would expend life judiciously. They most certainly wished to be led in a manner that did not needlessly place their well being in jeopardy. Although generally willing to forfeit their life and health if the situation so warranted, few were prepared to make such a heavy sacrifice without just cause or adequate reason. Many soldiers demanded that their leaders act with a degree of concern for their welfare, rather than with abandon and recklessness. David Bercuson has noted that soldiers "…go where they are sent, do the best they can, and accept the risks inherent in soldiering as part of the job. They trust their lives are not being endangered needlessly and that the missions they are sent to perform are doable and necessary, at least to somebody."[41] Delivered in the spring of 2000, the final report of the Croatia Board of Inquiry succinctly expressed this notion as well:

> Military units are designed to fight, or support those who do. The possibility of injury or death is ever present during military operations. Service personnel understand and accept this liability. At the same time, however, they expect a high degree of responsibility from those who make the decisions that may put them in harm's way.[42]

Likewise, in the words of Sergeant James Davis who served with the Royal Canadian Regiment (RCR) in Yugoslavia and the Cdn AB Regt in Rwanda:

> There must be an unwritten trust between a government and its soldiers. In return for offering to give up their lives to achieve the government's goals at home and abroad, the government must undertake to protect their soldiers and not throw their lives away needlessly. Looking out for their welfare must be a fundamental of building a reliable national army.[43]

Perhaps more so today than at any other time in the Canadian experience, the causes for which soldiers have been called upon to risk their lives have been obscure, ambiguous and even questionable. Confronted with situations in which the purpose of a particular task did not seem to justify the potential cost, some leaders have perceived the welfare of their troops to be of greater importance than achieving the desired end-state and have acted to protect their subordinates accordingly.[44] "One officer," when recounting his experiences on a recent deployment, "described at great length how he struggled with himself after having been given a dangerous mission, which in the end he refused because he could not reconcile its purpose with the dangers to which he would expose his troops."[45] Dilemmas of this type, in which the potential cost did not seem to justify the risk, are neither unique nor novel, and have apparently occurred with some frequency on both foreign and domestic operations.[46] New leadership doctrine is fully cognizant of these realities.[47] With this being said, however, soldiers did not desire their leaders to be detrimentally timid, overly cautious or entirely casualty adverse, but

CHAPTER 2

only conscious of the gravity and magnitude of the sacrifice that they might call upon their charges to make in the interest of necessity. When faced with certain situations that seemed unnecessarily dangerous or with leaders who were perceived to be acting without due regard for their welfare, soldiers either voiced their concerns before any action could be taken or, more rarely, refused to participate altogether.[48] S.L.A. Marshall once observed that a soldier will lose faith with the mission and his leadership "'…when he sees that casualties are wasted on useless operations or when he begins to feel that he is in any respects a victim of bad planning or faulty concepts.'"[49]

When confronted with an over-zealous officer who did not seem to have his soldiers' best interests in mind, Will Bird and his mates, all of whom belonged to the 42nd Battalion, CEF, engaged in mutiny to protest his actions. Although the details of this event seem somewhat exaggerated and sensationalized for effect, they are nevertheless instructive since they provide insight into the mindset of Canadian soldiers of the First World War-era and probably those of other periods as well. While describing the battle for Amiens in August 1918, he relates that on one particular afternoon, after hours of heavy and costly fighting, a new Lieutenant who had apparently "spent most of the war in lecture halls and on parade grounds" ordered Bird and his few remaining companions to charge headlong against a German machinegun that could fire unobstructed down a long deep trench owing to its advantageous placement. After one soldier observed that "it would be suicide to try it," another suggested quite sarcastically that "they were not going up the trench unless the officer chose to lead them," with the obvious implication being that he would be the first to die. Faced with the refusal of his subordinates to advance, the officer drew his revolver and exclaimed, "'I'm giving you an order.'" No sooner had he threatened his charges then one of Bird's companions levelled his rifle at the Lieutenant and implied that "just one more move would be his last on earth." The officer soon relented and was wounded shortly thereafter, much to the relief of all concerned. Free from such encumbrances, the men eventually captured the gun emplacement and suffered no casualties in the process.[50]

In this specific case, the lack of experience demonstrated by the officer in ordering such an attack and by quickly resorting to compulsion encouraged an act of protest that had the potential to end much worse than it did. Because Bird and his fellow soldiers perceived the Lieutenant to be acting without full regard for their lives, they took immediate action to prevent what they thought to be an unnecessary risk. As has been noted elsewhere, "Competent subordinates will sometimes accept an order's objectives as legitimate, but reject its formulation and methods as grievously ill-considered."[51] Bird's reaction should not really be surprising as one commentator has observed, "Few direct conflicts can shatter cooperation as quickly and completely as the issuance of illogical and impossible orders. In garrison, this can produce desertion and resentment; in combat, it can spur mutiny as a profound sense of unfairness arises."[52]

CHAPTER 2

During the Second World War as well, Canadian soldiers expected their leaders to remain conscious of the sanctity of life and to avoid unnecessary casualties and suffering whenever possible. When this expectation was not met, as before, discontent oftentimes resulted. In recounting his days with the Perth Regiment during the Second World War, Stanley Scislowski recalled, although he admitted that such stories were hearsay, that some regiments in Italy were considering not going into battle if ordered simply because they did not possess enough men to be effective, a situation that many thought would result in prohibitive casualties.[53] He also related how on one occasion during the Italian campaign, when attempting to breach the heavily-fortified Gothic Line, Captain William (Sammy) Ridge ordered elements of his company to advance across a minefield rather than follow an open roadway where German machineguns were situated and had already inflicted heavy casualties on the attacking Canadians. In his estimation, Ridge believed that the risk in traversing this ground was acceptable, especially given the fact that the Germans sometimes falsely marked minefields in order to fool their enemies into making an advance through more deadly killing fields. As soon as the order was given to climb the fence that denoted the edge of the field, however, many soldiers immediately began to protest since "no one wanted to commit suicide." Fearing censure from his companions if he appeared cowardly, as well as punishment if he refused, Scislowski decided to obey and so "with undisguised dismay and misgiving we climbed the fence, muttering oaths." The mines soon claimed many victims and the officer, realizing the predicament in which he had placed his soldiers, ordered those who remained to reform on the nearby road where the advance could be continued. With some dismay, Scislowski remembered that while in the field:

> Mixed feelings of fear, anger and even pride were going through me. Uppermost was the fear of dying. Next came anger over being made to sacrifice ourselves in a hopeless venture. And lastly, there was the pride in being brave enough to go ahead and do as we were ordered to do even while our comrades were going down all around us.[54]

Despite this failed crossing, Scislowski described Ridge as a leader who:

> ... led the company all through the Italian campaign and then through Holland with distinction and with firm and fair discipline. He wasn't the kind to waste lives through foolhardy ventures for the sake of quick promotion. And he wasn't the kind to go looking for medals at other people's expense. He did what had to be done, and we did what was expected of us in a manner that showed the kind of leadership we had. This reflected on us in the growing respect shown by our senior companies. What more could we have asked?[55]

In this particular instance, Ridge's actions encouraged vocal protests amongst his soldiers, but they did not pursue the matter any further and ulti-

CHAPTER 2

mately complied with his orders. Their willingness to follow, especially in such a dangerous situation as this, seems attributable to the strong sense of trust that had developed between themselves and their leader. In return for competent and effective leadership in the past, Ridge's soldiers generally respected his judgment for they believed, based on their prior experiences, that he would not waste their lives in the pursuit of futile goals and that he would only do that which had to be done. By ensuring their welfare in the past, Ridge developed a strong professional relationship with his soldiers that ultimately manifested itself through a more willing obedience when faced with a difficult situation. Moreover, his soldiers seemed prepared to forgive this costly mistake since he consistently led them well and, as a result, they had few reasons to doubt his competence. Had he not possessed the confidence, commitment and trust of his men, it is possible that this incident could have ended much differently. As Major-General Chris Vokes once observed, "Soldiers have more confidence in someone who has been with them right from the start, who knows the score and who has come up through the training programme with them."[56]

Even in the present-day, the belief that one's safety should not be needlessly compromised remains an essential belief of the Canadian soldier. As in the past, soldiers oftentimes engaged in some form of protest when they perceived their leaders to be acting without proper concern for the welfare. On a recent deployment, for instance, a vehicle driver refused to wear the shoulders flaps on his flak vest, as one of his senior NCOs had ordered him to do, for they would have prevented him from quickly withdrawing into the vehicle through the driver's hatch should an emergency occur.[57] In addition, during Operation HARMONY, a small number of soldiers from the PPCLI Battle Group allegedly attempted to poison their platoon warrant officer who, in their estimation, had been "leading recklessly, placing his platoon in jeopardy unnecessarily."[58] This particular incident is explored at length in Chapter 6.

Many leaders, however, appreciated their soldiers' attitudes and behaved in a manner that encouraged trust and respect, and by extension, a more willing compliance. Being an astute officer who understood his soldiers, an ability that undoubtedly derived from his considerable militia experience and the time that he spent in South Africa as a young subaltern, Adamson once wrote to his wife in late-November 1916 that "I am off up the line as we are retaliating in an hour's time and want to be there, not that I can do any good, but the men I think like to see one around."[59] Soldiers liked to see their leaders, especially their officers, sharing their difficulties with them, and more importantly, sharing their risks. As one modern-day soldier observed, "Troops need to see their leadership."[60] In another of his almost-daily letters home, Adamson wrote that his charges were sometimes protected from unnecessary danger by those set over them, a fact that they no doubt greatly appreciated:

> We are the only Regiment without a Chaplain. Before we left the last trenches, the C.O. read the funeral service on our men. We have refused to allow a Chaplain to hold a funeral service on our poor fellows who are out in front of our trenches and have been there for almost a year, it appears to be risking the lives of men for a sentiment.[61]

Adamson's willingness to be present and to protect the welfare of his charges undoubtedly contributed to their general willingness to follow him since they knew that he could be depended upon and, whenever and wherever possible, he would attempt to ensure their safety.

In like manner, soldiers frequently engaged in acts of disobedience when their leaders failed to accord them a degree of respect or to ensure their general welfare. Again, lapses in leadership encouraged the disaffected to engage in unacceptable, and oftentimes illegal, behaviour because "Nobody likes being treated like a monkey."[62] As one commentator has observed, no leader "…can command without order and discipline, but if he ignores the simple provisions that common decency demands in return for labours undertaken, he courts disaster."[63] Since they belonged to an institution that curtailed many of their individual freedoms – a soldier fighting in the Second World War once claimed that joining the Army "was like breaking your leg and learning to live with it" and that many soon submitted "without consciously realizing it, to army rules and regulations" [64] – their sense of fairness and justice became all the more attuned to arbitrary abuses. Soldiers consequently came to resent any infringements of their well being that they thought unnecessary or which they perceived as exploitative. From their perspective, if they were to willingly endure the hardships of military service, in which serious injury or death were very real possibilities, then those set over them were obligated to treat them in a fashion that was consistent with their sacrifices, that is, with consideration and dignity. In return for surrendering their "civil liberties on enlistment," many soldiers believed that the Army, and also their leaders, "had an almost feudal duty to care for their welfare."[65] Historian Jack Granatstein believed that the "primary task" of all leaders was to "look after their soldiers."[66]

Possessing a remarkable degree of endurance and resolve, and perhaps fearing punishment as well, many soldiers expressed their dissatisfaction with the conduct of their superiors only when it could be tolerated no longer. Throughout the past century, although soldiers have generally been willing to endure certain forms of "abuse" at the hands of their seniors – the screaming Sergeant-Major is a sufficiently understood example – there seems to have been a line that could not be crossed. As will become apparent, this threshold has recently become much lower.[67] Nevertheless, when this boundary was exceeded, wherever it may have been positioned, some form of action was the usual and predictable result. Aside from being able to demonstrate their competence on the battlefield, leaders who wished to prevent disobedience also required the ability to interact with their charges in a respectful manner.[68] "We must show the same respect and loyalty to our soldiers if we expect them in return," cautioned one modern-day officer.[69] He continued, "I believe the best approach ... is to simply treat one's soldiers with respect. If this is done, the junior officer will, in turn, earn their respect."[70] More often than not, leaders who treated their subordinates with basic dignity benefited immediately, and immensely, from this approach. Soldiers who believed themselves to have been treated fairly at the hands of their leaders were much more likely to follow their orders when the time came. Soldiers usually came to admire and respect those leaders who treated them well and, in return, they believed that following their orders was the very least that they could do to show their appreciation for such treatment.[71] A genuine respect and loyalty usually developed between a leader and his subordinates when interactions were cordial, and this respect usually resulting in a more willing, and indeed a more enthusiastic, compliance. In these situations, then, soldiers followed because they wanted to, not just because they had to. One serving officer remarked that the Golden Rule – do unto others as you would have them do unto you – was the first and last rule of leadership.[72] Another soldier-author similarly noted that a leader "must be a gentleman."[73] And finally, the Somalia Inquiry arrived at a similar conclusion when it observed that the best leaders realize "'...that being liked is not a sure road to success, but that the esteem he earns through his leadership performance is the best means of assuring the individual performance of his subordinates.'"[74] Kentish surely understood and appreciated these dynamics.

Any period of Canadian history offers excellent examples of soldiers reacting inappropriately to mistreatment. Again in his memoirs, Will Bird relates that one particular engineering officer, who felt the infantry to be "the lowest form of humans in uniform" exploited the men under his command who were responsible for digging deep trenches in which communication cables would eventually be placed. Aside from resorting to abrasive sarcasm throughout the night, the officer purposely measured the depth of the channel incorrectly so that he could exact more work from his weary charges. In response to his conduct, one individual dug a narrow yet very deep hole that caused the officer to fall violently into the trench when he attempted to measure the depth with a stick on which he leaned for support. This particular soldier responded not so much to the task at hand, but rather to the conditions of his treatment. Although willing to work, he demanded to be dealt with fairly and with respect, and when he was not, he took steps to demonstrate his displeasure.[75] As recent leadership doctrine has noted, "Substantial power applied with little consideration of its consequences is equivalent to the abuse of power and authority, and, over time, will create a psychologically stressful and toxic environment."[76] Whether or not this particular officer realized that one of his subordinates was attempting to send him a message,

CHAPTER 2

and whether he learned from this encounter and adjusted his conduct accordingly, is unknown.[77] Such instances, in which soldiers exacted a form of revenge in order to "even the score" and to satisfy their own personal sense of "natural justice" are explored at length in Chapter 9 of this volume, albeit in the context of the British Army.

Modern-day examples likewise reveal that soldiers demanded to be treated with respect. During the early-1990s, one particular company commander treated his subordinates with such disregard that they eventually exacted a form of revenge in order to express their dissatisfaction with his conduct. This officer, who few trusted, frequently pushed his soldiers out of his way and, on one occasion, incited their ire by removing a videotape that they were watching in the canteen tent so that he could watch one of his own. When the opportunity later presented itself, one or more of his soldiers defecated in his boots that he habitually left unattended outside of his tent. Owing to his behaviour, the officer was duly replaced by another. The new company commander, through his conscientious leadership, soon improved the morale of his now-exasperated soldiers. Being competent, approachable and genuinely concerned for the welfare of his subordinates, yet fair and firm in the administration of discipline, he gave the company little cause for complaint and it eventually became extremely effective and highly motivated.[78]

When faced with a leader whom they despised or did not trust, soldiers oftentimes failed to put their fullest effort into the task at hand. These actions negatively influenced group performance and, if serious enough, impeded mission success. If a leader had treated his subordinates poorly in the past or had not recognized or appreciated their contributions, soldiers oftentimes felt little incentive or obligation to work as hard as they could. In these cases, they tended to put forth the minimum effort required and little else. Being obligated by law, and perhaps fearing the ramifications of refusing a legal order, "a good soldier will do to a point anyways ... whether he respects the individual or not."[79] On the other hand, however, a leader who treated his subordinates with dignity, acknowledged their efforts and sacrifices, and generally treated them in a professional manner, usually encouraged his subordinates to follow his orders and to complete the task at hand in an exemplary manner since they understood that their efforts would not be wasted and were, in fact, greatly appreciated. Since they knew that they would be treated with respect and fairness for what they were doing, many felt an obligation to ensure that the job was done to the best of their abilities. As one modern-day soldier observed, "Thanks goes a long way," [80] because in terms of recognition, "Everybody needs it."[81]

Those leaders who failed to consider the welfare of their subordinates frequently encouraged disobedient acts within their respective commands. Once again, Bird relates that on one occasion, he and a small group of soldiers, who had just returned hungry and sleep-deprived from a lengthy tour at the front, were ordered by a newly commissioned and inexperienced lieutenant to fill shell holes in a nearby road. After marching past an idle labour battalion lazily enjoying their breakfast in the sun, the soldiers abruptly put down their tools and refused to work. To satiate their hunger, they eventually walked to the nearest canteen tent and purchased a well-deserved meal, which Bird partially paid for.[82] By forcing these men to perform tasks that were properly the preserve of others, in addition to failing to provide them with adequate rest and food, this particular lieutenant stimulated an act of protest (actually mutiny) by creating an unfair situation that grated against the reasonable expectations and needs of his subordinates. Although well within his legal prerogative to issue such an order, he apparently failed to understand or to consider the possible implications of his directive. Having endured so much, the soldiers believed that they were entitled to certain concessions. Being mistreated only added to the stress of recent days and prompted them to swiftly rectify the problem on their own. Kentish would undoubtedly have understood the catalysts behind this incident for he believed, first and foremost, that mistreating soldiers while they were supposed to be resting was exceedingly detrimental to morale, and by extension, discipline.

More modern examples demonstrate the same point. During the late-1970s, a large number of soldiers who were undergoing training as reconnaissance patrolmen refused to participate in any additional exercises when the behaviour of their leaders, in their opinion, became entirely unacceptable. Although generally willing to tolerate some verbal abuse, they objected to the fact that during their route marches, their leaders, both commissioned and non-commissioned, rode behind them in jeeps and constantly yelled profanities at them. Aside from increasing fitness, these route marches offered the soldiers no additional training and did not force them to implement any of the tactical measures that they had learned. They soon came to see these simplistic marches as exercise for exercise sake and thus of little value to their training as a whole. When such treatment could be tolerated no longer, they mutinied. After dismounting from a transport truck, they were again ordered on another pointless march. This time, however, they simply remained where they sat and refused to go any further until amends were reached.[83] Pointless work also led to other instances of disobedience. In Cyprus, Canadian infantrymen refused to mount a guard for a visiting dignitary when ordered to do so by remaining in their barracks. Their disobedience resulted from the fact that they had recently been working extremely long days on mindless and pointless projects, such as painting rocks, and these chores unfortunately left little personal time for showering, recreation and sleep. The company commander and sergeant-major were eventually disciplined for their lack of foresight and concern for the welfare of their soldiers.[84] As one veteran of the Korean War recalled, "Bored soldiers are not happy soldiers...."[85]

Moreover, during winter exercises at Canadian Forces Base (CFB) Petawawa, one particular officer incited the ire of his soldiers by unnecessarily taxing their welfare. His conduct, not surprisingly, encouraged his subordinates to exact revenge. In sum, so that he would not have to carry his own rucksack, he placed it on the toboggan that his men were struggling to drag through the bush. The sled already contained a fair amount of heavy equipment that the soldiers required to participate in the scheduled activities and the additional weight needlessly added to their burden. Because of this simple act, the soldiers later filled his rucksack with water which, given the extreme temperature, eventually turned to a block of ice that solidly encased his personal equipment. The officer was now forced to carry this now-exceptionally heavy load for the remainder of the exercise. Ironically, what had initially been an attempt to lighten his load resulted in him carrying a much greater weight. That the soldiers would go to the trouble of melting a considerable amount of snow in sub-zero weather, just to prove a point, illustrates how profoundly the officer's actions had affected them.[86]

In contrast, morale and discipline benefited greatly from conscientious officers and NCOs who took care to make certain that their charges were well looked after. Leaders who attended to their soldiers' welfare again were held in greater esteem than those who appeared less concerned and, as has been suggested, this esteem usually translated into a more willing obedience. During the North West Rebellion, for instance, Lord Melgund, the Chief of Staff to Frederick Middleton, the General Officer Commanding the Canadian Militia, served in the field alongside many Canadian soldiers. With the insurrection not yet suppressed, he returned to Ottawa and the men, realizing that they were losing a great supporter, lamented his early departure. Harold Penryn Rusden, a soldier serving with French's Scouts, remorsefully recalled:

> Lord Melgund ... had left, much to the regret of our corps with whom he was a universal favorite [sic]. He would always listen to our complaints and endeavor [sic] to rectify them if possible. He was a thorough soldier and a thorough gentleman, a sort of soldier that men would follow anywhere.[87]

In his memoirs, Scislowski likewise remembered one particular officer whom the men initially despised and even joked about shooting when an opportunity so presented itself. During the campaign in Italy, however, "Our contempt for him slowly turned to guarded admiration. It was nothing special or outstanding that he had done up there, only that he listened to us and our concerns and even helped carry the rations and water to the forward platoons on occasion."[88] Because their complaints were heard, and in many cases probably acted upon and rectified, Scislowski and his mates were left with little reason to pursue a disobedient course. The fact that this officer shared in the experiences and hardships of his men surely helped as well;

CHAPTER 2

modern-day personnel will attest that sharing in the hardships of one's soldiers is a quick and simple way for a leader to gain the trust and respect of his or her subordinates.[89] Had he brushed their problems aside, or remained entirely aloof, his soldiers might have engaged in behaviour that would have ensured that he noticed the difficulties under which they were suffering. Simply put, in the words of one modern-day soldier, "As long as someone was looking out for our interests we were satisfied"[90] and the possibility of disobedience became all the more remote. In much the same manner, one officer who served in Korea believed "'…that if you take care of your troops, they reciprocate in spades.'"[91]

In addition, the failure of leaders to ensure that their soldiers received an appropriate amount of food to sustain them has, throughout all of Canada's military commitments over the last century or so, encouraged complaint, some of which has translated into disobedient behaviour. Because soldiers expected their welfare to be looked after, food was consequently of great concern. When the quantity was insufficient, or the quality poor, discontent oftentimes resulted that could erupt into protest if not immediately checked or resolved.[92] While soldiers generally understood that their leaders were sometimes incapable of providing for them owing to circumstances well beyond their control, they became intently frustrated at those situations that could be easily rectified through a little effort and foresight; they were certainly not willing to tolerate shortages that resulted from negligence.[93] On his return to Port Hope, Ontario, after helping to suppress the North West Rebellion, Sergeant Walter Stewart of the Midland Battalion recorded in his diary that he had been:

> On the train all night, no sleep. On the train all day. Nothing to eat; no provisions had been made by the officers in charge to feed us. No stops were made and no supplies on the train; a bungled piece of business. But we were getting home. Otherwise there might have been a riot.[94]

For him, and probably his mates as well, the fact that he was returning home after being absent for many months was of greater significance than the amount of food that he was currently receiving. In this instance, with the prospect of returning to family and friends close at hand, he was willing to overlook this apparent oversight.[95] Not all soldiers were as forgiving though. David Morrison Stewart, a trooper serving with the Strathcona's Horse in South Africa, noted in his diary in mid-1900 that he and his companions thought the "Grub very poor" on one occasion and "a little kick about it" was the natural result.[96] Not surprisingly, the inability to prepare an adequate meal, even when food was to be had, caused great consternation. Lieutenant Richard Cassels recorded in his diary during the North West Rebellion that "Great profanity is indulged in when it is found that again we have no means of doing any cooking. The men are rapidly becoming mutinous."[97]

CHAPTER 2

Despite the fact that many meals failed to satisfy their recipients, whether owing to a lack of quantity, or quality, or both, some soldiers opted not to make their complaints known due to their understandable desire not to leave an unsatisfactory impression with their companions. After receiving one of his first meals in the Perth Regiment, a meal that he thought less-than satisfactory, Scislowski:

> … looked around hoping to see the orderly officer of the day to let him know how bad the food was, but he was nowhere to be seen. Then I thought it mightn't be a wise move on my part, being a newcomer, to start complaining the minute I joined the regimental family. It just might be asking for trouble later on down the line.[98]

For new men, the need to "fit in" and to gain acceptance was paramount and appearing weak would not have facilitated these goals. When they received food in the field, some soldiers were generally tolerant of the monotony and accepted this reality as a normal fact of military life. Although willing to tolerate unpalatable rations under certain conditions, they believed that when proper food was to be had, they should have it. Only two weeks after departing Toronto for the seat of the Rebellion, Cassels recorded in his diary:

> In the evening the men have an elaborate concert and interspersed with the songs are several capital speeches, the burden of which is complaint against the grub. Pork, beans, and hard tack are very delightful, and certainly, whatever may be the case now when we are in the wilds, we might have had something better when we were on a line of railway and in a well-settled district.[99]

In like manner, soldiers also expected to receive proper accommodations and meals upon their return to rest billets, especially when suitable facilities existed. Donald Fraser, for instance, recorded in his journal that when he was sent to a rest camp, he found the walls of his quarters to stop neither the daylight nor the cold; no clean or warm water was to be had either. Under these trying circumstances, which closely resembled those he had encountered in the trenches, he opined, "For a winter billet it was a crying scandal. Instead of a rest camp, it was torture." Fraser also commented upon the effect that poor billets had on morale and discipline:

> Housing soldiers under these conditions, miles behind the firing line, is very poor policy. It only helps to undermine their constitution and sow seeds of discord in the ranks. There is absolutely no reason, when there is a stationary front, why suitable reserve billets are not found.[100]

Again, Kentish would have agreed with Fraser's assessment. The discipline of the Canadian constables cum soldiers of the South African Constabulary

CHAPTER 2

suffered greatly when they were exposed to poor living conditions as well. As one observer has noted, "Housed in rudimentary shelter, poorly fed and with no literature, amusements or training routine, the men became careless, bored, restless and discontented. Drinking and fighting increased, morale fell, and men applied for transfer to other military units...."[101]

Such "discord in the ranks" sometimes, although rarely, manifested itself as mutiny. In early-January 1917, Arthur Lapointe, an intensely devout Roman Catholic who served overseas with the 22nd Battalion, CEF, recorded in his diary that a group of soldiers, of which he was one, refused to obey an entirely legal order as a means of illustrating their displeasure with the less-than satisfactory treatment that they had received. After spending a bitterly cold night in a billet with shattered windows and a broken heating stove, he later recalled, "This morning, after the distribution of a miserable ration, which none of us could eat, the men in our hut refused to parade. A sergeant ordered us out, but we told him: 'Better treatment, or we won't budge.'" An officer eventually induced the men to parade as ordered with the promise of more agreeable arrangements in the future.[102] In this particular instance, members of the group believed themselves to have been poorly treated and took what they thought were the appropriate steps to rectify the situation. Similarly, when a group of volunteers from the 180th Battalion, CEF, were ordered onto the parade grounds at Toronto's Exhibition Camp to drill, they "would not move" as none had had their breakfast. As one participant recorded in his diary, "The battalion sergeant-major gave us an order and not a man moved. Finally, [Lieutenant-] Colonel Greer [the CO] came and did the same, but still no one moved. We wanted our breakfast. He had to dismiss us and get a meal ready."[103]

In the present day as well, many soldiers protested those circumstances that they thought needlessly compromised their well being and which could easily be ameliorated. James Davis recorded in his memoirs that he and his fellow soldiers were frequently assigned the task of providing gate security at the entrance to their camp in Yugoslavia. So uncomfortable was this duty that they made their concerns known to those in command and the problems were ultimately rectified. "We spent a lot of hours out there, standing in the cold night air," he wrote. "Eventually, our protests were heard and a bunker was constructed at the front gate."[104] Just how exactly they expressed their displeasure remains unknown, but as with other soldiers, he apparently took some form of action to remedy what he thought was a needless and detrimental situation.

Despite the fact that soldiers demanded suitable billets when they were available, the historical literature strongly suggests that soldiers quite clearly understood that inhospitable conditions existed in the field that could rarely be ameliorated despite their best efforts to do so. Aside from grousing, another constant of soldierly life, few serious protests occurred at the front

CHAPTER 2

for "When we go up [the line] the boys soon accept the inevitable and copy the trench-rat's mode of life."[105] Only when soldiers returned from the field did they expect more amenable living conditions. As Adamson once related to his wife, "The men never complain when in the line of any kind of hardship, but when out in billets, supposed to be resting quite out of danger from anything but bombing [from the air], they expect comfort and shops and entertainments and they jolly well deserve them."[106] Adamson's soldiers no doubt appreciated his concern.

Moreover, many soldiers also valued those routines that provided them with relief from the strains and difficulties inherent in active service. Any changes to those practices that benefited their physical and mental welfare, in addition to their morale, frequently aroused considerable complaint and, on occasion, outright protest. In his memoirs, E.L.M. Burns, a signals officer during the First World War, recalled that during the winter of 1916-1917, the General Officer Commanding, 11th Infantry Brigade, Brigadier-General Victor Odlum, an avowed teetotaller, attempted to replace the soldiers' daily rum issue with hot cocoa. As might be expected, his "innovation got minus zero in the front-line opinion polls." Being wise to the needs of his men (and perhaps to prevent the further escalation of this issue), the General Officer Commanding, 4th Infantry Division, Major-General David Watson, eventually overruled his subordinate's proposal thereby ensuring that the "tot" remained an integral part of military routine, much to the obvious pleasure of those who partook.[107] While the specific methods by which the soldiers demonstrated their displeasure are unknown, the fact remains that they appear to have influenced the conduct of their superiors by expressing their "mutinous feelings."[108] Such were the benefits of this sweet liquor that "In an organization where soldiers had little if any power, the withholding of rum was important enough for them to raise their disenfranchised voices."[109]

The importance of rum, as historian Tim Cook has observed, cannot be overestimated. For some, the daily dram acted as a sedative, a painkiller or as a reward for enduring yet another day at the front; for others, it served as a combat motivator by steeling the will or numbing the nerves. Consequently, "When rum was issued, men were content. If it were withheld, it could lead to a plunge in morale" in which individuals "could turn mutinous or 'swing the lead,'" that is, malinger. Aside from failing to soldier as hard as they could in order to protest what they deemed to be an injustice, some soldiers demonstrated their displeasure by feigning sickness in order to temporarily remove themselves from the day's early chores and parades. On this point, one soldier asserted that "'more than half will parade sick in the morning'" if rum was denied.[110] Acts of this nature were intended to indicate that, for whatever reason, all was not well. Of course, the efficacy of these techniques depended heavily upon leaders recognizing them for what they were, namely expressions of discontent. As E.L.M. Burns once recalled, "Good officers

61

CHAPTER 2

paid attention to what the men were grousing about, and if there were reasonable grounds for it the officer tried to put it right. The men did not usually expect more than this."[111] Not to be eclipsed, however, NCOs performed a similar role:

> Discontent and morale problems can often be avoided or quickly resolved by timely intervention or advice. In this vein, senior NCOs provide clarity and context to transgressions in behaviour or perceived affronts or injustices. In addition, they provide a voice for aggrieved, intimidated and/or over-anxious subordinates, particularly young soldiers.[112]

In addition, soldiers disliked being exploited by those set over them and frequently made their views known to those who were responsible for such maltreatment. During the gold rush, the Canadian government created the Yukon Field Force in the hopes of preserving order amongst the booming population and the many speculators who now inhabited some of the nation's northernmost reaches. The soldiers, who came from Canada's Permanent Force, were oftentimes ordered to saw their own cordwood to provide fuel for cooking and to heat their billets. When they were finished, they were usually dismissed, apparently for the balance of the day. On one occasion in mid-January 1900, though, their officers attempted to exact more work from them. Edward Lester, a member of the Force, recorded in his diary that, in sub-zero weather, "We had about four cords to saw & we worked hard at it, getting through about 11 o'clock. Instead of being dismissed, however, as we were led to suppose, we were ordered to carry up wood from the pile till the 'Disperse' went." Evidently, the hour was still too early to set them at liberty. Lester's earlier premonition – "I am afraid they will increase our task if they find us getting through too fast" – came true, much to his dismay. From the soldiers' perspective, the extra work was nothing short of unfair, so "Curses deep, if not loud, were the natural result." Feeling himself aggrieved, Lester wrote, "This kind of treatment is doing incalculable harm to the temper of the troops & is fast destroying what little good feeling is left between officers & men."[113] Although there may have been a good reason behind the requirement to carry additional wood, it was apparently not explained.

His assertion that little amity remained between the officers and the soldiers was adequately founded and not unreasonable. On one occasion, for instance, what was thought to be a needless kit inspection almost caused a mutiny by bringing to a head the "general dissatisfaction which has been brewing." Having recently had a kit inspection, in which "all showed a good kit," Lester thought "it was certainly out of all reason to order them to show again." Many of the other soldiers thought so as well, as one company was "unanimously resolved not to show." Senseless, impractical and illogical orders, which soldiers perceived as a further drain, ultimately encouraged them to express their dissatisfaction with the manner in which they were being treated. In this case, the leadership style exercised by certain officers, who were "exasperating the company very much," led to a severe breakdown in discipline amongst members of the Force.[114] Again, the reason for the proposed inspection, if there was one, was apparently not explained.

Soldiers also expected their leaders to exercise a degree of fairness when dispensing discipline, or indeed, when dealing with them generally because they "...knew enough about their rights under the law to recognize arbitrariness and injustice."[115] Those individuals and practices that were deemed to be manifestly unfair could either encourage an act of protest or, more likely, damage soldiers' morale and commitment, and thus their willingness to put forth an extra effort when one was required. In the words of Field-Marshal Earl Wavell, "The soldier does not mind a severe code [of discipline] provided it is administered fairly and reasonably."[116] For instance, in South Africa, Frederick Dunham "thought it was an injustice" that he was punished for disobeying a recently published order that he was completely unaware of. At Belmont, he recorded in his diary with some regret:

> It seems that just after I had left the lines an order was issued forbidding all persons from going farther than 100 yards from the lines. After questioning for about 2 hours we were brought before the [Colonel]. I explained my case to him but it was no use. We each got 5 days [Confined to Barracks] fatigue duty.[117]

Similarly, in Canada, after being unjustly convicted and punished for a crime that he did not commit, Will Bird became "determined to buck" every representative of authority who abused their position and who failed to accord their charges a modicum of both respect and decency. This experience, in which he had been denied a reasonable opportunity to defend himself and to explain the situation, "changed me from a soldier proud to be in uniform to one knowing there was no justice whatever in the army."[118] Bird would surely have appreciated, and preferred, an officer who administered "discipline with a certain amount of humility and humanity."[119]

As with all else, individuals in positions of responsibility oftentimes received the esteem of their charges if they paid close attention to their sense of fairness and justice. Treating soldiers with respect, compassion and dignity in matters pertaining to their welfare, whatever those matters may have been, usually resulted in a positive and more amiable relationship between subordinate and superior. Adamson, who was "...more convinced than ever that nothing but a mutual understanding and a mutual feeling of respect can keep a Regiment together and make it do its best in the face of death,"[120] always attempted to treat his subordinates with decency and his manner toward them seems to have contributed to the esteem in which he was apparently held by

CHAPTER 2

his men. If the exchanges between a leader and a follower were congenial, the possibility existed that their relationship would be more pleasant and perhaps stronger. Historian and author Reginald Roy has noted the same phenomenon in his biography of George Randolph Pearkes, a highly-decorated First World War infantry officer and later both Minister of National Defence and Lieutenant-Governor of British Columbia. He wrote:

> Both officers and men remarked about his concern for the private soldier. 'He was always interested in the comfort of his men and their training,' wrote one of them later, and although Pearkes was strict, 'the troops admired him from the first day he took command [as Senior Major of the 116th Battalion, CEF] because they soon realized they would always get a fair hearing.'[121]

Such sentiments suggest quite strongly that these soldiers, since they were treated with respect and allowed to explain themselves fully, were more willing to abide by his decisions, even if they suffered from them in the end. The respect bestowed upon Pearkes seems to have derived, at least in part, from his willingness to listen to his charges.[122]

A soldier's sense of fairness was also satisfied when leaders gave adequate compensation for work performed. When, for instance, Edward Lester received additional time off or was exempt from certain duties because he had undertaken extra fatigues, like transporting goods throughout the night, he was more than content and did not feel the need to complain about the strenuous labour of late.[123] For the same reasons, Frederick Ramsay, who served in South Africa, felt content with the situation in which he found himself because "…we have been off now for two days on account of our company having had so much work lately."[124] Soldiers of all ages have certainly appreciated being somehow compensated for a "hard go."[125] In some instances, however, compensation also served to motivate dissatisfied soldiers. When in Korea, Dan Loomis found it quite difficult to motivate his charges to perform manual labour, many of whom apparently complained when they were ordered to do so. In recalling how he used an incentive to deal with their grievances, he noted:

> Try as I might I could not get the soldiers to dig as fast and as hard as they potentially could. I tried everything to increase their productivity without much success until one day I set a goal – four inches more in depth and then the rest of the night relaxing with only those on guard duty being fully vigilant. It worked. Now, rather than take the trenches down an inch or so over the whole night, they went down four times as fast with the soldiers getting an extra hour or so off every night. The grumbling ceased. Measurable goals and incentives are superior to generalized motivation ….[126]

In addition, some disobedience resulted from dysfunction within the chain of command. During certain exercises in Canada in the late-20th century, a particular platoon was plagued by miscommunication. Although the platoon lieutenant was a caring, intelligent and smart fellow, he had the unfortunate habit, perhaps owing to his inexperience or the lack of guidance given him by either his superiors or subordinates, of telling his privates and corporals exactly what should be done. While entirely within his legal prerogative, he circumvented the established chain of command with the unfortunate result that his orders were oftentimes countermanded when platoon NCOs issued a different set of orders to the same group of individuals. With instructions being received from so many authorities, the soldiers, who were becoming exceedingly frustrated at the lack of consistency, eventually performed their assigned tasks with minimal effort and drive, or not at all. From their perspective, there was no use in following one particular order, as they would only be told to do something entirely different. A sense of "why bother?" and "what's the point?" soon developed that affected their morale and thus their commitment. Many soon began to "drag their feet" and malinger. The platoon warrant officer astutely realized that the actions of the lieutenant were affecting the performance and discipline of his soldiers. Speaking with tact and respect, he informed this particular officer that he should make his wishes known to him alone and that he would then inform the section commanders as to what is to be done. When this approach was taken, morale and performance improved significantly since the soldiers now received clear direction and guidance from one source only, rather than from many.[127]

In parallel to the above, soldiers also expected to be kept informed of the situation in which they found themselves and also of the reasons why they were being asked to perform a particular task. Louis Keene, a Canadian artist who eventually received a commission in the British Army after enlisting in the first contingent of the CEF, reflected upon his promotion from the ranks in 1915 that "I am very glad that before being an officer I have been a private, because I now have the latter's point of view. I am going to try hard to be a good officer."[128] For him, success as a leader depended directly upon his knowledge of the attitudes and desires of those whom he was now to command. The familiarity with his subordinates' expectations, which derived from his earlier experiences and of course from his own needs and wants, allowed him to tailor orders in such a way as to encourage compliance. On one occasion, for instance, while commanding British troops, he "told them [of] the importance of the work we were to undertake. I have found it always a good thing to make the men think the job that they are doing is of great importance. Better results are obtained that way."[129] Although sheer expediency rather than deep concern for the feelings of his charges may have motivated Keene to explain the reasons behind his orders, these comments certainly suggest that soldiers valued a flow of meaningful and pertinent information through the chain of command which ultimately provided them

CHAPTER 2

with a greater sense of purpose. In earlier conflicts as well, Canadian soldiers expected no less. Historian Carman Miller has observed that during the South African War, Canadian officers:

> ...contended that Canadian soldiers worked better if they were treated as responsible persons, and were told the purpose or reason for their mission. Those officers who 'condescended to make clear the reason for a certain move' found their men more willing to adapt to changing circumstances, to initiate and think their way out of a difficult situation, a characteristic which some British generals ... professed to admire in colonial soldiers.[130]

Being told *why* they were to perform a certain task, rather than simply being ordered to do so without an explanation, as military culture has sometimes encouraged, appears to have satisfied at least one of the many expectations held by Canadian soldiers.[131]

Such conclusions are supported by sociological research. In describing how the possession of a sense of purpose increases the morale, motivation and commitment of soldiers, Anthony Kellett notes that:

> ... it has been shown that a group's cohesion is very much dependent on its having a mission or an objective. ... Though soldiers tend to be parochial in their outlook, they do need to have objectives by which they can measure the progress of the fighting and assess the importance of their own contribution. This need is demonstrated by the evident value of the dissemination of information.[132]

Those soldiers who understood why they were asked to perform a specific duty and why the duty itself was important tended to be more agreeable which, in the end, curtailed the possibility of an act of disobedience. On the other hand, when they believed a task to be useless or detrimental to their well being, discontent oftentimes resulted. In the words of one soldier:

> The most important troop-leading steps are telling your troops exactly what they are supposed to do, and why it's necessary to do it. It's also the very least soldiers deserve because if they know what's expected of them and why it's necessary, things have meaning and meaning sparks interest. When troops are interested they stay alert and stay alive longer. They will also come to trust that you know what you're doing.[133]

The dissemination of information also served to create commitment, the other pre-requisite for "the willing acceptance of leader direction and influence."[134] Leaders who took the time to explain to their subordinates why a task was important and why it had to be completed usually received their support, even if the task itself was dangerous or of questionable value. "If sub-units have things explained to them," noted one soldier, "then by and large they accept it, and they accept it if everybody is in the same boat."[135] When the reasons for specific tasks were not explained, disobedience sometimes resulted because if the soldiers "see no harm in not doing the mission, they won't."[136] Perhaps this accounts for the infantry corporal that Scislowski observed during the Italian campaign who, when detailed to venture into a nearby valley to listen for enemy activity, simply walked out of sight and allowed time to elapse. He recalled, "On the two standing patrols I'd been on, the corporal in charge took us down no more than ten yards. I guess he felt like the rest of us: 'It's no use sticking our necks out any farther than we have to.'"[137] Leaders could also create commitment by reassuring their soldiers that all necessary steps had been taken to ensure their safety, because "If you have a leader who wants to go on a certain path, and his subordinates or her subordinates don't see that path as looking after their safety and security, then they are going to act."[138]

Of course, taking the opportunity to explain the mission did not mean that the issue was open for discussion, debate or consensus, although leaders had to be willing to listen to their subordinates who offered their advice and suggestions, when and where appropriate.[139] And certainly, not all dangerous tasks could be explained. When time was of the essence, leaders frequently did not have the chance to explain the requirements of a particular mission or order to their soldiers. Because of trust, however, soldiers usually compiled since they understood, based on past experience, that their leader would not needlessly jeopardize their safety and that he or she would act in their best interest. The potential for disaster was always present when communication was lacking. "It's like driving your car with your eyes closed. It's a matter of time 'til something goes wrong."[140] If certain officers had taken the time to explain to the men of the Yukon Field Force why certain disagreeable tasks were necessary, it is possible that the animosity and breaches of discipline that they engendered may not have occurred at all.

Although leaders have not always been encouraged to inform their subordinates of the reasons as to why things are being done, such willingness to communicate seems to be a pre-requisite for effective leadership today. "A soldier will do damn near anything for you if you explain it to him why it's got to be done."[141] In the past, soldiers tended, and were indeed encouraged, to follow the orders of their leaders without question or hesitation. Being the product of a society that inculcated deference to authority, be it in the home, school or church, many willingly accepted the reality that "soldiers are not allowed to complain" and that they were to do as they were told "and like it."[142] Those who voluntarily offered their opinion on a particular point or questioned their superior's reasoning were sometimes given "a sharp reminder that ... my job was to obey orders."[143] For many, performing one's duty meant obeying. In

CHAPTER 2

the words of one Canadian soldier in a letter home from South Africa while serving as a lieutenant with Brabant's Horse, "we did our duty and obeyed."[144]

Today, however, the situation has changed drastically. Many individuals who are entering military service are much more aware of their rights, less deferential to authority and more willing to express their dissatisfaction. Historian Richard Holmes observed, "The leader of the late twentieth century must also relate to the soldiers produced by societies which are decreasingly deferential...."[145] Another commentator has noted, "The better educated recruits are more likely to share some of the individualistic values of a postmodern orientation, and hence are more likely to be the 'free thinkers' of their cohorts, conscious of their rights and sensitive to infringements perceived as arbitrary."[146] By the same token:

> The fact that we have entered a postmodern rights era probably means that some CF members will be more aware of their rights as individuals, less tolerant of perceived infringements on their rights, and more assertive in seeking redress. To a large extent, this is a direct consequence of higher educational attainment and the increases in literacy and social consciousness that comes with education.[147]

Rather than simply obeying without question, as the military culture of earlier years so encouraged, today's youth are prone to demand explanations. In the future, an even greater requirement will be placed on leaders, of whatever rank, to exercise a style of leadership that is cognizant of the many and varied expectations held by their subordinates. A changing society will place "additional pressure on leaders to be more candid, democratic, and responsive to subordinate voice."[148] Those who do, it seems reasonable to suggest given the above analysis, will probably encourage greater compliance amongst their subordinates than those leaders who fail to recognize the fact that today's soldiers are more willing to challenge authority, to exert their rights should they feel infringed upon and to voice their concerns. Leaders must be aware that "Authoritarian leadership is generally incompatible with mainstream liberal-democratic values, so that it tends to have a demoralizing effect on people accustomed to a high degree of personal choice."[149]

While the majority of disobedient acts that Canadian soldiers have participated in can be attributed, on the surface, to failings in leadership, some of their improper conduct also resulted from the environment in which they found themselves. In these cases, they reacted passively to their predicament and did not aggressively protest a particular circumstance. Despite their remarkable capacity to endure and their general willingness to tolerate adverse living conditions when required, soldiers could only be pressed so far before physical and mental exhaustion deprived them of their effectiveness and much of their will to continue. Over time, the hardships of campaigning

CHAPTER 2

imposed a heavy burden and exacted a heavy toll. Upon their arrival in Winnipeg after the conclusion of the North West Rebellion, for instance, the men of the Queen's Own Rifles from Toronto were so exhausted from their journey from Battleford that they simply could not exert themselves any further and thus established their camp where they saw fit, contrary to the orders of their officers:

> We find it is intended that we should pitch camp on the common near the emigrant sheds, a long distance away and on the outskirts of the city. Tired and hungry, the men wish to go no further and we accordingly pile arms and take off our accoutrements in a vacant lot …[150]

In much the same manner, Frederick Ramsay observed on one occasion in South Africa, "Our men were so tired after our forced march, we couldn't double as we were ordered so [we] quietly marched across and took up our position with the guns."[151] In both cases, these soldiers disobeyed their orders, which were not overly important in their opinion, simply because they could no longer exert themselves to the extent required. It is arguable, however, that these instances of disobedience, however benign, resulted from leadership failings; their officers, some might contend, should have been more attuned to their physical condition and adjusted their orders accordingly.

Taken together, the above examples of indiscipline within the Canadian Army over the course of the last century or so strongly suggest that disobedience and leadership are profoundly and intimately linked. Disobedience and mutiny are certainly not novel manifestations of discontent, but rather have for centuries represented viable, if somewhat risky, options through which soldiers could express their displeasure and frustrations.[152] All in all, Canadian soldiers expected much from those set over them. Aside from expecting to be led by competent leaders and in a manner that did not needlessly jeopardize their safety, they insisted that they be treated with respect and fairness and demanded that their general welfare be assured. When speaking about the First World War, Bill McAndrew commented on the numerous expectations held by Canadian soldiers of their leaders, especially their officers. His analysis could apply equally as well to the present:

> Anecdotal evidence suggests that soldiers respected officers who were courageous, considerate, honest, humane, responsible, had some military skill, and displayed a measure of common sense. Above all, soldiers wanted no part of an officer who foolishly exposed them to unnecessary hazards.[153]

Those individuals who neglected the needs and expectations of their subordinates not only harmed their sense of commitment and morale, but also tended, on the whole, to encourage diverse forms of protest that were meant to either correct the deficiency outright or to express dissatisfaction with the present state of affairs, all of which negatively impacted discipline.

Canadian soldiers did not complain about every instance of unfairness or inequality that they encountered. Rather, they tended to demonstrate against individual failings of leadership that would, if successfully resolved, result in an immediate improvement to their present condition. For the most part, they asserted "their own interests against authorities who always professed to know better."[154] They understood quite clearly that certain elements of military life could not be changed or altered. In the words of one soldier, the system of "discipline, with the death penalty behind it, was a canker we could not cure."[155] Since they protested for specific reasons and seldom participated in arbitrary attacks on either property or persons, soldiers' expressions of displeasure were usually directed toward the individual who was perceived to be immediately responsible for the situation at hand. Rarely did they pursue a disobedient course and risk punishment for a matter that was of little importance. A constant flow of complaints and calls for concessions would surely have antagonized those in a position to realize the desired change. Soldiers chose their battles wisely in order to add both weight and credibility to their complaints and, above all else, to ensure a reasonable degree of success.

In protesting an unfair or unjust circumstance, soldiers frequently employed a response that was in direct proportion to the perceived wrong: a minor issue encouraged a relatively meagre reaction while more serious and potentially life-threatening situations evoked more forceful interventions. A response tended to be more dynamic and sustained when, for instance, leaders disregarded the supremacy of life, as opposed to when they ignored some of the less significant, but nonetheless important, expectations held by their subordinates. Employing the appropriate means of protest allowed soldiers to deal with most situations in a prompt and usually successful manner. For many, demonstrating against a particular circumstance was not inconsistent with performing their duty well, for in their opinion, the matters against which they dissented needlessly impacted their well being. Few indeed were willing to quietly tolerate maltreatment. In protesting a specific situation, though, most soldiers did not endeavour to obtain more than that which was required for the immediate resolution of the present difficulty.

Those individuals who consistently met or exceeded the varied expectations of their soldiers appear to have been held in greater esteem, respect and trust than those who did not. Such feelings between leader and follower significantly lessened the amount of existing tension and, more importantly, reduced the probability that an act of protest would occur. When individuals in positions of responsibility adequately attended to both the physical and psychological needs of their soldiers, the latter was left with little or no reason to complain. Consequently, professional conduct ensured a fairly high standard of discipline. On the whole, the willingness of soldiers to pursue a disobedient course waned significantly when their most important expectations were satisfactorily met. Successful leaders seem to have understood that paying attention to the needs of their subordinates in the present would pay untold dividends in the future; those who neglected them did so at their own peril.

Good leaders surely encouraged disobedient behaviour from time to time, and probably for many of the same reasons as given above. With this being said, however, the need to resort to such activity was, by and large, considerably muted within their respective commands. Even if leaders met their subordinates' expectations in one regard, but failed to meet them in another, the chance that they would protest still remained, although they were less likely to pursue such a course with leaders who had done their best to ensure their welfare and to lead them in a professional and effective manner over time. Soldiers appreciated a responsive chain of command that was attuned to their problems and greatly valued those individuals who treated them with respect, who gave them a fair hearing and did all in their power to ensure their welfare whenever possible. When soldiers encountered leaders who valued them not only as soldiers, but as people as well, the novelty of these interactions was not lost and usually increased the respect of the former for the latter. The ability to understand the mind of one's charges, which more often than not came from close and prolonged contact with them, or in other words, experience, usually proved to be a welcome asset to a leader desirous of moving his or her subordinates toward a common goal.

The desire of Canadian soldiers throughout the ages to improve the general conditions under which they served prompted many to act in a manner contrary to the encouraged modes of behaviour. Soldiers of the First World War-era, and undoubtedly those from different eras as well, would probably have disagreed with the statement made in the British *Manual of Military Law* that "Provocation by a superior, or the existence of grievances, is no justification for mutiny or insubordination" and would have taken little comfort from the fact that "such circumstances would be allowed due weight in considering the question of punishment."[156] For many, if their leaders would not willingly treat them in a manner that was consistent with their expectations, they would demand it, and demand it they did. All in all, it would seem that disobedience tended to occur when leaders exercised "'too much militarism and too little humanity.'"[157]

ENDNOTES

[1] Canada, Department of National Defence [DND], *Leadership in the Canadian Forces: Conceptual Foundations* (Kingston: Canadian Defence Academy – Canadian Forces Leadership Institute, 2005), 59.

[2] Unaddressed Letter, 1 June 1916, File 6, Folder 2, Vol. 4121, Record

CHAPTER 2

Group [RG] 9, III-C-3, *Library and Archives Canada* [*LAC*]. Other British officers held similar views. Major-General Robert Baden-Powell, for example, instructed his subordinate commanders in the South African Constabulary that "'the rank and file were to be fairly treated'" and that they were also to "'treat their men as reasoning young Englishmen and not as mindless boys to be ordered about.'" See Carman Miller, "The Unhappy Warriors: Conflict and Nationality among the Canadian Troops during the South African War," *The Journal of Imperial and Commonwealth History,* Vol. 23, No. 1 (1995), 96. Likewise, historian Richard Holmes has noted that Sir John French, the first commander of the British Expeditionary Force during the First World War, "…was convinced that the performance of his troops depended upon good leadership." See Richard Holmes, *Acts of War: The Behavior of Men in Battle* (New York: The Free Press, 1985), 345. The link between leadership and disobedience was even noticed during the Crimean War. Captain Hedley Vicars of the 97th Regiment once wrote, "'… and all officers who treat men with the same feelings as their own, and take an interest in their welfare, find they do not see much insubordination nor want many courts-martial.'" See Anthony Kellett, *Combat Motivation: The Behavior of Soldiers in Battle* (London: Kluwer~Nijhoff Publishing, 1982), 135.

[3] This document must, of course, be used with caution. Employing courts-martial returns as a method to assess the overall state of discipline in a unit is a somewhat risky approach and may, in fact, lead to an inaccurate assessment altogether. To explain, a unit with a high number of trials may be very well-disciplined because those who break the rules are consistently punished, whereas a unit with few or no courts-martial may be poorly disciplined because serious infractions, and even those of a lesser nature, are either permitted to occur or are lightly punished.

[4] Brigade Order, 15 May 1916, File 6, Folder 2, Vol. 4121, RG 9, III-C-3, *LAC*.

[5] An example from February 1940 illustrates this point perfectly. When faced with an influenza epidemic, poor food, "some inadequate junior leadership" and "abysmal" accommodations and amenities, in which their billets were "unheated and sparsely equipped," some soldiers belonging to the Seaforth Highlanders of Canada refused to parade as a means to protest their treatment. Bert Hoffmeister, a company commander at the time, soon replaced those leaders who were incompetent, and the regimental cook as well, because he realized that his soldiers' morale "could not be ignored" and that his "future successes would depend on subordinate performance." In the words of historian Doug Delaney, Hoffmeister "believed that content soldiers who had faith in their leaders would perform better." His quick and decisive action in this regard increased his credibility amongst his soldiers since they now knew that he cared for their welfare and was someone "who could get things done." See Douglas E. Delaney, *The Soldiers' General: Bert Hoffmeister at War* (Vancouver: University of British Columbia [UBC] Press, 2005), 27-8.

[6] David Bercuson, *Bercuson Report*, "Getting and Keeping the Best People."

http://www.forces.gc.ca/site/minister/eng/Bercuson/BERCUSO3.htm. 23 December 2005. Richard Holmes has similarly observed, "The discipline enforced by the officer's pistol or the firing-squad's volley is avowedly inferior to that produced by mutual respect and affection." See Holmes, *Acts of War*, 340.

7   Major-General C.W. Hewson, *A Report on Disciplinary Infractions and Antisocial Behaviour Within FMC with Particular Reference to the Special Service Force and the Canadian Airborne Regiment* (Ottawa, 1985), 31.

8   Joel E. Hamby, "The Mutiny Wagon Wheel: A Leadership Model for Mutiny in Combat," *Armed Forces & Society*, Vol. 28, No. 4 (Summer 2002), 577.

9   During the First World War, for instance, "A soldier having a complaint to make will make it to his company commander through his company sergeant major. He must not go direct to an officer to complain or request indulgences." See Canada, Department of Militia and Defence, *Infantry Training for Use of Canadian Militia* (Ottawa: 1915), 4. See also, Lawrence James, *Mutiny in the British and Commonwealth Forces, 1797-1956* (London: Buchan & Enright, 1987), 10.

10   Although written to describe a naval setting, the same could also be said of the following for the Army as well: "When the formal and informal machinery for addressing grievances functioned properly, trouble was normally avoided. It was when the system clearly did not work, or when it encountered a situation it was not designed to deal with, that sailors were most likely to pursue drastic solutions to their complaints." Christopher M. Bell and Bruce A. Elleman, "Naval Mutinies in the Twentieth Century and Beyond," in Christopher M. Bell and Bruce A. Elleman, *Naval Mutinies of the Twentieth Century: An International Perspective* (London: Frank Cass, 2003), 269.

11   The possibility of attempted murder, however remote and unlikely, must be acknowledged since some evidence exists on point. See Stephen Pike, Gene Dow, ed. *World War One Reminiscences of a New Brunswick Veteran* (New Brunswick: Privately Published, 1990), 46-7. In the Royal Canadian Navy (RCN) during the Second World War, disgruntled sailors seem to have temporarily disabled their ship because they "had a grievance with their commanding officer." On HMCS *St. Laurent*, for example, ratings may have used sabotage as a way to express their dissatisfaction with their new Commanding Officer (CO) who apparently ran his ship "'by the book'" and "'had the knack of making everyone [around him] hostile.'" From initial impressions, leadership and disobedience seem to be connected in the RCN as well. See Lieutenant (Navy) Richard O. Mayne, "Protestors or Traitors? Investigating Cases of Crew Sabotage in the Royal Canadian Navy: 1942-45," *Canadian Military Journal*, Vol. 6, No.1 (Spring 2005), 55-6.

12   Bell and Elleman, "Naval Mutinies," 267.

13   Elihu Rose, "The Anatomy of Mutiny," *Armed Forces and Society*, Vol. 8, No. 4 (Summer 1982), 567.

14   See for instance, Richard Scougall Cassels, "The Diary of Lieutenant R.S. Cassels" in *Reminiscences of a Bungle by One of the Bunglers and Two*

Other Northwest Rebellion Diaries, R.C. Macleod, ed. (Edmonton: University of Alberta Press [UAP], 1983), 13 May 1885, 167, for an example of soldiers who lied to their officer (by overstating their present value and worth) in order to remain in comfortable billets.

[15] Desmond Morton, "'Kicking and Complaining': Demobilization Riots in the Canadian Expeditionary Force, 1918-19," *Canadian Historical Review*, Vol. LXI, No. 3 (1980), 343.

[16] Author's personal and confidential interview with Major Dave Lambert, CD, 21 July 2005.

[17] Fred Cederberg, *The Long Road Home: The Autobiography of a Canadian Soldier in Italy in World War II* (Toronto: Stoddart Publishing Co., 2000), 40.

[18] This was certainly true in the RCN where acts of mutiny "were spontaneous displays, precipitated by some local event and undertaken with a view to attracting the attention of immediate superior officers to a problem the sailors believed was within the power of those superiors to correct." Richard H. Gimblett, "What the Mainguy Report Never Told Us: The Tradition of 'Mutiny' in the Royal Canadian Navy before 1949," *Canadian Military Journal*, Vol. 1, No. 2 (Summer 2000), 88.

[19] In the Navy, "most mutineers [were] seeking to redress specific complaints rather than fundamentally upset the status quo...." The same can also be said of the Army. Bell and Elleman, "Naval Mutinies," 271.

[20] Director General – Land Capability Development, *Canada's Soldiers – Military Ethos and Canadian Values in the 21st Century – The Major Findings of The Army Climate & Culture Survey and The Army Socio-cultural Survey* (Ottawa: Land Personnel Concepts and Policy, 2005), 48.

[21] During the North West Rebellion of 1885, for instance, one individual from the Queen's Own Rifles from Toronto acted as "spokesman ... of the privates" until he was promoted corporal, a "two striped nuisance." Such a comment suggests that the airing of complaints and grievances was not an uncommon practice. See Cassels, "Diary," 24 June 1885, 208.

[22] Ascribing every disobedient act to a failure of leadership is admittedly naïve and unwise for other factors may also have contributed to the outbreak of disobedience. According to Joel Hamby, alienation, the environment, values and hopes, combat experience, training, discipline and primary groups all influence the outbreak of mutiny. See Hamby, "The Mutiny Wagon Wheel." In light of this reality, however, the sheer number of disobedient acts that took their impetus, at least in part, from failings in leadership, lends weight to the claim that the former and the latter are intimately connected. It is impossible in many cases to offer a more complex and satisfying explanation for the occurrence of certain acts of disobedience since all that remains of a particular episode is what a participant or observer recorded, and these recollections are seldom detailed. Had soldiers not recorded their perceptions, however, evidence of these acts would surely have been lost forever. Joe Sharpe and George Dowler argue in Chapter 6 that there are usually more complex explanations, beyond leadership, for those acts of disobedience that

have occurred in the past. While they are certainly correct, the paucity of evidence in some cases limits what can truly be known about the larger context in which these acts occurred. Time and space does not permit of a thorough investigation of each case that is presented herein.

[23] Historian Carman Miller has argued that differences in culture, class and national identity (which of course impacted on styles of leadership) contributed to outbreaks of disobedience amongst Canadian troops whilst they were serving under British command during the South African War. See Miller, "The Unhappy Warriors." Many commentators have also acknowledged the relationship between alcohol and disobedience. See, for instance, David Bercuson, *Significant Incident: Canada's Army, the Airborne, and the Murder in Somalia* (Toronto: McClelland and Stewart, 1996), 62, and Chris Madsen, *Another Kind of Justice: Canadian Military Law from Confederation to Somalia* (Vancouver: UBC Press, 1999), 23. Selection policies, in some instances, have had a negative impact on discipline as well. See, for example, Madsen, *Another Kind of Justice*, 109, where he admits in reference to the Korean War, "...officials accepted many men with objectionable backgrounds and little previous military training. As a result, Canadian soldiers committed numerous offences against service discipline and the Korean civil population." See also, Lieutenant-Colonel (now Colonel) Bernd Horn, *Bastard Sons: An Examination of Canada's Airborne Experience, 1942-1995* (St. Catharines: Vanwell, 2001), 236, where it is acknowledged that weak selection standards for the Canadian Airborne Regiment "'ultimately resulted in leadership shortcomings, ill-discipline, and the emergence of a small lawless element whose challenges to authority and intolerable actions in operations, disproportionately overshadowed and discredited the achievements of the remainder of the Regiment.'"

[24] When leaders did not have the opportunity to demonstrate their competence and their concern for their subordinates, trust and discipline tended to suffer. Major-General Hewson noted this reality in his report. He wrote, "The absence of junior leaders due to taskings and career courses, combined with a lack of job stability within units, prevents them from effectively knowing their men. ... The resulting failure to form a bond of trust between leaders and men is considered to be one of the key factors contributing to a breakdown of discipline." Hewson, *Report*, Executive Summary, Para 14. He similarly noted, "Junior leaders, particularly lieutenants and master-corporals, must spend as much time as possible with their men. Only through this constant contact does the bond of trust and confidence develop. In time, leaders come to intuitively know when something is wrong with an individual and, conversely, soldiers are more likely to discuss any problems with their leaders. The leader will be able to intervene at an early stage in the problem and thus avoid more serious complications at a later date." Hewson, *Report*, 28. As the Somalia Inquiry noted, "Most breaches of discipline reflect on leadership. Leaders who really understand their subordinates and have won their confidence will always be aware of the existence of a griev-

CHAPTER 2

ance long before the subordinates are driven to any concerted breach of discipline." See Canada, *Dishonoured Legacy: The Lessons of the Somalia Affair: Report of the Commission of Inquiry into the Deployment of Canadian Forces to Somalia*, Vol. 2 (Ottawa: Minister of Public Works and Government Services Canada, 1997), 370. See also, Bercuson, *Significant Incident*, 79-80.

25 Author's personal and confidential interview with Formation Chief Warrant Officer Robert Lamothe, MMM, CD, 18 August 2005. Similarly, leaders can build trust and respect by "continually building on and expanding one's level of professional competence." Warrant Officer T.N. France, "The Heart and Soul of the Company – The Principles of Leadership and the Role of the Company Sergeant Major," in *In the Breach: Perspectives on Leadership in the Army Today*, Lieutenant-Colonel (now Colonel) Bernd Horn, ed. (Kingston: Director General – Land Combat Development, 2004), 83.

26 Author's personal and confidential interview with Chief Warrant Officer Jules Moreau, MMM, CD, 20 July 2005.

27 Author's personal and confidential interview with Lieutenant-Colonel Mike Goodspeed, CD, 21 July 2005. And similarly, soldiers "… will be much more likely to follow a leader who knows what he is doing as opposed to one who has a vague understanding of tactics." See Captain A.D. Haynes, "The Importance of Building Credibility as a Junior Leader," in *In the Breach: Perspectives on Leadership in the Army Today*, Lieutenant-Colonel (now Colonel) Bernd Horn, ed. (Kingston: Director General – Land Combat Development, 2004), 106.

28 Leonard V. Smith, *Between Mutiny and Obedience: The Case of the French Fifth Infantry Division During World War I* (New Jersey: Princeton University Press, 1994), 249.

29 DND, *Conceptual Foundations*, 50.

30 As one commentator has observed, "The troops' lack of confidence in their officers or the officers' lack of understanding of the troops has been a feature of most mutinies…." Rose, "Anatomy of Mutiny," 567.

31 John Gardam, *Korea Volunteer: An Oral History From Those Who Were There* (Burnstown: General Store Publishing House, 1994), "Flip a Coin: Heads, Military College; Tails, McGill University," 149.

32 Gardam, *Korea Volunteer*, "Guardsman on Hill 355," 218.

33 Holmes, *Acts of War* 341.

34 Kellett, *Combat Motivation*, 156.

35 Dan Hartigan, "1st Canadian Parachute Battalion Assault on the Rhine. The Ride, The Drop, and the Objectives," 1st Canadian Parachute Battalion Association pamphlet, 1988, 4.

36 Hamby, "The Mutiny Wagon Wheel," 591.

37 Donald Fraser, Reginald H. Roy, ed., *The Journal of Private Fraser, 1914-1918* (Victoria, British Columbia: Sono Nis Press, 1985), 18 July 1916, 175. In all fairness, however, the inexperienced were oftentimes thrust into positions of leadership owing to the lack of suitably trained and prepared replacements. Agar Adamson, who served with the PPCLI, once wrote, "We

are also very short of good senior N.C.O.s having lost so many at Passchendaele and having to fill their places with inexperienced youngsters who do not know the job, either in or out of the line." See Agar Adamson, N.M. Christie, ed., *Letters of Agar Adamson, 1914 to 1919* (Nepean: CEF Books, 1997), Agar Adamson to Mabel Adamson, 21 January 1918, 331.

[38] Fraser, *Journal*, 26 September 1915, 30-1.

[39] Adamson, *Letters*, Agar to Mabel, 4 March 1915, 32.

[40] Bert Hoffmeister, as quoted in J.L. Granatstein, *The Generals: The Canadian Army's Senior Commanders in the Second World War* (Toronto: Stoddart Publishing Co., 1993), 198.

[41] Bercuson, *Significant Incident*, 149.

[42] Croatia Board of Inquiry, Executive Summary. Likewise, "In return for obedience, the fighting man expects to be sustained by his country and, when he is not, may demand his rights." See James, *Mutiny in the British and Commonwealth Forces*, 272.

[43] James R. Davis, *The Sharp End: A Canadian Soldier's Story* (Vancouver: Douglas & McIntyre, 1997), 269.

[44] A recent survey of Canadian Army personnel noted, "...Canadians can feel confident in the willingness of soldiers to place their lives at risk to defend Canada and in combat operations to defend Canadian citizens at home and abroad. Soldiers are less willing to endanger troop safety as operations stray further from defence of Canada toward operations other than war such as humanitarian and disaster relief missions." *Canada's Soldiers*, 27.

[45] Canada, DND, *The Debrief the Leaders Project (Officers)*, 11.

[46] In a similar vein, "It is not surprising that leaders in the field, when faced with ambiguous missions and unclear criteria for defining success, and aware of their responsibility for Canadians entrusted to their command find it difficult professionally and morally to put the imperative of the mission before the welfare of their own troops." And again, the *Debrief the Leaders Project* "discovered that many officers reported that they could not identify any important Canadian interest to be upheld which reasonably justified putting their troops in harms way." *Debrief the Leaders*, 13.

[47] For example, "Clearly, in wars of national survival, or in conflicts where vital national interests are at stake, the priority accorded the mission over own troops and self is virtually indisputable. However, in missions undertaken for other reasons – combating natural disasters, resolving other people's conflicts – it should not be assumed that mission accomplishment will always or automatically take priority over force-protection obligations or other values." DND, *Conceptual Foundations*, 20. In addition, "… members are legally and ethically obligated to perform their duties, but it is both unreasonable and imprudent to expect them to perform supererogatory (beyond the call of duty) acts for any and every operational rationale. Injuries and losses of life incurred on missions with ambiguous political goals, or of questionable military importance, or with a low probability of success, may not only seriously damage morale but may undermine mission legitimacy and public support. Good leaders and com-

CHAPTER 2

manders consider and weigh these kinds of risks before putting service members in harm's way, and as necessary, either explain to their subordinates why the risks must be assumed, or else attempt to convince their superiors why the mission should be reconsidered." DND, *Conceptual Foundations*, 24.

48 As one commentator has observed, "Superiors could not assume, as a matter of course, that highly dangerous orders would be obeyed without cavil. Inferiors had to be reasoned with and persuaded concerning the merits of a risky course of action. In fact, they had to be treated as parties in a negotiation." See Mark J. Osiel, *Obeying Orders: Atrocity, Military Discipline & the Law of War* (London: Transaction Publishers, 1999), 216. In addition, many of the French Army mutinies of the First World War "…arose in response to orders requiring troops to risk near-certain death when, in the soldiers' view, the objective of the assault either had become clearly unobtainable or had lost its strategic value." Osiel, *Obeying Orders*, 225.

49 As quoted in Hamby, "The Mutiny Wagon Wheel," 590.

50 William Richard Bird, *Ghosts Have Warm Hands ~ A Memoir of the Great War ~ 1916-1919* (Nepean: CEF Books, 1997), 110.

51 Osiel, *Obeying Orders*, 315.

52 Hamby, "The Mutiny Wagon Wheel," 586.

53 Stanley Scislowski, *Not All Of Us Were Brave* (Toronto: Dundurn Press, 1997), 318.

54 Scislowski, *Not All Of Us Were Brave*, 250-52.

55 Ibid., 38.

56 Major-General Chris Vokes with John P. Maclean, *Vokes: My Story* (Ottawa: Gallery Books, 1985), 80.

57 Author's personal and confidential interview with Corporal Al Hennessey, CD, 22 July 2005.

58 *Detailed Report of the Special Review Group – Operation HARMONY (Rotation Two)*. http://www.forces.gc.ca/site/reports/harmony_2/annexa1-e.asp. 23 December 2005.

59 Adamson, *Letters*, Agar to Mabel, 26 November 1916, 239.

60 Hennessey interview.

61 Adamson, *Letters*, Agar to Mabel, 21 February 1916, 149

62 Lamothe interview.

63 Richard Woodman, *A Brief History of Mutiny* (London: Robinson, 2005), 285.

64 Cederberg, *The Long Road Home*, 40.

65 Julian Putkowski, *British Army Mutineers, 1914-1922* (London: Francis Boutle, 1998), 18.

66 Jack Granatstein, *Granatstein Report*, "Responsibility, Accountability, Discipline, and the Regimental System." http://www.forces.gc.ca/site/minister/eng/Granatstein/gra2main.html. 23 December 2005.

67 Joel Hamby has noted a similar phenomenon: "Instances of mutiny are and will probably continue to be uncommon, but the threshold of what the average soldier will tolerate before surrendering to mutiny is lessening.

Examination of the circumstances of mutinies reveals that progressively less provocation seemed necessary as the century progressed." See Hamby, "The Mutiny Wagon Wheel," 593.

68   Those officers who imposed a strict regimen of discipline, which their subordinates thought to be too harsh or indeed unnecessary, sometimes encouraged acts of disobedience. In the 1st Canadian Parachute Battalion during the Second World War, a hunger strike was occasioned by a "new CO [who] was an exceptionally strict disciplinarian and in his enthusiasm had been punishing minor offences on a much too severe basis and in some respects had produced regulations, particularly concerning dress within the camp area, which were not entirely reasonable ones." The strike was also caused by the fact that many of the junior officers had not yet "grown to know their men as they should." The soldiers, "over-pampered and temperamental primadonnas," also disliked having to go through another training program, having just participated in operations in Normandy. See Para Battalion, File 2011, Vol. 12721, RG 24, *LAC*. Much tension was created in the Cape Breton Highlanders during the Second World War when new officers sent to replace the older ones imposed a strict discipline upon all. See Cederberg, *The Long Road Home*, 15-21. The reaction of these soldiers should come as no surprise as "…the imposition of tyrannical, inconsequential sanctions on fighting men has long led to detrimental performance in battle. It can feed the sense of discontent, and become the tinder seeking a spark." Hamby, "The Mutiny Wagon Wheel," 586.

69   Captain R. McBride, "Gaining Respect and Loyalty," in *In the Breach: Perspectives on Leadership in the Army Today*, Lieutenant-Colonel (now Colonel) Bernd Horn, ed. (Kingston: Director General – Land Combat Development, 2004), 93.

70   McBride, "Gaining Respect and Loyalty," 99.

71   As one officer noted, "If the officer looks after their interests, soldiers will undoubtedly look after him/her when the time comes." See Ibid., 98.

72   Goodspeed interview.

73   Author's personal and confidential interview with Sergeant Kurt Grant, CD, 14 September 2005.

74   *Dishonoured Legacy*, Vol. 2, 370.

75   Bird, *Ghosts*, 53-4. For an additional example of a soldier's reaction to being toyed with and teased while working, see Eedson Louis Millard Burns, *General Mud: Memoirs of Two World Wars* (Toronto: Clarke, Irwin & Company, 1970), 37.

76   DND, *Conceptual Foundations*, 64.

77   Desmond Morton has noted that bullying has rarely produced efficient and successful soldiers. He writes, "Present-day Canadians are no more impressed than their victorious ancestors by bullying and insults. It takes little historical research to discover that Canadians have never responded well to such treatment, nor have other effective warriors. Such behaviours … are evidence not of valued traditions but of weak self-confidence and low

CHAPTER 2

personal esteem." See Desmond Morton, *Morton Report*, "Leadership." http://www.forces.gc.ca/site/minister/eng/Morton/MORTONe.htm. 23 December 2005.

[78] Lambert interview. In this case specifically, the officer in question was removed on the grounds that he would be attending a course. The reasons for his "sacking" were not made public, although it was generally thought by many, both at the time and afterwards, that he was removed because of his inadquate performance. Regardless of the cause, his subordinates were happy to see him leave.

[79] Lamothe interview.

[80] Ibid.

[81] Moreau interview.

[82] Bird, *Ghosts*, 128-29.

[83] Author's personal and confidential interview with Major Brent Beardsley, MSC, CD, 15 July 2005.

[84] Beardsley interview.

[85] Gardam, *Korea Volunteer*, "Guardsman on Hill 355," 217.

[86] Author's personal and confidential interview with Lieutenant-Colonel Howard Coombs, CD, 12 September 2005.

[87] Harold Penryn Rusden, "Notes on the Suppression of the Northwest Insurrection," in *Reminiscences of a Bungle by One of the Bunglers and Two Other Northwest Rebellion Diaries*, R.C. Macleod, ed. (Edmonton: UAP, 1983), 285.

[88] Scislowski, *Not All Of Us Were Brave*, 213. One commentator on the phenomenon of mutiny has observed, "The leader must identify with his soldiers and take an active interest in their welfare. This welfare may take the form of delivering success on the battlefield, sharing risk and danger, ensuring fresh rations, or distributing mail or information. The group determines what the correct and sincere level of involvement with their lives is." Hamby, "The Mutiny Wagon Wheel," 589-90.

[89] Haynes, "The Importance of Building Credibility," 104.

[90] Davis, *The Sharp End*, 35.

[91] Gardam, *Korea Volunteer*, "Guardsman on Hill 355," 219. In like manner, Bert Hoffmeister's soldiers "respected him" since "he marched with them, he dug his own trenches [and] he looked after their welfare...." See Delaney, *Hoffmeister*, 27.

[92] In South Africa, soldiers belonging to William Otter's Royal Canadians were more than a little dismayed when they received their Christmas meal that consisted of "a small portion of chicken, spoiled fruit and vegetables, and an insufficient quantity of beer." The fact that their officers received a larger and more sumptuous meal only furthered their ire. See Carman Miller, *Painting the Map Red: Canada and the South African War, 1899-1902* (Montreal and Kingston: McGill-Queen's University Press, 1993), 81.

[93] The Somalia Inquiry observed, for instance, "Troops will accept shortages of weapons and equipment out of necessity but not due to lack of concern by their leaders. They are justified in their expectations that commanders will do everything possible to get the necessary equipment and supplies." *Dishonoured Legacy*, Vol. 2, 371.

CHAPTER 2

[94] *Canadian Letters and Images Project*, Department of History, Malaspina University College, British Columbia [*CLIP*], Walter F. Stewart Collection, Diary entry for 16 July 1885. http://web.mala.bc.ca/davies/letters.images/W.F.Stewart/diary.4.htm. 23 December 2005.

[95] A similar phenomenon has been noted elsewhere. The Hudson's Bay Company attempted to sell goods at exorbitant prices to Rusden and his mates on their eastward voyage home. The soldiers did not complain as they possessed adequate funds, and were so tired of the items that they had been forced to subsist on in the field that the goods, although expensive, came as a welcome change. Having suffered such deprivations, they willingly submitted to financial exploitation in order to improve their comfort and perhaps to celebrate their recent victory. See Rusden, "Notes," 301. By way of comparison, soldiers new to the Army who had not yet served in any significant capacity greatly resented financial exploitation. In the autumn of 1914 at Valcartier, Canada's initial mobilization camp, a civilian contractor repeatedly showed the same serial film time and time again without respite. After the soldiers could bear seeing *The Perils of Pauline* no longer, they pulled down the tent that doubled as a makeshift theatre and in the confusion that followed, the cashbox (and presumably all of its contents) vanished, while the tent itself caught fire. See Desmond Morton, *When Your Number's Up - The Canadian Soldier during the First World War* (Toronto: Random House, 1993), 19. Later, in late-1915, while en route to England from Halifax aboard the Cunard liner *Saxonia*, volunteer infantrymen ransacked a canteen causing "apples, ginger ale, biscuits and chocolate [to be] strewn about the deck in one grand mélange. It seems that the long-suffering troops had rebelled at paying ten cents for worm-eaten apples and mouldy chocolate, and … had staged a raid …." See Frank Byron Ferguson, Peter G. Rogers, ed. *Gunner Ferguson's Diary: The Diary of Gunner Frank Byron Ferguson: 1st Canadian Siege Battery, Canadian Expeditionary Force, 1915-1918* (Hantsport, Nova Scotia: Lancelot Press, 1985), 28 November 1915, 18-9.

[96] *CLIP*, David Morrison Stewart Collection, Diary entry for 17 June 1900. http://web.mala.bc.ca/davies/letters.images/D.M.Stewart/diary2.htm. 23 December 2005.

[97] Cassels, "Diary," 20 April 1885, 135.

[98] Scislowski, *Not All Of Us Were Brave*, 31-2.

[99] Cassels, "Diary," 15 April 1885, 131.

[100] Fraser, *Journal*, 8 February 1916, 93.

[101] Miller, "The Unhappy Warriors," 88.

[102] Arthur J. Lapointe, R.C. Fetherstonhaugh, tr. *Soldier of Quebec, 1916-1919* (Montreal: Editions Edouard Garand, 1931), 8 January 1917, 15.

[103] Deward Barnes, Bruce Cane, ed., *It Made You Think of Home: The Haunting Journal of Deward Barnes, Canadian Expeditionary Force: 1916-1919* (Toronto: Dundurn, 2004), 24 and 26.

[104] Davis, *The Sharp End*, 110.

[105] Stanley Arthur Rutledge, *Pen Pictures From The Trenches* (Toronto: Wm. Briggs, 1918), 29 March 1916, 105.

CHAPTER 2

[106] Adamson, *Letters*, Agar to Mabel, 21 November 1917, 316.
[107] Burns, *General Mud*, 14-5.
[108] Tim Cook, "'More a medicine than a beverage': 'Demon Rum' and the Canadian Trench Soldier of the First World War," *Canadian Military History*, Vol. 9, No. 1 (Winter 2000), 15.
[109] Cook, "Demon Rum," 15. Cook also mentions an incident where an officer of the 54th Battalion, CEF, refused to issue rum to his men immediately before a battle whereupon the "expectant soldiers" threatened him; they eventually received their tot! See Ibid., 12.
[110] Ibid., 15.
[111] Burns, *General Mud*, 63.
[112] Lieutenant-Colonel (now Colonel) Bernd Horn, "A Timeless Strength: The Army's Senior NCO Corps," *Canadian Military Journal*, Vol. 3, No. 2 (Spring 2002), 42.
[113] Typescript diary, 114-15, Edward Lester fonds, Manuscript Group [MG] 29-E105, *LAC*.
[114] Lester fonds, 24.
[115] Madsen, *Another Kind of Justice*, 51. Certainly, "…the citizen-soldier will not entirely relinquish the rights of the citizen." Smith, *Between Mutiny and Obedience*, 11.
[116] Field-Marshal Earl Wavell, *The Good Soldier* (London: Macmillan, 1948), 16.
[117] Typescript diary, Part II, entry for 10 December 1899, 4, Frederick Harold Dunham fonds, MG29-E89, *LAC*.
[118] Bird, *Ghosts*, 1-3.
[119] Vokes, *My Story*, 26.
[120] Adamson, *Letters*, Agar to Mabel, 18 April 1917, 275. As evidence of his concern for the manner in which he interacted with his men, Adamson related to his wife, "I am beginning to find out more about the men in the Company [by] sitting about and talking during the day." See Adamson, *Letters*, Agar to Mabel, 24 March 1915, 49. He also related, "I always ask each man if there is anything he would like to tell me about himself in private and I get many secrets and I think it is inclined to help the men if they know you take more than a general interest in them." See Adamson, *Letters*, Agar to Mabel, 24 November 1917, 317. Finally, Agar frequently asked Mabel to visit wounded men and officers who were recovering in English hospitals and to ask if there was anything that they needed or would like done for them. For one of many possible examples, see Adamson, *Letters*, Agar to Mabel, 25 October 1918, 346.
[121] Reginald H. Roy, *For Most Conspicuous Bravery: A Biography of Major-General George R. Pearkes, V.C., Through Two World Wars* (Vancouver: UBC Press, 1977), 66-7. For some impressions of George Pearkes as a soldier during the Second World War, see Vokes, *My Story*, 72-3.
[122] Soldiers serving with the PPCLI apparently respected Adamson for many of the same reasons. As a company commander, one of his responsi-

bilities was to censor his men's outgoing mail. One of his soldiers apparently wrote of him, "'Our Captain whose name is Adamson is a dear, good, fat old man who crawls about in the trenches like a porpoise and speaks to us like real men.'" See Adamson, *Letters*, Agar to Mabel, 4 March 1915, 32.

[123] Lester fonds, 60, 91 & 122.

[124] Typescript letter dated 30 December 1899, Frederick Ramsay fonds, MG30-E231, *LAC*.

[125] Hennessey interview.

[126] Gardam, *Korea Volunteer*, "Flip a Coin: Heads, Military College; Tails, McGill University," 148-49.

[127] Lamothe interview.

[128] Louis Keene, *"Crumps" ~ The Plain Story of a Canadian Who Went* (New York: Houghton Mifflin, 1917), 66.

[129] Keene, *Crumps*, 92. Agar Adamson also found that passing information downward through the chain of command had a salutary effect on the "spirit of the men." See Adamson, *Letters*, Agar to Mabel, 25 October 1917, 307.

[130] Miller, "The Unhappy Warriors," 96.

[131] Leaders could ensure the trust and confidence of their subordinates by keeping them fully informed. See France, "The Heart and Soul of the Company," 87. In a similar manner, "Inducing soldiers to comply with dangerous orders, in short, is mostly an emotional game with mirrors, requiring psychological sleight of hand. At the decisive moments, effective leadership consists in persuasively redefining the situation, reconstructing the soldiers' sense of reality, so that what initially seems a foolhardy or even suicidal course of action comes to seem possible, even indispensable." Osiel, *Obeying Orders*, 218.

[132] Kellett, *Combat Motivation*, 251.

[133] Major-General (ret'd) Guy. S. Meloy, United States Army, from *Reflections of a Former Troop Leader*, as cited in DND, *Conceptual Foundations*, 90.

[134] Ibid., 50.

[135] Goodspeed interview.

[136] Coombs interview.

[137] Scislowski, *Not All Of Us Were Brave*, 140. On this point, Anthony Kellet opines, "... outright disobedience is a relatively rare occurrence in combat because it too obviously invites sanctions. Yet in modern warfare soldiers have found ways of reducing the risks implicit in their orders without inviting retribution. That is, they may comply with the letter of their instructions, but not necessarily with the spirit." Kellett, *Combat Motivation*, 147.

[138] Author's personal and confidential interview with Chief Warrant Officer James (Jim) Boland, MMM, CD, 20 July 2005.

[139] Leaders could win their subordinates' trust by showing them respect and being willing to listen to their ideas and opinions. See Lieutenant-Colonel (now Colonel) Bernd Horn, "What Soldiers Want: A Perspective on Soldier Expectations," in *In the Breach: Perspectives on Leadership in the Army*

Today, Bernd Horn, ed. (Kingston: Director General – Land Combat Development, 2004), 35. See also Captain M.A. Blanchette, "Selected Experiences of a Platoon Commander," in *In the Breach: Perspectives on Leadership in the Army Today*, Bernd Horn, ed. (Kingston: Director General – Land Combat Development, 2004), 152.

[140] Goodspeed interview.

[141] Lamothe interview.

[142] Interview with D.D. Spencer, Royal Canadian Regiment, Accession 1980-0123, C07859(2) & C07860(1), Canadian Broadcasting Corporation, *LAC*.

[143] Bird, *Ghosts*, 112. Other authors have observed that "quietism," that is, keeping one's opinion private, was an integral component of many military cultures. See James, *Mutiny in the British and Commonwealth Forces*, 11-2. See also, Smith, *Between Mutiny and Obedience*, 250.

[144] Ramsay fonds, typescript letter dated 23 March 1900.

[145] Holmes, *Acts of War*, 341.

[146] Karol W.J. Wenek, "Looking Ahead: Contexts of Canadian Forces Leadership Today and Tomorrow", (Unpublished paper produced for CFLI, July 2002), 5. http://www.cda.forces.gc.ca/cfli/engraph/research/pdf/72.pdf. 23 December 2005. Another scholar has similarly observed, "…modern soldiers, better educated and used to a higher standard of living, have become progressively less willing to endure hardships imposed by the failure of any kind of leadership. With good or even adequate leaders, soldiers of all nations will usually perform to and usually beyond expectations, but without good formal leadership, a military unit will frequently fail to achieve its definition of success." See Hamby, "The Mutiny Wagon Wheel," 594.

[147] Wenek, "Looking Ahead", 20. See also, Bercuson, *Significant Incident*, 88-9.

[148] Wenek, "Looking Ahead", 20.

[149] DND, *Conceptual Foundations*, 64.

[150] Cassels, "Diary," 15 July 1885, 229.

[151] Ramsay fonds, typescript letter dated 8 January 1900.

[152] Edmund Fuller thought that mutiny "…is as old as the idea of authority itself, and though it will change its forms under changing circumstances, it is likely to exist as long as authority exists." See Edmund Fuller, *Mutiny! Being Accounts of Insurrections, Famous and Infamous, on Land and Sea, from the Days of the Caesars to Modern Times* (New York: Crown Publishers, 1953), ix.

[153] Bill McAndrew, "Canadian Officership: An Overview" in Bernd Horn and Stephen J. Harris, eds., *Generalship and the Art of the Admiral: Perspectives of Senior Canadian Military Leadership* (St. Catharines: Vanwell Publishing Ltd., 2001), 41.

[154] Morton, "Kicking and Complaining," 360.

[155] Bird, Ghosts, 25.

[156] Great Britain, War Office, *Manual of Military Law*, 1914. 6th Edition. (London: HMSO, 1914), 16.

[157] Miller, "The Unhappy Warriors," 98. Other historians have also realized the connection between leadership and disobedience, and as such, "It has often been argued that navies have to be less authoritarian, more consensual in their approach to 'human resources' if they are to function efficiently." See, Bell and Elleman, *Naval Mutinies*, xvii.

CHAPTER 3

Mutiny and the Royal Canadian Navy

Christopher M. Bell

> *Mutiny? Pure piffle, nonsense. They were perfectly orderly the whole time.*[1]

Mutinies, like the armed services in which they occur, reflect the societies that produce them. Throughout history, naval personnel have defied authority in pursuit of a wide variety of goals, ranging from the improvement of shipboard conditions to far-reaching political reform and, in rare cases, outright revolution. This chapter examines the Royal Canadian Navy's (RCN) experience with mutiny. It begins by providing a conceptual framework for understanding naval mutinies as a phenomenon across time and borders. Mutinies in the navies of modern, democratic states like Canada have traditionally differed in important ways from those in authoritarian regimes or less-developed societies. In the former, mutinies have usually been short-lived, non-violent and easily resolved. They sometimes spread from ship to ship, but the mutineers' demands mostly remained moderate and limited. In the latter, such incidents have been less frequent, but were more often characterized by violence, escalating demands and revolutionary intent.[2] This chapter also places the Canadian navy's experience into an imperial context. Britain's Royal Navy (RN) already had a centuries-old tradition of mutiny when the RCN was established in 1910. Canada's new service adopted or absorbed many of the RN's laws, customs and traditions, including those relating to matters of discipline and welfare. Thus, for many officers and ratings, their training and service with the RN shaped their attitudes toward mutiny. Finally, this chapter examines the RCN's own mutinies. These episodes were relatively modest affairs, with disgruntled ratings generally locking themselves into a mess deck to draw attention to complaints about matters such as leave, workload or treatment by officers. These protests, which authorities and participants alike were loath to label as mutinies, occurred periodically throughout the Second World War and continued into the post-war era, culminating in the outbreak of three mutinies over three weeks in early-1949.[3]

The term *mutiny* has traditionally been used to describe a diverse group of activities, many of which seem far removed from the dramatic and violent events normally associated with mutiny in the popular mind. The law does little to clarify the problem, as legal definitions of mutiny tend to be both broad and ambiguous. The United States' Uniform Code of Military Justice, for example, focuses on the intent of the mutineers as the defining feature of mutiny, reserving the charge for an individual who "with intent to usurp or override lawful military authority, refuses, in concert with any other person, to obey orders or otherwise do his duty." It also allows for an individual act-

CHAPTER 3

ing alone to be charged with this offence.[4] Britain's Naval Discipline Acts, on the other hand, have always defined mutiny as, fundamentally, a group activity, describing it most recently as "a combination between two or more persons ... to overthrow or resist lawful authority in Her Majesty's forces ...; to disobey such authority ...; or to impede the performance of any duty or service in Her Majesty's forces."[5]

Canadian usage has closely followed Britain's. When the RCN was established in 1910, Canada incorporated Britain's 1866 Naval Defence Act directly into its own Naval Service Act. Canadian ratings, like their British counterparts, were forbidden to combine with others "for the purpose of bringing about alterations in existing regulations or customs of the Naval Service."[6] Thus, individuals could seek the redress of grievances, but groups could not. The first uniquely Canadian code of discipline, the 1944 Naval Service Act, and its successor, the National Defence Act, clearly show their British heritage.[7] Canadian authorities now define mutiny as an act of "collective insubordination or a combination of two or more persons in the resistance of lawful authority in any of Her Majesty's Forces or in any forces cooperating therewith."[8] Canada's Code of Service Discipline does acknowledge, however, that all mutinies are not created equal. Those accompanied by violence are potentially punishable with life imprisonment, while those without are subject to lesser terms, except for individuals designated as "ringleaders," who may also be imprisoned for life.[9]

Distinguishing between violent and non-violent incidents may be helpful from a disciplinary perspective, but as a phenomenon, mutinies are best understood by focussing on the nature of the objectives that produce or sustain them. Most mutinies are conceived by what sociologist Cornelis Lammers calls "collective action to improve or maintain the position of the group [i.e., the sailors] with respect to its income or other work conditions."[10] They are thus similar in appearance and intent to an industrial strike, with mutineers motivated solely or primarily by relatively mundane issues such as pay, leave, working conditions, discipline or food. In some instances, however, mutinies at sea have had more profound causes. In the 20th century, sailors have turned to mutiny as a means to overthrow governments or achieve far-reaching social or economic reform. Probably the only feature that all mutinies share is that they constitute a deliberate and concerted defiance of legal authority. A recent comparative study of modern naval mutinies by Christopher M. Bell and Bruce Elleman outlines four basic types of mutiny, which will be labelled here as *minor*, *major* (or *political*), *seizure of power* and *secession*.[11]

Minor mutinies, the type that occur most frequently, consist of isolated incidents prompted, in most cases, by conditions unique to a particular ship. N.A.M. Rodger, in his study of the Georgian Royal Navy, notes that "collective actions by whole ship's companies" were actually quite common during that period.[12] He further claims:

> When other methods [of obtaining redress] failed, mutiny provided a formal system of public protest to bring grievances to the notice of authority. It was a sort of safety-valve, harmless, indeed useful, so long as it was not abused. It was part of a system of social relations which provided an effective working compromise between the demands of necessity and humanity, a means of reconciling the Navy's need of obedience and efficiency with the individual's grievances. It was a means of safeguarding the essential stability of shipboard society, not of destroying it.[13]

Mutiny often plays the same role in modern navies as well. In these cases, sailors' demands usually remain limited and moderate, in large measure to avoid the appearance that a mutiny is, in fact, taking place. Participants may even be unaware that passive acts of defiance legally constitute mutiny as well. And while officers generally do know this, they are usually no less eager than their subordinates to avoid using the term. Because a ship's officers have the power to satisfy basic grievances themselves, these incidents seldom turn violent and are generally resolved quickly and easily, often without the mutineers being punished.

The situation becomes more complicated when a ship's officers or the navy's local commanders cannot easily satisfy their sailors' grievances. In some instances, the complaints that spark a mutiny relate to problems that affect an entire fleet or navy. They sometimes stem from things as simple as pay, but may also reflect more systemic issues, such as social, national or racial tensions within the service. In most cases, *major* (or *political*) mutinies are still aimed at promoting sailors' work-related interests, but they are fundamentally different from the *minor* mutinies discussed above in that they attempt to exert pressure on their government rather than on naval authorities. This does not, however, signify an outright rejection of the government's authority or legitimacy. On the contrary, in these instances, the act of mutiny represents a desire by the participants to engage in their nation's political process by openly protesting decisions that adversely affect their interests. In democratic states, naval personnel are generally conscious of the rights enjoyed by their civilian counterparts when confronted with similar challenges, and the resort to mutiny is rationalized as an assertion of those same fundamental rights. In less-developed states, collective insubordination may represent one of the few means sailors have to exert influence on civil authorities.

A mutiny in the Royal Navy's Atlantic Fleet in September 1931 provides an excellent example of a *political* mutiny in a democratic state. In this instance, ratings mutinied when they learned that drastic pay cuts were about

CHAPTER 3

to be imposed on them by the government.[14] Relations between officers and men remained cordial throughout the mutiny, however. The sailors' complaints were not directed against their immediate superiors or the commander of the fleet, all of whom were clearly not responsible for the situation and were equally incapable of resolving it as well. The mutineers' decision to prevent ships from sailing was a calculated move to force concessions directly from the government, which alone had the power to moderate pay. A mutiny in the Brazilian navy in 1910, on the other hand, demonstrates how mutiny may be employed as a political tool in a less-developed state. On this occasion, Afro-Brazilian sailors protested against brutal discipline throughout the service by seizing control of warships in Rio de Janeiro's Guanabara Bay. To force the government into eliminating racial injustices in the navy, mutineers turned the fleet's guns on the nation's capital city, effectively holding the civilian population and the federal government hostage.[15] *Political* mutinies, therefore, have a different dynamic from *minor* mutinies. Because they stem from widespread issues, they are much more likely to spread beyond a single ship or squadron. And because they tend to generate greater demands, they are correspondingly more difficult to resolve and are more liable to involve violence.

In rare cases, mutiny represents a form of outright rebellion against the state. The majority of these incidents can be classified as *seizure of power* mutinies. When sailors' demands are so far-reaching that they cannot be accommodated within the existing political framework, they may resort to mutiny as a means to alter the political *status quo*. This is exactly what happened in the Soviet Union in March 1921, when naval ratings, disillusioned with the course that the revolution had taken, seized control of the Kronstadt naval base and demanded fundamental political reforms from the Bolshevik leadership. In instances such as this, where the survival of both parties is ultimately at stake, violence is virtually unavoidable. The Kronstadt mutiny was not resolved until the Soviet regime mounted a large-scale military operation against the mutineers. The mutineers were punished with great brutality after the base had been captured. There are instances, however, where insurgents have been successful. In 1918, for example, a mutiny in the German High Seas Fleet sparked the revolution that led to the establishment of the Weimar Republic.

Revolution is such a difficult and risky proposition, however, that the sailors' alienation from the state or naval authorities may manifest itself in an attempt to secure their autonomy. In a *secession* mutiny, sailors physically seize control of a warship in order to obtain mobility and firepower, both of which may be used to escape entirely from the state's authority and to avoid punishment. During the age of sail, mutineers who pursued this course would often turn to piracy or, as in the case of HMS *Bounty*, attempt to vanish into remote areas. In the last century, sailors have preferred to seek asylum from a sympathetic foreign government.

CHAPTER 3

Mutinies, especially large ones, are inherently chaotic events and do not always fit neatly into a single category. In the first place, mutineers may differ amongst themselves with respect to their objectives. When a French fleet mutinied in the Black Sea in 1919, for example, some sailors hoped only to improve local conditions of service (*minor* mutiny), others sought to pressure the government to demobilise them or end the intervention in the Russian civil war (*political* mutiny) and a handful wished to exploit the unrest to spark a communist revolution in France (*seizure of power* mutiny).[16] Second, mutineers may disagree with higher authorities about the nature of a mutiny. The latter often see political or revolutionary motives where none are intended, or recognise better than the mutineers, the potential of even minor incidents to undermine their authority and prestige. Finally, the objectives of a mutiny are not always static. The famous 1905 mutiny on the Russian battleship *Potemkin*, for example, began as an isolated protest against bad food (*minor* mutiny) but quickly developed into an attempt to spark a national revolution (*seizure of power* mutiny). When mutineers failed to achieve this goal, they sailed to Rumania in search of asylum (*secession* mutiny).

Bell and Elleman refer to the tendency for mutineers' demands to become more extensive or radical after a mutiny has begun as a process of *vertical escalation*. This progression is not automatic, however. In many mutinies, and especially in *minor* ones, sailors appreciate that their best chance of achieving a satisfactory outcome rests in keeping their demands limited and reasonable. The potential for escalation, though, is always present. Even when sailors are eager to downplay the seriousness of a mutiny, they also recognise that there is often little additional risk in making demands that go beyond the complaints that triggered the mutiny in the first place, provided that these other complaints are not of a political or radical nature. Moreover, because mutiny is such a drastic step to take, mutineers looking only to improve local conditions may inflate their list of grievances to reassure authorities that they have sufficient justification for their actions. This certainly appears to have been the case, for example, during the mutinies (discussed below) in HMCS *Rivière-du-Loup* and HMCS *Magnificent*. In the latter case, investigators concluded that the men's more mundane complaints were advanced "as a justification for the incident after it had happened and that many of the criticisms were cited as excuses for insubordination rather than a prior cause for its occurrence."[17]

Sailors' demands will also tend to escalate as a mutiny spreads from one ship to another, or from ships to shore establishments. As the size of a mutiny grows, so does the bargaining power of the participants. A mutinous fleet can expect to extract greater concessions from the government than can a single ship, and mutineers will often modify their goals to reflect newfound opportunities. Finally, the radicalisation of sailors' demands is closely linked to their expectations regarding the ultimate resolution of the mutiny. Once mutineers become convinced that a peaceful resolution is not possible, or that they will be severely punished for their actions, they will have little incentive left for moderation. This occurs rarely in democratic states, but authoritarian regimes and many less-developed states have both a low tolerance for dissent and a propensity toward violence. If mutineers feel that they have been backed into a corner, seeking autonomy or attempting to overthrow the government may become the only means to obtain a satisfactory outcome.

The tendency for a mutiny to spread has been described, again by Bell and Elleman, as a process of *horizontal escalation*.[18] As long as the complaints that provoke insubordination are restricted to a single vessel, there is little likelihood that this will happen, as sailors on other ships will have nothing to gain by joining the disturbance. But if grievances are widely shared, the potential for a mutiny to spread increases dramatically. There is normally much less risk involved in joining a mutiny than in starting one. Once one ship has taken the lead in defying authority, others may join the mutiny knowing that they are less likely to be singled out for punishment. There is, moreover, a certain safety in numbers. As a mutiny grows, the prospect of collective punishment tends to decrease. Sailors are well aware that it is not feasible to hang every sailor in a fleet. They also appreciate that joining a mutiny increases the pressure on either the naval authorities or the government, thereby improving their chances of success. Thus, once a mutiny begins to spread, it easily gains momentum. This may be accompanied by an increase in scope or in the severity of the mutineers' demands, but vertical and horizontal escalation are not necessarily linked. In democratic states especially, the tendency is for demands to remain moderate and focussed on the proximate causes of the protest. The two types of escalation are most likely to occur together when mutiny spreads in a service already plagued by serious systemic problems, or when naval grievances begin to merge with social, economic or political disputes affecting civilian society.

Because mutinies have the potential to escalate in dangerous and unexpected ways, the initial decision to defy authority is seldom taken lightly. In general terms, disgruntled sailors resort to mutiny when there are no legal means available to resolve serious grievances. In the case of *minor* mutinies, the ultimate source of the sailors' complaints is usually the ship's officers. If such leaders are unwilling – or appear to be unwilling – to address the complaints that have been put through the proper channels, sailors may decide that they must resort to extreme measures to resolve matters. Much the same is true of the other types of mutinies, except that in these instances, legal channels may simply not exist, they may be deemed inadequate, or the responsible authorities may oppose concessions altogether.

For mutiny to be a rational option, however, complaints must be serious enough to justify the risk. Punishment for mutiny can be severe. Many countries have retained the death penalty as a maximum punishment for this offence. In democratic states, mutineers still face the possibility of lengthy prison terms. Furthermore, the law does not always distinguish between ringleaders and other participants, or between active participants and passive supporters. Even bystanders can potentially face punishment. Canada's National Defence Act, for example, allows for life imprisonment of an individual who, "being present, does not use his utmost endeavours to suppress a mutiny," or, "being aware of an actual or intended mutiny, does not without delay inform his superior officer thereof."[19] There are numerous instances in the past century of sailors being executed for mutiny, although this seldom occurs outside of authoritarian regimes. In practice, democracies rarely apply harsh penalties. Western armed services go to great lengths to provide channels, both official and unofficial, for lower-ranking personnel to represent concerns about their working conditions. There is thus a realisation by naval and civilian authorities that when a *minor* mutiny does occur, it often stems from the failure of the ship's officers to address legitimate grievances. Moreover, because sailors will usually find means to express dissatisfaction with their working conditions long before a mutiny occurs, officers are expected to resolve such problems in a timely manner. Thus, as long as a mutiny does not turn violent and the sailors' complaints appear justified, it is usually the officers who are censured. Nevertheless, the existence of drastic penalties for mutiny serves as a powerful deterrent to would-be mutineers.

The complaints that can trigger a mutiny vary considerably. Ratings everywhere are usually resigned to a certain amount of inconvenience and are often willing to suffer additional or even extreme hardships out of a sense of duty, especially if such impositions are for a short duration or become necessary during wartime. Numerous factors, however, can undermine their willingness to do so. In the case of *minor* mutinies, where local conditions are the primary cause of discontent and seemingly trivial incidents may have a disproportionate impact, the critical consideration appears to be sailors' perceptions of what is fair and reasonable treatment. Again, these perceptions are neither static nor universal. Every navy possesses a unique set of values and traditions, and even individual ships will react differently to a given situation. Sailors accustomed to poor working conditions within the service and in civilian society are more likely to mutiny because of unusual hardships than over conditions, however bad, that are accepted as normal.

Other variables are also important in determining how a ship's company will respond to poor conditions. The first is the quality of the ship's captain and executive officer. Trusted and respected commanders inspire confidence in their leadership by demonstrating that their subordinates' grievances will be given a fair hearing. This reality makes recourse to mutiny less likely in the first place and helps to ensure that such incidents will be resolved quickly if they do occur. With unpopular leaders, however, the reverse is normally true. A second variable is the risk involved in openly defying authority. Sailors must carefully weigh their grievances against the likelihood of punishment and the severity

CHAPTER 3

of the penalties. As the perceived risk declines, the incentive to engage in mutiny increases. Finally, personnel will be less inclined to make sacrifices or accept risks if they become alienated from the state or from naval authorities, even if they are unlikely to cite this as a justification for their disobedience. This type of alienation can, however, become a primary motivating factor for mutiny if it becomes great enough. The difficulty facing mutineers in this case is that once local grievances are no longer the ostensible cause of their disobedience, the nature of the mutiny becomes fundamentally altered. In instances such as this, mutineers will opt for secession, an outcome that a single ship has a good chance of achieving. Anything more ambitious, such as forcing a change of government, quickly becomes problematic. Sailors who wish to achieve far-reaching political, economic or social reform have to overcome many obstacles, the most important being organisation. It is virtually impossible for a single ship acting alone to force major concessions from the civil authorities. Ensuring broad support for a mutiny, however, requires considerable preparation. This can be physically difficult when ships are at sea, and it carries with it much greater risk, as the likelihood of detection increases as the size of the conspiracy grows. Consequently, large-scale or revolutionary mutinies seldom begin that way; they are more likely to start as a minor mutiny and escalate.[20]

The RCN's approach to discipline was a natural offshoot of its close ties with the RN. Following the closure of the Royal Naval College of Canada in 1922, RCN officer cadets received an initial five years of training in Great Britain. After returning to Canada, officers continued to serve regularly in sea-going appointments with the RN and were eligible for courses and shore appointments, again in Britain.[21] Not surprisingly, Canadian naval officers absorbed British naval traditions and values, so much so that critics later charged that they were, as a group, more "British" than "Canadian." However, the methods that they acquired from the British were not necessarily ill-suited to a Canadian environment. The 20th century RN strove to instil in its officers a paternalistic attitude toward the lower deck. As one typical memorandum on the subject from the 1930s asserted, naval discipline "must be based on mutual confidence and respect between officers and men." It continued:

> This will only be achieved if officers regard their men as human beings with ambitions, hopes and fears, who have private lives and private troubles. They must also bear in mind that when men come under their command an early opportunity to show some tangible sign of sympathetic leadership should be sought, and thus early in the commission gain the confidence of the ship's company.
>
> The Commanding Officer has the main responsibility and has it in his power to prevent circumstances arising which might make for discontent. For example, in his proposals for commissioning, storing and sailing and for working-up practices he should endeavour to

CHAPTER 3

frame them so that they will not lead to undue hardship. If he is ordered to carry out a programme which, in his judgement, will put an undue strain on his ship's company, it is clearly his duty to represent the matter.[22]

Officers were thus expected to watch carefully over the interests of the men directly under their command so as to gain their confidence and be able to satisfy grievances before they began to undermine discipline.[23] As long as ratings knew that their legitimate complaints would receive prompt and sympathetic attention from their immediate superiors, Canadian naval officers, like their British counterparts, would have been confident that discipline was on a firm basis.

There is no evidence to suggest that this assurance was misplaced. On the contrary, the RN's paternalistic approach was largely successful as discipline was not a serious problem in the service at any time in the first half of the 20th century.[24] Mutinies did occur sporadically during this period, but these were almost all minor incidents motivated by local conditions and confined to single ships. Given the size of the RN during this period, the relative infrequency of mutiny suggests that relations between officers and men were generally sound, even if some individual officers failed to meet the Navy's expectations. On only two occasions in the interwar years did the service experience large-scale disturbances. The first occurred in a number of British ships and in a Royal Marine battalion that were supporting "white" forces in the Russian civil war. In this instance, mass unrest stemmed primarily from complaints relating to food, leave and pay, although war-weariness and a lack of enthusiasm for the intervention in Russia were important contributing factors as well.[25] The second major episode, the 1931 Invergordon mutiny, engulfed most of the British Atlantic Fleet, including four capital ships, for nearly two full days.

The Russian incident seems to have made little impression on either British naval officers or later historians, despite its potentially serious political implications. The Invergordon mutiny, on the other hand, had a deep and lasting impact. The mutiny itself was resolved relatively easily. The Admiralty grudgingly acknowledged the validity of the men's grievances and the government ultimately agreed to reduce its proposed pay cuts. The scale of the insubordination nonetheless came as a profound shock to naval officers. Because they were accustomed to thinking of mutiny in terms of minor incidents in which officers almost inevitably bore primary responsibility, they found it difficult to explain a fleet-wide mutiny as anything other than the manifestation of a general "loss of touch" between officers and men.[26] Notably, the officer corps blamed itself, rather than the lower deck, for this perceived failure. The Admiralty attempted to address this problem through several initiatives. First, the complements of officers on ships were reduced to allow junior officers more opportunities to develop their powers

95

CHAPTER 3

of command. Second, measures were taken to ensure a greater continuity of personnel in the Atlantic Fleet, so that officers and men would have enough time together to develop close ties. Third, the RN's welfare machinery was overhauled to ensure that ratings had to direct complaints to their divisional officers, rather than to the Admiralty, in order to reinforce the bonds between officers and men and to convince ratings that their officers could not be circumvented. Finally, a Director of Personal Services was established at the Admiralty to ensure that the views of the lower deck received careful attention at the highest levels.[27]

Canadian naval officers serving in RN vessels during the 1930s or taking courses in Britain would have been caught-up in the uncertainty that swept through the service in the aftermath of Invergordon. They would also have been exposed to the Navy's efforts to prepare officers to deal with future acts of mass insubordination. This was done primarily through confidential publications made available to officers in ships and shore establishments, and through lectures to junior officers on divisional courses and senior executive officers at the RN College Greenwich.[28] In this material, the Admiralty tacitly accepted that *minor* mutinies would continue to occur from time to time. What clearly haunted senior officers during the 1930s was not the possibility of mutiny, but of another large-scale incident like Invergordon. As one Admiralty official remarked in 1938, "A tiger having once tasted human blood is never supposed to be the same tiger again. So is the Fleet now alive to the fact as to what can be accomplished by a firm front [against authority]."[29] To ensure that future incidents remained localised, officers were instructed to take immediate and firm action to maintain or restore discipline in the face of mass unrest, something senior officers in the Atlantic Fleet had failed to do in 1931. A confidential memorandum issued in August 1932, for example, emphasised "the necessity of putting down any attempt at collective indiscipline promptly and with a strong hand." It continued:

> Should there be any evidence of general discontent which might develop into massed disobedience, or if such disobedience occurs, the action of all officers must be such as to indicate unmistakably that they intend to retain or regain control and to uphold discipline. Prompt action must be taken at the same time to make it clear to the men that their grievances will be investigated and, if found to be genuine, remedied with as little delay as possible, provided they continue to carry out their duties.[30]

The maintenance of discipline was therefore seen as essentially a question of leadership. Officers were reassured that any ship's company would contain only a small number of natural troublemakers and potential ringleaders, and that "the majority of men can be relied upon if they are given the proper lead by their officers."[31]

The Admiralty's concerns about the foundations of naval discipline were largely unfounded. The Invergordon mutiny was little more than a spontaneous reaction to drastic and unfair pay cuts, not a sign of systemic problems within the Fleet. Ratings were not alienated from their officers, but were forced to circumvent them because their real dispute was with higher authorities. The lower deck's success on this occasion did not, however, leave it more disposed to defy naval authority in the future. The RN experienced only one other notable mutiny before the outbreak of the Second World War, when ratings on the battleship HMS *Warspite* gathered on the ship's forecastle for an unauthorised meeting to discuss an unexpected curtailment of leave. A Board of Enquiry later reported that "no particular precautions were taken to keep this meeting secret," suggesting that "the men in fact wanted it to be discovered so that their grievance could be unmistakeably demonstrated."[32] This was just the sort of "safety valve" that the RN regarded as a normal part of service life. The incident would probably have attracted little attention if a handful of ratings had not exhorted the ship's company to continue the demonstration after being addressed by the captain, resulting in Marines being used to clear the quarterdeck.[33] This type of mutiny also occurred periodically in the RN during the Second World War without prompting serious concern at the Admiralty. All of this demonstrates that once the initial shock of the Invergordon mutiny had worn off, discipline in the RN quickly returned to "business as usual," with minor mutinies being treated by both ratings and officers as a relatively harmless means of drawing attention to grievances that could not be resolved through normal channels.

Such attitudes were in keeping with a tradition of mutiny in the RN that clearly stretched as far back as the Georgian period, when minor incidents were, as N.A.M. Rodger has shown, also a common occurrence, and an acceptable one at that, provided they conformed to certain "unwritten rules." According to Rodger, these rules were generally understood in the following terms:

1. No mutiny shall take place at sea or in the face of the enemy;
2. No personal violence may be employed (although a degree of tumult and shouting is permissible);
3. Mutinies shall be held in pursuit only of objectives sanctioned by the traditions of the Service.[34]

In a similar vein, David Divine's study of the Invergordon mutiny refers to "a community memory, on the lower deck, of success in the righting of past wrongs and of the methods and rules to be observed in the event of future necessity."[35] Divine is mistaken, however, in suggesting that fleet-wide disturbances such as Invergordon and its predecessor, the 1797 mutiny of the Channel Fleet at Spithead, were part of this tradition. In fact, on these two occasions, mutineers broke another "unwritten rule," namely that mutinies were to be confined to a single ship. Because they engulfed entire fleets,

CHAPTER 3

these incidents generated widespread alarm within the service. It is also important to recognise that the tradition of mutiny was not, as Divine implies, restricted to the collective memory of the lower deck. Officers understood this tradition at least as well as their men. Indeed, for the "rules" to work, there had to be a tacit understanding between officers and men that as long as protests stemmed from legitimate complaints, mutineers would not be subjected to draconian punishment.

The British tradition of mutiny would have been passed to both the officers and ratings of the RCN through their frequent contact with the RN. Canadian ratings, for instance, took courses in Britain and served on British ships during this period, ensuring that they would share their officers' familiarity with British naval customs and traditions.[36] As in the case of the RN, it is impossible to determine how often minor incidents occurred in Canadian vessels, as most would have been resolved by a ship's officers without higher authorities becoming aware that anything had happened. There are, in fact, few recorded instances of collective disobedience in the RCN prior to the Second World War. The earliest of these occurred in February 1918. On this occasion, a group of four Newfoundland sailors attached to HMCS *Niobe* in Halifax refused to work until their rate of pay (40 cents a day) was raised to match the higher rate ($1.10 to $1.20) of Canadian naval personnel. Their demand was ultimately met, which may have emboldened Canadian seamen and stokers to refuse several months later to put to sea in the minesweeper *TR 30*, where living conditions below deck were regarded as "intolerable." In this instance, however, the mutineers were sentenced to eighteen month's hard labour.[37]

No other mutiny is recorded prior to 1936 when sailors in the destroyer HMCS *Skeena* briefly barricaded themselves into the mess deck during the destroyer's annual spring cruise.[38] The ship had travelled as far south as Acapulco, where in previous years, a "tropical routine" had been adopted so that the men would not have to work in the tropical heat past noon. *Skeena*'s executive officer, Lieutenant-Commander (later Rear-Admiral) H. Nelson Lay, had informed the company that the change would be taking place that day, but the captain decided to continue the normal routine indefinitely. Learning that the men had decided not to fall in that afternoon, Lay resolved the situation in precisely the manner laid down by the Admiralty. According to his memoirs, he expressed his sympathy with the disgruntled sailors and warned them of the seriousness of their actions. "By refusing to 'fall in' when piped," he informed them:

> ... you have, in fact, started a mutiny, and a mutiny is a very dangerous thing to start. If you look out the scuttle you will see there is a British cruiser in Acapulco harbour and if you persist in the present situation, I will have to report to the Captain that the ship's compa-

ny refuse to obey orders. He will then send a signal to the Captain of the cruiser which has 100 Royal Marines on board. They will come over here, you will all be arrested and taken over to the cruiser and put in custody there. You will then be tried by Court Martial. Now, King's Regulations and Admiralty Instructions lay down that, 'the penalty for mutiny is death or such other punishment as is hereinafter mentioned.' So you see what a serious position you have put yourself in. Now, I am going to give you one chance. I'm going aft to the Quarter Deck and will pipe 'hands fall in'. If everyone falls in, I will not report this incident officially to the Captain. I will also try and persuade him to allow me to go into tropical routine as soon as possible.[39]

His words apparently settled the matter. The men returned to work that afternoon, the captain changed the routine the following day and no penalties were ever imposed.

Incidents of this nature continued to take place in the RCN during the Second World War. Vice-Admiral Ralph Hennessy later recounted how, as a young Sub-Lieutenant in HMCS *Assiniboine*, he had been astonished by the other officers' "relative acceptance" of a mess deck lock-in that took place in the ship in the late-spring or early-summer of 1940. This incident was probably typical in that the ship's officers treated it "as an internal event."[40] A similar protest in November 1942 in the armed yacht HMCS *Reindeer* did come to the attention of higher authorities, but clearly failed to generate much alarm. In this instance, the ship's captain, an unpopular Royal Canadian Naval Volunteer Reserve (RCNVR) lieutenant, was removed from command and no disciplinary action was taken against the sailors.[41]

In fact, only a handful of mutinies in Canada's wartime navy are well documented. The first of these, and probably the RCN's best-known wartime mutiny, occurred in July 1943 in the *Tribal*-class destroyer HMCS *Iroquois*.[42] Ratings had been unhappy for some time with their commanding officer, Commander W.B.L. Holms, RCN. As Michael Whitby has noted, the short-tempered Holms "showed little tolerance for mistakes, cursing loudly at and sometimes 'manhandling' ratings who did not perform to his satisfaction."[43] The ship's company also resented Holms' practice of stopping the leave of a whole mess when one of its members went absent over leave. Mutiny only broke out, however, when Holms cancelled leave for the entire ship because an eagle insignia stolen from the uniform of a German prisoner by one of the crewmembers was not returned. On the morning of 19 July, 190 sailors locked themselves in their mess decks and refused to fall in until their grievances had been brought to the attention of authorities ashore. The British officer responsible for the destroyers operating from Plymouth, Commander Reginald Morice, RN, who was summoned by *Iroquois*'s executive officer

CHAPTER 3

after Holms suffered an apparent heart attack, ultimately resolved the incident. Morice addressed the mutineers and informed them of the seriousness of their actions. He then offered to provide them with assistance in submitting their grievances through the proper channels and demanded that they immediately return to duty. All hands fell in later that day. The subsequent Board of Inquiry blamed Holms' leadership style for the incident, a verdict endorsed by both British and Canadian naval authorities.[44]

Another notable mutiny occurred in early-1944 in the newly commissioned RN escort carrier HMS *Nabob*.[45] The ship's company was composed of RCN, RN and British merchant service personnel; the commanding officer was Commander H. Nelson Lay, RCN. While *en route* from the Panama Canal to Norfolk, Virginia, a handful of junior ratings briefly locked themselves in their mess deck. Lay's memoirs do not indicate the nationality of the protesters, but both Canadian and British sailors had their grievances. The ship's RN ratings objected to being paid at a much lower rate than their Canadian brothers and RCN personnel were unhappy about the quality of the food, which was provided under RN rates. A possible U-boat sighting brought the protest to an end almost immediately, but morale continued to suffer. Lay's report to Canadian and British authorities suggested that his main concern was the crew's Canadian component. It was, he wrote, "an indisputable fact that the average R.C.N. rating is accustomed to [a] much higher standard of living, both in his home and in H.M.C. Ships that [sic] is expected by an R.N. rating." He also noted, presumably for the benefit of British authorities, that most of his RCN personnel were "in the Reserve forces who have not had a great deal of disciplinary training or experience in large ships. These ratings are undoubtedly in the habit of speaking their minds and demanding their rights in a much more definite manner than R.N. personnel."[46] Upon arriving in Norfolk, Lay informed the British Admiralty representative in Washington of the situation and stated that he "would not take the ship to sea until action had been taken on my recommendations." "If necessary," he later claimed, "I was prepared to be relieved in Command or to be Court Martialled!"[47] Lay then flew to Ottawa to put his demands to Canadian authorities, who agreed to put the ship on RCN rations and take over responsibility for the pay of RN personnel. The Admiralty approved both of these changes.[48]

The next incident to attract the attention of higher authorities occurred on 18 August 1944 in the *River*-class frigate HMCS *Chebogue*. As the men were sitting down for lunch, they were ordered to change into rig-of-the-day so that the vessel could be shifted to its anchorage from the oiler where it had been refuelling.[49] To show their resentment, the men fell in without having changed their clothing. The ship's new captain, an acting-Lieutenant Commander from the Royal Canadian Naval Reserve (RCNR), promptly ordered all ratings "who were not prepared immediately to change into the rig-of-the-day to shift ship" to step forward so that their names could be

CHAPTER 3

taken. Those sailors who did so were ordered to the mess deck while the ship was moved without their assistance.[50] The defiant crewmembers were later addressed by Commodore G.W.G. Simpson, RN, the Commodore (Destroyers) for the Western Approaches command, who had been informed of the incident by the captain. Simpson conceded that the "orders piped were not perhaps well thought out," but also reminded the men that they must submit their complaints through the proper channels. This effectively brought the incident to a close. No ratings were ever punished, even though Simpson later characterised the pretext for the mutiny as "totally frivolous."[51] Simpson placed the blame for the incident on the captain for his "lack of foresight and inconsiderate orders," but also suggested that the previous captain and executive officer should be investigated for their role in allowing discipline to deteriorate.[52]

The most serious wartime mutiny, if judged by the punishments awarded, took place during the final year of the war in HMCS *Rivière-du-Loup*, a corvette that was also attached to the Western Approaches command.[53] The ship had been an unhappy one for some time and the executive officer was especially unpopular with the crew who had little respect for his professional abilities. When the ship's captain, Lieutenant R.N. Smillie, RCNVR, went into hospital to have an infected hand treated, the men became alarmed by rumours that the first lieutenant would be taking the ship to sea the following day. On the morning of 10 January 1945, 47 sailors refused to turn in for duty and instead locked themselves in the forward mess. Smillie rushed back to the ship but was unable to gain access to the mutineers. Rear-Admiral R.H.L. Bevan, the Flag-Officer-in-Charge, Northern Ireland, decided to wait matters out rather than attempt to force an entry into the mess deck.[54] The mutineers surrendered several hours later and were escorted ashore. They left behind a long list of complaints to justify their action. The most serious charge, that senior officers (and especially the first lieutenant) were incapable of properly handling the ship, was clearly what had triggered the mutiny. Other complaints, which undoubtedly contributed to the men's general discontent, were presumably added to the list to bolster their case for engaging in mutiny. These included excessive drinking by the officers, the use of foul language to address ratings and other disrespectful behaviour.[55] The subsequent Board of Enquiry blamed the incident primarily on "injudicious and tactless handling of the ratings by the Executive Officer," and the crew's concerns about his competence.[56] Both the captain and the first lieutenant were relieved of their duties. Petty officers and leading seamen were reprimanded for failing "to notice trouble brewing" and were drafted to other ships. Forty-four of the 47 mutineers were sentenced to terms of between 42 and 90 days in Belfast Gaol.[57]

Thus, the RCN's own tradition of mutiny was well established by the end of the Second World War. Canadian ratings periodically employed passive mess deck lock-ins as a means to bring complaints to the attention of their superi-

CHAPTER 3

ors. In the case of *Nabob* and *Chebogue*, mutiny was apparently intended only to force the ship's captain to address the men's complaints. In *Iroquois* and *Rivière-du-Loup*, however, the goal was to have unpopular officers removed, and so the protest was meant to bring grievances to the attention of authorities ashore. In all of these ships, mutiny proved to be very effective. Authorities agreed that the men had legitimate complaints and prompt action was taken to address them. Just as important was the fact that the ratings had achieved their goals at an acceptable price. In every case where higher authorities became involved, blame was placed either primarily or solely on the ships' officers. As a result, the only ratings formally punished were those from HMCS *Rivière-du-Loup* who had disobeyed sailing orders in wartime, an offence too serious to overlook. Both Canadian and British authorities treated these incidents for what they were, isolated protests caused by conditions unique to the ship and the shortcomings of individual officers.

The early post-war years were chaotic for the RCN, for it had to cope with the rapid demobilisation of nearly 100,000 "hostilities only" personnel, while simultaneously attempting to expand its permanent peacetime manpower to more than triple the previous level.[58] Officials soon became aware of rising discontent within the fleet, as ratings employed a variety of means, including desertion, to demonstrate their unhappiness with peacetime service conditions. On 5 December 1946, a leading seaman in the destroyer HMCS *Micmac* attempted to organise a lock-in to obtain a "make and mend" routine (effectively giving sailors a half-day off) for the afternoon. He was subsequently court-martialled and sentenced to twelve months' detention (later reduced to three). Problems escalated during the following year. On 16 July 1947, a planned lock-in was aborted in the *Tribal*-class destroyer HMCS *Nootka* only because the ship had to depart hastily to assist *Micmac* which had been involved in a collision at sea.[59] Two months later, a more serious incident occurred on the cruiser HMCS *Ontario*.[60] On 22 August 1947, most of the ship's junior hands locked themselves in one of the mess decks.[61] The immediate cause of the unrest was later determined to be "the wearing of uniform, particularly of 'night clothing' and overalls, ... the capricious variation of the ship's routine, and ... general dissatisfaction with the Executive Officer."[62] The ship's commanding officer, Captain Jimmy Hibbert, immediately addressed the men and persuaded them to return to duty. As usual, the mutineers obtained their objective and escaped punishment. Authorities concluded that blame for the incident lay with the ship's executive officer who, incidentally, was quickly transferred from the ship with unseemly haste.

In Ottawa, the Naval Staff realised that it had to address the causes underlying the lower deck's discontent. A report on "Morale and Service Conditions," produced in October 1947, offered a number of recommendations including better pay and accommodation, the showing of films at sea and the creation of a lower deck magazine.[63] Steps had already been taken

CHAPTER 3

several months before to establish "welfare committees" in RCN ships and shore establishments. It was intended that these would provide "machinery for free discussion between officers and men of items of welfare and general amenities within the ship or establishment that lie within the powers of decision held by the Captain or his immediate Administrative Authority."[64] Some progress was made toward implementing these changes, but by 1949, considerable work still remained to be done. To make matters worse, the Navy's efforts to reform its rank and trade group structure resulted in ships' companies that were awash in chief and petty officers, but suddenly deficient in the seamen needed to perform the ships' more labour-intensive duties. This imbalance put greater demands on junior ratings, with an inevitable impact on morale.[65] As a result, 1949 proved to be a low point for discipline, with three mutinies taking place in rapid succession.[66]

The first of these occurred on 26 February 1949 in the destroyer HMCS *Athabaskan* while the ship was preparing to refuel at Manzanillo, Mexico. Approximately 90 ratings, nearly half the ship's company, locked themselves into the mess deck and demanded to meet with the captain, Commander M.A. Medland (formerly RCNVR). The men complained about the ship's failure to adopt a tropical routine, the enforcement of dress regulations that were more strict than other Canadian and American ships in the region and "unreasonable demands and minor criticisms" by certain officers, in particular the ship's executive officer. The captain spent 15 minutes in the mess deck listening to grievances and the men returned to work shortly afterwards. Some of the participants were subsequently cautioned for their part in this incident, but none were ever punished.

The next incident occurred in the destroyer HMCS *Crescent* while the ship was alongside in Nanking, China. On the morning of 15 March 1949, 83 men locked themselves in the mess deck. While the captain, Lieutenant-Commander D.W. Groos, attempted to discover the cause of the incident, a written list of complaints was posted on the door outlining the men's general dissatisfaction with the ship's captain and executive officer. The former was felt to be neglecting his duty to the ship as a result of the social and diplomatic obligations imposed on him as the Senior Naval Officer at Nanking. There was also considerable resentment that no effective welfare committee had ever been established on the ship, that frequent changes were made in their routine and that men were used as sentries for a wet canteen ashore, in addition to their normal duties.[67] The captain later addressed the mutineers, informing them that he was eager to hear their complaints, provided that they were advanced through the proper channels. He reassured them, moreover, that "since he wanted to find out all the facts and the reasons for the incident, he was not contemplating any disciplinary action thus far."[68] All hands subsequently reported for duty and the captain began interviewing individual ratings that afternoon.

CHAPTER 3

The next incident occurred less than a week later in the aircraft carrier HMCS *Magnificent*. On the morning of 20 March 1949, 32 of the ship's aircraft handlers refused to fall in for duty. *Magnificent* was not a happy ship when the incident occurred and the aircraft handlers, who "tended to consider themselves separate and distinct from the rest of the ship's company," felt that they were being subjected to heavier demands than their crewmates. This, according to investigators, made them "somewhat 'sorry for themselves.'"[69] The mutineers were also unhappy over more mundane matters like inadequate leave and entertainment, living conditions in their mess and a lack of consideration shown to them by the captain and executive officer. This incident was also quickly resolved. The captain, Commodore G.R. Miles, warned the men that collective action to present grievances would not be tolerated, but agreed to meet with men individually to discuss their complaints. The men promptly returned to duty and were never disciplined for their actions.

Individually, there was nothing remarkable about these incidents. The outbreak of three mutinies in such a short space of time, however, was too serious to be ignored. The Minister of National Defence, Brooke Claxton, quickly established a commission to investigate what had gone wrong in these ships and to look into the general state of morale and discipline in the Navy.[70] The committee's report, popularly known as the Mainguy Report after the chairman, Vice-Admiral Rollo Mainguy, dismissed politicians' fears that the incidents had been caused by communist subversion. Instead, the immediate source of lower deck discontent was determined to be a general dissatisfaction with the conditions of service, which included such issues as pay, food and accommodation. These, in turn, were held to be by-products of the Navy's post-war "growing pains" and "rapid peacetime expansion."[71]

To explain the breakdown of discipline in the fleet in 1949, the committee identified a number of problems. First, the executive officers on the three affected ships were all inexperienced and consequently did not handle men with sufficient skill. Second, frequent changes in personnel had made it difficult for officers and men to develop intimate relations. Third, the welfare committees had either not been set up or had functioned so badly that they had themselves become a cause of discontent. Fourth, ratings had learned from the 1947 mutiny in *Ontario* that mass disobedience could be used to obtain concessions at little risk. These factors would have been sufficient to explain the three incidents in 1949, but the committee also suggested that an "artificial distance" had grown up between officers and men throughout the fleet. The root of the problem, it charged, was the Canadian naval officers' initial training and periodic service in the Royal Navy. This, according to the report, "superimposed upon them a type of life and a style of leadership not only foreign to themselves and their own social background but also to the social background of the men whom they command. There is no form of artificial superiority which Canadians resent more", it concluded, "than the variety imported from another land."[72] In a similar vein, the committee asserted that men were unhappy about the lack of Canadian identifying features on their uniforms and ships.

The upper ranks of the Navy were understandably unhappy about suggestions that their training and performance had somehow been factors behind the mutiny. Privately, the Chief of the Naval Staff, Vice-Admiral Harold Grant, complained that the real problem was the influx of unsuitable Volunteer Reserve personnel into the new peacetime navy. Claxton, however, was pleased with the results, as they allowed him to press forward with the "Canadianisation" of the Navy, a goal that was, according to David Bercuson, "dear to his heart."[73] To address the absence of "Canadian identity," the decision was made to place "Canada" shoulder flashes on RCN uniforms and maple leaf emblems on ships' funnels. More usefully, the Navy overhauled its welfare committee system and the government began to provide the funds that were needed to address the various deficiencies detailed by the Mainguy Commission, many of which had already been identified in the 1947 report on morale and service conditions.

All of this was undoubtedly beneficial for the RCN, but the Mainguy Report's emphasis on the shortcomings of Canada's RN-trained officers and the lack of a national naval identity has left a distorted picture of the state of discipline in the service in 1949. The pre-war officer corps was generally well trained in matters relating to discipline. This was even tacitly admitted in the Mainguy Report, which praised officers for handling "their men with humanity and in the opinion of the highest officers of the Navy, with wisdom and perfect propriety."[74] Some officers undoubtedly failed on occasion to make the necessary allowances for the more egalitarian sensibilities and relaxed attitude of Canadian ratings, but most clearly did not have undue difficulty in this respect. Moreover, close association with the RN did not hopelessly tarnish a significant proportion of the Navy's post-war officers. Richard Gimblett's research has shown that, for example, of the 13 officers in HMCS *Crescent* in February 1949, only three (including the captain) had received comprehensive professional training with the RN.[75] The shortcomings of officers entering from the RCNVR, on the other hand, were not systematically examined and may have been greater than the commission was ready to accept.[76] Finally, as Gimblett has noted, despite "all of the fuss in the Report over 'Canada badges' (i.e. shoulder flashes), not one sailor providing testimony to the commission raised that as an issue critical to them, although when queried by the commissioners as to whether it was a good idea, they of course agreed."[77]

The Mainguy commission also ignored the long-standing tradition of mutiny in the RCN. Its report implied that the only precedent for the 1949 mutinies was the earlier incident in *Ontario*. The removal of the executive officer on

CHAPTER 3

that occasion was, it declared, "widely publicized and generally known throughout the Navy." Moreover, some of the ratings involved had subsequently been drafted to *Athabaskan* and *Crescent*. The commissioners were also impressed by the fact that men in *Magnificent* knew of the earlier incidents in the other ships. All this is true, of course, but by drawing such a clear link between these four particular incidents, the report obscured how widespread the knowledge and experience of mutiny would have been in the RCN by 1949. The commission was nevertheless correct in noting that the mutineers' success on these occasions and the absence of any punishments had made an impression on ratings. To prevent further mass insubordination, so it was asserted, "We can only recommend what the high ranking officers of the Navy have already determined, that any recurrence of such incidents be promptly and severely punished."[78]

This is a surprising statement in a document that exonerated ratings of blame in the four incidents it examined. It demonstrates, however, that naval authorities understood that the threat of punishment played a critical role in the maintenance of discipline. The outbreak of three mutinies in rapid succession could not easily be dismissed as a normal part of the Navy's tradition of mutiny. On the contrary, the 1949 incidents seemed to violate two "unwritten rules," namely that protests are to be restricted to a single ship and that they are not to be undertaken lightly. By the time that the mutiny occurred in *Magnificent*, it was becoming apparent that these incidents were somehow linked; that ratings had little fear of being punished for a mess deck lock-in; and that the complaints required to spark such protests were becoming increasingly minor. Thus, even though each of the 1949 incidents had its own unique causes, the Navy had reason to worry that if this trend continued, mutiny would become a routine occurrence rather than an exceptional means of drawing officers' attention to serious shipboard problems.

The 1931 Invergordon mutiny had shocked the Royal Navy because it appeared to violate an implicit understanding between officers and the lower deck about when mass insubordination was permissible. The RCN's three mutinies in 1949, although smaller in scale, had much the same effect, and for essentially the same reason. The resulting crises induced both navies to take a renewed interest in the welfare of the lower deck and to initiate a variety of reforms to remedy systemic problems that appeared to be undermining service discipline. In Canada, despite a great deal of attention being focussed on issues that had little bearing on the Navy's mutiny epidemic, such as the absence of visible symbols of the Navy's Canadian identity, service leaders appreciated that stability could only be achieved by impressing on ratings that mess deck lock-ins *were* legally acts of mutiny and that the penalties for this were potentially severe. The Mainguy commission concurred. When junior ratings in HMCS *Swansea* staged a mess deck lock-in in June 1949, armed troops were brought in and some participants were sentenced to hard labour and dishonourably discharged from the service.[79] This action sent a clear message to the fleet that mutiny had not become a risk-free undertaking. That no subsequent mutinies have been recorded suggests that officers and ratings effectively re-established the "unwritten rules" about when mutiny could be condoned.

Canada's naval mutinies have been modest affairs, and in this, they clearly reflect the nation's values and traditions. Mess deck lock-ins would have been almost unthinkable in a country like tsarist Russia where, for example, the spectre of revolution lurked behind every act of disobedience and even seemingly minor incidents carried the potential for bloodshed. The frequency of mutiny during the RCN's formative years is hardly surprising, however, given its close ties with the RN. Despite concerns in some quarters that the British approach to discipline was fundamentally unsuited to Canadian sailors, the RN's traditions actually served Canada well. As long as all of the parties involved observed the same ground rules, mutiny allowed sailors to demonstrate their dissatisfaction with service conditions when no other means were available or effective. Navies that have not shown this flexibility have generally experienced fewer mutinies, but often at a heavier cost. The absence of a "safety valve" in authoritarian societies ensured that when mutinies did occur, they easily turned violent and escalated out of control.

Probably the greatest barrier to understanding mutiny in the Canadian context has been the popular perception that the term only *really* applies when sailors physically seize control of their ship or assault their officers. The use of euphemisms like "incidents" and "sit-down strikes" [80] to describe these events has only obscured the fact that they *were* mutinies in a very real sense. In every instance, a group of sailors deliberately and collectively defied legally constituted authority. Where mutiny is concerned, however, naval authorities in Canada and other western states have placed themselves in an awkward position. The days when sailors might seize a ship and sail off to become pirates is long past, yet the term *mutiny* legally continues to apply to minor incidents that are generally agreed not to warrant serious punishment. Authorities are reluctant even to label them mutinies. And yet western states have not redefined the term to exclude acts such as "sit-down strikes," even though these are not considered mutinous and will almost never be punished as such. The reason for this, as events in 1949 demonstrate, is that the *threat* of harsh and potentially disproportionate penalties for collective action continues to serve a useful purpose by ensuring that ratings resort to mutiny only when they have serious and legitimate grievances. Thus, in a navy like Canada's, mutiny has *practical* distinction between minor protests and "real" mutinies, even if they are not ready to recognise this difference in law.

CHAPTER 3

ENDNOTES

I am grateful to Richard H. Gimblett, Bill Rawling, Bob Caldwell and Michael Whitby for their assistance.

1   Captain E. R. Mainguy, as quoted in Gordon McCallum, "No Mutiny on Uganda, Her Commander states," *Globe and Mail*, 11 August 1945, 3.
2   For a broad overview of naval mutinies during the last century, see Christopher M. Bell and Bruce A. Elleman, eds., *Naval Mutinies of the Twentieth Century: An International Perspective* (London: Frank Cass, 2003). The editors' concluding chapter analyses the nature and dynamics of naval mutinies during this period. Two good popular works on the subject are Leonard F. Guttridge, *Mutiny: A History of Naval Insurrection* (Annapolis: Naval Institute Press, 1992) and Richard Woodman, *A Brief History of Mutiny* (New York: Carroll and Graf Publishers, 2005). On the phenomenon of mutiny generally, useful studies include: Elihu Rose, "The Anatomy of Mutiny," *Armed Forces and Society*, Vol. 8, No. 4 (Summer 1982), 561-74; Cornelis J. Lammers, "Strikes and Mutinies: A Comparative Study of Organizational Conflicts between Rulers and Ruled," *Administrative Science Quarterly*, Vol. 14, No. 4 (December 1969), 558-72; and Jane Hathaway, ed., *Rebellion, Repression, Reinvention: Mutiny in Comparative Perspective* (Westport: Praeger, 2001).
3   A large literature has emerged in recent years on mutiny in the Royal Canadian Navy. The most important works include: Richard H. Gimblett, "Too Many Chiefs and Not Enough Seamen:" The Lower Deck Complement of a Postwar Canadian Navy Destroyer - The Case of HMCS *Crescent*, March 1949," *The Northern Mariner*, Vol. 9, No. 3 (July 1999), 1-22; Bill Rawling, "Only 'A Foolish Escapade by Young Ratings?' Case Studies of Mutiny in the Wartime Royal Canadian Navy," *The Northern Mariner*, Vol. 10, No. 2 (April 2000), 59-70; Richard H. Gimblett, "What the Mainguy Report Never Told Us: The Tradition of Mutiny in the Royal Canadian Navy before 1949," *Canadian Military Journal*, Vol. 1, No. 2 (Summer 2000), 85-94; Michael J. Whitby, "Matelots, Martinets, and Mutineers: The Mutiny in HMCS *Iroquois*, 19 July 1943," *Journal of Military History*, Vol. 65, No. 1 (January 2001), 77-103; and Richard H. Gimblett, "The Post-War 'Incidents' in the Royal Canadian Navy, 1949," in Bell and Elleman, *Naval Mutinies*, 246-63.
4   United States of America, *Uniform Code of Military Justice*, Article 94. 29 September 2005. http://www.constitution.org/mil/ucmj19970615.htm; United States of America, *Manual for Courts-Martial* (2000 edition), IV-26. 29 September 2005. http://www.jag.navy.mil/documents/mcm2000.pdf.
5   Great Britain, *Naval Discipline Act 1957* (as amended to 1 December 2000), Chapter 53, Part I, Section 8.
6   King's Regulations for the Canadian Navy, as reproduced in *Report on certain 'Incidents' which occurred on board HMC Ships Athabaskan, Crescent*

and Magnificent and on other matters concerning the Royal Canadian Navy (Ottawa: King's Printer, 1949), 27. [Hereinafter, Mainguy Report.]
7   Brigadier-General Jerry S.T. Pitzul and Commander John C. Maguire, "A perspective on Canada's Code of Service Discipline," *Air Force Law Review*, Vol. 52 (Winter 2002), 4-5.
8   Canada. *National Defence Act*, Revised Statutes of Canada, 1985 Act, Chapter N-5, Section 2. 29 September 2005. http://laws.justice.gc.ca/en/N-5/85073.html.
9   Canada. *National Defence Act*, Revised Statutes of Canada, 1985 Act, Chapter N-5, Part III, Code of Service Discipline, Section 79-80. 29 September 2005. http://laws.justice.gc.ca/en/N-5/85316.html. The maximum term that can be awarded for mutinies without violence is 14 years.
10 Lammers, "Strikes and Mutinies," 559.
11 Christopher M. Bell and Bruce A. Elleman, "Naval Mutinies in the Twentieth Century and Beyond," in Bell and Elleman, *Naval Mutinies*, 264-76.
12 N.A.M. Rodger, *The Wooden World: An Anatomy of the Georgian Navy* (London: Fontana Press, 1988), 237-44.
13 Rodger, *The Wooden World*, 243-44.
14 Christopher M. Bell, "The Invergordon Mutiny, 1931," in Bell and Elleman, *Naval Mutinies*, 170-92, and Christopher M. Bell, "The Royal Navy and the Lessons of the Invergordon Mutiny," *War in History*, Vol. 12, No. 1 (January 2005), 75-92.
15 Zachary Morgan, "The Revolt of the Lash, 1910," in Bell and Elleman, *Naval Mutinies*, 32-53.
16 Philippe Masson, *Le Marine Française et la Mer Noire* (Paris: Publications de la Sorbonne, 1982); Philippe Masson, "The French Naval Mutinies, 1919," in Bell and Elleman, *Naval Mutinies*, 106-22.
17 Mainguy Report, 11.
18 Bell and Elleman, "Naval Mutinies," 269-71.
19 Canada. *National Defence Act*, Revised Statutes of Canada, 1985 Act, Chapter N-5, Section 81. 29 September 2005. http://laws.justice.gc.ca/en/N-5/85316.html.
20 Bell and Elleman, "Naval Mutinies," 268-69.
21 William Glover, "The RCN: Royal Colonial or Royal Canadian Navy," in Michael L. Hadley, Rob Huebert and Fred W. Crickard, eds., *A Nation's Navy: In Quest of Canadian Naval Identity* (Montreal & Kingston: McGill-Queen's University Press [MQUP], 1996), 76-80.
22 Admiralty to Commanders-in-Chief, "Procedures to Avoid Indiscipline," 23 September 1937, ADM [Admiralty Records] 1/10277, *The National Archives of the United Kingdom* [*TNA*].
23 See Bell, "Invergordon Mutiny," 172-75.
24 Relatively few works address the question of discipline in the Royal Navy during this period. See Anthony Carew, *The Lower Deck of the Royal Navy 1900-1939* (Manchester: Manchester University Press, 1981); Jason Sears, "Discipline in the Royal Navy, 1913-46," *War and Society*, Vol. 9, No.

CHAPTER 3

2 (October 1991), 39-60; and Christopher McKee, *Sober Men and True: Sailor Lives in the Royal Navy, 1900-1945* (Cambridge: Harvard University Press, 2002).

25 Stephen Roskill, *Naval Policy Between the Wars* (London: Collins, 1976), Vol. I, 142 & 152-3; and Lawrence James, *Mutiny in the British and Commonwealth Forces, 1797-1956* (London: Buchan & Enright, 1987), 158-60.

26 Bell, "Lessons of Invergordon," 83.

27 Board of Admiralty Minute 2992, 28 July 1932, ADM 167/85, *TNA*.

28 Minutes by the Director of Training and Staff Duties, 3 November 1937 and 10 May 1938, ADM 178/133, *TNA*; Admiralty to Commanders-in-Chief Portsmouth and Plymouth *et al*, 16 December 1937, Ibid.

29 Undated Lecture by the Fourth Sea Lord, "Invergordon – 1931," *c*. early-1936, ADM 1/10923, *TNA*.

30 "Notes on Dealing with Insubordination," enclosure to Admiralty Letter NL 1201/32, 12 August 1932, ADM 178/133, *TNA*. This document was reissued in 1937 following the mutiny on HMS *Warspite* and again in 1944 as the Admiralty began preparations for operations in the Pacific.

31 Ibid.

32 Board of Enquiry Report, "Collective Indiscipline in HMS Warspite on the 30th June 1937," 23 September 1937, ADM 1/10277, *TNA*.

33 These details are notably absent from Stephen Roskill's early account of the *Warspite* mutiny. See Stephen Roskill, *H.M.S. Warspite: The Story of a Famous Battleship* (London: Collins, 1957), 167-69. In his book, Roskill suggests that the attention surrounding the mutiny was the result of one of the "trouble-makers" communicating details to the press.

34 Rodger, *Wooden World*, 238.

35 David Divine, *Mutiny at Invergordon* (London: MacDonald, 1970), 13.

36 Richard H. Gimblett, "Command in the Canadian Navy: An Historical Survey," *The Northern Mariner*, Vol. 14, No. 4 (October 2004), 47.

37 Michael L. Hadley and Roger Sarty, *Tin-Pots and Pirate Ships: Canadian Naval Forces and German Sea Raiders 1880-1918* (Montreal & Kingston: MQUP, 1991), 223; Bernard Ransom, "A Nursery of Fighting Seamen? The Newfoundland Royal Naval Reserve, 1901-1920," in Hadley *et al.*, *A Nation's Navy*, 253. Ransom notes similar protests by Newfoundlanders attached to HMS *Caesar* and HMS *Albion*.

38 This paragraph is based on the account given in Rear-Admiral H. Nelson Lay, *Memoirs of a Mariner* (Stittsville: Canada's Wings, 1982), 85-6.

39 Lay, *Memoirs*, 85.

40 Gimblett, "What the Mainguy Report Never Told Us," 87.

41 R.H. Caldwell, *Morale and Discipline in the Canadian Naval Service in the Second World War* (Unpublished Directorate of History and Heritage Naval History Narrative, 29 December 1998).

42 An early and inaccurate report of this incident appeared in Joseph Schull, *Far Distant Ships*: *An Official Account of Canadian Naval*

Operations in the Second World War (Toronto: Stoddart, 1987), 191-93. For a detailed and scholarly study, see Whitby, "Matelots, Martinets, and Mutineers," on which this account is primarily based.

43 Whitby, "Matelots, Martinets, and Mutineers," 86.
44 Ibid., 94-7; Report of Board of Inquiry, 28 July 1943, ADM 178/305, *TNA*.
45 Lay, *Memoirs*, 157-59.
46 Lay to Naval Board, Ottawa and British Admiralty Maintenance Representative, Washington, 8 March 1944, ADM 1/16045, *TNA*.
47 Lay, *Memoirs*, 159.
48 Lay to Flag Officer Carrier Training, Scotland, 10 April 1944, ADM 1/16045, *TNA*. This report lends credence to Lay's claims that he tried to bring his concerns to the attention of authorities several months earlier. It also suggests that the ship's problems were exacerbated by an "ineffective" executive officer, problematic petty officers, RCNVR officers with no experience on bigger ships and "a number of French-Canadian ratings (about 100) who due to racial education or environment are apparently not suitable for service in this type of ship." This group was, he claimed, responsible for "a majority" of the ship's disciplinary offences, including desertions.
49 Rawling, "'Foolish Escapade,'" 61-3.
50 Ibid., 61.
51 Gimblett, "What the Mainguy Report Never Told Us," 87.
52 Rawling, "'Foolish Escapade,'" 62-3.
53 Accounts of this mutiny have been published in Bill McAndrew, Bill Rawling and Michael Whitby, *Liberation: The Canadians in Europe* (Montreal: Art Global, 1995), 111-12; and Rawling, "'Foolish Escapade,'" 63-8.
54 Flag Officer in Charge, Northern Ireland to Commander-in-Chief Western Approaches, "H.M.C.S. 'Riviere du Loup' – Board of Inquiry," 17 January 1945, ADM 178/360, *TNA*.
55 "Complaints of Ship's Company," ADM 178/360, *TNA*. See also Rawling, "'Foolish Escapade,'" 63.
56 "Board of Inquiry," 12 January 1945, ADM 178/360, *TNA*.
57 In accordance with practices in the RN at this time, only two-thirds of these sentences were actually served.
58 Marc Milner, *Canada's Navy: The First Century* (Toronto: University of Toronto Press [UTP], 1999), Chapters 9 & 10.
59 These incidents are recorded in Gimblett, "What the Mainguy Report Never Told Us," 89-90.
60 On the HMCS *Ontario* mutiny, see Mainguy Report, 30-1; Gimblett, "What the Mainguy Report Never Told Us," 90; and Tony German, *The Sea is at Our Gates* (Toronto: McClelland and Stewart, 1990), 207-08.
61 The Mainguy Report suggests that 50 ratings were involved, but Gimblett's research indicates that the number may have been as high as 300. See Gimblett, "What the Mainguy Report Never Told Us," 86.
62 Mainguy Report, 31; Gimblett, "What the Mainguy Report Never Told Us," 90.

CHAPTER 2

[63] Gimblett, "Post-war Incidents," 253-54.
[64] National Service Headquarters, Ottawa, to Cangen 54, 25 July 1947, as printed in Mainguy Report, 26.
[65] Gimblett, "Too Many Chiefs and Not Enough Seamen."
[66] On the three 1949 mutinies, see in particular Milner, *Nation's Navy*, 189-92; Mainguy Report; and Gimblett, "Post-war Incidents."
[67] Mainguy Report, 16-7.
[68] Ibid.
[69] Ibid., 9-12.
[70] Gimblett, "Post-war Incidents;" Milner, *Nation's Navy*, 192-95; David J. Bercuson, *True Patriot: The Life of Brooke Claxton* (Toronto: UTP, 1993), 183-86; L.C. Audette, "The Lower Deck and the Mainguy Report of 1949," in *RCN in Retrospect, 1910-1968*, James A. Boutilier, ed. (Vancouver: University of British Columbia Press, 1982), 235-49.
[71] Mainguy Report, 33-4.
[72] Ibid., 51.
[73] Bercuson, *True Patriot*, 186.
[74] Mainguy Report, 31.
[75] Gimblett, "Post-war Incidents," 252.
[76] Milner, *Nation's Navy*, 194; Gimblett, "Post-war Incidents," 258.
[77] Gimblett, "Post-war Incidents," 258.
[78] Mainguy Report, 31.
[79] Gimblett, "Post-war Incidents," 260.
[80] For example, Gilbert Norman Tucker, *The Naval Service of Canada: Its Official History*, Vol. 2, *Activities on Shore During the Second World War* (Ottawa: King's Printer, 1952), 328.

CHAPTER 4

Beyond Mutiny? – Instrumental and Expressive Understandings of Contemporary "Collective Indiscipline"

Christopher Ankersen

> *Duty cannot exist without faith.*
> Benjamin Disraeli

At an academic conference in 2004, three panellists presented papers that described mutinies throughout Canadian military history. At the conclusion of their presentations, a currently-serving senior officer stood up and stated that there was little utility in examining such historical episodes because today's Canadian Forces (CF) were more or less immune to mutiny. Organisational innovations such as the redress of grievance system and the Office of the Ombudsman have reduced the chances of mutiny to almost nil, he said. Mutiny, if it were to occur, would be a "failure of individual leadership" and not something that the CF would need to address in a systematic manner.

My incredulity at this reaction is the genesis of my involvement in this volume. At the time, I stated that many leaders present in the room that day (including me) could testify to having observed acts that teetered on the precipice of mutiny, if not full mutiny itself. On operations in the Balkans, for instance, there were occasions where troops cowed their officer and refused to follow an order and where the troops' "right to grumble" approached collective indiscipline. I did not, and do not, share the confidence of that senior officer: the CF is not immune to the threat of mutiny. To think otherwise is arrogant. Let this chapter, therefore, serve as a warning: beware the pride before the fall.

Today's CF, it is alleged, is "beyond mutiny" because of structural mechanisms (such as the redress of grievance and harassment investigation procedures) which serve to give "voice" to serving personnel. Certainly, these institutional arrangements are progressive and impressive, and indeed, may be seen as the fruit of earlier mutinous activity, but are they enough to forestall mutiny *forever*? If they are, it is an amazing development, for Canadian military history and contemporary experience are replete with examples of mutiny and mutinous behaviour.

Overall, though, mutiny is under-analyzed and what analysis that does exist tends to focus on the particularities of historical examples.[1] Since mutiny as a field of study has been dominated by history (as an academic discipline), it tends to be under-theorised as well. Furthermore, mutiny tends to be neglected by the military; it is seen as an aberration and, other than having disciplinary regulations in place to handle its occurrence, the military does not discuss the matter with any candour. The reality is that the potential for mutiny transcends any single historical period; its causes, forms and functions may mutate across time. There is, therefore, value in examining historical instances of mutiny with a view to discerning the enduring aspects that commanders (and others) should bear in mind.

While my aim is to illustrate that the CF is not beyond mutiny, this chapter centres on the question of why people choose mutiny. Rather than looking for *causes* of mutiny, this chapter focuses on mutiny's *function*. In so doing, it may be possible for military leaders to appreciate aspects of the complex relationship with followers that are often overlooked. It concludes, therefore, with suggestions for changes to leadership doctrine and training. This chapter examines the function of mutiny as a concept and does not rely on any particular historical example. In this sense, this chapter has a dual purpose. On the one hand, the reader is invited to use it as a lens through which other studies might be viewed. Perhaps its conceptual curvature will allow the empirical case studies that follow in the subsequent volumes to come into sharper focus. On the other hand, the numerous empirical chapters may act as tests to what amounts to a theoretical hypothesis.

Mutiny Happens

The *sine qua non* of any mature study of mutiny and its relevance to contemporary military life must be that *mutiny happens*. As a possibility, it can never be ruled out. Militaries are human organizations that, when put into conditions of stress, may act in any number of ways. This fact is what leads Joel Hamby to claim, "There is no set formula to explain the circumstances necessary for mutiny, a form of military rebellion that can happen to any military formation, in any war."[2] As many of the studies in the following two volumes illustrate, though, combat is not the only crucible of mutiny. Lest we shrug off the "non-spectacular" incidents, Elihu Rose reminds us that:

> Few would argue that the refusal of a rowdy group to disperse is different from the refusal of a unit to advance in the face of the enemy but, by definition, the difference is one of degree, not of kind. Twentieth-century mutinies have indeed run the gamut of behaviour. One finds cases of assaults upon officers, the threatening of bodily harm, the destruction of property, the presenting of petitions, the passive refusal of duty, and various gradations between.[3]

As certain chapters in this volume ably demonstrate, most of these kinds of mutinies have happened in the Canadian experience and each has the potential to happen again.

Although mutiny has existed since the beginning of organized warfare, as a term it was born in 16th century France. Defined then as "collective military insubordination, a revolt of troops against lawfully constituted military authority," conceptually it has not changed much in five hundred years.[4] Within Canada's *National Defence Act*, for instance, mutiny "means collective insubordination or a combination of two or more persons in the resistance of lawful authority."[5] Now, as then, mutiny need not involve violence [6] and is "amenable to broad interpretation."[7]

Interpretation aside, two elements are of note. First, mutiny is a collective activity. Individual disobedience may be labelled insubordination or dealt with in a number of other ways. Collective action, of course, connotes conspiracy and collaboration and it is for this reason that mutiny has always held an almost magical quality. Images of sinister gangs, and later communist agitators, are emblematic of mutiny and conjure up the dread of mob rule or mass disorder. Second, mutiny consists of defying authority that is duly constituted. It is therefore, by that very fact, a criminal act and cannot be confused with, say, refusing to follow an overtly illegal or immoral order, an action that is wholly legitimate and provided for within military law. Taken together, these two elements make it clear why mutiny is such a threat: mutiny is the collective defiance of legal authority, something which, if left unchecked, can rock the military to its very foundations. In this sense, mutiny has long been regarded as "the antithesis of discipline."[8]

The awesome potential of mutiny may well explain the lack of appreciation on the part of most military leaders. Commanders are strangely hesitant to label even clear cut incidents of collective insubordination as mutiny, preferring to use labels such as "unrest, incident, affair, collective protest, insubordination, strike, disaffection, collective indiscipline, [or] combat refusal."[9] Canadian commanders have not been different in this regard, as such euphemisms as "sit-down strikes," "lock-ins" and "incidents" were used to describe both wartime and postwar mutinies in the Royal Canadian Navy.[10]

Mutiny: Now…and Here?

Perhaps stories of "near misses" or whispered recollections around a stand-up table in a mess somewhere are not enough to worry Canadian military commanders. Even if this is so, there are examples from other militaries engaged in large-scale, sustained military operations that should serve as warnings. For instance, in October 2004, "18 reservists from the 343rd Quartermaster Company [of the United States Army] didn't accompany a…fuel supply convoy" as they had been ordered. Their commanders may have deemed it an "isolated incident,"[11] but it is instructive nonetheless. Take, for instance, the fact that "…officials in Iraq are steering clear of the 'M' word, referring instead to a platoon's refusal to take part in a supply convoy as 'temporary breakdown in discipline.'"[12] That "breakdown," though, involved not only a refusal to follow orders, but was coupled with a high-profile information campaign. The soldiers involved "phoned their parents and begged them to tell members of

Congress that this was a 'suicide mission' because of the miserable condition of their unarmored vehicles."[13] In the end, no charges of mutiny were laid. The military's initial report on the incident stated that the soldiers "raised some valid concerns" about the convoy mission. Despite being in a combat zone, where the full weight of the United States' Uniform Code of Military Justice would have applied – meaning that if found guilty of mutiny, those involved could have faced the death penalty – mutiny did occur. Afterwards, things improved: the soldiers did not carry out their "suicide mission" and – thanks *not* to official chains of command, or systems of redress, or even a visit to the padre – their trucks were fixed and heavily armed escorts were provided for subsequent convoy operations of this type. As one reporter remarked, "The reservists in the 343rd made a conscious choice between the risk of court-martial and the risk of a combat mission, based on their gut feelings about their equipment, training, leadership, and the likelihood of survival."[14] Let there be no doubt: mutiny happened in October 2004, *and it worked*.

But, critics will say, that is not Canada: it could not happen here. It is true that there are no reports of mutinies in recent Canadian operations, but there is evidence to suggest that there *could be*, given the right circumstances, and while merely suggestive, such a possibility should not be overlooked too quickly. In 2001, the CF conducted a survey of more than 800 officers who had served on operations, ranging from the first Gulf War to NATO's Kosovo campaign. The report on what was known as *The Debrief the Leaders Project (Officers)* revealed some troubling sentiments amongst its respondents. "Almost 50 % of those interviewed," the report said, "expressed serious reservations concerning the chain of command and especially NDHQ [National Defence Headquarters]."[15] Because they saw little in what they were doing that made sense to them, "more than 30 %" of the leaders polled, "stated that they would automatically put the safety of their own troops before the maintenance of the mission."[16] Reporting four years on, researchers from the Royal Military College of Canada found a similar trend: in seven of eight operational scenarios presented, when asked "Which is most important—mission accomplishment or troop safety?," a majority of respondents chose troop safety.[17] See Table 4.1

Only in combat operations meant to defend Canadian territory or citizens was "mission accomplishment" the clear winner. It is heartening to know that this is so; however, since neither of these scenarios is likely to present itself, it is instructive to note that in precisely the kinds of operations in which the CF finds itself engaged, there may be an expressed desire to put safety before success. If ordered to do otherwise, it is *conceivable* that mutiny could occur. Even in terms of combat operations, there may be cause for concern, at least according to certain survey data. For instance, when the researchers measured "willingness to put life at risk" through combat, they found that total obedience could not be guaranteed. Overall, they found that 6.8 percent of some 4,000 soldiers surveyed said they would "avoid going" or "refuse to go" into combat.[18]

CHAPTER 4

Which is more important - mission accomplishment or troop safety?	
Scenario	% choosing troop safety 'slightly' or 'absolutely' (combined)
Humanitarian operations throughout the world	84.6
Disaster relief in Canada	83.4
Peace support operations	71.8
Search and Rescue operations in Canada	71.3
Aid to the civil power operations in Canada	60.9
Combat operations abroad in defence of an ally of Canada	52.9
Combat operations to defend citizens at home or abroad	24.2
Combat operations to defend Canadian territory	17.3

Table 4.1: Mission or Troops?

As noted in the report for *The Debrief the Leaders Project*, these types of findings reflect a fundamental change from the classic formulation of "mission, troops, self." It certainly calls into question the certainty of obedience in times of doubt. Survey data may not be a completely accurate forecast of how leaders and troops will act in combat, but they certainly raise the spectre of "combat refusals" and "collective disobedience." Such information suggests that mutiny may not be a thing of the past or something that only others need worry about after all.

How, in the face of this, can we view the remarks of the senior officer introduced above? By examining his main thesis – that personnel now have a "voice" and therefore have no need of mutiny – it is possible to see that such measures are the right answer to the wrong problem.

Mutiny: A Functional Analysis

It is true that the CF has a robust and efficient system that allows for the voicing of grievances. It springs from the principle that commanders must hold the welfare of their subordinates in high regard. There are three outlets for "voice" within the CF. The first is the notion that all members of the CF have the right to bring forward concerns to their superiors, which is enshrined in such practices as "the divisional system," "platoon commander's hours" and

CHAPTER 4

"open door policies," whereby opportunity is given to all ranks to air their complaints or signal problems to the chain of command.

This first routine channel has been augmented by a second, the system of "redress of grievance," wherein members of the CF who believe that they have been mistreated or unfairly treated may, formally and in writing, seek some sort of correction, whether it be a posting, a promotion or a payment.[19] A variety of layers and safeguards have been added to this system, including the provision of an assisting officer to aid in the research and written expression of the grievance; strict time limits for commanders to reply; and the right of appeal, up the chain of command, all the way to the Chief of the Defence Staff (CDS). This process is bolstered by the existence of a high-level staff directorate, a toll-free number and the existence of an independent Canadian Forces Grievance Board. Ultimately, members of the CF may even challenge the CDS' decision in federal court.

The third mechanism available to members of the CF is the Office of the Ombudsman. The Office was created in 1998 to serve as "an neutral and objective sounding board, mediator, investigator and reporter on matters related to DND [Department of National Defence] and the CF."[20] It is intended that the Ombudsman will "serve to contribute to substantial and long-lasting improvements in the welfare of employees and members of the DND and CF community."[21] The Ombudsman has been a vocal and active advocate for the rights and welfare of CF members and has demonstrated on several occasions the kind of autonomy and freedom of action required to fulfil the Office's mandate.

Each of these administrative avenues certainly gives personnel ample opportunity to voice their concerns and have injustices corrected. When combined, it is easy to see from whence our senior officer's confidence stems. Why is it, then, that I insist mutiny is still a possibility? To answer that, it is necessary to understand what is meant by "voice" by examining the pioneering work of Albert O. Hirschmann, an economic and political theorist, known for his radical perspective.

Hirschmann's Exit, Voice and Loyalty

Working in the 1960s, Hirschmann, in contrast to most economic and political theorists of the time, examined organizations in decline. Surrounded by the tumultuous times of civil disquiet and protest in the United States, he wanted to understand how firms, organisations and states reacted to failure. Decline, he believed, was omnipresent, but most academic theory (at least in terms of economics, business and political science) addressed issues that revolved around success. Such a perspective was unhelpful:

> Under any economic, social, or political system, individuals, business firms, and organizations in general are subject to lapses from effi-

cient, rational, law-abiding, virtuous, or otherwise functional behavior. No matter how well a society's basic institutions are devised, failures of some actors to live up to the behavior which is expected of them are bound to occur, if only for all kinds of accidental reasons.[22]

Simply put, in reaction to such decline, individuals (be they consumers, shareholders, members of an organisation or voters) have three choices. First, they may remain loyal, despite the "lapses" of the kind described by Hirschmann. Individuals who choose to be loyal put their faith in the fact that the organization will "come through in the end," that decline is temporary or that they have no other choice. Second, individuals may choose to exercise "voice," that is, lodge a complaint. It is hoped that through such actions, conditions will change, either for the individual alone or for all.

These two choices are readily identifiable within a military organization. Loyalty is certainly seen as the most desirable state of affairs. Troops are required to be loyal to their superiors. However, this requirement rests upon an implicit "contract," whereby, in exchange for obedience, the chain of command will see to the needs of its personnel and ensure that they are well cared for.

As a tacit acknowledgement of the fact that not all commanders honour this contract all the time, some mechanism of voice is also available within the military, although only in tightly prescribed channels. It can be argued that such circumscribed application of voice actually commutes it into a form of loyalty: if individuals are willing to "work inside the system" in the hope of some form of redress, then they are displaying incredible loyalty. Despite harbouring some feeling of dissatisfaction, these aggrieved members of the military are content to *follow the rules* and allow the chain of command to provide a solution. Voice, in this light, is neither disruptive nor disloyal, but rather "part of the game." Such captured voice is, in reality, nothing more than "vocal loyalty." While it may be a CF member's *right* to exercise his or her voice, that right does not include the use of all available means of expressing that voice. Even the vaunted Ombudsman's power to act as a mechanism of member voice is constrained for there are several instances which the Ombudsman "shall not investigate," including anything related to a military judge or trial. True voice, such as speaking out on parade, banding together to sign a petition or complaining to the press, is not legitimate and is really a form of "exit," in that it represents a departure from the organization's sanctioned behaviour. Put another way, "voice within bounds" is actually a form of loyalty, in that a member of an organization willingly submits to the host of rules surrounding the time, manner and form in which voice is expressed.

The third choice that individuals might choose to follow is "exit." In many situations, exit is a straightforward choice: consumers switch brands, voters elect other parties and employees quit their jobs. Despite its regularity, organ-

CHAPTER 4

izations must take note of exit for the loss of staff, customers and followers cannot be ignored. While it may be possible to live with the less than desirable reactions of loyalty, as expressed through suffering or even loudly voiced dissatisfaction, exit must be addressed. No organization can survive without customers, supporters or members. This is why, in the face of such definite disapproval, normal "market theory" tells us that "management is impelled to search for ways and means to correct whatever faults have led to exit."[23] For this reason, Hirschmann claims, "the exit option is…uniquely powerful."[24] Hirschmann expressed in simple terms how voice, exit and loyalty operated within different kinds of organisations. See Figure 4.1 below.

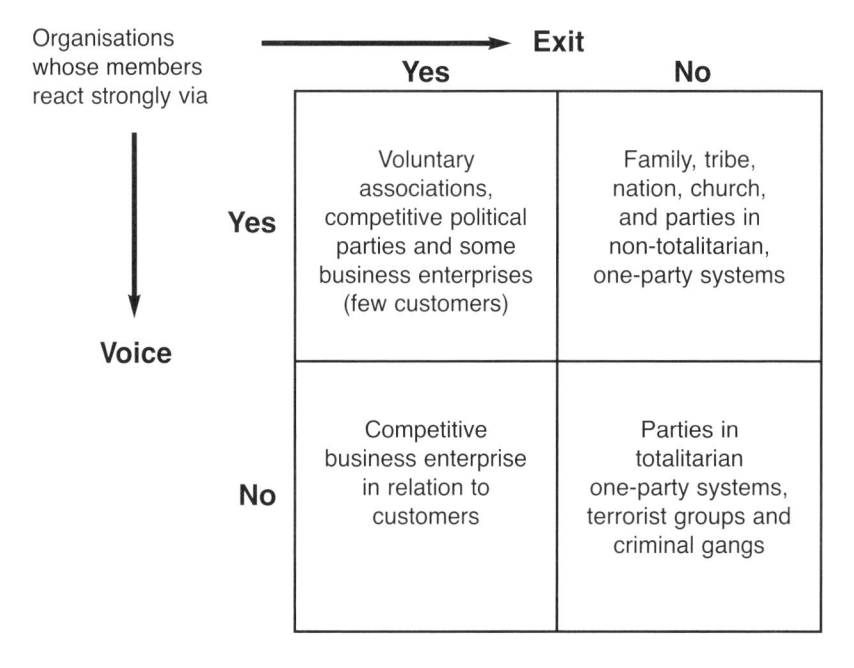

Organisations whose members react strongly via

Exit

	Yes	No
Voice — Yes	Voluntary associations, competitive political parties and some business enterprises (few customers)	Family, tribe, nation, church, and parties in non-totalitarian, one-party systems
Voice — No	Competitive business enterprise in relation to customers	Parties in totalitarian one-party systems, terrorist groups and criminal gangs

Figure 4.1: Exit and Voice by Organisational Type.

Large firms with many customers in non-specialised markets (lower left quadrant) tend to ignore complaints, but pay attention to "loss of market share" instead. Political parties (upper left quadrant), on the other hand, are wedded both to opinion polls (a form of voice) and to membership (a reflection of exit).

While members may leave the military, they may only do so in accordance with specific regulations, which are subject to change and "the needs of the service." Exit is not a right in the same way that voice is. For organizations like the military, Hirschmann reminds us, "exit has often been branded as *criminal*, for it has been labelled desertion, defection, and treason."[25] Unlike voice, which can be tamed by being supported and facilitated, exit within the military is seen as subversive and is thus discouraged. In Hirshmann's lower right quadrant, exit is punishable by death and even in the upper right quadrant, exit from a family, tribe or church means estrangement, exile or excommunication.

From an organizational point of view, then, loyalty is the most desirable option. Even in the face of severe sanction, however, neither voice nor exit can be removed from the pallet of choice. In Hirschmann's words, "There are probably no organizations that are wholly immune to either exit or voice on the part of their members. The ones that are…are those that, in their intended structure, make no explicit allowance for either mechanism."[26] In order to compensate for such a lack of immunity against exit, organizations, like the CF, try and inoculate themselves by shoring up voice as an option. Better to suffer the slings and arrows that may arise from within the system than to be confronted by the power of exit. It certainly seems that, at least to the senior officer central to this study, such efforts have created a false sense of protection. As Hirschmann points out, even in those organizations in which they are "severely penalised," voice and exit "will be engaged…in when deterioration has reached so advanced a stage that recovery is no longer either possible or desirable." In such cases, "voice and exit will be undertaken with such strength that their effect will be destructive rather than reformist."[27]

Mutiny can be seen, therefore, as a form of exit. Rather than choosing to follow the rules or putting faith in the system to change a particular set of circumstances, mutineers decide to "exit" the system and take matters into their own hands, either by refusing to work or by taking charge. This is often accompanied by the exercise of what I have called "true voice," intense vocalization of demands or complaints. While there are many examples, the mutiny in Iraq by the 343rd Quartermaster Company mentioned above illustrates this nicely.

What does "bad enough" look like?

If things get *bad enough*, mutiny may occur, despite efforts to siphon off discontent through other means. But what is "bad enough" to warrant a reaction as radical as mutiny? Upon reviewing the historical record, Rose contends that there are three broad "categories of discontent" which can give rise to mutiny. They are:

1. working conditions: bad food, harsh discipline, racial discrimination;
2. demobilization; and
3. legitimacy: the "why," not the "how," of employment.

A closer analysis of these categories reveals some useful insights. First, there are not really three categories at all. Rather, demobilization is a time period in which both working conditions and legitimacy tend to be subject to close review

CHAPTER 4

by the troops; it is merely a "when" that allows the "how" and the "why" to come the fore. There are other "whens," such as after long periods of heavy fighting (as in the case of the French Army mutinies during the First World War) or during "unpopular wars" (such as American involvement in Vietnam).

This leaves us with two categories of discontent that have historically led to mutinies. Members of the military, it can be said, have chosen to "exit" over *material* issues (such as working conditions) and *existential* issues (such as legitimacy). If they use mutiny to improve material concerns, then mutiny can be said to be instrumental. However, if mutiny occurs as a result of existential concerns, then mutiny may be less instrumental than expressive. According to Leo Charbonneau, a social psychologist whose research includes work on how emotions translate into behaviour, the "emotional antecedents" underpinning what he calls *mutiny* are very different from those of what he calls *redress*. For him, mutiny is expressive; its antecedents are "resentment and exasperation." This contrasts strikingly with the more instrumental concept of redress, which is triggered by "anger and disgust." Correspondingly, the goal of mutiny is the "assertion of autonomy" while the goal of redress is "restoring order."[28]

While material issues are easily understood, the idea of existential discontent requires further explanation. Existential concerns centre on the idea of "existence." Survival, therefore, is something that motivates soldiers to mutiny. However, existential motivations go beyond life and death. They deal with the quality of existence as well. Followers must feel that their existence is worth something, that they are valued and that they are not taken for granted.

Hamby's study of mutiny includes such a perspective. He lists eight factors that can lead to mutiny and three of them are clearly existential in nature: alienation, values and hope. Alienation, for instance, can include feelings of powerlessness, meaninglessness, normlessness, isolation and self-estrangement.[29] Hamby's factors accord with what Emile Durkheim called *anomie*, a condition of extreme "deregulation" in society. According to Durkheim, *anomie* means that "people did not know what to expect from one another" because "norms (expectations on behaviours) are confused, unclear or not present." This normlessness, then, leads to "deviant behaviour."[30] Mutiny is one such deviant behaviour, according to Hamby:

> When a soldier's group recognizes that its values and hopes run contrary to those of higher authority, the group has taken a critical step toward disobedience. No longer can higher authority take it for granted that their soldiers will fight, a strike at the very heart of discipline.[31]

Such a perspective, however, is not often adopted by scholars. Much more common is Geoffrey Parker's summary of mutineers: "they acted out of despair, fatigue, or momentary anger at the appalling conditions in the trenches, at the arbitrary punishments imposed, or at the lack of leave. [They were] desperate and frightened men reacting to short-term material or psychological pressures."[32] Such a materialist perspective is fraught with conceptual difficulties. Occasions where soldiers endured hardships and continued to fight outnumber those in which they resorted to mutiny. Soldiers may be quite willing to follow the rules when engaged in a war and the notion of victory over the enemy ties them to their leaders and the greater organization, even if that means dying. Such service or sacrifice could be seen to be meaningful given the framework of war, which places individual action into the context of a collective effort that is directed toward a greater goal. However, once that framework is gone and the enemy safely defeated, soldiers may feel that continued service (often merely "waiting" to be shipped home) is not preferable. Hardships (such as cramped conditions, boredom, poor food) are not worth it. They may even feel that their leaders are taking their continued obedience for granted. In this way, what may appear to be a mutiny over "working conditions" may actually be about more deeply seated feelings of disrespect or even the need to assert oneself, to stand up and be noticed. Working conditions themselves may not be "bad enough" to warrant mutiny until they are combined with unacceptable existential feelings.

What can be done?

We are now closer to understanding the confusion surrounding the notion that the Ombudsman might be able to prevent mutiny. *If* one were to take the perspective that mutiny is only about material concerns, then the Ombudsman may well be instrumental in reducing mutinies: over 90 percent of the Ombudsman's case load in 2004-2005 dealt with material issues.[33] Over 50 percent of the cases concerned benefits, recruiting and release. While the Office is likely to improve working conditions over time and may perhaps contribute to an increase in feelings of legitimacy and loyalty as a result, it is specious to claim that mutiny will be eradicated as a result.

We are still left wondering why the material school of thought is believed in the first place. Let me suggest here two theoretical reasons, both linked to forms of arrogance. First, many regard the "lower ranks" as unsophisticated and animalistic. Soldiers have historically been less well educated and have come from lower socio-economic classes than either officers or scholars. It may be easier, therefore, for their grievances to be viewed as "basic and immediate."[34] Such a "classist" view of mutiny is reminiscent of the larger, but related issue, of revolution, where both socialist organizers and patrician elites agreed that masses were revolting. From this arrogant perspective, paternalistic solutions are easily seized upon. Since soldiers are dominated by material concerns, and use mutiny as a "routine tactic in the negotiating repertoire,"[35] one may avoid mutiny simply by improving conditions (food, pay and housing).

CHAPTER 4

The second school of thought is related to the first. As Rose describes, institutional vanity sees "mutiny as antithetical to an ethos whose fundamental tenets are duty, loyalty, honor, and patriotism, and the unit that participates in a mutiny brings discredit upon itself, its officers, and its service."[36] Mutiny, therefore, cannot be about deep dissatisfaction or fundamental questions of value and worth. It must be about material concerns, esoteric and addressable. To admit otherwise would be to damage the *existential framework of the leadership*. It is easier, therefore, to see "disloyal" troops as "occupationally oriented" (in that they see the military as just another "job") and loyal troops and their leaders as "institutionally focused" (in that they truly value the military as a "way of life").[37]

Whatever the reason behind it, mutiny is not dealt with adequately in the CF. The feeling that "it couldn't happen here" pervades most discussion and is reflected in the recent leadership manual. The sole mention of mutiny is contained in a section that deals with "resistance," one of the options that people may choose as a response "to the exercise of authority and influence:"[38]

> Resistance refers to delaying, avoidant, or non-compliant behaviour with attitudinal opposition; behaviour and attitude are congruent but negatively so. Resistant or oppositional followers either refuse to pursue the leader's goals or else pursue antithetical goals (e.g. *American soldiers who engaged in mutiny and 'fraggings' in the Vietnam War*) and cannot be reliably controlled by organizational norms, promise of reward, or threat of punishment.[39]

Just how far removed mutiny is from the Canadian imagination is illustrated by the fact that, despite many "home grown" historical examples, the example given in the text is not even Canadian.

Mutiny must be studied and examined if it is to be understood, and understood if it is to be avoided, or at least reduced. Volumes such as this one are positive first steps, but a systematic introduction of mutiny into leadership doctrine must follow. If, for instance, mutiny hinges on matters of meaning and value, then leaders must be aware that these are important leadership issues. The key role of a leader may be, as stated by Robin Higham and Gilles Paquet, "making sense of people's experience."[40] This is a far more complex undertaking than merely providing food and shelter or even administrative avenues to channel complaints.

The threat of mutiny cannot easily be dismissed. It happens and it works. However, it is a complex phenomenon, fuelled by a mixture of material and existential factors. Under the pressure of combat, or the frustration of ambiguous operations, this mixture *may* ignite, with mutiny being the result. It may be tempting for some to claim that military personnel have all the necessary administrative mechanisms at their disposal to negate the need to resort to "collective indiscipline." To make such a claim, however, both denies the lessons of history and, paradoxically, takes a very "old fashioned" approach to the form and role of mutiny in today's military. It is instructive, perhaps, to consider an analogous example to fully understand the contemporary imminence of mutiny. One might claim that since industrial working conditions have improved greatly since the brutal scenarios of the Industrial Revolution, strikes are no longer a necessary part of labour relations. Such a claim would be confronted by the reality that strikes *do* exist and the reason that they do is that they continue to play a defining role, both in terms of the workers' tactics and their identity. It is unlikely that strikes will ever disappear from the world of labour, no matter how many mechanisms are put in place to prevent them. Similarly, mutiny is not a relic of the past, but a real possibility. A policy of management through understanding (informed by history and theory), rather than neglect through ignorance, is the best approach to deal with it.

ENDNOTES

1   Geoffrey Parker, "Foreword," in *Rebellion, Repression, and Reinvention: Mutiny in Comparative Perspective*, Jane Hathaway, ed. (Westport: Praeger, 2001), ix.
2   Joel E. Hamby, "The Mutiny Wagon Wheel: A Leadership Model for Mutiny in Combat," *Armed Forces & Society*, Vol. 28, No. 4 (2002), 576.
3   Elihu Rose, "The Anatomy of Mutiny," *Armed Forces & Society*, Vol. 8, No. 4 (1982), 568.
4   Ibid.," 561.
5   Canada. *National Defence Act*, Chapter N-5, Paragraph 2.
6   Ibid., Part III, Code of Service Discipline, Sections 79-81.
7   Rose, "The Anatomy of Mutiny," 561.
8   Ibid., 562.
9   Ibid., 562-63.
10 See, for instance, Richard Gimblett, "What the Mainguy Report Never Told Us: The Tradition of 'Mutiny' in the Royal Canadian Navy before 1949," *Canadian Military Journal*, Vol. 1, No. 2 (2000), 85-92.
11 Gerry J. Gilmore, "Alleged Troop Mutiny was 'Isolated Incident,' General Says," *Armed Forces Information Service*, 18 October 2004.
12 Julie Rawe, "Mutiny on the Convoy?," *Time*, 25 October 2004, 24.
13 Rawe, "Mutiny on the Convoy?," 1.
14 Phillip Carter, "The Reserve Mutiny: How the Iraq war is crippling the Army Reserve," *Slate*, 18 October 2004. http://slate.msn.com/id/2108357/. 18 August 2005.
15 Canada, Department of National Defence [DND], *The Debrief the Leaders Project (Officers)*, 7.
16 Ibid., 11.
17 Director General – Land Capability Development, *Canada's Soldiers –*

CHAPTER 4

Military Ethos and Canadian Values in the 21st Century – The Major Findings of The Army Climate & Culture Survey and The Army Socio-cultural Survey (Ottawa: Land Personnel Concepts and Policy, 2005), 26. A ninth scenario, Promoting Canadian Societal Values, was also offered. However, this seems to be incongruous with the remaining choices; therefore, it has been left out of this discussion. The result in this scenario was to be expected: 84.1 percent in favour of troop safety.

[18] Taken from the Army Culture-Climate Survey (2004) as reported in *Canada's Soldiers*, 34.

[19] Canada, *Queen's Regulations and Orders*, Chapter 7, Grievances.

[20] Canada, *Ministerial Directives*, "Ombudsman Mandate, General Duties and Functions," Paragraph 3.1.a.

[21] Ibid., Paragraph 3.1.c.

[22] Albert O. Hirschmann, *Exit, Voice, and Loyalty: Responses to Decline in Firms, Organisations, and States* (Cambridge: Harvard University Press, 1970), 1.

[23] Hirschmann, *Exit, Voice, and Loyalty*, 4.

[24] Ibid., 21.

[25] Ibid., 17.

[26] Ibid., 121.

[27] Ibid.

[28] Leo Charbonneau, "How do I hate thee?" *Affaires Universitaires* (April 2005), 23-4.

[29] Hamby, "The Mutiny Wagon Wheel," 576-79.

[30] Emile Durkheim, *The Division of Labour in Society* (New York: Free Press, 1984).

[31] Hamby, "The Mutiny Wagon Wheel," 582.

[32] Parker, "Foreword," viii.

[33] Canada, Office of the Ombudsman for the Department of National Defence and the Canadian Forces, Statistics. http://www.ombudsman.forces.gc.ca/statistics/main_e.asp. 2 December 2005.

[34] Parker, "Foreword," viii.

[35] Rose, "The Anatomy of Mutiny," 573.

[36] Ibid., 563.

[37] These orientations are taken from Charles Moskos, "From Institution to Occupation: Trends in Military Organisation," *Armed Forces & Society*, Vol. 4, No. 1 (1977), 41-50.

[38] Canada, DND, *Leadership in the Canadian Forces: Conceptual Foundations*. (Kingston: Canadian Defence Academy – Canadian Forces Leadership Institute, 2005), 72. The other responses are commitment and compliance.

[39] DND, *Conceptual Foundations*, 72. Emphasis added by present author.

[40] Robin Higham and Gilles Pacquet, "The Challenges of 2020: A Citizen's Perspective," Discussion Paper (Ottawa: Center of Governance, University of Ottawa, 2000), 4.

CHAPTER 5

A Law Unto Themselves? – Elitism as a Catalyst for Disobedience

Bernd Horn

The concept of an elite has always been distasteful to most western democratic societies. Most pride themselves with being egalitarian and maintaining the unassailable virtue that all humankind is created equal. Elitism automatically destroys those precepts. The term alone conjures up notions of favouritism, privilege, superiority and standards that are unobtainable by the majority, which immediately creates angst. As a whole, the military institution also parallels society's disdain for elites. Most military establishments have historically despised such groups. For example, Thomas Adams, a former Director of Intelligence and Special Operations at the United States Army Peacekeeping Institute, revealed that "the US military, particularly the Army, has long distrusted the whole idea of elite units on the general principle that such organizations have no place in the armed forces of a democracy."[1] Martin Kitchen, a professor of history, believed that "the very mention of the idea of a military elite is enough to set the alarm bells ringing in sensitive democratic souls."[2]

In the military, elites are often seen as resource intensive and particularly divisive. Their privileged status, which includes special badges and dress, special equipment and training, and streamlined access to the chain of command, as well as special consideration, runs counter to a very hierarchical, traditional organization that prides itself on uniformity, standardization and rigid adherence to military norms, values and traditions. But the greatest dissension over elites is their tendency to act as a "law unto themselves," a reality that ultimately fuels disobedience to lawful authority. Their demanding and rigorous selection standards, strenuous training, immense capability and privileged status normally creates and feeds a "cult of the elite" mentality that is inwardly focused and that rejects those from outside the group, regardless of rank or position. Responsive only to their respective group, members of elite formations frequently disregard and openly flaunt military conventions, rules and regulations because of their special membership. As such, elitism is a catalyst for disobedience.

Before examining the relationship between elites and disobedience however, it is necessary to define what exactly constitutes "an elite." The word is often used, or more accurately, misused, by the press, the public and even the military itself. It is a term that oftentimes carries negative connotations, the reasons for which are relatively clear. The concept of an elite invariably generates enmity. Respected military analyst and author Tom Clancy once observed, "As always, those who dare rise above the crowd and distinguish themselves will spark envy and resentment."[3] Similarly, "elitism," acknowledged one former member of an elite unit, "is counter-productive, it alienates you from other people."[4] Elites are often generally defined as "exclusive" and as "a class or group possessing wealth, power, and prestige."[5] The term usually refers to individuals and groups that are ranked in the upper levels of a stratified hierarchy; they normally possess greater power, influence, mobility, status and prestige than other individuals or groups ranked beneath them.[6] In its purest form, the term elite translates into "the choice or most carefully selected part of a group."[7]

Generally speaking, there are four traditional types of elites. The first is an aristocracy or any other group that enjoys particular hereditary privileges. These individuals constitute an elite of birth. The second is an elite of merit that includes the intellectual elite (e.g. academic, medical, scientific), and now, in a more contemporary setting, sport and entertainment celebrities as well. In short, this group is composed of people with outstanding merits and qualities. The third is a functional elite, comprised of individuals who hold particular positions in society that are essential for its efficient and effective operation, such as key civil servants; certain members of the military are occasionally included in this bureaucratic elite also. The fourth and final type is a power elite. This group consists of individuals who hold and wield political and / or economic power and has now grown to include the contemporary cultural elite, or more specifically, those people (often holding political and economic power as well) who are capable of influencing the terms of public debate on such topics as the environment or social issues.

But, regardless of the specific type of elite in question, there are a number of common features that explain the link between elitism and disobedience in a military context. Sociologists and political scientists have tended to define elites as a unified minority that holds the power of decision-making in any given group or society. They further note that the chief strength of a given elite is its autonomy and cohesiveness, both of which are born from an exclusiveness that is protected by rigorous entrance standards. Furthermore, elites are extremely homogeneous and self-perpetuating.[8] In short, the term elite connotes a select minority within a group or society that holds special status and privilege. Traditionally, this has meant those who have held political, administrative and economic power.[9] Simply put, "elites are viewed as the 'decision-makers' of a society whose power is not subject to control by any other body in society."[10]

In addition, elites (or ruling minorities) are usually constituted in such a manner that the individuals who comprise such groups are distinguished from the mass of the governed by qualities that give them a certain material, intellectual or even moral superiority; alternatively, they may be the heirs of individuals who possessed such qualities.[11] This includes, for some, the interpretation that elites can also be elite because they are the "sole source of values in the society or constitute the integrating force in the community without which it may fall apart."[12] Sociologist John Porter's 1965 study of Canadian elites, *The Vertical Mosaic*, revealed that in Canada, the traditional political and economic elite represented less than ten percent of the population and was almost exclusively white, English-speaking and protestant. Furthermore, he revealed that they attended the same schools, belonged to the same country clubs and sat on the same Boards of Executives for many corporations and committees. Moreover, they socialized, married and did business largely within their own strata.[13] Although the central tenets of elitism, namely autonomy and exclusivity, have not changed, the composition of elites in society most definitely has. The new elites are now defined as those who control the international flow of money and information, preside over philanthropic foundations and institutions of higher learning and manage the instruments of cultural production. Within this new elite, the term elite is often meant to convey the simple concept that implies those who are "highly successful."[14] The new elites are "far more cosmopolitan … restless and migratory, than their predecessors."[15]

Historically, the concept of a "military elite," at least for sociologists and political scientists, has centred on its impact on the politics of a given society. The Prussian military and its role in the creation of the state and its caste-like structure is a prime example.[16] In the case of military elites, the focus does not necessarily centre on cultural, economic or political power. Most often, it relates to the relationship of a given group within its own institution. With this being said, however, the question of what exactly constitutes a military elite is not as clear as most people think. The term is often misused by both the press and the public, as well as by military personnel, owing to a lack of understanding on their part. Many different groups, such as submariners, search and rescue technicians, paratroopers, fighter pilots and even military police, just to name a few, have all been labelled as elite at one time or another. In most cases, however, the term is used incorrectly.

The confused and inappropriate labelling of groups should come as no surprise when one considers the myriad of concepts that exist to define the term "military elite." For example, the famous writer James Jones believed that "an elite unit is only elite when the majority of its members consider themselves already dead."[17] Clearly, he was referring to elitism as a military "forlorn hope," the force of last resort or only resort. An Algerian veteran of the French Foreign Legion, who succinctly captured the sentiments of his peers, shared this view. "We were the elite," he proclaimed, "because of our will to obey and fight and die."[18] Such romanticized depictions are often utilized by the media who ultimately feed to the public a more stereotypical Hollywood image of military elites, an image that centres on the belief that "elite units require troopers who can ignore pain and exhaustion, eat just about anything that grows or crawls, and fight on no matter what the danger."[19] To others, military elitism is primarily a question of command. Ducournau, a French Second World War general, once insisted that "average soldiers [are] commanded by elite leaders."[20] He defined elitism as a quality imposed from above springing from a small, highly-trained group of skilled officers. Similarly, Eva Etzioni-Halevy, in her study of Israeli forces, defined the military elite as "the most senior officers, holding the rank of colonel and above."[21]

From a different perspective altogether, Richard Szafranski, a military analyst with the Toffler Associates, asserted that "elite means people and forces selected, organized, trained and equipped to rapidly adapt to, and even shape, changing or unforeseen circumstances."[22] His underlying belief centered on individuals and / or organizations of greater intellect, ability and decision-making powers who were capable of exercising control over their own destiny. Moreover, Roger Beaumont, author and former military policeman, characterized military elites as those organizations that are relatively free from ordinary administration and discipline and where entry to such units is often through the survival of an ordeal – a "rite of passage" – requiring tolerance of pain or danger and subsequent dedication to hazardous roles.[23] Similarly, French author Gilles Perrault insisted that military elites are cults who possess special rites, a specialized language or vocabulary, including passwords, their own apostles and martyrs, and their own distinct uniform. In addition, he stipulated that elites have a simple and very defined view of the world: there are those who belong to the group and the rest who do not.[24]

Renowned scholar Eliot Cohen developed specific criteria to define elite military units. "First," he stated, "a unit becomes elite when it is perpetually assigned special or unusual missions – in particular, missions that are, or seem to be, extremely hazardous." For this reason, he insisted, "airborne units have long been considered elite since parachuting is a particularly dangerous way of going into battle." His second criterion is based on the premise that elite units conduct missions that "require only a few men who must meet high standards of training and physical toughness, particularly the latter." Finally, he argued, "an elite unit becomes elite only when it achieves a reputation – justified or not – for bravura and success."[25] For the strategist Colin Gray, the designation of "elite" pertained directly to the standard of selection and not to the activity that soldiers were selected to perform.[26] Conversely, military historian Douglas Porch utilized conventional measures of performance to determine elite status. As a result, he relied on such benchmarks as "battlefield achievement, military proficiency, or specialized military functions."[27] Similarly, Eric Morris, another military historian, defined units as elite by virtue of the fact that "they were required to demonstrate a prowess and military skill of a higher standard than more conventional battalions."[28]

Prowess and skill are indeed the most common themes. Tom Clancy believed that:

its not just the weapons you carry that matter, but also the skill, training and determination of the troopers .... Elite is as elite does. Elite means that you train harder and do somewhat more dangerous things – which earns you the right to blouse your jump boots and strut a little more....[29]

In the same vein, military analyst and author Mark Lloyd defined military units as elite by reason of their superior training and equipment, or greater combat experience.[30] David Miller likewise argued that military elites:

are selected and trained for a special role, for which conventional troops do not have either the special weapons or training needed [or] ... are given a special designation earned by a particularly meritorious performance in battle and are then expected to set an example which other elements should follow.[31]

Along this line, Clancy also noted that military elites are "fit volunteers, trained to a razor's edge and beyond."[32] For this reason, Major-General Robert Scales stated, "Elite soldiers who are carefully selected, trained and well led always perform to a higher standard."[33] Not surprisingly, the *Creed* of the US Army Rangers contains the conceptual definition of a military elite based on the premise that "My country expects me to move farther, faster and fight harder than any other soldier."[34]

Yet, there are still other interpretations. Dennis Showalter, a professor of history, argued that some elite military units during the Second World War achieved their status not through personnel selection, but rather through their functionalism, which was "based on learned skills [and their] professionalism [which] facilitated employing ways of war inapplicable to homogenized mass armies."[35] For this reason, author James Lucas, whose work focuses primarily on the history of the German military during the same conflict, believed that military elites were so designated because they were "given the hardest military tasks to perform."[36] Altogether different, Martin Kitchen claimed that modern military elites are the "classless, highly trained killers who have a wide popular appeal."[37] Numerous other military analysts, researchers and scholars have applied a comparable approach, in that they have used the designation of elite simply because individuals and units were not representative of their conventional brethren by virtue of the quality or type of personnel, training or mission.[38] Quite simply, unique equalled elite.[39]

Perceptions of what constitutes a military elite are clearly wide ranging and oftentimes the criteria are somewhat contrived and misleading. Simply put, being different and / or performing a unique task is far from being a *de facto* "elite." Therefore, for the purposes of this chapter, a military elite, borrowing heavily from Eliot Cohen, will be defined as an organization that bases

CHAPTER 5

its selection on rigorous screening processes that demand extremely high standards of mental and physical ability and fitness, professional experience and skill levels, maturity and motivation. In addition, to be considered elite, those organizations must also have assigned to it an exclusive and special mission or role (either conventional or unconventional or both) that is actually exercised. And finally, it entails a recognized reputation for excellence (based on the level of training, expertise and professionalism of the group or on its success in operations). Considering these criteria, it becomes evident that not all units with "unique characteristics" warrant elite status. For instance, so-called elite units may demonstrate different skill sets than conventional units, however, they do not necessarily reflect a qualitative superiority over the latter.

Although elites are generally resisted in the military, they do provide certain benefits. First, they are extremely cohesive with an unquestioned solidarity amongst their members. Within such groups, officers and men normally undergo identical training and are faced with the same tests of courage, endurance and strength. They have generally all passed the rigorous selection standards as well. In short, there are no shortcuts and no distinctions for anyone. With respect to paratroopers, for instance, Colonel Peter Kenward, the last Commanding Officer of the Canadian Airborne Regiment, recognized that "it is impossible to hide weakness in the Airborne."[40] As a result of the exacting standards that all must meet, as well as the shared hardships that all must suffer, a bond is created based on group identity, mutual respect and solidarity. Membership in the fraternity cannot be bestowed due to affluence, connections or rank. It must be earned.

To be sure, unique and shared experiences build strong group cohesion. Sociologists have argued that high standards and requirements to enter into a group result in a greater sense of commitment and value placed on membership to that group by successful candidates.[41] More simply, the greater the degree of challenge, hardship and danger, the greater is the development of mutual respect and affiliation.[42] Samuel Stouffer, in his monumental study of battlefield behaviour, entitled *The American Soldier,* indicated that 80 percent of respondents believed that strong group integration was the main reason for stamina in combat. This study also observed that motivation is primarily dependent on group cohesion and that group cohesion, in turn, is the decisive factor for combat efficiency. The steadfast self-confidence in oneself and in one's fellow soldiers engenders a belief and philosophy that there is no mission that cannot be accomplished.[43] As such, elite units provide a very reliable and effective combat force regardless of the difficulty of the task.

Furthermore, elite units also act as a "leadership nursery." Members have the opportunity to acquire additional expertise, particularly advanced leadership skills, through their exposure to different training and operational experiences. The opportunity to interact with more experienced, mature and highly-skilled personnel also facilitates the same end. Ultimately, members return to their former units and share the expertise and skills that they have attained. In addition, elite units are often a preferred testing ground for new tactics and procedures since they represent smaller, more experienced and more talented organizations. As such, it is easier to test new processes, tactics, equipment and techniques within such units and then refine them prior to introducing them to the wider organization.

Despite the possible benefits that can be derived from elite units, they are generally resisted. Almost universally, they face bureaucratic hostility from the larger conventional institution to which they belong. According to most military commanders, this reality is based on the detrimental impact that elite units can have on the larger organization. First, such units are perceived to be "skimming the cream," that is, taking for themselves the best individuals from conventional units, thereby leaving the latter with less leadership capability. "Almost invariably the men volunteering," explained historian Philip Warner, "are the most enterprising, energetic and least dispensable."[44] It was for this reason that Field-Marshal Sir Alan Brooke, Chief of the Imperial General Staff, never agreed with Winston Churchill's sponsorship of special, elite type units. He felt that it was "a dangerous drain on the quality of an infantry battalion."[45] The legendary Field-Marshal Viscount Slim was in strong agreement. He noted that special units:

> were usually formed by attracting the best men from normal units by better conditions, promises of excitement and not a little propaganda. ... The result of these methods was undoubtedly to lower the quality of the rest of the Army, especially of the infantry, not only by skimming the cream off it, but by encouraging the idea that certain of the normal operations of war were so difficult that only specially equipped corps d'élite could be expected to undertake them.[46]

Elite units are also seen to be bad for the morale of the larger institution. Military leaders consistently acknowledged the negative consequences of failing to meet the high standards normally imposed during selection. Brooke and Slim, for example, were both convinced that failing to gain admission into an elite unit undermined one's confidence.[47] Moreover, the nature of highly-selective units created an impression that everyone else was second best. Indeed, many that had been admitted to elite units believed that they were superior to all others. "I was glad they [those not selected] left camp immediately and didn't say any awkward farewells," confessed one successful candidate, for they "were social lepers and I didn't want to risk catching the infection they carried."[48] This attitude is dangerous and, more importantly, it underlines the chasm that develops between those in the group and those external to it.

CHAPTER 5

Furthermore, when the return is compared to the investment, many commanders perceive elite units to be resource intensive, if not an actual waste of men and materiel. Detractors argue that elites are "expensive, independent, arrogant, out of uniform, [operate] outside normal chains of command, and [are] too specialized for [their] own good."[49] Tom Clancy observed that elite "units and their men are frequently seen as 'sponges,' sucking up prized personnel and funds at the expense of 'regular' units."[50] Critics of special or elite units often liken their efforts to "breaking windows by throwing guineas [gold coins] at them."[51]

However, the most emotive criticism that generates the greatest amount of resistance and animosity, and that which is the most relevant to the question of disobedience, is the issue of the "cult of the elite" mentality, specifically the arrogance and rejection of conventional military discipline, practice and protocol that elites demonstrate. It is this attitude, what some scholars, analysts and military personnel have described as the phenomenon of elites being a "law unto themselves," that serves as the connection between elitism and disobedience. Simply put, the rejection by members of an elite group of the authority or the validity of anyone outside of the group, combined with their oftentimes arrogant behaviour and flagrant flouting of military rules, regulations and protocol, generates an environment where only internal values, norms and rules are followed and where external guidelines are ignored. This phenomenon is exacerbated by the fact that the elite leadership often ignores such non-conformist behaviour. Military analyst and author Roger Beaumont described elites as "virtually encapsulated delinquency."[52] In short, membership to an elite, more often than not, actively promotes disobedience to lawful authority.

This mentality is probably the greatest seed of discontent amongst conventional military leaders with respect to elites and a major reason for their resistance, animosity and active hostility toward them. To those on the outside, units that do not fit the conventional mould, specifically those described as elite, special or unique, are frequently seen as rogue outfits and divisive in relation to the greater institution. In his studies of military culture, former Canadian lieutenant-colonel and current sociologist Charles Cotton noted that "their [elite] cohesive spirit is a threat to the chain of command and wider cohesion."[53]

Such a situation is often the result of the fact that the leadership and discipline are informal within elite units and the normal protocol and emphasis placed on ceremony and deportment is generally relaxed. Professor Eliot Cohen revealed that "an almost universally observed characteristic of elite units is their lack of formal discipline – and sometimes a lack of substantive discipline as well." His research determined that "elite units often disregard spit and polish or orders about saluting."[54] As evidenced by the testimony of former members of a wide range of elite fighting units, Cohen was entirely correct in his assessment. For instance, as a junior officer in the British Special Air Service (SAS), General De La Billiere recalled, "The men, for their part, never called me 'Sir' unless they wanted to be rude."[55] In addition, historian Eric Morris has noted that "the LRDG [Long Range Desert Group] and other like units did offer a means of escape from those petty tediums and irritants of everyday life in the British Army. Drills, guards, fatigues and inspections were almost totally absent."[56] Another military historian has likewise observed that the commander of 2 SAS Brigade, mad Mike Calvert, "like many fighting soldiers was not particularly concerned by the trivia of, for example, military appearance [since] uniformity and smartness have little bearing on a unit's ability to fight."[57] But, without a doubt, this "trivial" aspect has an enormous impact on how the respective unit is perceived by others, namely outsiders.

This reality was not lost on the members of elite organizations. "We were already conspicuous by our lack of dress code," confessed one SAS non-commissioned officer (NCO), since "The green army always dresses the same."[58] One neophyte American Special Forces soldier recalled his amazement after arriving at his new unit. "Sergeants Major are the walking, breathing embodiment of everything that's right in the US Army," he explained. Yet, his first glimpse of his new sergeant-major caught him unprepared. "This guy looked like Joe Shit the Ragman," he exclaimed. "His shirt was wide open and he wore no T-shirt. His dog-tags were gold plated. His hat was tipped up on the back of his head, and he wore a huge, elaborately curled and waxed handlebar moustache."[59] The fact of the matter is that elite units realize that their lax discipline and dress codes irritate the conventional military. Such tension is part of their appeal, as is their need to clearly differentiate themselves from the "regular" military. Their behaviour, as might be expected, generates a good deal of enmity from the conventional hierarchy as well. Nonetheless, much of this dynamic is based on the type of individuals that actually join these units. David Stirling, the founder of the SAS, reflected that the "Originals" were not really "controllable" but rather "harnessable."[60] The Rangers were acknowledged to consist largely of "mavericks who couldn't make it in conventional units."[61] "Commanding the Rangers," explained William Darby, their first commanding officer, "was like driving a team of very high spirited horses. No effort was needed to get them to go forward. The problem was to hold them in check."[62]

American Special Forces (Green Berets) were later similarly described as those "who wanted to try something new and challenging, and who chafed at rigid discipline."[63] Furthermore, General De La Billiere observed that "Most officers and men here do not really fit in normal units of the Army, and that's why they're here in the SAS, which is not like anything else in the Services."[64] He assumed that most of the volunteers, like himself, "were individualists who wanted to break away from the formal drill-machine discipline" which existed in the army as a whole.[65] A similar pattern is noticeable elsewhere. According to General Peter Schoomaker, who joined Delta Force under its founding commander, Colonel Charlie Beckwith, "Beckwith was looking for a bunch of bad cats who wanted to do something different."[66]

This element of self-selection, combined with the feeling of accomplishment, as one of the few who has successfully passed selection, and the self-confidence born from challenging, difficult and hazardous training, creates an aura of invincibility and an intense loyalty to what is perceived as a very exclusive group. An intimate bond is further generated through shared hardship and danger. Members of these "special" groups frequently develop an outlook that treats those outside the "club" as inferior and unworthy of respect. "The more the group is centred on itself, thus increasing its cohesion," observed Professor Elmar Dinter, "the less it is interested in its environment." He argued that "an already existing behavioural pattern is thereby reinforced. ... What matters to the group is only what affects it directly." Dinter added, "The desire to distinguish the group from other groups is not restricted to insignia and ritualism, but leads, in addition, to a spiteful attitude towards others."[67] Often, this sense of independence from the conventional army, as well as the lack of respect for traditional forms of discipline, spawns what some analysts describe as the emergence of units that are more akin to militant clans than military organizations.[68] Needless to say, this type of organization and institutional attitude is anathema to a military that prides itself on decorum, tradition and uniformity.

Not surprisingly, the arrogance and deliberate insubordination of individuals in elite units often fuels the fire. No image is more representative than the scene from *Black Hawk Down* when a captain gives direction to a group of senior NCOs. After he has finished his explanation, the group, less one, acknowledges the orders. The captain quickly confirms with the recalcitrant NCO if he understood the direction. The Delta Force sergeant replies nonchalantly, almost contemptuously, "Yeah, I heard ya." Such an exchange is a classic case of art reflecting reality. Moreover, one operator laughingly described how he had failed to salute two "crap-hat" (regular army) captains. When brought to task for this clear omission of military protocol, he flippantly explained that he "couldn't because he was smoking and couldn't do two things at once."[69] Such a situation echoed the behaviour of paratroopers in the Canadian Special Service Force in the 1980s who consistently refused to salute "LEG" officers and were not held accountable by their chain of command.[70] Further examples of disobedience to authority generated from elitism are readily available. In another instance, which is representative of numerous cases, a former support officer of an elite organization revealed that "assaulters would refuse to listen to others regardless of rank because 'you hadn't done selection.'"[71] Similarly, an executive assistant to a Sector Commander in Bosnia disclosed that "whenever they [members of elite units] didn't like what they were told, they went in to see the commander," thereby circumventing the chain of command.[72]

CHAPTER 5

The issue of circumventing or ignoring the chain of command is a bitter and long standing one. Many see it as one of the most common examples of disobedience by elites. It also tends to raise the accusation that elites are in essence "Private Armies" that usually "become an object of suspicion to the public army."[73] This perception often results from the fact that elite units value concrete action and have little patience for bureaucracy. Coupled with an "end justifies the means attitude," it is not surprising that conventional feathers are easily ruffled. "One danger of the private army," commented one senior officer, "is certainly that it gets into the habit of using wrong channels."[74] He was entirely correct. conceded that "A private army ... short-circuits command."[75] One need only listen to stories from the various operations that have been conducted in the recent past and those currently underway to realize that this situation has not changed.

In the end, the arrogance and aloofness that is bred from a cult of elitism, which is often endemic within groups that are specially selected, develops and nurtures an "in-group" mentality that is dangerously focused inward. They trust only themselves, that is, those who have passed the rigorous selection standards and tests. Anthropologist Donna Winslow confirmed the negative aspects that often arise from an emphasis on the exclusivity of this "warrior cult." It nurtures an unassailable belief, she insisted, that "only those who have done it know, or can be trusted, or more dangerously yet, can give direction."[76] Alan Bell, formerly of the SAS, confessed that we "tended to have an arrogance that we knew it all, did it all, and had nothing to learn." Moreover, he acknowledged that they would work only with Delta Force or SEAL Team Six – no one else. "We figured," he confessed, that "it wasn't worth our time."[77]

And so it becomes clearly evident that elitism, whether real or imagined by its members, actively contributes toward the disobedience of lawful commands. Elites tend to define conformity in a different way, that is, in consonance with their own particular culture and standards of discipline and obedience. When this reality is combined with their overt rejection of conventional military conventions, practices and protocols, which their command element quite often sanctions, it creates an almost *de facto* disobedience to authority.

ENDNOTES

[1] Thomas K. Adams, *US Special Operations Forces in Action - The Challenge of Unconventional Warfare* (London: Frank Cass, 1998), 9-10.

[2] Martin Kitchen, "Elites in Military History," in A. Hamish Ion and Keith Neilson, eds., *Elite Formations in War and Peace* (Wesport: Praeger, 1996), 8. Brigadier-General (ret'd) R.G. Theriault astutely noted that in Canadian society, it is not a good thing to produce a group who is favoured above others. Interview with author, 28 April 1998.

[3] Tom Clancy, *Special Forces* (New York: A Berkley Book, 2001), 3.

CHAPTER 5

[4] Andy McNab, *Immediate Action* (London: Bantam Press, 1995), 381.
[5] Katherine Barber, ed., *The Canadian Oxford Dictionary* (New York: Oxford University Press, 1998), 454.
[6] *Elites*. 18 April 2001. http://www.webref.org/sociology/e/elites.htm.
[7] Kitchen, "Elites in Military History," 7.
[8] See John Porter, *The Vertical Mosaic - An Analysis of Social Class and Power in Canada* (Toronto: University of Toronto Press, 1965), 27 & 207; Robert Putnam, *The Comparative Study of Political Elites* (Englewood Cliffs: Prentice-Hall, 1976), 4; Geraint Parry, *Political Elites* (New York: Praeger, 1969), 30-2; Sylvie Guillaume, ed., *Les Elites Fins de Siècles - XIX-XX Siècles* (Editions de la Maison des Sciences de L'Homme D'Aquitaine, 1992), 27; and M.S. Whittington and Glen Williams, eds., *Canadian Politics in the 1990s* (Scarborough: Nelson Canada, 1990), 182.
[9] Hervé Bentégeant, *Les Nouveaux Rois de France ou La Trahison des Élites* (Paris: Éditions Ramsay, 1998), 19.
[10] Parry, *Political Elites*, 13. This also includes leadership positions in special interest groups. Those who lead such organizations are often designated as "elites," as opposed to the "non-decision making" mass of their membership. Leo V. Panitch, "Elites, Classes, and Power in Canada," in Michael S. Whittington and Glen Williams, eds., *Canadian Politics in the 1990s*, 3rd ed. (Scarborough: Nelson Canada, 1990), 182.
[11] Moshe M. Czudnowski, ed., *Political Elites and Social Change - Studies of Elite Roles and Attitudes* (Northern Illinois University Press, 1983), 221.
[12] Parry, *Political Elites*, 13.
[13] Porter, *The Vertical Mosaic*.
[14] Reg Jennings et al., *Business Elites. The Psychology of Entrepreneurs and Intrapreneurs* (New York: Routledge, 1994), 10.
[15] Christopher Lasch, *The Revolt of the Elites and the Betrayal of Democracy* (New York: W.W. Norton & Co., 1995), 3, 5, 25-6. See also Guillaume, *Les Elites Fins de Siècles*, 112-13. In accordance with this study, an elite must fulfil two conditions. First, it must be recognized by the respective "local society" as an elite (by definition, the author states that the elite is of small composition). This aspect is symbolic in nature. The second requirement is that the elite must have control of and power over the cultural infrastructure of the society.
[16] Parry, *Political Elites*, 75-6.
[17] Douglas Porch, "The French Foreign Legion: The Mystique of Elitism," in A. Hamish Ion and Keith Neilson, eds., *Elite Formations in War and Peace* (Wesport: Praeger, 1996), 131.
[18] Porch, "The French Foreign Legion," 126.
[19] Steve Payne, "Hell is for Heroes," *The Ottawa Sunday Sun*, 19 March 1995, 6.
[20] Porch, "The French Foreign Legion," 118.
[21] Eva Etzioni-Halevy, "Civil-Military Relations and Democracy: The Case of the Military-Political Elites' Connection in Israel," *Armed Forces and Society*, Vol. 22, No. 3 (Spring 1996), 401.

[22] Richard Szafranski, "Neocortical Warfare? The Acme of Skill," in John Arquilla and David Ronfeldt, eds., *In Athena's Camp: Preparing for Conflict in the Information Age* (New York: Rand, 1999), 408.

[23] Roger A. Beaumont, *Military Elites* (London: Robert Hale and Co., 1974), 2-3.

[24] Gilles Perrault, *Les Parachutistes* (Paris: Éditions du Seuil, 1961), 42.

[25] Eliot A. Cohen, *Commandos and Politicians* (Cambridge: Center for International Affairs, Harvard University, 1978), 17.

[26] Colin S. Gray, *Explorations in Strategy* (London: Greenwood Press, 1996), 158. The question of selection is an important one. Using Special Operations Forces (SOF), which are universally seen as elite, as an example, their selection / status is based on a three-tiered structure. For instance, "Tier One" SOF consists primarily of "Black Ops," or counter-terrorism. Normally, only 10 to 15 percent of those attempting selection are successful. What makes this number so impressive is that a large percentage of those trying to gain admission are already second or third tier SOF members. Organizations that fall into this category include the US 1st Special Forces Operational Detachment - Delta, the German *Grenzschutzgruppe*-9 (GSG 9), and the Canadian Joint Task Force - 2 (JTF 2). "Tier Two" SOF reflects those organizations that have a selection pass rate of between 20 to 30 percent. They are normally entrusted with high value tasks such as Strategic Reconnaissance and Unconventional Warfare. Some examples include the American Special Forces (also referred to as the Green Berets), the American SEALs, and the British, Australian and New Zealand SAS. "Tier Three" SOF consists of those units, such as the American Rangers and the British Royal Marine Commandos, that have a selection success rate of 40 to 45 percent, and whose primary mission is Direct Action. See Colonel C.A. Beckwith, *Delta Force* (New York: Dell Publishing Co., 1985), 123 & 137; Interview with Major Anthony Balasevicius; Leroy Thompson, *The Rescuers - The World's Top Anti-Terrorist Units* (London: A David & Charles Military Book, 1986), 127-28; General Ulrich Wegener, Presentation to the RMC Special Operations Symposium, 5 October 2000; Judith E. Brooks and Michelle M. Zazanis, "Enhancing U.S. Army Special Forces: Research and Applications," US Army Research Institute for the Behavioral Social Sciences Special Report 33, October 1997, 8; General H.H. Shelton, "Quality People: Selecting and Developing Members of U.S. SOF," *Special Warfare*, Vol. 11, No. 2 (Spring 1998), 3; Commander Thomas Dietz, CO Seal Team 5, Presentation to the RMC Special Operations Symposium, 5 October 2000; John D. Leary, "Searching for a Role: The Special Air Service Regiment in the Malayan Emergency," *The Journal of the Society of Army Historical Research*, Vol. LXXIII, No. 296 (Winter, 1995), 265; and Colonel Bill Kidd, "Ranger Training Brigade," *US Army Infantry Center Infantry Senior Leader Newsletter*, February 2003, 8-9.

[27] Porch, "The French Foreign Legion," 117.

CHAPTER 5

[28] Eric Morris, *Churchill's Private Armies* (London: Hutchinson, 1986), xiii. See also David Chandler, "Indispensable Role of Elite Forces," *Military History Quarterly*, Vol. 15, No. 3 (Spring 2003), 77-8.

[29] Tom Clancy, *Airborne* (New York: Berkley Books, 1997), xviii.

[30] Mark Lloyd, *Special Forces - The Changing Face of Warfare* (New York: Arms and Armour, 1995), 11.

[31] David Miller, *Special Forces* (London: Salamander Books, 2001), 15. Similarly, author Duncan Anderson defines military elites as "a relatively small highly trained force specializing in extremely hazardous operations, often of a militarily non-conventional nature." See Duncan Anderson, *Military Elites* (London: Bison Books Ltd., 1994), 7.

[32] Tom Clancy, with General Fred Franks, *Into the Storm - A Study in Command* (New York: G.P. Putnam's Sons, 1997), 119.

[33] Major-General (ret'd) Robert H. Scales Jr., *Yellow Smoke - The Future of Land Warfare for America's Military* (New York: Rowman & Littlefield Publishers Inc., 2003), 69.

[34] Matt Labash, "The New Army," *The Weekly Standard*, Vol. 6, No. 31, 30 April 2001.

[35] Dennis Showalter, "German Army Elites in World Wars I and II," in A. Hamish Ion and Keith Neilson, eds., *Elite Formations in War and Peace* (Wesport: Praeger, 1996), 152.

[36] James Lucas, *Storming Eagles - German Airborne Forces in World War II* (London: Cassel & Co. Ltd., 2001), 14.

[37] Kitchen, "Elites in Military History," 26.

[38] See D.R. Segal *et al.*, "Paratroopers as Peacekeepers," *Armed Forces and Society*, Vol. 10, No. 4 (Summer 1984), 489, and Donna Winslow, *The Canadian Airborne Regiment in Somalia - A Socio-cultural Inquiry* (Ottawa: Commission of Inquiry into the Deployment of Canadian Forces to Somalia, 1997), 128-38. Gideon Aran stated that: "Jumping can be viewed as a test which allows those who pass it to join an exclusive club, to be initiated into an elite group." See Gideon Aran, "Parachuting," *American Journal of Sociology*, Vol. 80, No. 1, 150.

[39] This emphasis on discernable differences between the "special" units and their "conventional" brethren became the core of the Canadian military's understanding of elite. Many senior Commanders defined and treated the Canadian paratroopers as elite, at least prior to the Somalia debacle, based on the higher levels of fitness required of them, their distinctive uniform and their ability to jump. Colonel Painchaud, a former Airborne Regimental Commander, was representative of many when he asserted, "the airborne soldier is the elite of the Canadian Army. He must be in top shape compared to any other soldier, in physical fitness and shooting and weapon handling." Dick Brown, "Hanging Tough," *Quest*, May 1978, 12. See also Commission of Inquiry into the Deployment of Canadian Forces to Somalia, *Information Legacy - A Compendium of Source Material from the Commission of Inquiry*, CD-ROM (1998), Hearing Transcripts, Volume 36, 22 January 1996, testimony of Lieutenant-Colonel Morneault, 6898.

CHAPTER 5

[40] Interview with author, 4 October 1996. One sergeant-major of the British 2nd Parachute Regiment stated that the officers and men rely on one another in airborne units. He explained, "a special bond was created because of the fact that the men knew that the officers, like them, endured the same difficult training prior to arriving at [the] Regiment." See Rory Bridson, *The Making of a Para* (London: Sidgwick & Jackson Ltd., 1989), 81. Major-General A.S. Newman declared, "There's a close bond between the airborne soldier and his officer, because each knows the other has passed the jump test. And they continue to do so together. Each believes the other will be a good man to have around when things get sweaty." See Major-General A.S. Newman, *What Are Generals Made Of?* (Novato: Presidio, 1987), 193.

[41] E. Aronson and J. Mills, "The Effect of Severity of Initiation on Liking for a Group," *Journal of Abnormal & Social Psychology*, (1957), 157-58. Elliot Aronson of Stanford University and Judson Mills of the U.S. Army Leadership and Human Research Unit established this linkage in their laboratory experiments. They stated, "Subjects who underwent a severe initiation perceived the group as being significantly more attractive than those who underwent a mild or no initiation." See also R.B. Cialdini, *Influence - Science & Practise*, 3rd ed. (Arizona: Harper Collins, 1993), 70 & 74; and Major James McCollum, "The Airborne Mystique," *Military Review*, Vol. 56, No. 11 (November 1976), 16.

[42] W.D. Henderson, *Cohesion: The Human Element in Combat* (Washington: National Defence University Press, 1985), 14.

[43] Elmar Dinter, *Hero or Coward: Pressures Facing the Soldier in Battle* (London: Frank Cass, 1985), 41, and Anthony Kellet, *Combat Motivation* (Boston: Nijhoff Publishing, 1982), 45-6.

[44] Philip Warner, *Phantom* (London: William Kimber, 1982), 11.

[45] Morris, *Churchill's Private Armies*, 90.

[46] Field Marshall Sir William Slim, *Defeat Into Victory* (London: Cassel and Co. Ltd., 1956), 547.

[47] Slim, *Defeat Into Victory*, 546, and Morris, *Churchill's Private Armies*, 243.

[48] Command Sergeant Major Eric L. Haney, *Inside Delta Force. The Story of America's Elite Counterterrorist Unit* (New York: A Dell Book, 2002), 97.

[49] Adams, *US Special Operations Forces in Action*, 162.

[50] Clancy, *Special Forces*, 3-4.

[51] Cohen, *Commandos and Politicians*, 61.

[52] Beaumont, *Military Elites*, 192.

[53] Charles A. Cotton, "Military Mystique," Canadian Airborne Forces Museum files.

[54] Cohen, *Commandos and Politicians*, 74.

[55] General Sir Peter De La Billiere, *Looking For Trouble - SAS to Gulf Command* (London: Harper Collins Publishers, 1995), 117.

[56] Eric Morris, *Guerillas in Uniform* (London: Hutchinson, 1989), 15.

CHAPTER 5

[57] Adrian Weale, *Secret Warfare* (London: Coronet Books, 1997), 154.
[58] Cameron Spence, *All Necessary Measures* (London: Penguin Books, 1997), 43.
[59] Haney, *Inside Delta Force*, 20.
[60] Anthony Kemp, *The SAS at War* (London: John Murray, 1991), 11.
[61] Charles M. Simpson III, *Inside the Green Berets - The First Thirty Years* (Novato: Presidio, 1983), 14, and Charles W. Sasser, *Raider* (New York: St. Martins, 2002), 186.
[62] William O. Darby and William H. Baumer, *Darby's Rangers - We Led the Way* (Novato: Presidio, reprint 1993), 184.
[63] Darby and Baumer, *Darby's Rangers*, 21.
[64] De La Billiere, *Looking For Trouble*, 236.
[65] Ibid., 98.
[66] Greg Jaffe, "A Maverick's Plan to Revamp Army is Taking Shape," *Wall Street Journal*, 12 December 2003.
[67] Dinter, *Hero or Coward*, 70.
[68] John Talbot, "The Myth and Reality of the Paratrooper in the Algerian War," *Armed Forces and Society*, Vol. 3, No. 1 (November 1976), 75; Cohen, *Commandos and Politicians*, 69; and Winslow, *The Canadian Airborne Regiment in Somalia*, 135-41.
[69] Spence, *All Necessary Measures*, 43.
[70] Interviews with Lieutenant-Colonel Ken Watkin and Lieutenant-Colonel Peter Bradley, 4 June 1998 and 15 September 1997, respectively. The derogatory term "LEG" originates from the Second World War. Regular infantry wore canvas "leggings" as part of their uniform. The "elite" paratroopers were spared this ordeal. They were issued with high cut "jump boots" into which uniform trousers could be tucked. Needless to say, the paratroopers quickly christened their brethren with the contemptuous label of "LEGs." A more contemporary version translates the meaning to "Lacking Enough Guts." This is not surprisingly a peacetime mutation. Beyond the obvious that "leggings" are no longer worn, the act of parachuting is seen as a test of individual courage. It has taken on an importance of far greater proportion than it did during the war. Since virtually all infantrymen saw combat, and those in the regular line infantry for longer periods than those in airborne units, the question of individual courage was rather mute.
[71] Interview with a confidential source, September 2002.
[72] Interviews with confidential sources, 25 October 2002.
[73] Colonel J.W. Hackett, "The Employment of Special Forces," *Royal United Service Institute Journal*, Vol. 97, No. 585 (February 1952), 35.
[74] Hackett, "The Employment of Special Forces," 39.
[75] Ibid. Examples of this are legendary. For instance, Prime Minister Winston Churchill took great interest in the development of the commandos and he supported other similar aggressive, unorthodox type units. General George Marshall personally pushed his subordinates to support the establishment of the American Rangers, and his political master, President Franklin

CHAPTER 5

D. Roosevelt, allowed the director of the Office of Strategic Services (OSS) to maintain direct contact with the White House. Later, President John F. Kennedy heaped lavish attention on the American Special Forces, much to the chagrin of his conventional chiefs of staff. Recently, Secretary of Defence Donald Rumsfeld personally ensured that American SOF received starring roles in US operations, as well as hefty increases in manpower and budgets. Examples of SOF operators conducting operations in complete isolation, if not in contempt of local command arrangements, are also numerous. One need only speak with individuals who assumed leadership.

[76] Winslow, *The Canadian Airborne Regiment in Somalia*, 126-33.

[77] Allan Bell, formerly of 22 SAS, presentation to the RMC Special Operations Symposium, 5 October 2000 and RMC War Studies 586 class, 19 March 2004.

CHAPTER 6

Combat Stress Reaction and the Act of Disobedience:
Does the Significance of Acts of Disobedience Diminish Under the Pressure of Combat Stress?

Gordon (Joe) Sharpe and George Dowler

It is practically inconceivable to any officer or senior Non-Commissioned Officer (NCO) in the Canadian Forces (CF) that the people that they lead would attempt to render him or her ineffective as a result of being perceived as having a "gung-ho" attitude. Yet in 1999, that was precisely the message that Warrant Officer (WO) Matt Stopford, a retired member of the 2nd Battalion, Princess Patricia's Canadian Light Infantry (2 PPCLI), received when he was hand-delivered a letter on behalf of the Canadian Forces Provost Marshal. This letter stated that the Canadian Forces National Investigation Service (CFNIS) was about to commence an investigation into the allegation that he, as a platoon warrant officer, had been poisoned by his own troops while deployed to Croatia in 1993. Stopford claims that he was asked not to go public with the letter before the investigation was complete; Peter Worthington, however, made the contents public in the *Toronto Sun*. The letter stated in part:

> ... Information has recently come to light that indicates you may have been the victim of systemic ingestion of naphtha gas during your tour to Croatia in 1993 ... it is alleged that minute amounts ... of naphtha gas were covertly put into your coffee on a regular basis by other servicemen over an extended period of time ... [and] may have included the majority of your time in theatre.[1]

In the same column, Worthington also reported Stopford's reaction to the claims that were made in the letter. The latter asserted:

> I know my men, the guys I served with, and if anyone was out to get me, I'd have known it. Besides, how could you drink coffee with gasoline in it and not know? Gasoline floats on water. As for battery acid in my food — it makes no sense.[2]

Stopford clearly did not believe that this type of action could have been taken by his own troops and neither did other members of the Battalion's leadership cadre. A number of the people who had served with Stopford rejected these allegations outright. Master Warrant Officer Daniel Hartford, for instance, stated to the Croatia Board of Inquiry (CBOI):

> And it is simply with regards to the allegation that Warrant Stopford was being poisoned by his own troops. That is patently the most ridiculous piece of bullshit I have ever heard. I mean most people that have any kind of familiarity with the life are of the same mind.[3]

CHAPTER 6

Stopford believed that the CF was simply trying to divert attention away from a serious environmental contamination issue.[4] Nonetheless, in 2000, after reviewing much of the evidence collected by the CFNIS, Stopford finally accepted the fact that the troops in his platoon had indeed tried to render him ineffective. The *Canadian Press* news service later quoted him as saying that he was deeply hurt by the idea that his own men had turned on him and that "… maybe they were really scared and cowardly."[5]

After the CFNIS investigation, Inspector Russ Grabb of the Royal Canadian Mounted Police (RCMP) presented the findings at a press conference on 30 May 2000. He stated:

> The evidence in this case supports the following conclusions. Firstly, during Roto 4 [sic], a number of identified soldiers did in fact place substances such as naphtha, anti-freeze, anti-irritant eye drops like Visine, and boot blackener in coffee intended to be consumed by Matt Stopford. … How do we know this? Many of the people who were involved, many of the soldiers about which I'm speaking, confessed not only to fellow soldiers but to police during our criminal investigation. The alleged motive for these acts was to temporarily render him unable to carry out his position of command. The evidence also supports the conclusion that a number of other substances including battery acid was also contemplated. The evidence supports the conclusion that no permanent harm was intended. And the identified soldiers also contemplated placing similar substances in the coffee of other leaders in their company. Again, how do we know this? The people directly involved made incriminating statements not only to their fellow soldiers who in turn gave us witness statements but in some cases some of these individuals confessed to having placed the substances in coffee intended to be consumed by Matt Stopford.[6]

Although some members of the unit found his statements virtually unbelievable, other soldiers alluded to these findings during their testimony to the CBOI. For example, on 22 September 1999, one witness stated:

> …soldiers were being unnecessarily exposed to dangerous situations and I am going to point to D Company because I think D Company … I heard the stories out of D Company from about five or six different sources. Stories of, you know, graves being dug for a couple of guys in senior ranks of that company. Guys carrying an extra couple of rounds around in their pockets to if they got a chance to use them. There was a cowboy mentality out there and there was a reckless treatment of the soldiers.[7]

Given the above background, this chapter examines the types of conditions that contribute to incidents of disobedience in otherwise well performing units, that is to say, the type of conditions under which soldiers who experience combat conditions decide that for their own well being they must effectively remove their leaders from command. Specifically, it examines the factors that most probably contributed to the suspected poisoning of WO Stopford during the deployment of 2 PPCLI to Croatia in 1993 and 1994 and asks the question of whether or not a foreseeable reaction to combat stress should be considered in the same vein as mutiny.

Combat Stress Reaction

The last fifteen years have seen Combat Stress Reaction (CSR) become an increasing fact of life for Canadian soldiers, although it has often been interpreted as something else. For example, in 1999, numerous veterans of Operation HARMONY, the Canadian contribution to the United Nations Protection Force (UNPROFOR) in the Balkans, were identified as suffering from a wide variety of undiagnosed illnesses. The CF called a Board of Inquiry to investigate whether exposure to environmental contaminants in Croatia had caused the problems that the veterans of that deployment had encountered in the years after their return to Canada. While the environmental conditions in Croatia were far from pristine, they were not the culprits in this case, and the Board concluded that combat stress was a much more significant issue.

In a background paper prepared to assist the Board of Inquiry in understanding CSR, Dr. Allan English observed that this phenomenon has been around, and has adversely affected soldiers, for a very long time – nearly as long as historical records have been kept. Nonetheless, modern militaries are still grappling with how to develop a culture that both understands and contributes to the reduction of this often-debilitating condition. He concludes:

> The GWS [Gulf War Syndrome] debate is a clear example that the issues surrounding illnesses that may have been caused by exposure to combat or intense operations are far from resolved. The opinions expressed in the debate run the whole gamut of beliefs about the subject, and most are based on paradigms that have been used in the past to try to explain the various illnesses not directly related to physical injuries that have afflicted soldiers. For those investigating perplexing subjects like CSR, they will continue to encounter many competing explanations based on the paradigms of the experts providing each interpretation. To date, we can only say that no explanation has been generally accepted to account for the precise causes of illnesses that may result from the stress of combat or intense operations. It may be that, like our predecessors, we are still grappling with problems beyond our capacity to solve.[8]

CHAPTER 6

The United States military, and American society in general, became painfully aware of the reality of this phenomenon during the Vietnam conflict of the 1960s and 1970s. More recently, similar combat stress related problems resulting from the war in Iraq have freshened awareness of this issue. The United States Army's approach to dealing with the issue of combat stress has matured since Vietnam and is well described in an official Field Manual entitled the *Leaders' Manual for Combat Stress Control*. This manual includes a chapter devoted to stress and combat performance and draws a direct link between exposure to combat stress and the resulting behaviour of the soldiers involved. The term combat stress behaviour is defined as "… the generic term which covers the full range of behaviors in combat, from behaviors that are highly positive to those that are totally negative."[9]

Of particular note is that this approach identifies both positive and negative combat stress reactions. The positive stress reactions are considered adaptive, while the negative ones are identified as dysfunctional. This manual places behavioural types in three categories. It observes:

1. Positive Combat Stress Behaviors include the heightened alertness, strength, endurance, and tolerance to discomfort which the fight or flight stress response and the stage of resistance can produce when properly in tune. Examples of positive combat stress behaviors include the strong personal bonding between combat soldiers and the pride and self-identification which they develop with the combat unit's history and mission (unit esprit). These together form unit cohesion – the binding force that keeps soldiers together and performing the mission in spite of danger and death. The ultimate positive combat stress behaviors are acts of extreme courage and action involving almost unbelievable strength. They may even involve deliberate self-sacrifice. *Positive combat stress behaviors can be brought forth by sound military training (drill), wise personnel policies, and good leadership.*

2. Misconduct Stress Behaviors – Examples of misconduct stress behaviors range from minor breaches of unit orders or regulations to serious violations of the Uniform Code of Military Justice (UCMJ) and perhaps the Law of Land Warfare. As misconduct stress behaviors, they are most likely to occur in *poorly trained, undisciplined soldiers. However, they can also be committed by good, even heroic, soldiers under extreme combat stress.*

3. Battle Fatigue – Battle fatigue is also considered a combat stress reaction or combat fatigue. Examples of battle fatigue are hyper alertness, fear, anxiety, irritability, anger, rage, grief, self-doubt, guilt, physical stress, complaints, inattention, carelessness, loss of confidence, loss of hope and faith, depression, insomnia, impaired duty performance, erratic actions, outbursts, freezing, immobility, terror, panic running, total

exhaustion, apathy, loss of skill and memories, impaired speech or muteness, impaired vision, touch or hearing, weakness or paralysis, hallucinations, and delusions. Those battle fatigue behaviors listed [at the beginning of this paragraph] may accompany excellent combat performance and are often found in heroes, too. These are normal, common signs of battle fatigue. Those that follow ... indicate progressively more serious or warning signs.[10]

Some of the factors that the US military has identified as potentially contributing to misconduct stress behaviours are boredom and monotonous duties, especially if combined with chronic frustration and tension; commission of atrocities by the enemy; failure of expected support, such as reinforcement or relief; inadequate re-supply; inadequate medical support and evacuation; the loss of confidence in leaders; and of course, a soldier's fear of dying. Some misconduct stress behaviours that can result include: either opting not to take or killing enemy prisoners; mutilating enemy dead; torturing prisoners; using excessive force or brutality; killing animals; looting, pillaging and raping; killing non-combatants; fighting with allies; being absent without leave or deserting; self-inflicted wounds; malingering; drug and alcohol abuse; refusing to obey an order; and threatening to kill or killing unit leaders or other soldiers. The manual goes on to explain that:

> Threatening to kill or attempting to kill unpopular leaders as related to combat stress (rather than some other grudge) may involve an individual or group of individuals that are under the perception that the intended victim is excessively eager to commit the unit to danger, grossly incompetent, and/or unfair in sharing of the risks.[11]

The most widely recognized and publicised form of this particular manifestation of misconduct stress behaviour has come to be referred to as "fragging" and derives from the term that was commonly used by US forces during the Vietnam War. During that period, this term commonly meant the assassination or attempted assassination of an unpopular member of one's own fighting unit by dropping a fragmentation grenade into his tent at night. Fragging most often involved the killing of an unpopular or (perceived) incompetent officer or senior non-commissioned officer. If the victim was incompetent, fragging was seen to be in the interest of self-preservation. It was also believed that fragging sent a warning to others, especially junior officers, to avoid earning the ire of the enlisted men by commanding through recklessness, cowardice or lack of leadership.

According to statistics used by the US television network, *NBC News*, while reporting on a suspected fragging in Iraq in June 2005,[12] the American Army stated that, between the years 1969 and 1971, 600 fragging incidents killed 82 military members and injured 651. In 1971 alone, there were 1.8 frag-

CHAPTER 6

gings for every 1,000 American soldiers serving in Vietnam, not including gun and knife assaults. The news report also explained that as President Richard Nixon began to withdraw US forces from Vietnam, troops started to feel as if they were fighting a lost cause and thus became unwilling to die for it. Although there have been many documented cases of individual military personnel, and in some isolated instances, complete units, that disobeyed direct orders, it was not until the latter part of the Vietnam War that the problem of "combat refusal" received widespread recognition in the US military. Today, it is recognized as one of the indicative behaviours of combat stress. During Vietnam, however, this form of mutiny occurred when soldiers refused, disobeyed, or negotiated an order to go into combat and was, in the majority of cases, a result of many of them believing that they were putting their lives in danger unnecessarily.

The similarities in the situation that developed around WO Stopford, according to the CFNIS investigation, and the many documented examples of fragging in Vietnam, raise the question of whether or not similar dynamics may have been at play in Croatia in 1994. Certainly, Delta company, of which Stopford's platoon was a part, could be described as exhibiting many of the positive combat stress behaviours listed above, especially during the period leading up to and including the time that they spent in the Medak Pocket. At the same time, however, the alleged poisoning of WO Stopford is clearly a misconduct stress behaviour, but, as noted earlier, even good, heroic soldiers under extreme stress can behave improperly. Were the circumstances right in Croatia in 1994 for CSR to have been the root cause of the alleged behaviour of Stopford's subordinates?

There are many challenges that can arise in a specific command situation, any one of which can impact the ultimate willingness of a unit and / or individual members of a unit to disobey an order. Soldiers may, for instance, attempt to pre-empt an unpopular order by removing a superior from his or her position of authority or to limit his or her authority in some way. Often, the simplistic explanation for this behaviour, after the fact, relies on assigning it to a failure on the part of the leader. Certainly, the quality of leadership has an impact on the subordinates' decision to obey or not; however, in many cases, other factors influence the outcome to a much greater extent. In order to better understand all of the factors that can influence the outcome of a challenging command situation, a standard, repeatable model can be useful to investigators.

Command and Control Model

The stressful command environment that existed for the entire chain of command of the 2nd Battalion of the PPCLI Battle Group, referred to as CANBAT 1, in Croatia in 1994, can be analysed by using the Pigeau / McCann model of Command and Control.[13] This particular model is helpful as it has been validated by analysing a large number of challenging CF command situations – largely army-oriented – that were taken from real experiences. The model has been introduced to the students and staff at the Canadian Forces College over the last several years and is finding growing acceptance as an analytical tool. The model goes well beyond the traditional leader-centred approach and, using a three-dimensional representation, links three essential aspects of command: individual competency; legal and personal authority; and, extrinsic and intrinsic responsibility. These three factors provide the acronym for the model, CAR. An essential part of this model is the assumption that the exercise of command is not limited to the commander alone, but rather that every member of an organisation has the ability to effect command within their specific sphere. Consequently, this analytical approach to understanding the command dilemma can be used all the way down to the ordinary soldier in a rifle platoon, thus allowing for an understanding of the command environment from the perspective of the individual soldier. A cursory overview of the model is adequate to see its applicability to the situation that evolved in Croatia for CANBAT 1.

Competency, as it applies to the abilities required for military personnel, is divided into four general categories: physical; intellectual; emotional; and, interpersonal. The first two categories, physical and intellectual, are straightforward and are articulated through an emphasis on physical fitness and professional development. In the infantry, the importance of physical competency has never been debated, and the deployment to Croatia in 1994, like all others, proved that soldiers must be fit. Intellectual competency may not have been considered as important as physical competency for line soldiers in the past, but as both the infantryman's technology improves and the nature of peacekeeping operations becomes more complex, the significance of this aspect of competency will surely become more salient.

The importance of the last two competencies, emotional and interpersonal, became evident during this deployment as well. Traditionally, the CF has not focussed a lot of attention on interpersonal competency and even less on emotional competency. However, as the operational tempo experienced by CF members increases, along with the increased possibility of casualties, this will need to change. In all probability, for the CF, resource constraints will continue to force command compromises and create situations where emotional and interpersonal competency can become even more important than physical and intellectual. Pigeau and McCann point out that military members are subjected to the full range of negative emotions – guilt, anxiety, anger, frustration, boredom, grief, fear and depression – but are still expected to command effectively under all conditions. Because of this fact, they place great emphasis on emotional competency, which is described as an individual's resiliency, hardiness and ability to cope under stress. They conclude:

CHAPTER 6

> Command demands a degree of emotional 'toughness' to accept the potentially dire consequences of operational decisions. The ability to keep an overall emotional balance and perspective on the situation is critical, as is the ability to maintain a sense of humour.[14]

Interpersonal competency is somewhat more familiar to most military members, but has customarily been interpreted as the ability to communicate verbally and in writing with superiors, peers, subordinates and outside agencies. The CAR model expands on this basic concept to include a broader range of social skills, including empathy. All four competency areas – physical, intellectual, emotional and interpersonal – played a role in the command circumstance that Rotation 2 of Op HARMONY experienced in Croatia, but emotional and interpersonal competency are especially critical to understanding the decisions that the chain of command, down to the platoon level, made on the ground.

Authority is particularly important to military commanders and was clearly an issue with some of the decisions that the Commanding Officer (CO) of CANBAT 1 made during this deployment. Authority is defined by Pigeau and McCann as "… the degree to which a commander is empowered to act, the scope of this power and the resources available for enacting his or her will."[15] They elaborate on authority, identifying both the legal and personal aspects of it, and show that personal authority – that which is gained through one's personal credibility with superiors, peers and subordinates – is dangerous without legal authority and that legal authority, without personal authority, is forced to be rigid and direction-based. Command capability is best exercised when both the appropriate legal authority has been assigned and the personal authority has been developed. An essential element of legal authority, and one that is easy to overlook, is the assignment of sufficient personnel and materiel to allow the commander to fulfil his or her responsibilities.

The third category that constitutes command capability is responsibility, defined by Pigeau and McCann as the degree to which an individual accepts the legal and moral liability that goes along with the command. Again, as in authority, there are two components to responsibility. The first is externally or extrinsically imposed by the legal chain of command, and once accepted, closely resembles accountability. Responsibility applies down the chain of command as well, and demands that the individual uses the authority, both personal and legal, that he or she has been given appropriately. When a situation develops where a commander is unwilling to be held accountable for the authority that he or she has been given, serious abuses of authority can occur. The other very powerful attribute of responsibility is internally or intrinsically imposed. Intrinsic responsibility is the self-generated sense of obligation that a leader brings to a mission and is traditionally thought of as one's sense of duty. When the degree of intrinsic responsibility is high, but authority is low, as in the case where materiel or personnel are insufficient for the mission, the commander is faced with an ineffectual command situation and thus placed under tremendous psychological pressure.

When specific command situations are analysed using the CAR approach, a three-dimensional plot can be produced that represents a plane upon which a commander exercises his or her command capability. The model depicts this as a command envelope and describes it as "balanced" if all aspects of the command situation are correct. However, if one or more elements of the command circumstance are not correct, then the envelope is described as "unbalanced." The value of the Pigeau / McCann model is that it provides a consistent and repeatable framework within which to understand what actually went wrong, or right, within a specific command situation. Simplistically, if a mission fails, the default position is to blame the person in command, and while that may be correct some of the time, the rest of the time this explanation tends to obscure serious, underlying problems, and does little to draw out the fundamental lessons that can be learned in order to prevent similar circumstances from developing in the future.

A major advantage of the CAR model is that it focuses on the human element in command and thus it can be applied to any situation independent of the organisational structure involved. Operations under the auspices of the United Nations (UN) have some very complex command and control arrangements, the implications of which are easily missed when looking at the results of certain missions. Led by Lieutenant-Colonel Jim Calvin, the CF Battle Group (BG) encountered a command situation in Croatia in 1994 that was extremely complicated, owing both to the UN framework within which it worked and the unique reserve / regular force make-up of the BG itself.

Situation for 2 PPCLI Battle Group – Op HARMONY

On 4 April 1993, the third rotation[16] of the BG (CANBAT 1), which was based on 2 PPCLI and heavily augmented by personnel from 66 regular and reserve units from across Canada, assumed the responsibility for peacekeeping duties in Sector West of Croatia. Although this was neither the first nor the last Canadian BG to serve in Croatia as part of UNPROFOR,[17] it was in all probability the one that experienced the greatest period of change as the situation in the Balkans continued to deteriorate. The BG began preparing in January 1993 with the arrival in Winnipeg of approximately 550 reservists from across Canada, as well as about 150 or 160 augmentees – cooks, technicians and medics – from other regular force CF units, all of whom supplemented the core of approximately 320 experienced PPCLI soldiers. In the three months available before the deployment, all were subjected to intense training in order to turn them into a cohesive unit. In the end, an operationally competent BG of 870 personnel emerged, albeit with a significant percentage of minimally trained reservists assigned to the rifle companies. One

CHAPTER 6

member of Delta Company, a Sergeant, stated to the CBOI, "In Delta Company, of which I was a part of, was made up of mostly reservists. I believe 90 to 95 per cent."[18]

Only after completing his in-theatre reconnaissance in January was the CO fully aware of the physical danger that the BG would face in Croatia. During this visit, for instance, he observed a Canadian Armoured Personnel Carrier (APC) being lured into an ambush and then destroyed by a Serbian anti-tank rocket.[19] This was his first indication of the nature of what lay ahead, and upon his return to Canada, the intensity and focus of the training changed significantly. Prior to deploying, the entire BG underwent a rigorous 75-day training program in Canada, as well as at Fort Ord and Fort Hunter Ligget in the United States. The CO stated to the CBOI that:

> We began a training plan that would see us in about 75 days turn an ad hoc, thrown-together unit into a cohesive unit that could actually handle weapons under stress and protect themselves in a very dangerous situation. ... So we went from 550 reservists down to about 385 and we basically formed the tight teams of section and platoon and company level that were, by and large, going to carry us through the tour.[20]

As with previous Canadian battalions, this BG deployed with their full complement of weaponry and equipment, including M113 APCs fitted with Browning .50 calibre machine-guns to transport and protect the rifle companies. Weapons at the company level consisted of C-7 automatic rifles and C-9 light machine-guns, complemented with C-6 medium machine guns and 84 mm Carl Gustav anti-tank rocket launchers. There was also a heavy weapon Support Company that, operating 81mm mortars and TOW (Tube-launched, Optically-tracked, Wire-guided) anti-armour guided missiles aboard purpose-built APCs, augmented the rifle companies.

In late-March 1993, CANBAT 1 deployed to their initial Area of Responsibility (AOR), Sector West of Croatia, and assumed responsibility for the UN Mandate there from 3 PPCLI on 4 April 1993. At this time, there were three other UN contingents in Sector West besides the Canadians – the Nepalese, Argentineans and Jordanians – but they dealt with only the Serbs or Croats. CANBAT 1, which was also designated as the Force Commander's Reserve, was the only one that actually had a dividing line between the Serbs and Croats and thus had the most volatile situation to contend with. Their mission was to effectively enforce the peace, protect the unarmed and confiscate any weapons that they found. At the company and platoon levels, day-to-day work consisted of conducting foot, anti-ambush and vehicle patrols, establishing static observation posts, disarming any civilians found to be carrying weapons and protecting the existing UN Protected Areas. One soldier

CHAPTER 6

described this phase of CANBAT 1's deployment as "...we were sort of running the gamut ... of a low intensity conflict."[21] Although there were certainly tense moments, the conditions in this area were fairly stable since the Rules of Engagement were well established and understood.

In Sector West, the area that was considered to be the most stable in the country, the two belligerents were not actually conducting open warfare. While all the weapons had been, at least in theory, removed from the sector, there were still clashes between the two warring factions – ambushes of each other's police forces, the placement of anti-personnel mines, booby traps and so on – which made the situation dangerous for the Canadians, but comparatively quiet. CANBAT 1 demonstrated to the belligerents that they were not only there to keep the peace, but to enforce it as well. Their abilities and efforts soon earned them the recognition as one of the most effective units in UNPROFOR. This was not achieved, however, without the personal sacrifice of every soldier on the ground. There was no such thing as an eight-hour or even a ten-hour day. In the words of Major Dan Drew, the Officer Commanding, Delta Company, 2 PPCLI:

> The tempo itself was 27 and 7. The guys worked a minimum 12-hour shift every day and then from there they had to do weapons and vehicle maintenance. They had other – sometimes we would get bugged out and they would have to – they would have to stop what they were doing or get up out of bed and deploy.[22]

Added to this prolonged and intense workload were the constant concerns of possible mine strikes, occasional sniper fire, booby traps and the unvarying belligerence of the combatants toward the soldiers themselves. All the same, CANBAT 1 carried out their mission in this sector for three months and came to consider this period as the relative calm before the storm, a calm that was dramatically altered by circumstances beyond the control of the men and women in the rifle companies. The atmosphere was probably best put by a soldier speaking to the CBOI who stated, "Sector West overall was fairly – fairly calm."[23]

Lieutenant-Colonel Calvin was well aware that at the same time CANBAT 1 was functioning in Sector West, the UN was grappling with how to reassert their credibility and authority in the more explosive southern area of the country. The UN had suffered a severe setback to their reputation earlier in the year when a French battalion under UN command had withdrawn in the face of a Croatian attack on a power dam. Incidentally, neither the Serbs nor the Croats trusted the French – the former believing that they had at least been aware of an earlier attack on them by the latter – and thus their utility to the Force Commander, French Army General Jean Cot, was limited. As a result of their demonstrated effectiveness, CANBAT 1 was tasked in early-July 1993 by Cot to move into Sector South to enforce the newly-signed

CHAPTER 6

Erdut Ceasefire Agreement. The Agreement was intended to create four buffer zones in the region in an effort to de-escalate the fighting in the most hotly contested region of Croatia, Sector South. Unfortunately, Cot had neither the quantity nor the quality of forces that he needed in this sector to implement the Agreement and the UN could not afford another failure. Accordingly, he issued a warning order to CANBAT 1 for the Canadian commander to be prepared to split the Canadian battalion in half and move it 500 kilometres to the south to reinforce the sector and implement the Agreement; their responsibilities in Sector West would not change though.

The order was implemented in mid-July and Calvin split his force, including the administration and support elements. On 16 July, Charlie and Delta Companies commenced moving to Sector South. The soldiers arrived in the area of the Peruca Dam 36 hours later, having transported themselves and all of their required equipment the 550 kilometres to their newly assigned AOR. The operational area that the Canadians moved into with half a battalion was, in the words of a military historian researching the issue for the CBOI:

> … in the territory where the Croats and the Krajina Serbs directly confronted one another and, as a result, was bitterly contested by both the Serbs and Croats. Canadian troops often found themselves on the receiving end of artillery shells, small arms, and heavy machine gun fire. The land was littered with anti-tank and anti-personnel mines. Deployed into the middle of the war, the Canadians were often the targets of such weapons in attempts to intimidate the peacekeeping forces.[24]

During the next three to four weeks, Charlie Company worked at establishing the battalion's presence through patrols, etc., while Delta Company was moved to bolster the French battalion to their north. Living conditions in Sector South were abysmal as there were no established "camps;" by comparison, living conditions in Sector West, although not ideal, were, in the eyes of one soldier, "well established."[25] Consequently, the troops lived in bombed-out buildings with no running water or facilities and slept on the cots that they had brought with them. All of the required supplies, including water and fresh food, had to be transported from Sector West. The resulting meals consisted of part hard and part fresh rations. Phone contact with families back in Canada was lost once they went south and environmental conditions deteriorated as they crossed the mountains (temperatures reached into the 40 to 50 ° C range for days on end). The manpower situation was so critical that from mid-July onward, all leave except for the 17-day leave back to Canada (as required by the existing CF policy) was cancelled for members of CANBAT 1. After their first month in Sector West, by comparison, soldiers were granted 72 hours of leave each month. For some members, that meant that they went for up to 80 days without a single day off in some of the toughest conditions

CHAPTER 6

that they had ever encountered. The loss of the first battalion member in a road accident in Sector West added to the deteriorating mood.

Additionally, unlike the fairly stable situation that had been encountered in Sector West, Sector South was still in a very volatile state. Partly due to the fact that there had been no noticeable UN presence in that area since January 1993, both the Croatians and Serbians were trying to establish a territorial advantage over the other. Both Charlie and Delta Companies were trying to re-establish UN control and, as a result, were working longer hours in a heightened state of alert and under the constant threat of being fired upon or shelled. As one Master-Corporal stated at the CBOI:

> And then I got a new appreciation for danger once we went down to Sector South. Things became far worse and I mean we were repeatedly shelled with shells and rounds landing metres from some of our positions. In fact, some people had sustained some shrapnel injuries as a result of some of those rounds coming in.[26]

After several weeks, the Canadian BG began to reassert UN presence in the critical areas in Sector South and regained some of the respect that the French contingent had lost earlier in the year. As a result, General Cot asked that the full Canadian BG be moved to Sector South so that the UN could move ahead with the implementation of the Agreement. In mid-August, after the Canadian Government agreed, the remainder of the Canadian BG moved to the region. Calvin took advantage of this move to restructure CANBAT 1 into a three-company BG in order to facilitate the handover with the incoming three-company Canadian contingent that would arrive in October. After collecting Delta Company, the complete battalion moved 100 kilometres north where, after replacing the French battalion, the various companies were placed strategically to enforce the Erdut Agreement.

Delta Company moved to what was considered to be the most volatile location that had been assigned to the battalion, the area overlooking the Maslenica Bridge. There they were ordered to establish observation posts that the UN considered critical to ensuring an ongoing monitoring of the situation in the area. Both the Croatians and Serbians considered this particular area to be strategic. The Serbians tried to cut the bridge while the Croats tried to maintain it; Delta Company was in the middle. Both sides considered the Canadians to be an obstacle to their goals, and as a result, they were shelled almost consistently for hours at a time. As described by Calvin during his testimony six years later to the CBOI, the intensity of operations was hard to imagine:

> ... we had to maintain the OP [observation post] and we were literally having people going up to the OP, and when the shells started running back to the bunker and things like this. And for four days

CHAPTER 6

soldiers maintained their position at that bunker. Now, to be honest, the company commander and the sergeant major maintained their positions there and we tried to rotate soldiers in and out so that any one soldier didn't have to go through the whole period of time. I'm not certain how effective that was. But those were the kind of decisions we had to do if we were going to ... [restore the UN reputation] ... with the Serbs and get credibility. If they see that every time something happens we run away, we would be no better than the contingent that was there before us. So there was a degree of we had to show that we were there to do our job even if the going got tough and there was also the very real requirement to keep observation on the Maslenica Bridge.... But I had to say that down in the B Company area at Miranje they were shelled. They had OPs that were shelled regularly and I would say in general that somewhere in our sector every single day shells were falling.[27]

Captain D.R. Gosse echoed these remarks. He observed, "...Delta Company and C Company were continuously exposed to constant shelling from the time we deployed into the French battalion area to the time we left."[28] Another witness commented on the stress that the soldiers were under, stating "People were stressed out because of not knowing, especially in Delta Company, not knowing whether they were going to survive the evening or not."[29]

The last chapter in CANBAT 1's experience in Sector South was written in the Medak Pocket, a part of the operation that has been more widely reported on in the last few years.[30] The Medak Pocket operation started with an intense Croat artillery barrage on the town of Medak on 9 September; an attack that included tanks followed immediately.[31] The Serbs, initially caught by surprise, eventually began to reinforce their positions. Their actions resulted in a standoff, with the Serbian-populated town of Medak caught in the middle and in Croatian hands. On 13 September, CANBAT 1, reinforced by two French companies, was ordered to establish a buffer between the two sides, which would require the Croatian forces to leave Medak. On 15 September, during their move into position to do this, one of the Canadian companies came under intense Croatian fire, which they returned.

In a face-to-face meeting with Calvin, the Croatian commander agreed to withdraw, but insisted that they needed until noon of the next day to do it. Waking up the next morning to the sound of small arms fire and the sight of smoke rising from several locations, the Canadians realized that the Croatians were systemically ethnically cleansing the area and destroying the evidence before they left. Every soldier in 2 PPCLI knew why the Croatians had delayed their crossing. Standing there helplessly throughout the night, they could hear the gunfire and screams of the victims. As one member of Delta Company put it:

CHAPTER 6

>What the delay was, was the Croatians weren't finished their job yet. They weren't finished their ethnic cleansing. And we stood as soldiers, watched, listened and waited for them to finish what they had to do. And as a soldier and what you are trained to do, to stand up and listen to that is the hardest thing I ever had to do as a human being.[32]

Finally, at noon on 16 September, the Canadians moved forward and encountered a Croatian defensive position complete with a T-72 tank. Mines had been placed along both sides of the road as well as across it and the Croatians were again refusing to allow them to advance. Both sides, fully armed, with weapons cocked and aimed, remained in a standoff for over 90 minutes while negations went on to convince the Croatians to pull back, thus allowing the Canadians to move forward. Recognising the Croatian objective of keeping the world on their side in the larger conflict, Calvin brought up a number of reporters from the international media to monitor the event, an action that immediately diffused the situation and motivated the Croats to begin to dismantle their defences. Eventually, after this confrontation, the Canadians managed to move forward with Delta Company leading. When the Canadians eventually moved into the area, they found that the Croats had not left a single living thing alive in the Pocket – human or animal – and that they had not had the time to hide all of the evidence of their crimes.

The next few days proved to be what many of those there believed to be the most difficult of the whole tour. Not only were they attempting to enforce the newly declared buffer zone, but they were also working with both civilian and UN personnel to sweep the area for evidence of ethnic cleansing. Every building in the immediate area had been razed. Even the livestock had been shot and then dumped into the local wells in many places. Throughout this period, they found evidence of the inhumanity of man against man, which not only played heavily on their minds at the time, but which also continues to haunt many of them to this day. Shortly thereafter, CANBAT 2 relieved them and a very arduous deployment was complete.

Colonel George Oehring described the results of the Canadian action at Medak when he testified to the CBOI on 10 November 1999. Oehring had been the Canadian officer who commanded UNPROFOR Sector South from September 1993 until May 1994, and who then assumed the position of Deputy Commander of the Canadian contingent until September 1994. He related:

>First, what was seen as a Canadian success at Medak restored some degree of credibility in the UN, and marked a first for UNPROFOR; that is to say, some land that had been captured by military action had been subsequently surrendered, neutralized and then occupied by the UN. I don't think that happened anywhere at any time in UNPROFOR other than at Medak. The local Serbs were most

CHAPTER 6

favourably impressed by the courage, discipline and impartiality of CANBAT 1, and never hesitated to tell me of it, even as I was saying goodbye to them a year later. Even the Croats expressed their grudging admiration for what CANBAT 1 did. One of the Operational Zone Commanders with whom I frequently dealt was often heard to say, 'The Canadians do everything professionally.'[33]

In order to establish the context within which the alleged poisoning and other harmful actions against WO Stopford took place, it is important to emphasize the extreme stress, fatigue and anxiety that members of Delta Company were operating under during this deployment. From the start of their training phase in Winnipeg in January 1993 to their deployment to Sector West in March, and their eventual unscheduled move into the unknown of Sector South in the late-summer, their workload and level of anxiety continued to build. While testifying before the CBOI in the fall of 1999, numerous witnesses at all rank levels stated that as things unfolded, the stress and anxiety that they began to feel was like nothing else that they had ever experienced in their careers as professional soldiers. For example, one NCO stated that when the mission started, "in Sector West, it was a fast-paced, a very furious sort of a tour of duty." After moving to Sector South, however, he was struck by how much more serious and intense things had become. In his words, he "got a new appreciation for danger" after being repeatedly shelled with rounds landing metres from some of their positions.[34] When he testified on 28 October 1999 to the CBOI, WO Stopford, the platoon warrant officer of Delta Company, gave an overview of the hours that he and his people had worked both prior to and during their deployment. He stated that during the training phase, normal days had consisted of 15 or 16 hours; in Sector West, a typical day had averaged between 16 and 18 hours; and after the Battalion's move to Sector South, 18- and 19-hour days became the norm.[35]

Analysis

That there are both positive and negative behaviours associated with exposure to combat stress is a reality that is now widely accepted. Equally, there can be no argument that the conditions experienced by CANBAT 1 during Rotation 2 in Croatia in 1994 constituted combat stress, particularly with respect to Delta Company. The testimony provided by Colonel Oehring to the CBOI clearly describes the most positive combat stress behaviour. And yet, according to the CFNIS investigation of the allegations regarding the poisoning of WO Stopford, at least some of this same group of soldiers behaved in a manner that can only be described as disobedient. Unfortunately, virtually all of the subsequent attention paid to this operation has focussed on the misconduct stress behaviour, and much of this attention has given the impression that the problem was related to failures in leadership. In order to move beyond this superficial assumption and to identify the real issues, the question that must be

CHAPTER 6

answered is: "Was the root cause of the disobedience in Stopford's platoon a leadership failure or was it a result of predictable (and potentially, avoidable) circumstances beyond the control of the chain of command?"

Using the CAR model of Command and Control discussed above, it is evident that this deployment was not a perfectly balanced command situation. The first area to consider is competency – physical, intellectual, emotional and interpersonal. To say that this was a physically demanding deployment is a gross understatement. Even a cursory review of the testimony given to the CBOI reflects the extreme physical conditions that the BG operated under. Due to factors beyond the unit's purview, a number of health concerns existed throughout the deployment; things like clean drinking water and access to emergency medical care were frequently problematic. Nonetheless, from the platoon perspective, physical competency was never in question. Indeed, the overall level of physical competency shown by the entire company was extraordinary. Although the intense operational tempo may have taken an unseen psychological toll, which was made unnecessarily more severe by concerns about access to emergency medical care, there is no evidence to suggest that the physical demands proved beyond the capacity of the leadership or the troops.

Considering intellectual competency, it is quite clear that despite the rapidly changing operational picture, which was driven by shifting strategic objectives, the BG and company leadership were able to stay on top of the situation and produced rapid and effective plans to deal with it. At the platoon level, there was some concern about WO Stopford's judgment in taking risks, with some members of the platoon allegedly stating that they felt that he was exposing them to unnecessary danger through his aggressive drive to accomplish the mission. However, on balance, there is no reason to assume that the level of risk-taking significantly exceeded that which was necessary for mission accomplishment. The most telling gauge is that no members of his platoon were seriously injured during the six months that they were deployed. Indeed, it might even be supposed that the degree of aggressiveness shown by the platoon warrant officer even saved lives.

The third competency area, emotional competency, is one that is frequently overlooked in post-operational lessons learned activities, yet when missions become heavily involved in scenarios like the one that unfolded in Croatia, it is perhaps one of the more important elements. In this case, it is highly unlikely that the majority of riflemen at the platoon level, particularly the young and inexperienced reservists, were prepared emotionally to handle the type of atrocities and operational tempo that they were exposed to. On the other hand, the chain of command, from the platoon level upwards, consisted of largely experienced, regular force members who, owing to their previous peacekeeping operations, had a certain familiarity with and perspectives

161

on such stressors. Thus, while they were subjected to the same stress levels and traumatised by the same atrocities, the latter had a better chance of maintaining an emotional balance throughout the operation.

The fourth competency area relates to interpersonal competency. This is largely a personal trait and the information that is available through transcripts and other such material that has been released does not provide a great amount of direct detail in this area about either WO Stopford or his subordinates. However, as interpersonal competency requires attributes such as trust, respect, perceptiveness and empathy, it could be concluded that mixing the regular force and reserve cultures to the extent that they were within Delta Company, particularly at the platoon level, may have produced difficulties in this area. This conclusion is reinforced by the initial reaction of Stopford to the news that his men had attempted to poison him, as well as the reaction of other senior NCOs of the leadership cadre.

The second command capability identified in the Pigeau / McCann model is authority. Although authority is more often thought of in the legal context of the right to command, legal authority has a strong resource component associated with it. Unless the resources are available to carry out his or her will, a commander's authority is hollow. Authority also has a robust personal component, that is, an individual's credibility in the eyes of his or her peers and subordinates. Both aspects of authority need to be balanced in order for a situation to unfold properly. There was no apparent issue within CANBAT 1 in regards to the legal aspects of command; however, from the beginning of the deployment, resource shortages, especially with respect to defensive stores, beleaguered the BG. These shortages were exacerbated once elements of the BG moved south. Combined with the extreme operational tempo and the intermittent hazards of combat, the resulting combat stress levels were very high.

While Delta Company's chain of command had legal authority, albeit diminished somewhat by resource difficulties, personal authority may have been more problematic. The high percentage of reserve members and the number of augmentees combined to make it difficult for members at the platoon level to know individual members of the chain of command well. Personal authority takes a relatively long period of time to develop and requires that those being led observe their commanders in action. Only then is a level of trust developed that allows for the full development of personal authority. In the absence of personal authority, increased use is often made of legal authority that, in the end, can create resentment. The very short period of time allowed to build trust and confidence in the chain of command prior to deployment could very well have contributed to the overall command challenge in this operation.

The third command capability deals with responsibility. Responsibility can be imposed from external sources, referred to in the model as extrinsic, or can be generated by the individual's own sense of responsibility, called intrinsic. Extrinsic responsibility is associated with accountability, but differing in that while a superior can impose specific accountabilities, an individual must accept them in order for extrinsic responsibility to exist. Similarly, subordinates impose a degree of extrinsic responsibility because of their expectations concerning leader behaviour, and an individual commander, in order for extrinsic responsibility to exist, must accept these expectations too. When authority is exercised without the requisite degree of extrinsic responsibility, serious abuses of authority can result. Intrinsic responsibility is the characteristic most closely associated with the traditional concept of duty, and is reflected in the degree of commitment the individual feels toward the mission and the troops associated with it. In the simplest of terms, extrinsic and intrinsic responsibility is the degree to which an individual accepts the legal and moral liability associated with command.

Within Delta Company, there did not appear to be any issues associated with extrinsic responsibility, although in the minds of some of the line soldiers, there was a belief that WO Stopford was taking too many risks and placing their lives in danger. Specifically, there was nothing to suggest that he or anyone in Delta Company's chain of command had any reluctance to accept accountability for the mission or the welfare of their troops. However, at the individual level, there may have been a difference in the level of intrinsic responsibility felt, based on whether they came from a regular force or a reserve force background. It would not be surprising, given the different levels of experience, if a higher percentage of the reserve members felt less commitment to the mission. The CO described this aspect of the situation when he testified to the CBOI that:

> So when we went back, you know, during the course of our reconnaissance, we determined that because of the low level of training that the reserves were coming to us, you know, I am not being pejorative in any way to the reserves. In fact, I have a tremendous amount of respect for them. But as soldiers they came with a very low level of knowledge. They didn't even have familiarity on some of the weapon systems that they were going to be manning. They weren't familiar with 50 calibre machine guns, some of the higher calibre anti-armour weapons, and we had to make a cohesive unit very quickly that was able to be able to deal with those kind of situations.[36]

Overall, this very cursory analysis would suggest that this was not a well-balanced command environment within which Delta Company was operating. While the physical, intellectual and emotional competency of the leadership was not an issue, interpersonal competency was compromised by the short period of time that the platoon members were exposed to the platoon leadership in order to build up trust and confidence prior to experiencing intense

CHAPTER 6

operations. At the level of the individual soldier, physical and intellectual competency was not a factor. However, both emotional competency and interpersonal competency were compromised, especially for the high percentage of reservists who had neither the previous experience, nor the training, to handle the situations that they were exposed to. None of the members had the training that would have prepared them for the emotional trauma that they were to experience. The legal authority of the entire CANBAT 1 chain of command was compromised by the numerous resource constraints that they operated under, particularly in Sector South. More significant, however, was the limited personal authority enjoyed by the platoon leadership due to the relatively short period of time that the reserve members had to workup prior to deployment. When there is little time to allow personal authority to develop, the use of legal authority increases to compensate. And finally, neither extrinsic nor intrinsic responsibility was a factor with the leadership of this BG; however, the lower experience levels associated with many of the riflemen at the platoon level raises questions about their level of intrinsic responsibility.

The question at the beginning of the above analysis was: "Was the root cause of the disobedience in Matt Stopford's platoon a leadership failure, or was it a result of predictable (and potentially, avoidable) circumstances beyond the control of the chain of command?" Given the unbalanced nature of the command situation, the root cause of the disobedient acts appears to lie in the structure of the organisation, rather than in the leadership itself.

Complicating, and perhaps even masking the organisational problems, is the reality that combat stress often creates the types of misconduct stress behaviours that were allegedly carried out against the platoon WO, as well as the extremely positive combat stress behaviours observed in the Medak Pocket. By examining the circumstances that Delta Company experienced during their deployment, it becomes apparent that all of the factors that have been identified as contributing to combat stress reactions were present from the very beginning. CANBAT 1 experienced a pace and intensity of operations that had been unknown to Canadian soldiers since the Korean War. Delta Company worked an average of 15 to 18 hours a day while enduring extremely poor living conditions, especially once they moved to Sector South. They tolerated days of shelling while manning the OPs at the Maslenica Bridge as they themselves became the targets of the belligerents. On 16 September, while trying to move into and enforce the UN buffer zone around Medak, they were involved in an extremely dangerous and tense standoff with the Croatian Army for over 90 minutes. They not only witnessed ethnic cleansing in Medak but, in fact, encountered evidence of it through out their tour in both Sectors West and South.

Clearly, stress related training can reduce the incidents of misconduct stress behaviour and the CF has made great strides in introducing this. However, in 1993 when 2 PPCLI began preparations for their tour, training concerning combat stress and how to handle it was non-existent for either leaders or individual soldiers. The training for the mission, although intense, was based on what Canadian soldiers had experienced on previous UN peacekeeping missions. Once on the ground, however, circumstances changed dramatically. When all of these factors are weighed, it becomes extremely believable that some soldiers of WO Stopford's platoon did in fact attempt to render him ineffective as alleged by the CFNIS investigation.

Although much has changed since 2 PPCLI deployed to Croatia, the lessons that can be learned from that experience continue to apply. All units must be trained specifically for the mission that they are tasked to do and leaders must be taught how to recognize stress, not only in themselves, but also in the people that they are charged to lead. Personnel must be taught to recognize the warning signs of combat stress and to seek help when necessary. One of the most important lessons continues to be that sufficient resources must be applied to every mission, and whether regular or reserve, soldiers must have time to get to know each other and their leaders before they enter operations. Leadership failure was not the root cause of what occurred in Delta Company and similar reoccurrences can be avoided in the future.

ENDNOTES

[1] Peter Worthington, *Toronto Sun*, 12 August 1999, "Military Tells Soldier His Own Troops May Have Tried to Kill Him," 6.

[2] Worthington, "Military Tells Soldier," 6.

[3] Master Warrant Officer Daniel Hartford, Croatia Board of Inquiry [CBOI] Testimony, 24 November 1999.

[4] Many of the soldiers who had deployed on Operation HARMONY felt that the variety of troubling medical symptoms that had begun to appear after they had returned to Canada were related to their exposure to some toxic substance in the environment that they had operated in. The "red dirt," which turned out to be bauxite, was frequently blamed for their problems. When neither the Department of National Defence (DND) nor Veterans Affairs accepted their claims, they suspected a cover-up that was intended to avoid the high cost of paying hundreds of claims.

[5] John Ward, *Canadian Press* wire service, 18 January 2001, "Canadian 'Peacekeepers' Poisoned One Of Their Own Intentionally."

[6] DND Press Conference, National Defence Headquarters, Ottawa, Ontario, 30 May 2000, Statement by Inspector Russ Grabb, RCMP.

[7] Captain (ret'd) Kelly Brett, CBOI Testimony, 22 September 1999.

[8] Dr. Allan English, *Historical and Contemporary Interpretations of Combat Stress Reactions*, paper prepared for the CBOI, 26 October 1999, 14.

[9] Field Manual No. 22-51, *Leaders' Manual for Combat Stress Control*, Headquarters, Department of the Army, Washington, D.C., 29 September 1994.

CHAPTER 6

[10] Field Manual No. 22-51, Section 2-9. Emphasis added by author.
[11] Ibid.
[12] *NBC News* and news services, 16 June 2005, "Military files murder charges in Iraq killings – U.S. sergeant accused of 'fragging' officers had been disciplined by them."
[13] Dr. Ross Pigeau and Carol McCann, "Re-conceptualizing Command and Control," *Canadian Military Journal*, Vol. 3, No.1 (Spring 2002), 53-64. This article provides an excellent overview of the Command and Control model that Dr. Pigeau and Carol McCann have developed and since validated using numerous case studies from CF command experiences. It is particularly effective in looking at command situations where problems have arisen that may appear, on the surface, to be leadership related, but have on further analysis been shown to be far more complex in terms of causes.
[14] Pigeau and McCann, "Re-conceptualizing," 58.
[15] Ibid.
[16] Referred to as ROTO 2. The initial deployment (1 Royal 22^e Regiment BG) is referred to as ROTO 0, while the second deployment (3 PPCLI BG) is referred to as ROTO 1.
[17] Five Canadian BGs deployed to Croatia during the life of UNPROFOR, from March 1992 to November 1994.
[18] Sergeant Chris Byrne, CBOI Testimony, 25 November 1999.
[19] Calvin described this incident during his testimony to the CBOI on 16 September 1999. From his statements, it is clear this was no accident. He stated, "We were going into a theatre where Canadian soldiers could be specifically targeted. This was no accident. It wasn't in any way, shape [or form] that anyone was getting in the way of anything. They had planned an incident. They had drawn a Canadian APC and group of soldiers to it and they had attacked that APC."
[20] Lieutenant-Colonel Jim Calvin, CBOI Testimony, 16 September 1999.
[21] Major Dan Drew, CBOI Testimony, 21 October 1999.
[22] Major Dan Drew, CBOI Testimony, 21 October 1999. The actual transcript of this testimony reads "27," whereas he probably meant "24."
[23] Major Dan Drew, CBOI Testimony, 21 October 1999.
[24] Dr. Ken Reynolds, *Canadian Forces Operations in the Balkans, 1991-1995*, paper prepared for the CBOI, 12 September 1999.
[25] Major Robert Ferguson, CBOI Testimony, 24 September 1999.
[26] Master-Corporal Steve Atkins, CBOI Testimony, 19 October 1999.
[27] Colonel Jim Calvin, CBOI Testimony, 16 September 1999.
[28] Captain D.R. Gosse CBOI Testimony, 20 September 1999.
[29] Chief Warrant Officer M.B. McCarthy, CBOI Testimony, 20 September 1999.
[30] See, for instance, Carol Off, *The Ghosts of Medak Pocket: The Story of Canada's Secret War* (Toronto: Random House, 2004).
[31] According to testimony at the CBOI, approximately 500 rounds fell

CHAPTER 6

on the town of Medak, a village with about 50 homes in an area about the size of Parliament Hill in Ottawa, in the first 24 hours. Four members of CANBAT 1 were wounded.

[32] Sergeant Chris Byrne, CBOI Testimony, 25 November 1999.
[33] Colonel (Ret'd) George Oehring, CBOI Testimony, 10 November 1999.
[34] Master-Corporal Steve Atkins, CBOI Testimony, 19 October 1999.
[35] Warrant Officer (ret'd) Matt Stopford, CBOI Testimony, 28 October 1999.
[36] Colonel Jim Calvin in testimony to the CBOI, 16 September 1999.

CHAPTER 7

"But ... It's Not My Fault!" – Disobedience as a Function of Fear

Bernd Horn

> *Lt. [Lieutenant] Newlands rose up a little from me and gallantly endeavoured to signal us forward by a sweep of his hand, but the time was inopportune and no one moved. He himself was hardly up, when he was wounded and fell back into the shell hole.*[1]

Obedience to orders and lawful command has always been, and remains, a critical component of military effectiveness. Although leadership [2] is critically important in achieving military success, often it is not enough to propel individuals into the "valley of death." Rather, at times, it is the unflinching, instantaneous adherence to orders and unquestioning obedience, particularly during periods of chaos, crisis and great danger, that ensures that the battle is won. It was for this reason that Frederick the Great believed that soldiers must fear their officers more than their enemy. Fortuitously, leadership theory and practice have evolved since then. Nonetheless, adherence to lawful command is still essential to good order and discipline, not to mention success on the battlefield.

Because of its importance, disobedience to authority is not tolerated and transgressors normally face the full weight of military justice. But are there circumstances that mitigate, if not excuse, disobedience? Specifically, is fear, a natural reaction of most individuals in the face of danger, not a compelling circumstance? After all, war literature, memoirs and anecdotal accounts are filled with references to the paralyzing and numbing effects of fear. One veteran who seemed to capture the universal sentiment explained, "We remained frozen by the danger, unable to judge its magnitude. Our stupor was too great; we were like paralyzed mice facing a snake."[3] And so it appears that fear can create such angst, anxiety and terror that individuals are unable, or feel that they are incapable, of following orders. As such, is fear a component of disobedience? Moreover, if fear is so pervasive and paralyzing, can an individual in such a state be held accountable?

To address this dilemma, it is first necessary to examine the actual concept of fear. In the simplest of terms, it is an emotion, "a state characterized by physiological arousal, changes in facial expression, gestures, posture, and subjective feeling."[4] Once evoked, fear causes a number of bodily changes to occur such as rapid heartbeat and breathing, dryness of the throat and mouth, perspiration, trembling and a sinking feeling in the stomach. It can also have more obvious, if not embarrassing, manifestations. "And urine poured down our legs," confessed one veteran, "Our fear was so great that we lost all thought of controlling ourselves."[5] Similarly, Sergeant John Kite, a British commando during the Normandy invasion on 6 June 1944 revealed:

169

CHAPTER 7

> I was so scared, all the bones in my body were shaking. I said to myself, Pull yourself together, you're in charge and supposed to show an example. When the ramp went down dead on 0600 [hours], I looked around, and there were pools of water by men. It wasn't sea water.[6]

The body's reaction during emotional arousal is easily explained. It is caused by the activation of the sympathetic division of the autonomic nervous system as it prepares the body for emergency action – the fight or flight reflex. In short, it prepares the body for energy output. It does this by way of a number of bodily changes, which need not occur all at once. They include:

1. Blood pressure and heart rate increase;
2. Respiration becomes more rapid;
3. Pupils dilate;
4. Perspiration increases while the secretion of saliva and mucous decreases;
5. Blood-sugar levels increase to provide more energy;
6. The blood becomes better able to clot in case of wounds;
7. Blood is diverted from the stomach and intestines to the brain and skeletal muscles; and
8. The hairs on the skin become erect causing "goose pimples."[7]

These changes all have a specific purpose. As already stated, the sympathetic system activates the body for emergency action by arousing a number of bodily systems and inhibiting others. For example, sugar is released by the liver into the bloodstream for quick energy; the heart beats faster to supply blood to the muscles; the respiration rate increases to supply needed oxygen; digestion is temporarily inhibited, thus diverting blood from the internal organs to the muscles; pupils dilate to allow more light to enter the eyes; perspiration increases to cool the agitated body; and the blood flow to the skin is restricted to reduce bleeding.[8]

Of great importance is the fact that the bodily changes that occur can actually assist the individual. "It's amazing what fear does for you," revealed Alan Bell, a former British Special Air Service (SAS) senior Non-Commissioned Officer (NCO).[9] Not surprisingly, "The man who recognizes fear can often make it work in his favor," concluded war reporter Mack Morriss, "because fear is energy. Like anger, fear shifts the body into high."[10] John Dollard, a social anthropologist, explained in his seminal research into the subject that "Fear is a normal, inevitable, useful reaction to danger." He added, "It is a danger signal produced in a man's body by his awareness of signs of danger in the world around him."[11] Once the crisis is over, however, the parasympathetic system reverses emotional arousal and calms and relaxes the body.

Overall, research has shown that there are two types of fear. The first is *acute fear* that is generally provoked by tangible stimuli or situations, for instance, a loud bang or a snake suddenly slithering by. It normally subsides quite quickly when the frightening stimuli is removed or avoided. The second type of fear is *chronic fear*. This kind is generally more complex and may or may not be tied to tangible sources of provocation. An individual who persistently feels uneasy and anxious for unidentified reasons, such as the fear of being alone, is a good example.[12] Regardless of the type, it need not be immediate or the result of personal experience, since fear is a learned reaction. "Men and animals," reported John T. Wood, "experience fear in the face of present, anticipated, or imagined danger or pain."[13] Jeffrey Alan Gray, a professor of psychology at the Institute of Psychiatry in London, agreed. He asserted, "Fear … is due to the anticipation of pain."[14]

As such, fear knows no borders. As Colonel S.L.A. Marshall, the well-known American combat historian explained, "Fear is general among men … The majority are unwilling to take extraordinary risks and do not aspire to a hero's role."[15] Research in the field has supported this view. It has been conclusively confirmed that everybody experiences fear. "Fear," adjudged scholar Elmar Dinter, "is the most significant common denominator for all soldiers."[16] Studies have also established that fear in younger and unmarried soldiers is marginally less than in older, married ones, and that junior officers and NCOs show a little less fear than the other ranks.[17] Not surprisingly, most people appear to be more susceptible to fear when they are alone.[18]

And so, everyone is prone to fear. This is not surprising, particularly amongst military personnel, who in conflict are exposed to a myriad of stimuli, especially on the battlefield. An understanding of the causes and effects of fear sheds light on why and how fear can lead to, or at least become a component of, disobedience. The first major cause of fear in a military context is the fear of the unknown and the unexpected. "What a man has not seen," stated the ancient Greek general Onasander, "he always expects will be greater than it really is." Retired combat veteran and military theorist, Major-General Robert Scales Jr., opined, "soldiers fear most the enemy they cannot see."[19] The Medical Officer assigned to the original "L" Detachment of the British SAS in North Africa in 1941 wrote, "Why did we fear, and of what were we afraid? It was the continual uneasy anticipation and mental torture of anxiety."[20] Not surprisingly, anecdotal evidence indicates that fear increases in foggy conditions or when it is dark, or with the loss of orientation following an unexpected enemy attack from the rear.[21] This reality is in fact timeless and had particular relevance to the soldiers who fought in the tightly packed phalanxes of ancient times:

Men in the rear ranks can have had little idea of what was happening, even if they did not have their hearing and vision seriously restricted by a Corinthian helmet. They could not know whether a collapse at another point in the phalanx was imminent. If they were slow in realizing that their own phalanx had broken, they were more likely to be amongst those caught by the pursuing and vengeful enemy. Phalanxes spent a battle on the verge of panic, moving near-

171

CHAPTER 7

er to it as the battle progressed and they failed to win, or at least to continue advancing. The men in the rear ranks had to cope passively with the stress of this fear. Although they were not in direct physical danger until the phalanx was broken, battle was still a great ordeal for the rear ranks. In some respects it may have been worse for them than the men in the lead who were occupied facing the more tangible threats of combat.[22]

A second major cause of fear originates from a feeling of hopelessness. This is often due to a perceived or actual inability in the face of danger to influence the probable outcome of events. Simply put, it is caused by a feeling of being threatened without the power to do anything about it. "A soldier cowering alone in the bottom of his foxhole finds himself alone and isolated from his buddies," explained one veteran. "This feeling of isolation leads inevitably to vague imaginings and apprehensions - not only of dying, but of helpless inaction and the intense fear of being left to die alone."[23] Captain Adolf Von Schell, a First World War veteran, agreed. "When a soldier lies under hostile fire and waits, he feels unable to protect himself," Schell explained, and when "he has time; he thinks; he only waits for the shot that will hit him." He added that the soldier "feels a certain inferiority to the enemy. He feels that he is alone and deserted."[24] Little wonder that individuals in such a state may decide to abandon their positions or simply cower and hide.

A survey of 6,000 airmen by researchers during the Second World War showed that the factors of helplessness and hopelessness were responsible for major increments in fear. "Fear," asserted Professor S.J. Rachman from the Institute of Psychiatry at the University of London, "seems to feed on a sense of uncontrollability: it arises and persists when the person finds himself in a threatening situation over which he feels he has little or no control." Research demonstrated that "Being in danger when one cannot fight back or take any other effective action, being idle or being insecure of the future, were the elements that tended to aggravate fear in combat."[25]

Noise is yet another common stressor and a major cause of trepidation. "As we had feared, we heard the roar of war again," wrote one Second World War German veteran of the Eastern Front. "The noise," he stated:

> ...in itself was enough to send a wave of terror through the ... Men trapped beside the water ... Every man grabbed his things and began to run ... Frantic men were abandoning everything on the bank and plunging into the water to try to swim to the opposite shore ... Madness seemed to be spreading like wildfire.[26]

An airborne officer reported that in Tunisia, in 1942, he witnessed a group of American ammunition carriers shocked into inactivity "simply by the tremendous noise of real fighting. Instead of getting the ammunition forward to a machine gun these men were huddled together, hugging the ground, shaking - pitifully unaware that their route was protected by a hill."[27] Sergeant Peter Cottingham revealed, "It is impossible to describe the terror which the sound of even one incoming artillery shell can instill in a person."[28]

But, it is not only the sound of munitions that can create a state of fear and panic. Even the dreaded Scottish Highlanders were overcome by the "appalling yells of the Canadians and Indians" at Fort Duquesne in 1758 and broke away in a wild and disorderly retreat. "Fear," said Major Grant of the Highlanders, "got the better of every other passion; and I trust I shall never again see such a panic among troops."[29] Their experience was not isolated. As a young officer, George Washington witnessed similarly panicked troops during Major-General Edward Braddock's infamous defeat at the Monongahela River in 1754. "And when we endeavored to rally them," recounted Washington, then an officer assigned to Braddock's staff, "it was with as much success as if we had attempted to stop the wild bears of the mountains."[30] The battle cries of the North American Indians consistently unnerved their white opponents. One contemporary account captured the prevailing phenomenon. "The war cries of the Indians," reported one chronicler, "'ravenous Hell-hounds ... yelping and screaming like so many Devils' - came from every direction, terrifying men whose imaginations had fed on tales of how Indians tortured and mutilated their prisoners."[31] Similarly, Second World War German infanteer, Hans-Heinrich Ludwig, noted with fear the "wild choir of stormy Russian hurrahs." He acknowledged, "The tendency of Russians to trumpet their assaults with bloodcurdling screams unsettled many Landsers [German infanteers]." Leopold von Thadden-Trieglaff, another veteran of the Russian Front, also wrote home of the "fanatical [Russian] cries of hurrah ... which shattered us."[32] Overcome with terror, individuals are often swept up by emotion and do not always listen to reason or think rationally.

A third source of fear, although associated with noise, is the immobility caused by shelling or fire. "Each time a black iron oval [shell] broke the horizon," wrote First World War German veteran Ernst Junger, "one's eye sized it up with that instantaneous clarity of which a man is only capable in moments of life and death."[33] In his monumental study of the American soldier in the Second World War, Samuel Stouffer reported that many veterans testified that the "severest fear-producing situation they encountered in combat was just such immobilization under artillery or mortar fire."[34] American veteran Glenn Searle acknowledged, "No matter how gung-ho you are, after about fifteen minutes of artillery shells screaming in and exploding all around you, you start to quiver not unlike a bowl of gelatin and your teeth chatter." He conceded, "We did a lot of screaming."[35] Canadian paratrooper Jan de Vries felt that "shelling was probably the worst thing to have to live through."[36] Fellow veteran, Private Mervin Jones,

CHAPTER 7

agreed. "One day we were shelled for 12 hours straight," he remembered. "No one was hurt, but it was sure hard on the nerves."[37] The effect was the same on both sides. "Those who weren't struck dumb with fright howled like madmen," wrote German veteran Guy Sajer.[38] "For soldiers on the receiving end," explained American Major-General Scales, "firepower creates a sense of stress and alarm made all the more fearsome by its impersonal and anonymous nature."[39]

Yet another cause of fear is deprivation. All soldiers need sleep, food and drink regardless of their level of physical fitness. Practical experience in the Second World War, and all of the conflicts since, demonstrated that the physical and psychological factors that lowered morale and sapped men's courage were fatigue, hunger and thirst.[40] Paradoxically, there is a symbiotic relationship between fatigue and fear. The more fatigued a person is, the more susceptible they become to fear; the greater their fear, the greater is the drain on their energy. Colonel S.L.A. Marshall observed in his decades of battlefield studies that "Tired men fright more easily" and "frightened men swiftly tire."[41] Extreme fatigue ultimately makes it impossible for some men to continue to function. "We learned," asserted Corporal Dan Hartigan, "that the lack of sleep was the worst of all deprivations, far worse than hunger or thirst."[42] One Second World War German veteran stated, "The exhaustion we had been dragging about with us for days increased the fear we could no longer control." He explained that the "fear intensified our exhaustion, as it required constant vigilance."[43] Lieutenant-Colonel Michael Calvert, a wartime Chindit commanding officer and later SAS Brigade commander, explained in a 1943 report on Chindit operations that it was necessary to "march methodically and don't overtire yourselves or men, as lack of sleep and tiredness makes cowards of us all."[44] Psychologist F.C. Bartlett agreed. "In war," he insisted, "there is perhaps no general condition which is more likely to produce a large crop of nervous and mental disorders than a state of prolonged and great fatigue." This situation is the result of four factors: 1) physiological arousal caused by the stress of existing in what is commonly understood as a continual fight-or-flight arousal condition; 2) cumulative loss of sleep; 3) the reduction in caloric intake; and 4) the toll of the elements such as rain, cold, heat and the dark of night.[45]

Surprisingly, scholars and researchers have shown that the fear of killing is another predominant stress for soldiers. From an early age, Western culture encourages individuals to cherish the value of life and the abhorrence of killing others is deeply rooted in the psyche of soldiers. The lack of "offensive spirit" was widely reported in the Second World War. For instance, one 1943 report noted that the "average Jack was quite amazingly lethargic."[46] A British tank commander once conceded that the enemy "sprang at Allied tanks like wolves, until we were compelled under the murderous rain of their fire to kill them against our will."[47] Lieutenant-Colonel Robert Cole lamented that "not one man in twenty-five voluntarily used his weapon" even though they were under attack.[48] S.L.A. Marshall, based on his Second World War battlefield studies, reported that on average only 15 percent of infantrymen fired their weapons during an engagement.[49] Similarly, a Canadian military instructor complained in 1951 during the Korean War that "the problem is not to stop fire, but to start it."[50] Once again, this deep-seated fear can easily become a catalyst for disobedience by simply not engaging an enemy.

Another root cause of fear is the threat of being killed or wounded. "I suddenly felt terribly afraid," confessed one German veteran, "It would probably be my turn soon. I would be killed, just like that ... as my panic rose, my hands began to tremble ... and I sank into total despair."[51] Although this fear is self-explanatory and completely understandable, it does not appear to be the predominant cause of the fear expressed by combatants. Israeli military psychologist Ben Shalit was surprised to find the low emphasis on fear of bodily harm and death, and the great emphasis on "letting others down."[52] This phenomenon will be discussed in detail later in the chapter.

Undeniably, fear is capable of being, and throughout history has been, a key ingredient of many failed military endeavors. Moreover, it has also proven to be a catalyst for disobedience to authority. In its grip, individuals and groups have found themselves unable, or unwilling, albeit at times unintentionally, to perform their duties, and sometimes their inactivity resulted in catastrophe. British Colonel Ian Palmer, a professor of defence psychiatry, reported, "unfortunately, once given into, fear colours our cognitions leading us to expect the worst." He explained, "this contagion and catastrophic thinking is a real threat to the effectiveness of military operations." Palmer also noted that fear may often lead to "freeze" and "flight" reactions.[53] Both fly in the face of military duty and thus lead to a *de facto* disobedience of authority. But this should not be surprising. After all, the manifestations of fear are quite significant and they go a long way in explaining how disobedience, even though unintentional, can occur.

The effect that fear has on both individuals and units must now be considered, and the consequences can be devastating. First, fear impacts performance. Studies have shown that physical manifestations include "weight loss, tremors, abuse of alcohol and tobacco, insomnia, nightmares, cardiac irregularities, loss of confidence, and general nervous breakdown."[54] Moreover, Marshall determined that "in the measure that the man is shocked nervously, and that fear comes uppermost, he becomes physically weak." He added that the "body is drained of muscular power and of mental coordination."[55] Anecdotal accounts from Omaha Beach during the D-Day invasion of 6 June 1944 demonstrate that some men "were so weak from fear that they found it physically impossible to carry much more than their own weight." Staff Sergeant Thomas Turner revealed, "we were all surprised to find that we had suddenly gone weak. ... under fire we learned that fear and fatigue are about

CHAPTER 7

the same in their effect on an advance."[56] Remarkably, combat veterans discovered that "some frightened men have spent two hours negotiating the distance, which calmer ones cover in six minutes."[57] Research conducted in Bomber Command during the Second World War demonstrated a similar result. It determined that fear, or flying stress, rendered individuals mentally and physically tired.[58] But the effect on performance is even more pervasive. In many cases, it often debilitates individuals. Dan Ray of the U.S. 36th Infantry Division recalled that when preparing to ambush a group of German soldiers in the Colmar Pocket, "I was shaking so bad from fright" that "I had to brace my knees against the sides of the hole so that I could be ready to function."[59] Similarly, Walter Pippen, who served with Merrill's Marauders in Burma, admitted, "I couldn't speak. My vocal cords seemed to have jelled. It was as though my legs had been severed at the knee."[60]

Professor John Dollard discovered that fear also led to over-caution. Of those he questioned, 59 percent stated that there were occasions when they were too cautious and had had their efficiency reduced by fear. When fear leads to panic, performance suffers even more. "The men from what storys they had heard of the Indians in regard to their scalping and Mawhawking," wrote a British officer in his journal, "were so pannick struck that their officers had little or no command over them."[61] Similarly, "The Men of Coll: Dunbar's party hearing of our defeat, were extreamly frightened, so much so, that upon seeing 2 or 3 of our own Indians returning, the greatest part began to run away."[62] In the same vein, at Gallabat in November 1940, elements of the 1st Battalion, Essex Regiment, broke and fled under an Italian air attack, thereby destroying General W.J. Slim's chance of capturing the Italian fort, which was his objective.[63] As the Roman poet Virgil remarked, "Fear lent wings to his feet."[64]

Similarly, visual stimuli can trigger fear which, in turn, can impact negatively on performance. During a German counter-attack following the invasion of Sicily in 1943, German armour advanced toward American lines on Hill 41. One historian described how the Germans' menacingly long 88-millimeter cannons shone in the sun at the same time as they opened fire. "As if on cue, infantrymen of the 2nd Battalion of the 16th Regiment scrambled out of their holes and began rushing pellmell to the rear," he wrote. "At first it was only a handful, then more and more joined in, until within minutes two-thirds of the Big Red One battalion had urgently departed."[65] Likewise, Dominic Neal, a British officer in Burma recounted:

There was rifle fire ahead, and rounds were hitting the trees ahead of me. I saw the British Other Ranks ahead running back shouting 'Japs.' There was confusion in extreme up front. The leading platoon came rushing back with a look of terror in their eyes. The sight of fleeing soldiers is very infectious. My men, in sympathy, turned about, and started running.[66]

CHAPTER 7

In Vietnam, United States Marine Corps (USMC) lieutenant Philip Caputo confirmed the timeless, infectious nature of panic. He witnessed a tough sergeant curse at and kick a soldier who had collapsed in tears, unable to take any more combat. "None of us did a thing to stop Horne because we felt the same terror," he confessed. "And we knew that that kind of fear was a contagion and the marine a carrier ... beat him, kick him, beat that virus out of him before it spreads."[67] The belief that fear could be spread was widely held. Dollard found that 75 percent of the veterans that he questioned expressed the view that "fear can be contagious [and] that it can be transmitted from one soldier to another."[68]

Direct performance aside, fear can also cause severe emotional stress and psychiatric breakdown. Scholar Stephen G. Fritz noted that:

> Fear was the real enemy of most Landsers: fear of death or of cowardice, fear of the conflict within the spirit ... or, a simple fear of showing fear. Men felt haunted, hollowed on the inside by pockets of fear that would not go away, caught in the grip of something enormous about to overwhelm them.[69]

German veteran Will Thomas recognized the mental strain that fear exacted. "The psychological load," he explained, "presses harder than the burden of the almost superhuman physical exertions."[70] Similarly, Harry Mielert emphasized the "enormous amount of psychological stress demanded of each soldier." He asserted that the "physical is the smallest part of the strain."[71] The effect was universal. An American commander observed, "Gradually, your numbers are whittled down, your men grow jumpy, and approach the cracking point."[72]

Professor Anthony Kellet's examination of Second World War studies led him to believe that "More than anything else, fear itself is the critical ingredient in psychiatric breakdown in combat ... [and] causes a strain so great that it causes men to break down."[73] Stouffer's seminal work reported that 83 percent of those questioned asserted that they had the experience of seeing "a man's nerves 'crack up' at the front."[74] The potential impact of fear becomes clearly evident owing to its effects on individuals and the reality that it can cascade through the ranks. Seventy percent of 1,700 American veterans surveyed in Italy in 1944 said that they became nervous or depressed, or their morale suffered, at the sight of another man's psychiatric breakdown.[75]

Finally, fear can also impact adversely on decision-making. US Army research has shown "that during stressful combat-like training, every aspect of cognitive function assessed was severely degraded, compared to the subjects' own baseline, pre-stress performance." Moreover, the magnitude of the deficits was greater than those typically produced by alcohol intoxication or treatment with sedating drugs. One study team concluded that "on the battlefield, the severe

CHAPTER 7

decrements we measured ... would significantly impair the ability of warfighters to perform their duties." Specifically, the team determined that extended periods of pressure and fear lead to over-reaction, an increase in wrong decisions and inconsistency.[76] Similarly, Professor Dinter noted that fear and exhaustion will also reduce the willingness to make decisions at all.[77] These results are not surprising and anecdotal evidence provided in war literature and interviews with veterans clearly endorses these findings.

What becomes worrisome is the fact that fear is seemingly incontrovertible. Most revealing indeed is the fact that frightening experiences do not toughen an individual. The reality that fear has a cumulative effect is largely unknown. Dollard's research indicated that fear increases in proportion to the duration of the engagement and the number of frightening incidents endured by an individual.[78] Scottish historian Hew Strachan concluded, "the battle-hardened veteran was a mythical figure." He discovered that "sustained exposure to danger did not harden a soldier but eroded his limited resources."[79] Canadian military historian Desmond Morton agreed. He observed, "Most men [during the First World War] arrived at the front fearful of the unknown, mastered it if they survived, and then, in days, months or years, wore out their courage."[80] Marshall also explained that "sustained fear is as degenerative as prolonged fatigue and exhausts the body's energy no less."[81] Lieutenant-Colonel Dave Grossman determined from his research that "In sustained combat this process of emotional bankruptcy is seen in 98 percent of all soldiers who survive physically."[82] Another contemporary report concluded, "All soldiers have a breaking point beyond which their effective performance in combat diminishes."[83] Quite simply, even the most psychologically strong person will eventually succumb. No one ever becomes accustomed to fear – it is just a matter of trying to control it.

One study conducted during the Second World War by Lieutenant-Colonel J.W. Appel and Captain G. W. Beebe observed, "Each moment of combat imposes a strain so great that men will break down in direct relation to the intensity and duration of their exposure ... the average point at which this occurred appears to have been in the region of 200-240 aggregate combat days." The British estimated that a rifleman would last for about 400 combat days, the longer period being attributable to the fact that they tended to relieve troops in the line for a four-day rest after approximately twelve days.[84] Another study confirmed that around 200 to 240 days of combat, the average soldier became "so overly cautious and jittery that he was ineffective and demoralizing to the newer men."[85]

That fear affects performance, by increasing fatigue, by changing bodily function, by decreasing one's capability to perform or by leading to panic, is irrefutable. As such, is it surprising that fear can, and does, fuel disobedience, unintentional as it may be? As a result of fear, individuals are often rendered psychologically, as well as physically, incapable of responding effectively to, or carrying out, direction. If their fear is so uncontrollable that it leads to panic, it can result in one of the most serious of transgressions – desertion in the face of the enemy. One senior officer discovered upon stopping some troops who were retreating in the face of the enemy, that "Someone had given the order" to retire. He lamented, "Oh that 'someone' who takes concrete shape in the imagination of overwrought men and gives them concrete, disastrous orders!"[86] Clearly, when the emotion of fear takes over, individuals often act impulsively to save themselves without thought to the implications of their actions. At other times, they may consciously decide that the risk of official sanction is the better course than facing their fears. Either way, fear is the catalyst that drives disobedience. But, does fear absolve the individual or the leadership cadre for the failure in personal or group performance?

As prevalent and understandable as fear may be, it is controllable. "The basis of fear is the awareness of danger," explained Field-Marshal Bernard Law Montgomery, and "In itself this is healthy; for a man who is aware of danger automatically takes steps to provide against it."[87] The important point here is how one manages and controls his or her fear. In fact, as noted earlier, fear can be a positive influence on performance if managed properly. "We fought," maintained Guy Sajer, "from simple fear which was our motivating power."[88] Fear also sharpens an individual's senses and makes one more alert, mainly because of the release of adrenalin in the body. Panama veteran Sergeant First Class James Coroy of the 101st Airborne (Air Assault) Division noted, "Fear is not that bad, because it heightens your senses."[89] In fact, a Second World War US Air Force study found that 50 percent of the airmen reported that fear sometimes improved their efficiency so that they, in the end, were more accurate in their work.[90]

The key factor identified by combat veterans was not the fact that someone felt afraid, but rather "the effort to overcome the withdrawal tendencies engendered by intense fear."[91] Stouffer determined that when a person regards fear reactions as a normal response to a dangerous situation, they are less likely to be disturbed, once the danger has subsided, by self-reproaches of cowardice, unmanliness or other accusations that lower self-esteem. Moreover, in the face of danger, a potential source of conflict is eliminated if one accepts the notion that he need not fear the loss of status and esteem in the eyes of his fellows if he trembles, gasps or exhibits other marked fear symptoms while carrying out his job.[92] The Iroquois provide a compelling example of what happens when this attitude is not accepted. As historian Carl Benn explains:

> Iroquois society, with its emphasis on personal stoicism and bravery, may have failed to address the instinctive fear that a person feels when preparing to engage in mortal combat. At the beginning of the battle of Fort George, one Iroquois tried to rally the warriors with the

CHAPTER 7

simplistic declaration, 'The warrior knows no anxiety for his safety.' This was rhetoric, not the truth, and dangerous rhetoric because it conflicted with the immediate experience of people who heard it. Fear, and its attendant symptoms, such as uncontrollable trembling or bowel movements, are due to rapid involuntary muscular action designed to warm up the body for the anticipated fight. Most combatants experience such symptoms, yet warriors seem to have grown up hearing only about the fearlessness of their ancestors and the courageous exploits of the war with reference to the reality of fear in anything but contemptuous terms. Therefore, when they had to confront their own terror, some presumably believed they were cowards, not the 'men' of their culture's tradition, and they responded by fleeing if they could not bring their fear under control.[93]

As the numerous, yet far from definitive, examples throughout the text have shown, fear frequently leads to the disobedience of legal orders. However, quite often, this adverse military performance is indicative of more fundamental problems, such as a failing in training, leadership or group cohesion. Israeli research has shown that effective leadership is directly linked to acts of courage. Moreover, the Israeli findings maintain that training, practicing skills and confidence building are critical components in developing courage and avoiding the negative consequences that can result from fear.[94] Simply put, there are strategies for controlling fear and limiting the potential of disobedience that can result from its insidious effects on individuals.

First, coming to grips with the fact that fear is a normal occurrence can ultimately control it. Individuals must not repress their fear, nor should those who articulate it be ridiculed. Rather, the topic should be freely discussed. Research has indicated that eight out of ten combat veterans felt that it was better to admit fear and discuss it openly before battle. The belief that "the man who knows he will be afraid and tries to get ready for it makes a better soldier," was shared by 58 percent of those surveyed.[95] "If it [fear] is allowed to back up in a man, unspoken and unaired in any way," explained war correspondent Mack Morriss, "it can form a clot and create an obstacle to normal action."[96]

Another vital method for controlling fear is training and education.[97] Flavius Renatus asserted in A.D. 378 that "the courage of the soldier is heightened by the knowledge of his profession." Knowledge is the key as it provides confidence, not only in oneself, but also in one's comrades, equipment and tactics. This is achieved through realistic training, as well as a complete understanding of the realm of conflict. Such training reduces the fear of the unexpected and the unknown. It is for this reason that the British parachute school adopted the motto, "Knowledge Dispels Fear." Moreover, General Slim asserted, "Training was central to the discipline soldiers needed to con-

CHAPTER 7

trol their fear, and that of their subordinates in battle; to allow them to think clearly and shoot straight in a crisis, and to inspire them to maximum physical and mental endeavour."[98] In addition, realistic training (e.g. battle simulation, full combat loads, non-templated enemy action, intense tempo, stress, physical exertion and fatigue) creates reasonable expectations of how far an individual or unit can go and how long they can fight. Such training is also valuable to the extent that it inculcates in soldiers the realization that they can survive on the battlefield. Major John Masters, a Second World War Chindit commander, explained that it is "easy … to be brave when a little experience has taught you that there is nothing to be afraid of."[99]

In like manner, Dollard explained that "fear is useful to the soldier when it drives him to learn better in training and to act sensibly in battle."[100] Stouffer believed that fear aroused in training could serve a useful purpose as well. He argued that it "can motivate men to learn those habits which will reduce danger in battle." He explained that "training benefits by accustoming - taking away the unknown unfamiliar element." He concluded, "A certain amount of adaptation to the extremely loud noises and other stimuli probably takes place with repeated exposures so that when the stimuli are encountered in battle they elicit less fear."[101] As such, it is critical to add the element of ambiguity and the unknown to all training activities. In addition, training should be conducted at night, in poor light and in unknown surroundings. Moreover, it should include situations where things go wrong. In tandem, this will assist in inoculating individuals to the fear of the unknown and accustom them to dealing with adversity. It is for this reason that demanding Adventure Training in austere and harsh regions is invaluable. This form of training is almost always varied from the routine and incorporates real, unexpected events that must be dealt with on the spot.

The beneficial effect of realistic training is undisputed. Research and studies have shown that:

> The general level of anxiety in combat would tend to be reduced insofar as the men derived from training a high degree of self-confidence about their ability to take care of themselves … troops who expressed a high degree of self-confidence before combat were more likely to perform with relatively little fear during battle.[102]

Major Reg Crawford of the Australian SAS commented, "We wouldn't be able to do the things we do if a guy knew he was going to be faced with a degree of danger and didn't have the confidence to confront that and carry out the task regardless."[103] Similarly, Specialist Matthew Eversmann said of his combat experience in Mogadishu in October 1993, "seeing the men perform gave me the confidence and reassurance that I needed."[104] The issue of confidence is an important one since self-assurance is perhaps the greatest

CHAPTER 7

source of emotional strength that a soldier can draw upon. "With it," insisted behavioural expert Bernard Bass, the soldier "willingly faces the enemy and withstands deprivations, minor setbacks, and extreme stresses, knowing that he and his unit are capable of succeeding."[105] Numerous studies have shown that well led and cohesive units tend to have fewer stress casualties than units in which these qualities are not as pronounced.[106] In sum, self-confidence can be achieved through training, education and fitness, as well as through sound leadership, team cohesion and dependable equipment. In essence, it has been repeatedly demonstrated that troops that expressed a high degree of self-confidence before combat were more likely to perform with relatively little fear during battle. This, of course, also mitigates against disobedience toward lawful authority as a result of fear.

The value of training is also derived from its ability to create instinctive reactions. Drill, for instance, is utilized to teach automatic responses to commands. "What is learnt in training," insisted commando leader Lord Lovat, "is done instinctively in action - almost without thinking down to the last man."[107] In the same manner, discipline and responses to leadership are crucial variables that shape attitudes among combat veterans. The role of discipline is one of providing a psychological defence that helps the soldier to control fear and ignore danger through technical performance. "It is a function of discipline," extolled Field-Marshal Montgomery, "to fortify the mind so that it becomes reconciled to unpleasant sights and accepts them as normal every-day occurrences ... Discipline strengthens the mind so that it becomes impervious to the corroding influence of fear ... It instills the habit of self control."[108]

Another vital method for controlling fear is the maintenance of routine and habit. The adherence to simple daily routines, such as the ritual of shaving, provides individuals with a sense of normalcy. This is vital in maintaining an equilibrium that allows individuals to perform consistently. "It was not the food [deep in the Burmese jungle] that refreshed and renewed us," insisted Major Masters, "as much as the occasion."[109] Lord Lovat summed up the situation when he declared, "habit is ten times nature."[110]

There are a number of other strategies that can also be used to manage fear in a positive manner. Humour is the most important form of self-discipline and acts to release tension. Second World War veteran Howard Ruppel of the American 517th Parachute Infantry Regiment observed that "when circumstances become unbearable, the experienced soldier with some sense of humor and the ability to laugh at one's self has a better chance to retain his sanity than the serious minded fellow."[111] In regard to the fear and strain of long hours in covert observation posts, one long time intelligence operator serving with a highly classified unit in Northern Ireland commented, "the unit ran on a sense of humour."[112]

For others, religion and faith provide a foil for fear. Max Kocour of the German 90th Infantry Division revealed that faith among combat soldiers was usually a general belief in God and was not centered on any particular religion or denomination. "We developed faith," he divulged, "regardless of religions, which had been created by man, we felt we were on the right side of faith, under the protection / care of a truly fine Supreme Being." Arlo Butcher, a paratrooper with the 101st Airborne Division disclosed, "No matter what kind of protection you've got, or how deep the hole is, I sure realized the mighty power of God. It was your prayers … that helped us through this awful mess."[113]

Still others rely on more artificial tools for controlling their angst. Alcohol and drugs are time-honoured methods of dealing with pain, fear and stress, and their use is often more widespread than is generally acknowledged. One officer in colonial North America revealed that soldiers were often made "beastly drunk to be brought to the attack."[114] British regiments fought at the Battle of Waterloo in 1815 with barrels of whisky in the centre of their squares. "Had it not been for the rum ration," testified one British medical officer to the 1922 Shell Shock Committee, "I do not think we should have won the war."[115] Prior to Dieppe, the British commandos were given a breakfast served with rum, which at least one veteran of the raid credited with allowing them to keep the contents of their stomach despite the devastation, carnage and death that they faced that morning.[116] The Japanese and Russians regularly plied their soldiers with alcohol prior to their fanatical charges.[117] The American and Russian experiences in Vietnam and Afghanistan, respectively, are laden with accounts of substance abuse as a means of coping. Although drugs and alcohol have often been used to help control fear, their success is always of marginal value. While both temporarily alleviate anxiety, they reduce one's ability to act in a rational and coordinated manner. In addition, there are often long-term consequences of use.

A more effective tool for fear management, and one with less harmful side effects, is the timely and accurate passage of information. In the chaos of battle, information is almost a means of power. Individuals are hungry for anything that may shed light on events that are about to impact their future. Quite simply, knowledge dissipates the unknown and dampens groundless rumours. "If a soldier knows what is happening and what is expected of him," explained a veteran British officer, "he is far less frightened than the soldier who is just walking towards unknown dangers."[118] Theodore Roosevelt insisted, "fear can be checked, whipped and driven from the field when men are kept informed."[119] The passage of information is predicated on effective communications that are equally vital to staving off the effects of fear. It is critical to keep personnel informed as much as possible about virtually everything. It is not only the content of the message that is important, but also the process itself. Regular communications ensure that everyone knows that they are not alone and that they are still part of a team. It is for this reason that communications

CHAPTER 7

should always be maintained at all costs. Initially, during the Second World War, the Allies believed that German and Japanese night attacks were amateurish and disorganized because of the excessive amount of yelling that occurred. They later discovered, however, that this was deliberately done, not only as a means of control, but also as a method by which fear could be managed. Sajer provides a graphic example. "Nobody move!" the veteran commanded authoritatively. "In our terror," he conceded, "we obeyed him. His voice sounded more confident than the sergeant's."[120]

Simple activity is also essential for managing fear. Once again, Dollard found that veteran soldiers quickly learn that to be busy means to be less afraid. He wrote, "When fear is strong, keep your mind on the job at hand."[121] Major-General T.S. Hart, former Director of Medical Services in the United Kingdom agreed. "There is no doubt," he asserted, "that inactivity at a time of tension breeds fear and that the best antidote ... is purposeful action."[122] Colonel Palmer noted that "actions such as giving and receiving orders reduce fear by focusing the minds of those giving and receiving them."[123] Naval surgeon R.N. Villar confessed, "I found waiting the most worrying and doing the most relaxing."[124] Similarly, Ted Barris acknowledged, "I flew twenty-two missions ... and it's only when I have time to think that I realize how scared we were...."[125] Finally, Robert Crisp, a tank troop commander in North Africa in 1941, summarized, "When the race is begun or the innings started, the fullness of the moment overwhelms the fear of anticipation. It is so in battle. When mind and body are fully occupied, it is surprising how unfrightened you can be."[126]

Yet, another powerful tool for controlling fear is strong group cohesion or primary group relationships. As already noted, the greatest fear felt by most combat soldiers is the fear of letting down their comrades. This is a powerful impetus not to allow fear to lead to panic. Paratrooper John Agnew explained that "Pride in Regiment and Division and being able to depend on each other makes individuals courageous regardless of fear, don't let your comrades down."[127] S.L.A. Marshall asserted, "I hold it to be one of the simplest truths of war that the thing which enables an infantry soldier to keep going with his weapons is the near presence or the presumed presence of a comrade."[128] Conversely, fighter pilots suffered the greatest stress due both to their isolation while flying alone, as well as to the strain caused by the unpredictability of their adversaries in combat.[129]

This sense of obligation, coupled with a sense of responsibility for ensuring the well being of others, also generates a feeling of responsibility for upholding the reputation of the unit. It should be noted that this sense of responsibility also helps to alleviate fear. Creating demanding expectations of combat behaviour in members and then linking soldiers' self-esteem to the reputation of the unit and the welfare of their mates is a powerful control mechanism. Many believe that a man behaves as a hero or coward according to the expectations of others of how he is to behave. "The overwhelming majority of men," reported Dollard, "felt that they fought better after observing other men behaving calmly in a dangerous situation."[130] General Slim's subordinates were all in agreement that his "remarkable calmness in crisis, despite his own inner fears and anxieties, contributed significantly to a lessening of the storm of panic which erupted at every new and unexpected Japanese move."[131]

In that vein, Marshall insisted, "No matter how lowly his rank, any man who controls himself automatically contributes to the control of others." He added, "Fear is contagious but courage is not less so."[132] This reality was also borne out in research. Studies of Second World War submarine crews demonstrated that they suffered extremely low rates of psychiatric breakdown. The authors attributed this to a number of factors: 1) all members of the crew were volunteers who were required to meet rigid educational and physical standards for entry; 2) the training required was very thorough; 3) morale and confidence were high; and 4) a successful rotation scheme was used. Of a grand total of 126,160 patrols carried out by these crews, there were only 62 cases of psychiatric difficulty, or 0.00044 percent of the total.[133] Similarly, in John Flanagan's 17 volume report on performance of US combat air crews during the Second World War, he concluded, "The primary motivating force which more than anything else kept these men flying and fighting was that they were members of a group in which flying and fighting was the only accepted way of behaving."[134] Similarly, it has generally been acknowledged in the historical literature on German forces during the Second World War that the key to their success, despite the worsening situation, was the strength of the primary group. Clearly, when the primary group develops a high degree of cohesion, morale is usually high. More importantly, such bonds negate the influence of fear and decrease the likelihood of disobedience to command.

But, leadership is also a critical element in controlling fear. Dollard noted that 89 percent of those surveyed emphasized the importance of getting frequent instructions from leaders when in a tight spot.[135] Furthermore, evidence clearly indicates that leaderless groups normally become inactive.[136] Not surprisingly, Stouffer found that "cool and aggressive leadership was especially important" in pressing troops forward in dangerous and fearful situations such as storming across a beach raked by fire.[137] This finding is based on the fact that "role modeling" has an extremely important influence on a person's reaction to threatening situations. With regard to the evocation of courageous behaviour, American enlisted men in the Second World War told interviewers that leadership from the front was very important.[138] Most research has reinforced the intuitive deduction that "men like to follow an experienced man ... [who] knows how to accomplish objectives with a minimum of risk. He sets an example of coolness and efficiency which impels similar behaviour in others." In this regard, the presence of strong, thoughtful leadership creates "a force which helps resist fear."[139] For instance, a USMC private in the Pacific campaign was devastated by the death of his company commander. He revealed that his Officer Commanding "represented stability and direction in a world of violence" and when he died, "We felt forlorn and lost."[140] A wounded veteran from North Africa put it in perspective. He explained, "Everybody wants somebody to look up to when he's scared."[141] Sir Philip Sidney encapsulated the above sentiment. "A brave captain," he affirmed, "is as a root, out of which, as branches, the courage of his soldiers doth spring."[142] This effect, however, is only present if trust in the leadership exists. Soldiers must believe that leaders mean what they say. Body language, tone and eye contact all betray insincerity. Actions must match words. In the end, it comes down to setting the example. A leader must never ask, or expect, troops to do that which they themselves are unwilling to do. Stouffer's study showed that what the officers did, rather than what they said, was important. "I personally recall," wrote Sergeant Andy Anderson:

> when in the advance in Germany, our Platoon was 'on point' and we suddenly came under small arms fire from our front and my men all took to the ditches. I was peering about, under some cover to get a fix on the enemy. In a matter of minutes, I felt a poke in my back from a walking stick and it was the Brigadier with a smile. His comment was simply, 'not to hold up the entire Division,' so 'press-on' which is what we did. The point is, that you have no idea what confidence is carried to the troops when you have great leadership."[143]

In the end, fear is a real and powerful force. But, the essence of the issue is not whether one experiences fear, but rather how it is dealt with. It can be controlled and utilized to benefit the effectiveness of individuals and units in times of danger. Conversely, the failure to recognize the reality of fear and its effects can have serious repercussions that manifest themselves at the most disadvantageous moments. Unfailingly, it can, and will, cause disobedience to lawful command if not managed properly. As such, it is important to ensure that the necessary steps are taken to ease anxiety and fears. It is also important to discuss the issue to ensure that the perceptions and expectations of leaders and subordinates alike are realistic. Leaders must also imbue confidence in individuals, teams and equipment, and develop strategies to allow all to feel a sense of control over their destiny, regardless of activity or operation. Moreover, they must develop contingency plans and undertake additional training and education so that individuals are better able to cope with the unknown or unexpected.

Although the very complex and unpredictable nature of war mitigates against assurances that individuals or group will not allow fear to take control of their actions, the overwhelming and compelling human desire not to let down comrades, combined with solid leadership, training and strong unit cohesion, provide the necessary foil to disobedience due to fear. However, should

CHAPTER 7

these components not be present, or if any part thereof is weak, one should not be surprised if individuals break and fail to complete their mission in the face of crisis, chaos or danger. Although individuals must always be held accountable for their actions in these instances, events must be analyzed in detail to determine such mitigating circumstances. And, importantly, the command element responsible for leading, training and creating a cohesive team must also be examined. In the end, fear can and does lead to disobedience, albeit most often unintentionally. Nonetheless, fear is controllable and ensuring that the proper educational, training and leadership regime is in place must be a priority of all military leaders at all levels.

ENDNOTES

[1] Donald Fraser, Reginald Roy, ed., *The Journal of Private Fraser* (Victoria: Sono Nis Press, 1985), 207.
[2] Effective military leadership is defined as "directing, motivating, and enabling others to accomplish the mission professionally and ethically, while developing or improving capabilities that contribute to mission success." Canada, *Leadership in the Canadian Forces: Conceptual Foundations* (2005), 30. Kingston: Canadian Defence Academy-Canadian Forces Leadership Institute.
[3] Guy Sajer, *The Forgotten Soldier* (New York: Brassey's, 1990), 198.
[4] Dennis Coon, *Introduction to Psychology,* 8th ed. (New York: Brooks / Cole Publishing Co., 1998), 429.
[5] Stephen G. Fritz, *Frontsoldaten* (Lexington: University Press of Kentucky, 1995), 139.
[6] Douglas Brinkley, "What They Saw When They Landed," *Time*, 31 May 2004, 41.
[7] Rita Atkinson *et al.*, eds., *Hilgard's Introduction to Psychology,* 12th ed. (New York: Harcourt Brace College Publishers, 1996), 379-80.
[8] David M. Myers, *Psychology*, 4th ed. (Holland: Worth Publishers, 1995), 433. See also Coon, *Introduction to Psychology*, 431.
[9] Alan Bell, Presentation on the Special Air Service (SAS) Regiment's deployment and operations during the Falklands War, 19 March 2004, Fort Frontenac, Kingston, Ontario.
[10] John C. McManus, *The Deadly Brotherhood - The American Combat Soldier in World War II* (Novato: Presidio, 1998), 251.
[11] John Dollard, *Fear in Battle* (Westport: Greenwood Press Publishers, 1944), 56. Dollard's research was based on his study of 300 American volunteers who fought in the Spanish Civil War.
[12] S.J. Rachman, *Fear and Courage* (San Francisco: W.H. Freeman and Co., 1978), 6.
[13] John T. Wood, *What Are You Afraid Of?* (Englewood Cliffs: Prentice Hall, 1976), 22.
[14] Jeffrey Alan Gray, *The Psychology of Fear and Stress,* 2nd ed. (Cambridge: Cambridge University Press, 1987), 19.

CHAPTER 7

[15] John Keegan, *The Face of Battle* (London: Penguin Books, 1978), 71.
[16] Elmar Dinter, *Hero or Coward: Pressures Facing the Soldier in Battle* (London: Frank Cass, 1985), 12.
[17] Dinter, *Hero or Coward*, 24.
[18] Rachman, *Fear and Courage*, 84.
[19] Major-General (ret'd) Robert H. Scales Jr., *Yellow Smoke - The Future of Land Warfare for America's Military* (New York: Rowman & Littlefield Publishers Inc., 2003), 168.
[20] Malcolm James, *Born of the Desert - With the SAS in North Africa* (London: Greenhill Books, reprint 2001), 125.
[21] Dinter, *Hero or Coward*, 18 & 98, and Wood, *What Are You Afraid Of?*, 28-9.
[22] A.K. Goldsworthy, "The Othismos, Myths and Heresies: The Nature of Hoplite Battle," *War in History*, Vol. 4 (1997), 23.
[23] Scales, *Yellow Smoke*, 58.
[24] Captain Adolf Von Schell, *Battle Leadership* (Quantico: The Marine Corps Association, reprint 2000), 13.
[25] Rachman, *Fear and Courage*, 50-2.
[26] Sajer, *The Forgotten Soldier*, 257.
[27] Don Wharton, "Bringing the War to the Training Camps," *The Reader's Digest*, Vol. 42, No. 254 (June 1943), 37.
[28] Peter Layton Cottingham, *Once Upon A Wartime - A Canadian Who Survived the Devil's Brigade* (Private Printing, 1996), 103.
[29] Charles Hamilton, ed., *Braddock's Defeat - The Journal of Captain Robert Cholmley's Batman; The Journal of a British Officer; and Halkett's Orderly Book* (Norman: University of Oklahoma Press, 1959), 50. See also Francis Parkman, *Montcalm and Wolfe* (New York: Modern Library, reprint 1999), 333.
[30] George F.G. Stanley, *Canada's Soldiers - The Military History of an Unmilitary People* (Toronto: The Macmillan Co. of Canada Ltd., 1960), 66, and Paul E. Kopperman, *Braddock at the Monongahela* (Pittsburg: University of Pittsburg Press, 1992), 70.
[31] Quoted in Fred Anderson, *Crucible of War* (New York: Vintage Books, 2001), 102.
[32] Fritz, *Frontsoldaten*, 151.
[33] Ernest Jünger, *Storm of Steel* (London: Allen Lane, reprint 2003), 214.
[34] Samuel A. Stouffer et al., *The American Soldier - Combat and its Aftermath*. Vol. II. (Princeton: Princeton University Press, 1949), 83, and Rachman, *Fear and Courage*, 82.
[35] McManus, *The Deadly Brotherhood*, 250. Private Donald Fraser insisted that: "Gunfire so precise and methodical in its execution strikes terror, even into the bravest hearts." He added, "Standing up to shellfire of such method and accuracy is the hardest part by far of a soldier's trials." Roy, *Journal of Private Fraser*, 150-51.
[36] Interview with author, 18 January 2001.

37 Jean E. Portugal, *We Were There - The Army - A Record for Canada*. Vol. 2. (Toronto: The Royal Canadian Military Institute, 1998), 953.
38 Sajer, *The Forgotten Soldier*, 192.
39 Scales, *Yellow Smoke*, 57.
40 Major P.B. Deb, "The Anatomy of Courage," *Army Quarterly*, Vol. 127, No. 4 (October 1997), 405.
41 S.L.A. Marshall, *The Soldier's Load and the Mobility of a Nation* (Quantico: The Marine Corps Association, 1950), 46.
42 Arthur Max, *Men of The Red Beret - Airborne Forces - 1940-1990* (London: Century Hutchinson, 1990), 163; 1st Canadian Parachute Battalion War Diary, 9 June 1944, Vol. 15299, Record Group 24, *Library and Archives Canada*.
43 Fritz, *Frontsoldaten*, 121, and Rachman, *Fear and Courage*, 25.
44 Quoted in Julian Thompson, *War Behind Enemy Lines* (London: Sidgwick & Jackson, 1998), 155.
45 Lieutenant-Colonel David Grossman, *On Killing* (New York: Little, Brown and Co., 1996), 69.
46 Joanna Bourke, *An Intimate History of Killing* (London: Granta Books, 1999), 73-4.
47 Ian Baxter, *SS - The Secret Archives - Western Front* (London: Amber Books Ltd., 2003), 111.
48 S.L.A. Marshall, *Men Against Fire* (Alexandria: Byrrd Enterprises, Inc., 1947), 72.
49 Marshall, *Men Against Fire*, 54.
50 Captain W.R. Chamberlain, "Training the Functional Rifleman," *Canadian Army Journal*, Vol. 4, No. 9 (February 1951), 29.
51 Sajer, *The Forgotten Soldier*, 245.
52 Grossman, *On Killing*, 52.
53 Colonel Ian Palmer, "The Emotion That Dare Not Speak Its Name," *The British Army Review*, No. 132 (Summer 2003), 33.
54 Allan D. English, "A Predisposition to Cowardice? Aviation Psychology and the Genesis of 'Lack of Moral Fibre,'" *War and Society*, Vol. 13, No. 1 (May 1995), 17.
55 Marshall, *The Soldier's Load*, 41.
56 Ibid., 43-4.
57 Wharton, "Bringing the War to the Training Camps," 35.
58 English, "A Predisposition to Cowardice?," 18.
59 McManus, *The Deadly Brotherhood*, 251.
60 Ibid., 252.
61 Walter O'Meara, *Guns at the Forks* (Pittsburg: University of Pittsburg Press, 1965), 147. This quotation was correctly transcribed from the original.
62 Hamilton, *Braddock's Defeat*, 53. This quotation was correctly transcribed from the original.
63 Robert Lyman, *Slim - Master of War* (London: Constable, 2004), 75.

CHAPTER 7

64   Quoted in Palmer, "The Emotion That Dare Not Speak Its Name," 31.
65   William Breuer, *Drop Zone Sicily - Allied Airborne Strike, July 1943* (Novato: Presidio, 1983), 119-20.
66   Thompson, *War Behind Enemy Lines*, 155.
67   Philip Caputo, *Rumour of War* (New York: Ballatine Books, 1977), 273-74.
68   Dollard, *Fear in Battle*, 28, and Rachman, *Fear and Courage*, 76.
69   Fritz, *Frontsoldaten*, 134.
70   Ibid., 138.
71   Ibid.
72   Captain T.M. Chacho, "Why Did They Fight? American Airborne Units in World War II," *Defence Studies*, Vol. 1, No. 3 (Autumn 2001), 81.
73   Anthony Kellett, *Combat Motivation* (Ottawa: DND, 1980), 268. Operational Research and Analysis Establishment [ORAE] Report No. R77.
74   Stouffer, *The American Soldier*, 124-25, 134 & 208-9. See also Rachman, *Fear and Courage*, 61 & 76-8.
75   Ibid.
76   H.R. Lieberman *et al.*, "The Fog of War: Documenting Cognitive Decrements Associated with the Stress of Combat," *Proceedings of the 23rd Army Science Conference,* December 2002, abstract.
77   Dinter, *Hero or Coward*, 82.
78   Dollard, *Fear in Battle*, 22.
79   Quoted in Brigadier-General Denis Whitaker and Shelagh Whitaker, *Rhineland - The Battle to End the War* (Toronto: Stoddart, 2000), 351.
80   Desmond Morton, *When Your Number's Up* (Toronto: Random House, 1993), 230.
81   Marshall, *The Soldier's Load*, iii.
82   Grossman, *On Killing*, 84.
83   Jeremy Manton, Carlene Wilson and Helen Braithwaite, "Human Factors in Field Training for Battle: Realistically Reproducing Chaos," in Michael Evans and Alan Ryan, eds., *The Human Face of Warfare - Killing, Fear and Chaos in Battle* (St. Leonards, Australia: Allen & Unwin, 2000), 188.
84   Richard Holmes, *Acts of War - The Behaviour of Men in Battle* (New York: The Free Press, 1985), 215.
85   William Ian Miller, *The Mystery of Courage* (Cambridge: Harvard University Press, 2000), 61. Yet another research report confirmed that after approximately 30 days of combat, soldiers experienced a noticeable decline in performance. See Manton *et al.*, "Human Factors in Field Training for Battle," 188.
86   John Masters, *The Road Past Mandalay* (London: Cassell, reprint 2003), 270.
87   Field-Marshal Bernard L. Montgomery, "Discipline from Morale in Battle: Analysis," in Canada, *The Officer - A Manual of Leadership for Officers in the Canadian Forces* (Ottawa: DND, 1978), 66. In addition, "If

there are men who know no fear they are probably a danger to themselves and to others." Quoted in Major-General F.M. Richardson, *Fighting Spirit - A Study of Psychological Factors in War* (London: Leo Cooper, 1978), 112.
[88] Quoted in Fritz, *Frontsoldaten*, 135.
[89] Gregg Zoroya, "As war looms, young soldiers confront fear; 'Black Hawk Down' scenario among worries," *USA Today*, 18 March 2003, A1.
[90] Rachman, *Fear and Courage*, 60.
[91] Ibid., 200.
[92] Ibid., 205.
[93] Carl Benn, *The Iroquois in the War of 1812* (Toronto: University of Toronto Press, 1998), 82.
[94] Palmer, "The Emotion That Dare Not Speak Its Name," 32.
[95] Dollard, *Fear in Battle*, 2-3 & 24. They also felt that thinking the enemy is just as scared as you is also helpful in controlling fear.
[96] McManus, *The Deadly Brotherhood*, 251. It must be noted that some psychologists believe that an unnecessary focus on fear or sharing your feelings about being afraid may actually enhance your fears. See Palmer, "The Emotion That Dare Not Speak Its Name," 33 & 34.
[97] Training is defined as "a predictable response to a predictable situation," as opposed to education which is "the reasoned response to an unpredictable situation - critical thinking in the face of the unknown." Professor Ronald Haycock, former Dean of Arts, Royal Military College of Canada, "Clio and Mars in Canada: The Need for Military Education," presentation to the Canadian Club, Kingston, Ontario, 11 November 1999.
[98] Lyman, *Slim - Master of War*, 78.
[99] Masters, *The Road Past Mandalay*, 271.
[100] Dollard, *Fear in Battle*, 2-3, and Stouffer, *The American Soldier*, 195.
[101] Stouffer, *The American Soldier*, 223.
[102] Rachman, *Fear and Courage*, 63-64.
[103] Major Reg Crawford and Phil Mayne, "Professionals Accept High-Risk Employment," *Army*, No. 907 (27 June 1996), 3.
[104] Russell W. Glenn, *Capital Preservation - Preparing for Urban Operations in the Twenty-First Century* (Santa Monica: RAND Arroyo Center, 2001), 423.
[105] B.M. Bass, *Leadership and Performance Beyond Expectations* (New York: Free Press, 1985), 69.
[106] J.G. Hunt and J.D. Blair, *Leadership on the Future Battlefield* (New York: Brassey's, 1986), 215.
[107] Will Fowler, *The Commandos at Dieppe: Rehearsal for D-Day* (London: Harper Collins, 2002), 55.
[108] Montgomery, "Discipline from Morale in Battle," 66.
[109] Masters, *The Road Past Mandalay*, 198.
[110] Quoted in Fowler, *The Commandos at Dieppe*, 55.
[111] McManus, *The Deadly Brotherhood*, 247.
[112] Mark Urban, *Big Boys' Rules* (London: Faber & Faber, 1992), 178.

CHAPTER 7

[113] McManus, *The Deadly Brotherhood*, 233-34.
[114] Jeffrey Amherst, *Journal of William Amherst in America, 1758-1760* (London: Butler & Tanner Ltd., 1927), 24.
[115] Holmes, *Acts of War*, 249.
[116] Fowler, *The Commandos at Dieppe*, 138.
[117] Throughout history, all belligerents have used alcohol as a fortifying agent. For example, see Jünger, *Storm of Steel*, whose memoirs are filled with references to the use of alcohol to control fear.
[118] Lieutenant-Colonel Colin Mitchell, *Having Been a Soldier* (London: Mayflower Books, 1969), 41.
[119] Quoted in Canada, *CDS Guidance to Commanding Officers* (Ottawa: DND, 1999), 230.
[120] Sajer, *The Forgotten Soldier*, 180.
[121] Dollard, *Fear in Battle*, 3.
[122] Kellett, *Combat Motivation*, 281. Dollard's study found that 71 percent felt fear most acutely just before going into action, owing to the fact that they did not know what to expect.
[123] Palmer, "The Emotion That Dare Not Speak Its Name," 132.
[124] Holmes, *Acts of War*, 139.
[125] Ted Barris, *JUNO - Canadians at D-Day - June 6, 1944* (Toronto: Thomas Allen Publishers, 2004), 209.
[126] Kellett, *Combat Motivation*, 282.
[127] Chacho, "Why Did They Fight?," 80.
[128] Miller, *The Mystery of Courage*, 214.
[129] English, "A Predisposition to Cowardice?," 17.
[130] See Dollard, *Fear in Battle*, 28, and Rachman, *Fear and Courage*, 76.
[131] Lyman, *Slim - Master of War*, 108.
[132] Miller, *The Mystery of Courage*, 209.
[133] Rachman, *Fear and Courage*, 23 & 237.
[134] Ibid., 50.
[135] Dollard, *Fear in Battle*, 44.
[136] Dinter, *Hero or Coward*, 92.
[137] Stouffer, *The American Soldier*, 68.
[138] Kellett, *Combat Motivation*, 299.
[139] Dollard, *Fear in Battle*, 44.
[140] Anthony Kellet, "The Soldier in Battle: Motivational and Behavioural Aspects of the Combat Experience," in Betty Glad, ed., *Psychological Dimensions of War* (London: Sage Publications, 1990), 224.
[141] Stouffer, *The American Soldier*, 124.
[142] Grossman, *On Killing*, 85.
[143] Letter, Sergeant Andy Anderson to Bernd Horn, 10 January 2003.

CHAPTER 8

Disobedience of Professional Norms: Ethos, Responsibility Orientation and Somalia

George Shorey

> *Any army, ancient or modern, is a social construction defined by shared expectations and values. Some of these are embodied in formal regulations, defined authority, written orders, ranks, incentives, punishments, and formal task and occupational definitions. Others circulate as traditions, archetypal stories of things to be emulated or shunned, and accepted truth about what is praiseworthy and what is culpable. All together, these form a moral world that most of the participants most of the time regard as legitimate, "natural", and personally binding.*[1]

This chapter explores the relationship between Canadian military ethos, perceptions of responsibility and the impact of some of the social-psychological factors that can undermine professional behaviour during military operations. Reference to the Somalia incident involving Canadian Forces (CF) members in 1993 will be included in an effort to extend these concepts beyond the theoretical to the applied. This operational context has also been selected because it sheds light on the inextricable link between ethos, responsibility and action, and it offers lessons on how to minimize the likelihood of violating professional norms in the future. Prior to discussing how the role and interrelationship of ethos, individual responsibility and leadership apply to the disobedience of professional norms, the body of this chapter will address the Somali incident in terms of social-psychological factors that may, in part, explain why a number of individuals apparently diverged from their professional norms; the key role that individual perceptions of personal responsibility hold in terms of behaviour in situations calling for professional judgment and action will also be alluded to.

On 16 March 1993, a young Somali was detained in a bunker in the custody of two members of the Canadian Airborne Regiment (Cdn AB Regt), a master-corporal and a private soldier. Over the course of approximately four hours, and within earshot of other members of the regiment, Shidane Arone was subjected to a brutal beating that ultimately culminated in his death.[2] As a result of this incident, a range of charges and punishments (including dismissals from the CF and prison terms) were imposed on several participants. In turn, this incident contributed significantly to the decision to disband the regiment.

Whereas the *Report of the Commission of Inquiry into the Deployment of Canadian Forces to Somalia* (the Somalia Inquiry) emphasized failures in leadership as the overriding factor that influenced the conduct associated with this incident, other accounts highlighted the potential destructiveness of

CHAPTER 8

extreme in-group loyalty and the "hyper-investment" of certain Cdn AB Regt members in a "rebel-warrior" identity and sub-culture.[3] Two accounts, which provide an historical analysis and perspective on the Canadian Army in general and Airborne Regiment in particular, suggest that much of the conduct in question stemmed from a significant erosion of military professionalism, which was supplanted by careerism, and a diluted sense of responsibility amongst the CF officer corps.[4] As well, former members of the Cdn AB Regt's 2 Commando who served with the Unified Task Force (UNITAF) likely hold strong personal views based on their own first-hand experience as to what, how and why things went wrong.

Since this incident, and in part as a result of it, considerable attention has been focussed on military professionalism and leadership in the CF. A clear statement of the Canadian military ethos was enunciated in 2003 with the publication of *Duty with Honour: The Profession of Arms in Canada*.[5] In 2005, two companion works that articulate CF leadership doctrine and core concepts were endorsed by the Chief of the Defence Staff and released as foundation documents for leader training and education in the CF.[6] Central to these documents is an emphasis on certain core values, such as integrity, courage and humaneness, that are considered integral to the profession of arms in Canada.

Perceptions of personal responsibility and leader accountability in situations where ethically questionable direction has been given or actions (including inaction) have been observed, can vary in accordance with what individuals perceive as their principal obligations.[7] In relation to legitimate authority within a hierarchy where norms of obedience are strong, notions of personal responsibility are inclined toward a rule or role-oriented view. Both rule and role-oriented perceptions of responsibility can manifest themselves as individual acquiescence to legally and / or morally questionable observed actions, orders or directions. Value-based perceptions of responsibility, however, offer a counter to the potentially damaging responses that can result from rigid adherence (e.g., "just following orders" and "no one else questioned it") to distorted notions of certain obligations. Value-based perceptions imply the inclusion of independent moral judgment in situations where professional norms and the core values associated with them are being violated.[8]

Social-Psychological Factors in Somalia

This section focuses on the apparent lack of response on the part of many service personnel (bystanders) who either overheard or directly observed fellow members of the CF abusing the Somali detainee. The aim here is to draw attention to certain situational and group influences that can undermine bystander intervention, despite an awareness of wrongdoing and need for help. At least, these social-psychological forces may partially account for the responses and reported inaction of individuals in proximity to the bunker where Arone was being held. Research has revealed four factors that often negatively influence or undermine bystander willingness to intervene in the aid of others who are in physical distress or danger. They are:

1. the *bystander effect* and two related concepts, *diffusion of responsibility* and *normative social influence*;

2. *psychological distance,* which concerns the matter of relational distance between victims and witnesses to their distress;

3. *authorization,* which includes both formal and perceived tacit authority that legitimizes normally illegitimate behaviour or misconduct; and

4. concern regarding *personal consequences* or one's private assessment of the pros and cons of choosing to aid someone under threat or in distress.

Each of these factors may have influenced the behaviour of the bystanders who briefly visited or were near the bunker where Arone was being detained on the evening of 16 March 1993.

Bystander Effect

The March 1964 *New York Times* headline, "37 Who Saw Murder Didn't Call Police," concerned the murder of Catherine Genovese who, over a 30-minute period and within 100 feet of her apartment, was victim to three separate stabbing attacks.[9] With the exception of one man calling out from an upper-storey apartment window ("Let that girl alone!"), not one of some 36 other "observers" took any action to assist Genovese who several times screamed and cried out for help. This incident triggered considerable research into the question of what factors influence one's decision to either help others who are in physical distress or not. While it is a very complex issue, the research findings about bystander behaviour warrant attention in order to further a better understanding of both the Genovese affair and the Arone tragedy that occurred in Somalia some 29 years later.

It may seem reasonable to assume that the larger the number of people who witness a situation where someone in distress needs assistance, the more likely it is that the person in distress will receive help. In other words, the odds are increased that someone in the group of observers will take it upon him- or herself to intervene or assist in some way. The opposite, however, often proves to be the case. Awareness of the presence of other witnesses to an emergency or situation that calls for assistance can, in fact, undermine individual (observer) initiative and attempts to assist. This phenomenon has been well researched and is referred to as the *bystander effect*. It concerns the finding that people are often less likely to provide help when others are present.[10]

CHAPTER 8

Testimony given to the Somalia Inquiry (and other resources) make it clear that several individuals near the bunker where Arone was being beaten could hear his periodic screams, howling and crying-out. The *Report* concluded:

> During the time that Mr. Arone was being tortured and beaten to death, there were a number of Canadian soldiers in both the command and sentry posts. The distance from the command post to the bunker was 84 feet; from the sentry post to the bunker, 59 feet; from the bunker to the observation tower in Service Commando (across the road from the 2 Commando compound), 214 feet. One witness recalled hearing a 'yelp' from the bunker, and stated 'I recall everybody kind of looking in the direction of the bunker, and then just kind of went back to what they were doing.' There was also evidence that soldiers in the observation tower heard screaming (at a distance of 214 feet). Certainly, Arone's howls were heard by many over the operating noise of a nearby diesel generator.[11]

In addition to those "bystanders" outside of the bunker who could hear portions of what was happening, it was estimated by another, detailed account of the incident that "… during the course of the evening perhaps seventeen individuals came by the bunker, looked in, and left without commenting or interfering."[12]

Closely aligned to the *bystander effect* is the finding that individuals often feel that they have less responsibility to act in situations where multiple witnesses are present. This notion of *diffusion of responsibility* suggests that while, in general, people may feel some responsibility for helping others in distress, often "…when other people are present, the feeling of responsibility gets diffused. Every single person feels less responsible to act." With few exceptions, most people who are faced with a sudden need to act are much less likely to respond if other people actually are, or are believed to be, available.[13] Given the proximity of the command and sentry posts to the bunker, it is reasonable to suggest that those in the bunker vicinity might well have assumed that others (in particular those on duty that evening and / or functioning in a leadership capacity) were "believed to be available" to intervene. As in the Genovese case, individuals were aware that many others were co-bystanders to the incidents, which therefore reinforced a diffused sense of responsibility.

Another factor that can reinforce the *bystander effect* is the undercurrent of anxiety that can arise over possibly being evaluated by others who are present at an incident. A possible negative evaluation and the resulting disapproval of other bystanders and / or seniors (through appearing foolish or incompetent, or by engaging in behaviour considered by others present to be inappropriate) are of particular concern to potential participants. This concern can inhibit action if witnesses conclude that the "appropriate" response or situational norm is *not* to take any helping action at all. The influence (on individuals) of cues on how to respond, based on the actions of those around them, should not be underestimated:

> The evidence shows that by what they say, by what they do, or by their inaction people affect others' reactions to emergencies. They do this by affecting the interpretation or perceived meaning of the stimulus, whether it is an emergency or not, by affecting the assessment of appropriate reaction to it, or by producing compliance with their interpretation and with their implied expectation about how to react.[14]

Certain testimony in the Somalia Inquiry *Report* [15] reinforced the notion that the underlying attitude and dominant "cue" amongst bystanders to the Arone killing may have been the idea that some punishment of "infiltrators" would serve as a deterrent. Such a rationalization could have fuelled a degree of acceptance, captured in such comments as "...the tougher we look the better respect we'll get" and "we're going to sort them out. We're going to teach them a lesson." This element underlying the *bystander effect* has been termed the *normative social influence*. The critical factor here is what the bystander believes others think is appropriate. If one believes that it is normatively appropriate to help, then others' awareness of the bystander's behaviour should facilitate helping.[16] Conversely, if no one is observed taking action to assist, as in the Genovese murder and arguably in the case of Arone, such a collective response of inaction can prove to be an inhibiting influence.

It is important to note that "...often people are likely to act not according to *generalized* expectations about behaviour embodied in norms, but according to *specific* expectations implied or communicated by other people who are present, even if the specific expectations are contrary to normative expectations."[17] That is, the behavioural responses of those involved in the immediate dynamics of the situation may result in collective behaviour contrary to what might normally be considered an appropriate or commonsense response. In essence, situational forces can at times impel individuals to act out of character. As such, this component of the *bystander effect* may certainly have contributed to the failure of witnesses and bystanders in the vicinity of the 2 Commando bunker to intervene. While the *bystander effect* and its associated *diffusion of responsibility* and *normative social influence* aspects have received considerable support in the psychological literature as powerful forces that can undermine observer intervention, other factors may also have contributed to bystander inaction during Arone's detention.

Psychological Distance from the Victim

What was the nature of the relationship between those who briefly visited, or were in the immediate vicinity of the bunker, and the young Somali who was

CHAPTER 8

being beaten therein? Several accounts, including the *Report*, highlight the issue of camp security as having been an ongoing concern. For instance, the *Report* stated:

> ...one of the most aggravating problems facing the Canadian Airborne Regiment Battle Group (CARBG) was theft. Security for the Canadian base in the layout used in Belet Huen was hindered by insufficient wire for the perimeter of the compound. By the end of January, the troops were dealing routinely with individuals and small groups of Somalis trying to steal Canadian equipment, supplies and personal property. Sometimes only scrap and other minor items such as water cans were taken; however, other things were also stolen, including food, water, gear, radios and parachute equipment.[18]

Other UNITAF contingents also found the issue of theft and penetration into their bases to be a "major concern." Further, it has been reported, "at the end of January 1993, the infiltration had become endemic. ... To make matters worse, Somalis armed with knives or small arms began setting up roadblocks near Belet Huen after dark, robbing people and challenging the authority of the Canadian contingent."[19] A soldier quoted in a study prepared for the Somalia Inquiry stated:

> I don't think anybody likes a thief. There is nothing worse than a liar and a thief. The guys were getting tired of it. Very, very frustrated. And you got to remember, if you're sleeping, it's like, Gurkha [sic] used to come in and slit peoples throats. Internal security really threatens people. That sort of victim feeling, that emptiness.[20]

Irrespective of the labels assigned to those Somalis who breached the compound boundaries – "infiltrator," "thief," "looter" – they were considered to be a significant threat and an ongoing problem. As to how to describe the relationship between Arone and those who either saw or heard him over the four hours that he was being beaten, it would seem that he was largely viewed impersonally, or in other words, as an unknown thief warranting little empathy. Based on testimony given to the Board of Inquiry and on research related to "helping behaviour," there is much to suggest that this was indeed the case. Coupled with being marked as an intruder and a thief, the cultural and social gap between Arone and his captors only increased the psychological distance between them. Donna Winslow's study of the Cdn AB Regt in Somalia provides several testimonial accounts of this "gap" and offers a particularly striking example that captures a number of the issues that increased the psychological distance between Airborne soldiers and the Somalis. As one individual noted:

> A lot of the guys had problems with the culture as well. In the sense of the poverty that they saw and for a lot of the guys they had a hard

time to see how the women were treated. In the sense that men didn't do a lot of the work, the women did all the household chores, if you want to call them that – going to get the water, the food, the wood for fire. So it seemed that the women were being unjustly treated and the men were being very lazy. Because you would see the men in groups, talking and talking. Also they hold hands. When the guys saw that well everyone thought, "Everybody's gay here! What's going on!" Of course that's the way the Somalis express their friendship. You never saw that, men and women holding hands there. That's taboo, as far as the Muslims are, but still to a lot of soldiers that part of the world is bad, it's wrong. They don't know how to live.[21]

Social science research on the nature of the bystander-victim relationship has consistently demonstrated that people exhibit greater empathy in response to the distress of "similar others" than the distress of "dissimilar others." Studies of ethical decision-making have found that people care more about other people who are close to them (socially, culturally, psychologically or physically) than they do for people who are distant.[22] Similarly, other studies have noted, "guilt and blame for not helping, would likely be relatively high when feelings of closeness, attraction ... or we-ness characterize the bystander-victim relationship."[23]

While it is not the intent here to imply a direct comparison of the Somalia episode to the My Lai massacre of some 400 unarmed villagers by US servicemen in March 1968 during the Vietnam War, some of the underlying causes of both incidents are indeed similar. Interestingly, research into the latter event highlighted the extreme implications of psychological distancing. "Dehumanization" was found to be a key element that underscored sanctioned massacres. Specifically, "psychological distancing often occurs when the victims have been dehumanized – categorized as inferior or dangerous beings and identified by derogatory labels – so that they are excluded from the bonds of human empathy and protection of moral rules."[24] In particular:

> ...victims must be stripped of their human status. Insofar as they are dehumanized, the usual principles of morality no longer apply to them; ...often the victims belong to a distinct racial, religious, ethnic, or political group regarded as inferior or sinister. Labels help deprive the victims of identity and community, as in the epithet "gooks" that was commonly used to refer to Vietnamese and other Indochinese peoples.[25]

Although the Somalia Inquiry *Report* made reference to both the use of derogatory slurs of a racial nature (e.g., "smufties" and "nig-nogs") and a limited understanding amongst some Cdn AB Regt soldiers as to what constituted racist behaviour, it did not conclude or imply that the unit was racist. In fact, soldiers felt that many of the comments highlighted in media reports were presented out of context. Soldiers did acknowledge that some members held racist attitudes, but they did not consider them out of proportion to their civilian counterparts in Canadian society. For instance:

> What the army does, and does pretty well, is teach men to work with others, even though they may not want to. To some degree there is more tolerance in the army than in most civilian occupations. So while there is racism, it isn't the same as Civvy Street. And when you think about it, it's how you treat people that counts, not what you think of them privately.[26]

And again:

> They were called thieves, looters, not Somali harvesters picking up things, not recyclers but looters. A lot of Somali behaviour was classed as looting, which I think is a derogatory assumption. They were dirty and looters, these are the two concepts that seemed to be understood by Airborne soldiers.[27]

The label of "thief" or "looter" generally carries strong negative connotations and usually categorizes the individual as being outside the community of decent citizenry. Those deemed to be guilty of theft, and who therefore pose a threat to security, are generally viewed as deserving of punishment, to both right the wrong(s) committed and to contain the threat that they pose. There was probably little that was positive in bystander attitudes toward Shidane Arone, given his probable classification as a thief, and thus a threat to the compound. It is worth noting that, given the interdependent nature of military service and the high value placed on mutual trust, an individual exposed as a thief within the military is looked upon with particular disdain. The foregoing is certainly not meant to suggest that the bystanders were prepared to ignore or sanction a murder, but rather that their psychological distance from Arone fostered (likely in combination with other factors such as the *bystander effect*) an apparent apathy toward actively responding to the abuse that was taking place. Having discussed the potential impact of both the *bystander effect* and the matter of *psychological distance*, the influence of *authorization* needs to be considered. As will be seen, tacit authorization can at times prove as potent as authority that is formally sanctioned.

Authorization

While captured Somali intruders were not prisoners of war (PW), they were nonetheless to be treated within the spirit of the Geneva Conventions of 1949 and the relevant aspects of the Additional Protocols to the Conventions. The basic rules of International Humanitarian Law provide treatment guidelines for PWs and certain fundamental guarantees for those held in custody:

> ... Among the fundamental guarantees, it is specified that the person, the honour, the convictions and religious practices of all such persons must be respected. The following acts in particular are prohibited under any pretext whatever, whether committed by civil or military agents:
>
> 1. violence to the life, health and physical or mental well-being of persons, particularly: murder; torture of all kinds; corporal punishment; mutilation;
>
> 2. outrages upon personal dignity, in particular humiliating and degrading treatment, enforced prostitution and any form of indecent assault;
>
> 3. the taking of hostages;
>
> 4. collective punishments; and,
>
> 5. threats to commit any of the foregoing acts.[28]

Contrary to these obligations under humanitarian law and the CF guidelines espoused in leader education and training concerning the treatment of captured combatants or civilians who pose a threat to security, abusive treatment of detainees was authorized at a Orders Group on the morning of 16 March 1993 by the Officer Commanding (OC), 2 Commando. This officer testified later at his own court-martial that he had said, "I don't care if you abuse them but I want those infiltrators captured.... Abuse them if you have to. I do not want weapons used. I do not want gun fire."[29] Interpretation of this order – as to the nature and degree of abuse that had been advocated – varied amongst platoon and section commanders. It was not clear whether such treatment was restricted to the capturing of infiltrators or applicable throughout their detention once in custody. Irrespective of these nuances, the use of physical force had been authorized.

Furthermore, the powerful influence of authorization can spawn a certain loss of restraint and moral suspension:

> Thus when acts of violence are explicitly ordered, implicitly encouraged, tacitly approved, or at least permitted by legitimate authorities, people's readiness to commit or condone them is considerably enhanced. The fact that such acts are authorized seems to carry automatic justification for them. Behaviorally, authorization

obviates the necessity of making judgments or choices...normal moral principles become inoperative.[30]

The extent to which bystanders to the incident were aware that at least a degree of abuse had been formally authorized is not clear. For instance, not all section commanders privy to the instructions given by the OC chose to pass them on to their section members. Additionally, some CF personnel who were bystanders to the incident were not members of 2 Commando, and therefore likely not aware of any explicit authorization to abuse detainees.

While several of the bystanders may not have been aware of any "formal" authorization, they might well have assumed that the abuse taking place had at least the tacit, "informal" approval of duty, staff and other officers and non-commissioned officers in the vicinity. Research that addresses the issue of crimes committed under seemingly tacit authorization has noted that:

> A similar mechanism operates when a person engages in antisocial behaviour that was not ordered by the authorities but was tacitly encouraged and approved by them – even if only by making it clear that such behaviour will not be punished. In this situation, behaviour that was formerly illegitimate is legitimized by the authorities' acquiescence.[31]

At issue, then, is that authorities can wield influence in terms of what constitutes acceptable actions and what does not, not only through overt communication channels, but equally, at times, through what they condone or fail to take any apparent stand on. For the bystanders who were at least partly aware of the severe beating being inflicted on Arone, it would seem reasonable that they might have regarded those authorities and others in leadership positions who were in the vicinity as approving of the beating. This apparent *authorization* of abuse, in conjunction with the *bystander effect* and the *psychological distance* from the victim, could certainly have contributed to the lack of bystander response associated with this tragedy.

Personal Consequences

The fourth and final social-psychological factor to be considered is the perception of bystanders as to the *personal consequences* that could result from either helping or not helping someone in distress. It is a subjective, somewhat intuitive, and often rapid personal assessment of the pros and cons of getting involved. Social research on this issue describes the "costs" that bystanders weigh as two distinct types – the costs of helping and the costs of not helping. Such research concludes that the "Costs of helping include physical and material costs, time, embarrassment, and feelings of inadequacy if help is ineffective. Costs of not helping include self-blame, public censure, and in some situations prosecution as a criminal."[32]

CHAPTER 8

Given that the beating of Arone had received tacit approval and that the responsibility to help had been diffused owing to the large number of soldiers who were within earshot of the beating, the perceived costs of *not* helping (such as public censure and fear of prosecution) were probably minimal. Indeed, the 4 March 1993 shooting of two suspected infiltrators by members of the Cdn AB Regt's Reconnaissance Platoon, in which one Somali, Mr. Aruush, was killed, and the other, Mr. Abdi, wounded, may have softened soldier attitudes toward the perceived severity of Arone's treatment and any serious concerns regarding the consequences of not coming to his aid. Certainly, the Somalia Inquiry *Report* highlighted the handling of the shooting incident by the chain of command as "weak" and "unjustifiable" and based on a "cursory Summary Investigation," strongly suggesting it "...may have made possible the torture death of a Somali youth 12 days later."[33] The *Report* essentially implies that the response of the senior leadership to the 4 March incident may well have sent the message to certain Airborne soldiers that they need not fear adverse consequences should they be involved in any questionable captures and / or mistreatment of Somali nationals in the future.

The potential negative costs of helping (such as being perceived as somewhat disloyal to the unit, embarrassing oneself and / or inviting a backlash from others who authorized or at least condoned the beating of Arone) were likely salient. This is suggested given that certain variables, namely, authorization, a weak bystander-victim relationship and a collective group mentality that seemingly condoned the violence that was taking place, were likely powerful influences in the context of the situation. As well, a final, subtle element – unit cohesion – may have played a role in bystander inaction. Unit cohesion is defined as "the bonding together of soldiers in such a way as to sustain their will and commitment to each other, the unit, and mission accomplishment, despite combat or mission stress."[34] The Cdn AB Regt's isolation in an outer sector of a strife-torn, foreign country, combined with their mutual dependence and need for collective security, could well have undermined the willingness of some who felt the need to assist Arone. That is, bystanders might have believed that they ran the risk of being perceived by their peers as somehow being disloyal and weakening solidarity if they voiced their concerns or otherwise acted to challenge what was knowingly taking place. The importance and power of cohesion, particularly for deployed units given their isolation, cannot be overestimated:

> Whether the small unit is the dominant primary group for the individual soldier is of the utmost importance. Primary social affiliation within the unit is an extremely significant indicator of cohesion because it means that the small military unit has replaced other influences such as the family as the primary determinant of the soldier's day-to-day behaviour. In such a unit, the soldier becomes bound by the expectations and needs of his fellow soldiers. Such relationships

completely overshadow other obligations and claims on his loyalties.... The soldier merely recognizes that more immediate considerations and relationships have displaced family, parents, and friends as the prime determinant of his behaviour. Despite the intensity of the relationship, it is not usually seen as permanent but as one that is limited to a specific period or to the duration of the conflict.[35]

Considering the importance placed on building and maintaining unit solidarity, particularly for operational units, cohesion should be recognized as a force that may have prevented bystanders from helping Arone. This is where the potential dark side of strong cohesion can surface, whereby maintaining unity at all costs becomes a dominant norm, irrespective of what the situation demands. In short, the personal costs to bystanders associated with *not* helping Arone were likely perceived as limited, while the potential consequences of intervening were not seen to warrant the effort. On the balance, as in the Genovese case, it would seem that for the majority of bystanders who were at least partial witnesses to Arone's final few hours, complicity and the personal decision not to get involved proved dominant.

At this point, it should be evident that the social-psychological processes associated with being one of several bystanders witnessing a tacitly authorized beating, combined with having little or no relationship with the victim, or concern regarding the repercussions of not challenging the abuse being inflicted, were powerful forces that undermined intervention. Although these factors alone do not fully account for the lack of bystander response associated with Shidane Arone's death, nor do they provide any condolence for those personally affected by the tragedy, they can serve to further our understanding by providing a degree of explanation as to why so many knowingly stood by. While the foregoing is an accurate account of the majority reaction, it would be remiss to give the impression that all bystanders and unit leaders simply stood by or condoned the order to abuse detainees. There were a few individuals who let their seniors know that they were concerned about the treatment of Arone; there were also some leaders who were not prepared to pass on the abuse authorization to their section members.[36] Unfortunately, the follow-up to these actions was non-existent, insufficient or too late to check what was continuing to unfold in the bunker.

Responsibility Orientation

Although awareness of the possible insidious effects of the social-psychological influences that can surface in Somali-like contexts is an important starting point on the road to minimizing their impact, what additional factors offer a potential counter to their rise? Distinct features within the triad of individual responsibility orientation, leadership and overarching ethos should, it is suggested, come to the fore. The concept of *responsibility ori-*

entation concerns what individuals serving in a hierarchical organization (such as the military) regard as their principal responsibility obligation(s). That is, which obligations hold sway, for example, when they are under pressure to respond in the face of direction or tacitly authorized behaviour that is ethically questionable. Researchers addressing the subject of crimes of obedience note, "…we consider it likely that subordinates' conception of their own responsibility plays an important role in their actual response to questionable orders: in their relative sensitivity to binding or opposing forces and in their tendency to obey or disobey."[37] One's conception of their own responsibility, or *responsibility orientation*, can be categorized under three general types: 1) rule-based; 2) role-based; and, 3) value-based.[38]

Of note is that persons operating at the lower levels in hierarchies within a distinct chain of command are prone to adopt either rule- or role-based responsibility orientations. Rule-oriented subordinates are inclined to follow whatever appears to be authorized in an effort "to get by and stay out of trouble" and perceive responsibility "in terms of sanctions administered for non-compliance."[39] They tend to feel somewhat powerless to question authority and may defer personal culpability for their own actions to superiors in the chain of command with defences akin to "just following orders."

Ultimately, the actions of role-oriented subordinates are similar to those of rule-oriented individuals; the motives underlying the behaviour of the former, however, are based on a different rationale. *Responsibility orientation* aligned exclusively to one's role "leads subordinates to obey in order to do their duty and live up to authoritative expectations; responsibility is seen in terms of the obligations that adhere to the subordinate role."[40] In effect, subordinates that adhere to this orientation are susceptible to the distorted notion of equating loyalty to unquestioning obedience. Obedience is therefore viewed as an overriding obligation, amounting to, potentially, blind acceptance of questionable orders and the authority's definition of the situation and / or modes of behaviour that are harmful to others, yet seemingly condoned by their superiors.

As opposed to rule- and role-orientations, a value-orientation is characterized by the inclusion of independent judgment. That is, value-oriented individuals typically:

> …adhere to the rules and accept the role obligation to support and obey the authorities, but they bring independent judgement to bear on the authorities' demands, using their personal values as criteria. … applying independent judgement and making support and obedience contingent on its outcome (such as consequences to those affected by soldier actions) are essential features of this orientation.[41]

CHAPTER 8

Additionally, a value-oriented organization will hold individuals at all levels in the chain of command responsible for the consequences of those actions stemming from the directives and authorizations that led to them. The Somalia Inquiry *Report* noted this requirement for accountability when it observed, "Individuals can delegate the authority to act, but they cannot thereby delegate their assigned responsibility in relation to the proper performance of such acts."[42]

In a military context, value-orientation implies a personal and professional commitment to the values that distinguish professionalism in military service. For example, the principles underscoring the Law of War provide guidance in the formulation of targeting decisions and rules of engagement. Invariably, such values invoke moral parameters. Application of the principle of proportionality in the use of force is but one example. That detainees held by CF personnel are to be fairly and humanely treated, in accordance with the *spirit and intent* of the principles of the Third Geneva Convention is yet another.[43] Additional Canadian military values, such as moral courage and the concept of duty, supplementing those central to the Law of War and aligned to concepts of military professionalism and leadership, constitute the essentials of a value-oriented view of responsibility.

Given that the demands of contemporary operations can and will necessitate the application of professional judgment in isolated, high-stress situations at potentially all levels of the chain of command, a values-based orientation to responsibility would appear consistent with the need for self-confident, adaptive, thinking soldiers. The advent of mission command leadership from a tactical perspective denotes increased freedom of action, decision-making powers and use of initiative (within the parameters of the Commander's intent) and also highlights the relevance of an orientation that asserts responsibility. Indeed, the mission command philosophy in action serves to empower subordinates and incline them toward a professional, values-based orientation through encouraging lower level influence, judgment and responsibility. Emphasis on the development of an orientation that asserts responsibility should reinforce adherence to professional norms and in turn reduce the likelihood of disobedience.

Professional Ethos

The notion and importance of a values-oriented perception of responsibility is aligned to the concept of military ethos, which comprises values and beliefs considered fundamental to professionalism. Given that the values one respects can significantly shape behaviour, the importance of inculcating a sound professional military ethos cannot be overstated:

> Warrior's honor was both a code of belonging and an ethic of responsibility. Wherever the art of war was practiced, warriors distinguished

between combatants and non-combatants, legitimate and illegitimate targets, moral and immoral weaponry, civilized and barbarous usage in the treatment of prisoners and of the wounded. Such codes may have been honored as often in the breach as in the observance, but without them war is not war – it is no more than slaughter.[44]

Integral to the notion of warrior honour is the commitment to an abiding military ethos. Commitment here implies that the core values underscoring the ethos are consistently reflected in the actions of individual soldiers and their leaders, most critically when tested under the potential moral strains and physical threat(s) confronted on operations.

In the Canadian context, a recent statement of the Canadian military ethos has been formally promulgated with the publication of *Duty with Honour*, the profession of arms manual.[45] Its title makes explicit that professional military service is bounded by certain ethical obligations, select values and principles. A brief description of the Canadian military ethos will serve to define its scope and principal features. The framework of the ethos affirms a set of military values – duty, courage, integrity and loyalty – that are aligned to one's allegiance to Canada, the rule of law and the values expressed in the Canadian Charter of Rights and Freedoms. Buttressing the framework are four elements considered fundamental beliefs and expectations: 1) the acceptance of unlimited liability; 2) the maintenance of a high standard of personal discipline; 3) an emphasis on teamwork; and, 4) the cultivation of a fighting spirit committed to the primacy of operations.[46]

With reference to the apparent suspension of professional norms on the part of those in Somalia who chose not to intervene (despite their awareness of actions taking place that severely violated professional standards), the ethos appeals strongly to the concept and role of honour and how it is forged:

> Honour itself flows from practising the military ethos. It comes from being loyal to your unit and faithful to comrades in fulfilling your duties. It comes with adhering fully to the law of armed conflict, especially in humane treatment of prisoners of war. Honour insists that all non-combatants be protected and accorded the dignity and other considerations their situation may entitle them to ....[47]

Clear articulation of what comprises the professional military ethos is an essential first step in reducing resistance to authority by providing a foundation to guide early socialization and ongoing professional development efforts. The implementation of educational objectives on common training courses that promote the military ethos and unique requirements of the profession of arms will help ensure a common understanding of what it means. The publication of what might be regarded as a professional military *code* (i.e., the statement of the Canadian military ethos), combined with its inclusion on initial qualification and periodic professional development courses, serves the "formal," and in effect, the "theoretical" dimension of such an ethos.

The "practical" application of the ethos is dependent far more on the "informal," day-to-day attitudes and behaviours expressed by one's peers and leaders (i.e., the example set by those who most influence on a regular basis). The extent to which the "theoretical" is solidified or nullified (i.e., becomes an internalized, shared set of values and assumptions) will be directly proportional to the type of values practised and reinforced in the work setting. Research to this effect has observed that:

> ...formal socialization processes are often only the "first round" of socialization. The informal second round occurs when the newcomer is placed in his designated organizational slot and must learn informally the actual practices of his department. Whereas the first wave stresses general skills and attitudes, the second wave emphasizes specified actions, situational applications of the rules, and the idiosyncratic nuances necessary to perform the role in the work setting.[48]

Leadership Aspects

And in this capacity, leaders play a central role in cultivating a strong professional military ethos. When considering the matter of leadership and the Somali incident, the idea that the lack of intervention by bystanders in the chain of command can perhaps be explained by contextual influences (the social-psychological factors outlined earlier), comes up short. While these situational influences are real and can indeed undermine right action, commissioned officers, in particular, cannot hide behind such explanations. It is a truth that:

> In leadership, character matters. This is not to deny that evil people can bring about good things or that good people can lead the way to moral ruin. Rather, leadership provides a moral compass and, over the long term, both personal development and the common good are best served by a moral compass that reads true.[49]

The enduring principle of "leadership by example" stands out as the missing catalyst in adherence to the obligations of the professional military ethos (and those inherent in an Officer's Commission).

The earlier discussion on *responsibility orientation* highlighted the importance of forging a values-based perception of responsibility. The Canadian military ethos is consistent with this notion and reinforces the ethical dimension of professional military service. Leadership doctrine based on distrib-

CHAPTER 8

uted, values-based leadership, further supports this emphasis on the distinct values underlying the profession of arms and one's responsibility to uphold them. Leading by example implies just that, standing by the core values of the profession, particularly when faced with pressures to waiver from them. While much more easily pronounced than lived, compelling examples from history nonetheless serve as beacons. In David Grossman's compilation on the psychology of killing, one such instance provided by Glenn Gray, a Second World War intelligence officer who interviewed a German defector, offers pause for thought:

> In the Netherlands, the Dutch tell of a German soldier who was a member of an execution squad ordered to shoot innocent hostages. Suddenly he stepped out of rank and refused to participate in the execution. On the spot he was charged with treason by the officer in charge and was placed with the hostages, where he was promptly executed by his comrades. In an act the soldier has abandoned once and for all the security of the group and exposed himself to the ultimate demands of freedom. He responded in the crucial moment to the voice of conscience and was no longer driven by external commands...we can only guess what must have been the influence of his deed on slayers and slain. At all events, it was surely not slight, and those who hear of the episode cannot fail to be inspired.[50]

Even if not recognized by those associated with it at the time, the incident in Somalia was extreme, calling for some decisive intervention to put a stop to it. A young Somali in detention was being beaten and tortured, so much so that within a few hours he would die as a result. The needed action, however, did not take place. Most tragically, a life was lost. In turn, the event resulted in an attempted suicide by one of the perpetrators, the imprisonment of others, the destruction of careers, the disbandment of a regiment, and the smearing of an army and the Canada's armed forces. While it can only be inferred, the relevance to the incident of responsibility orientation, professional ethos and leadership by example, is by no means slight.

On the matter of inculcating ethos through informal socialization, the dominant, day-to-day attitudes and behaviours exhibited by fellow service members and leaders forge the unspoken norms that either strengthen or erode the values of the profession. Again, the example set by all, but in particular, by the leadership, will shape the culture and abiding ethos of the unit and institution. While operations can serve to test the strength of the ethos, ethos is cultivated over time in garrison, on challenging collective training, in unit and sub-unit efforts that foster cohesion and in the seemingly benign daily interactions and relationships of those in uniform. Similarly, it has been argued that well before operations begin, commanders should support the development of shared implicit intent which is based on unit members holding common expectations, values and beliefs which will ultimately support the explicit orders and direction communicated in-theatre.[51] While acknowledging the demanding personnel tempo at all levels in the Army, the development of ethos cannot be viewed as something to be relegated to periodic inoculation on professional development courses or in any way dismissed as a given or of secondary importance.

While this account is limited to a brief exploration of the interrelationship and application of ethos, responsibility orientation and leadership to the Somalia incident of 1993, these elements are deemed critical in complex operational situations that invoke the moral element. The stressors associated with contemporary missions can generate a simmering undercurrent of emotions, from frustration and anger, to despondency, guilt and revenge. Under such conditions, maintenance of a disciplined, professional self- and unit-perspective may prove one of the core demands confronting deployed military personnel in the 21st century. Ultimately, professionalism in the military equates to service with honour, the ongoing challenge will be for those in uniform to maintain that ideal as their central tenet.

ENDNOTES

[1] Jonathan Shay, *Achilles in Vietnam: Combat Trauma and the Undoing of Character* (New York: Touchstone, 1994), 6.

[2] *Dishonoured Legacy: The Lessons of the Somalia Affair* (*Report of the Commission of Inquiry into the Deployment of Canadian Forces to Somalia*, 1997), Vol. 1, Ch. 13 & 14. See also, B. Bergman and L. Fisher, "A Night of Terror: The Shocking Account of how Canadian Soldiers Tortured and Killed a Somali," *Maclean's*, 28 March 1994, 26-8.

[3] Donna Winslow, *The Canadian Airborne Regiment in Somalia: A Sociocultural Inquiry* (Ottawa: Minister of Public Works and Government Services Canada, 1997).

[4] David Bercuson, *Significant Incident: Canada's Army, the Airborne, and the Murder in Somalia* (Toronto: McClelland and Stewart Inc., 1996). See also, Peter Desbarats, *Somalia Cover-Up: A Commissioner's Journal* (Toronto: McClelland and Stewart, 1997).

[5] Canada, Department of National Defence [DND], *Duty with Honour: The Profession of Arms in Canada* (Kingston: Canadian Defence Academy - Canadian Forces Leadership Institute, 2003).

[6] DND, *Leadership in the Canadian Forces (Doctrine); Leadership in the Canadian Forces (Conceptual Foundations)*, (Kingston; Canadian Defence Academy - Canadian Forces Leadership Institute, 2005).

[7] Herbert C. Kelman and V. Lee Hamilton, *Crimes of Obedience* (New Haven: Yale University Press, 1989), 233-34.

[8] Kelman and Hamilton, *Crimes*, 316-17.

[9] M. Gansberg, "37 Who Saw Murder Didn't Call the Police," *New York Times*, 27 March 1964, 1 and 38.

[10] Latane, Bibb and Nida. "Ten Years of Research on Group Size and Helping," *Psychological Bulletin*, Vol. 89 (1981), 308-24. See also, J.F. Dovidio, "The Social Context of Helping" in L. Berkowitz, *Advances in Experimental Psychology*, Vol. 17, 1984, 398-99.
[11] *Dishonoured Legacy*, Vol. 1, 324.
[12] Peter Worthington and Kyle Brown, *Scapegoat: How the Army Betrayed Kyle Brown* (Toronto: McClelland-Bantam, 1997), 130. See also, Bergman and Fisher "A Night of Terror," 26, which provides brief testimonial accounts of several visits by different individuals to the bunker over the course of Arone's detention. As well, this article purports that a minimum of 16 people either heard or witnessed first-hand the assaults against him.
[13] Latane and Darley, "The Unresponsive Bystander: Why doesn't He Help?" in E. Staub, *Positive Social Behaviour and Morality*, Vol. 1, Ch. 3, 1978. Also see, Latane, Nida and Wilson (1981) in J.F. Dovidio, *Advances in Experimental Psychology*, Vol. 17, 399, 1984.
[14] E. Staub, "Positive Social Behavior and Morality" (Vol. 1, Ch. 3: *Determinants of People Helping Other People in Physical Distress*, 81, 1978).
[15] See especially, Volume 1.
[16] J.F. Dovidio, "The Social Context of Helping", 401, in L. Berkowitz, *Advances in Experimental Psychology*, Vol. 17, 1984.
[17] E. Staub, "Positive Social Behavior and Morality," Op. Cit., 89.
[18] *Dishonoured Legacy*, Vol. 1, 293.
[19] Bercuson, *Significant Incident*, 233.
[20] Winslow, *The Canadian Airborne Regiment in Somalia*, 241.
[21] Ibid, 232.
[22] T.M. Jones, "Ethical Decision Making by Individuals in Organizations: An Issue-contingent Model," *Academy of Management Review*, Vol. 16 (1991), 376-77. See also, the discussion of the concept of psychological distance as a moral buffer in David Grossman, *On Killing: The Psychological Cost of Learning to Kill in War and Society* (New York: Little, Brown & Co., 1995).
[23] J.F. Dovidio, Op. Cit., 404.
[24] Kelman and Hamilton, *Crimes*, 336.
[25] Ibid., 19.
[26] Worthington and Brown, *Scapegoat*, 61.
[27] Winslow, *The Canadian Airborne Regiment in Somalia*, 253.
[28] International Committee of the Red Cross, *Basic Rules of the Geneva Conventions and Their Additional Protocols* (Geneva, 1983). The CF adopted this document as DND Publication A-JS-007-008/JD-006. See also, the reference to the training of Canadian soldiers in the laws of war in Bercuson, *Significant Incident*, 5-6.
[29] *Dishonoured Legacy*, Vol. 1, 319.
[30] Kelman and Hamilton, *Crimes*, 16.
[31] Ibid., 16-7.

CHAPTER 8

[32] E. Staub, Positive Social Behaviour and Morality, (Vol. 1: *Stimulus Characteristics That Affect Helping*), 109.

[33] *Dishonoured Legacy*, Executive Summary, ES-35.

[34] E. Meyer (1982) in Gal and Mangelsdorff, *Handbook of Military Psychology*, 457.

[35] W.D. Henderson, *Cohesion: The Human Element in Combat* (Washington, D.C.: National Defense University Press, 1985), 14.

[36] *Dishonoured Legacy*, Vol. 1, 320-23. Although largely overshadowed by events and the reaction of the majority, the actions referred to and briefly mentioned in this section of the Somalia *Report* are worthy of note. They seem, at least, like attempts by certain unit personnel to counter both the abuse order and to make superiors aware of the severity of the treatment inflicted on Arone.

[37] Kelman and Hamilton, *Crimes*, 315.

[38] Ibid, 315-21.

[39] Ibid, 317.

[40] Ibid.

[41] Ibid.

[42] *Dishonoured Legacy*, Vol. 2, 393.

[43] Commander Land Force Command, *Dispatches: The Law of Armed Conflict*, Vol. 4, No. 2 (1997), 28-9.

[44] Michael Ignatieff, *The Warrior's Honor: Ethnic War and the Modern Conscience* (Toronto: Penguin Books, 1999), 117.

[45] *Duty with Honour*, Ch. 2.

[46] Ibid.

[47] Ibid, 32.

[48] J.V. Maanen, *People Processing: Strategies of Organizational Socialization* in Organizational Dynamics, Summer 1978, 22-3.

[49] B.M. Bass and P. Steidlmeier, *Ethics, Character and Authentic Transformational Leadership Behavior*, Leadership Quarterly, 1999, 193.

[50] Grossman, *On Killing, 225-26*.

[51] Carol McCann and Ross Pigeau in *Future Force: Concepts for Future Army Capabilities*, (Kingston, ON: DLSC, 2003), 104-06.

CHAPTER 9

"We Don't Like You, Sir!" – Informal Revenge as a Mode of Military Resistance in the British Army

Charles Kirke

It was only after the forward observation party had returned to camp that the captain realized that he had lost his pistol. The consequences were clear: he would be court-martialled for such a serious offence, thus ending his career. The weapon must have disappeared during the exercise, but he could not determine exactly when, and his crew were of no help. They shrugged their shoulders politely, but did not express any direct concern or sympathy, and proceeded to clean their vehicle. The captain did not sleep well that night, in spite of being tired after several days in the field. Two days later, however, the pistol suddenly reappeared, if in a rather muddy state. To say that the captain was relieved would have been a gross understatement. He was an ambitious officer and the blow had laid him very low indeed. But how could his pistol have turned up so mysteriously?

The truth was never officially known, but it came out later, albeit informally. The roots of this incident were long-standing. The captain was a strict disciplinarian, which was acceptable but tedious to his soldiers, and he combined his overbearing manner with a lack of any apparent interest in his men. He found little time to get to know them and he did not listen to them. Furthermore, he was not very skilled in those minor everyday chores that add to the credibility of a soldier of any rank. In particular, he neglected his personal weapon (i.e., the pistol), for he neither cleaned it properly nor ensured that he knew where it was at all times. A gulf soon resulted between the captain and his men in which the soldiers harboured a deep lack of soldierly respect for him. The crew were frustrated with their officer and wanted to send him a powerful message that he could not mistake, so they had done something about it. While he had been asleep during the last night of the exercise, they had taken his pistol and buried it not far from the vehicle, fully knowing the consequences that he would suffer for losing his personal weapon.

In taking this action, the soldiers had committed at least two potentially serious offences under military law, as set out in the British Army Act 1955.[1] They had caused the loss of Service property (contrary to Section 44(1)) [2] and, in taking concerted action against a superior officer, had engaged in conduct to the prejudice of military discipline (contrary to Section 69).[3] The key player in the series of events that led to the recovery of the pistol was the Battery Sergeant-Major who had noticed the poor relationship between the captain and his crew. He eventually took the crew commander, who was a junior Non-Commissioned Officer (NCO), to one side, and told him that the captain had now learned his lesson and that the pistol had better reappear before the following morning. In spite of the technical seriousness of what they had done, no disciplinary action was ever taken against the perpetrators and the incident officially remained a mystery.

This episode, which is based on real events in a unit of the British Army some time during the past twenty-five years, has a number of characteristics that are highly relevant to this chapter. On the surface, it appears to be a manifestation of what the anthropological literature calls "resistance" or counter-action by the weak and underprivileged against their oppressors. As will become evident, however, this form of activity has a special place in the British Army's organizational culture that distinguishes it from the normal field of resistance. For the moment, it is sufficient to note that the action was reversible, that no permanent damage was done, and that those who carried it out were not punished, although the Battery Sergeant-Major, a key member of the disciplinary chain, had in fact identified them. In short, it was a low-key event that did not upset the smooth running of life in the unit, but it carried a profound message.

This chapter concerns this very particular form of resistance in the British Army, called here "informal revenge," and how it is played out in the context in which it takes place. This chapter will begin with a consideration of the generic subject of resistance and will then consider the organizational culture of British military units, which provide the context. A few case studies will then be examined and some conclusions about the phenomenon of "informal revenge" will be drawn. Finally, the relevance of "informal revenge" to the Canadian Forces (CF) will be considered. In accordance with good anthropological practice, all examples and interview material used in this chapter are anonymous and names, when used, are pseudonyms. The significant social context, however, has been preserved.

Resistance

The topic of resistance as a manifestation of how the oppressed seek to redress or undermine the balance of power set against them has attracted a great deal of interest and effort over the past 30 years.[4] A concerted focus appears to have begun in the 1980s and the subject has been a perennial issue ever since in the social science literature. It is in the spirit of late-20th and early-21st century social science to seek out and expose oppression in many different forms, and resistance has been identified and expounded upon in those fields where political or social oppression has been found.[5] Areas that have attracted a great deal of attention, for example, have been the oppression of ethnic minorities, class and economic oppression, and gender oppression.

A significant criticism of the resistance literature is not so much that it is misguided *per se*, but rather that a particular concentration on resistance takes

CHAPTER 9

the researcher's eye away from other important social processes that may be occurring. For instance, Sherry Ortner has detected processes that she calls "sanitizing politics" (reducing politics to the single issue of oppression and resistance), "thinning culture" (ignoring the rich complexities of culture in the search for resistance) and "dissolving subjects" (not giving individual human agents a voice or a point of view).[6] In a similar vein, Michael Brown has warned against an excessive preoccupation with resistance that, in his view, reduces the study of rich and complex societies to a single issue.[7] In light of such critiques, then, this chapter will demonstrate that the social significance of cases of resistance in the British Army can only be understood when the wider organizational culture is considered.

Of the body of literature on resistance, the one work selected as the main starting point for this chapter is James C. Scott's *Weapons of the Weak*.[8] Not only is it regarded as one of the seminal volumes on practical resistance, but it also deals primarily with what he calls "everyday resistance," the constant, low-key reaction by the oppressed against the powerful. Scott contrasts such "everyday resistance" with the dramatic acts of resistance – rebellions, revolutions and attempts to establish alternative governments – that are rare in history, but attract far more attention because they are easily noticeable.[9] We can similarly contrast the type of "everyday resistance" in a military unit, as exemplified by "informal revenge," with much more rare and dramatic acts such as mutiny.

Scott's views arose from his study of life in a peasant village in Malaysia where a considerable economic gulf between rich and poor existed. A government irrigation scheme, which had been set in motion before his study was undertaken, had led to double-cropping and the wealth thus released had led to the eventual replacement of manual labour by mechanical implements such as tractors and combine-harvesters. Thus, the rich became more efficient and rich, whilst the poor could no longer sell their labour to enhance their income and thereby became poorer. The result was a growing differential of power between rich and poor. Scott describes the processes involved at great length, and in the second half of his book, he considers the ways in which the poor resist the power of the rich and counter their ideology and interests. The methods he identifies are usually so pitched as to express frustration and anger, but not to invoke punishment. Such methods include gossip (inherently behind the back of the person being maligned), petty acts of non-compliance that are not in themselves blameworthy, foot-dragging, dissimulation and so on. Where such acts are illegal, they are carried out anonymously. As Scott notes:

> Nearly all the resistance we have encountered in Sedaka is the kind of resistance that rather effectively "covers its own tracks". A snub on the village path can be excused later by haste or inattention.

What appears to be a boycott of transplanting can be rationalised as a delay or difficulties in assembling the workforce. And of course, acts of theft, sabotage, and vandalism have no authors at all. Thus, while there is a fair amount of resistance in Sedaka, there are virtually no publicly announced resistance or troublemakers.[10]

The match between Scott's model and the incident of the captain's missing pistol is a reasonable fit. In the latter, there was a power gap between the members of the crew and the officer, in that the captain had authority over them as conveyed by his superior rank and reinforced in law by the disciplinary code contained within the *Manual of Military Law*.[11] The act of removing the pistol, illegal as it was, had had "no authors at all."

More specifically, John Hockey has provided a British military example of resistance in *Squaddies: Portrait of a Subculture*.[12] This work is an ethnographic account of infantry soldiers first in recruit training, then in a formed unit in barracks after training, and finally on operations in Northern Ireland. It is an important work because it was the first attempt at the time to describe the Army's organisational culture at the unit level, albeit purely from a private soldier's viewpoint, and it remains one of only a very small number of works on this subject.[13] One of his principal theoretical contributions is the characterization of what he calls the "negotiated order" in the Army. Drawing on earlier work by Strauss *et al*,[14] he notes that private soldiers have the capacity to make officers and NCOs look less competent by carrying out what he calls "unofficial" activity. In response, officers and NCOs protect themselves by making life less difficult for the privates. Hockey notes:

> Evasion by skiving [avoiding work], making life more comfortable by scrounging [taking ownership of useful objects found lying around] and giving barely or less than adequate work performances to embarrass superiors, the use of ridicule, mimicry and even the application of official procedures to inconvenience those in command such as 'saluting traps' [several soldiers approaching officers singly to make them salute over and over again], were all gambits in evidence. ... Superiors are well aware that good working relationships are mandatory for units to function well, be they Brick [small patrol] or Battalion. The result is the operation of a negotiated order in the way I have described, in which a relaxed interpretation of military law is traded-off for effective role performance.[15]

The "negotiated order," as Hockey sees it, thus lies in the balance between the potential formal power of the officers and NCOs and the potential for the soldiers to make life difficult for them. In short, this is resistance for a purpose, that is to say, changing the application of power by the powerful. Hockey's main contribution in this area is showing how apparently powerless individuals and groups at the bottom of the British military hierarchy can act effectively against those with institutional power to curb their use of that power. The case of the captain's pistol might therefore be seen as a reaction by the vehicle crew against their officer's behaviour towards them: in giving him a severe fright (by threatening his career), they were raising the stakes in the negotiation.

British Army Unit Organizational Culture

The present chapter goes beyond the level of analysis offered by both Scott and Hockey, important as it is, and locates acts of resistance within a model of British Army unit organizational culture developed by the author during research in the British Army, mainly between 1993 and 2002.[16] Such an approach will add further dimensions to the two-dimensional image of polarization between the powerful and oppressed, the authorities and the resisters. A more complete account of British Army organizational culture at unit level appears in another volume that is soon to be released by the Canadian Forces Leadership Institute.[17] What follows is a summary only. British Army organizational culture at the unit level can be modelled using "social structure" as a core element. "Social structure" as a general concept has been under sustained attack in the past 20 years or so, and for very sound reasons. Early social scientists such as Emile Durkheim appeared to treat the organizing principles and structural forces in society as an empirical entity, a vital ingredient that was greater than the sum of its individual human parts.[18] This entity, "social structure," seemed to be thought of as in some way compelling the members of that society to behave in accordance with itself. In more recent times, those like Anthony Giddens, whose analytical frameworks are the individual agent and the processes of everyday life, have successfully attacked this position.[19] In essence, consideration of agency and process conceptually liberates the social scientist from any idea that the members of a human group are pawns compelled by the overarching pressures of "society." They could always "have acted otherwise."[20]

The present study, arising out of the author's research, uses the idea of "social structure," but in a way that is conceptually different from Durkheim and his followers. Rather than being an empirical entity, "social structure" is treated here as a model that helps us to understand what is going on in the everyday life of a British Army unit. It represents a shared body of ideas, rules and conventions of behaviour that guides groups of people or individuals in organizing and conducting themselves, vis-à-vis each other. The concept is therefore a way of modelling the background to, and framework for, the daily lives of all members of the unit. These individual agents navigate their own way through the various situations and contexts in which they find

CHAPTER 9

themselves, using the "social structure" as a reference point and guide. Like all models, it does not fit every possible situation, but it is a considerable aid to describing, analysing, explaining, and in some cases predicting, soldiers' behaviour. In the context of this model, and indeed the present chapter, "soldier" refers to any member of a unit regardless of rank.

Social Structures

After a fruitless search for a single "social structure" that might model soldiers' behaviour in all contexts, four separately identifiable "social structures," that is, bodies of ideas, rules and conventions of behaviour, were characterized, each concerned with different and separable elements in a soldier's life in the unit.[21] They are:

1. The *formal command structure*, which is the structure through which a soldier at the bottom receives orders from the soldier at the top. It is embedded in, and expressed by, the hierarchy of rank and the formal arrangement of the unit into layer upon layer of organizational elements. It contains the mechanisms for the enforcement of discipline, for the downward flow of orders and instructions, for the upward flow of reports, and it provides the framework for official responsibility. It also determines, through the formal Unit Establishment document, the exact position of each member in the organization.

2. The *informal structure*, which consists of unwritten conventions of behaviour in the absence of formal constraints, includes behaviour off-duty and in relaxed duty contexts. An important element in this structure is the web of informal relationships within the unit that are explored below.

3. The *loyalty / identity structure*, which is encapsulated by the concept of "belonging." Belonging is manifested most obviously in the nesting series of different sized groups that are defined by opposition to, and contrast with, other groups of equal status in the *formal command structure*. This nesting series consists of the various organizational levels from the small to the large that are the structure of all military units. A British infantry private soldier, for example, has full membership of his fire team, his section, his platoon, his company, his battalion and (above battalion level) his regiment. The level at which he exercises his membership at any particular moment depends on the level of comparison. This same infantry soldier would express his identity as a member of his platoon and feel loyalty to it in competition with other platoons of the same company. However, where his company is in competition with other companies, these attitudes and feelings would be transferred to the company, rather than to the platoon, and this process can be continued up to levels beyond the unit (and down to those below the platoon). The

social structure, the "body of ideas, rules and conventions of behaviour," consists in the attitudes, feelings and expectations of soldiers toward these groups and their membership. These attitudes and feelings can be effectively captured in the overarching concept that "we are the best," at whatever organizational level the "we" is placed.

4. The *functional structure* consists of attitudes, feelings and expectations connected with being "soldierly" and properly carrying out "soldierly" activity.

A significant feature of this model is that an individual only operates in a single social structure at any one instant, although he or she may transit from one social structure to another, sometimes very rapidly. Thus, for example, when a group of soldiers who are maintaining a vehicle take a "smoke break," they move from the *functional structure* (working on the vehicle) to the *informal structure* (relaxing and chatting). Similarly, a group of soldiers present on morning parade (*formal command structure*) transit to the *functional structure* when they are dismissed to begin their morning's work. The social structure of the moment is called the *operating structure* in the model.

Informal Relationships

This model has been extended in a number of ways, two of which are highly relevant to the area of resistance. The first addresses the range of social relationships encountered in the *informal structure* and the second addresses the ways in which soldiers bend or break formal rules. The importance of informal relationships in the present chapter is that they provide simultaneous channels of communication for every soldier, through his or her personal network, regardless of rank differences. At first sight, it might be deduced that informal relationships are a matter of free choice as they are not subject to formal rules, but it was found during the research that there is a distinct and generally accepted set of conventions in this area that are seldom broken. These conventions can be captured by breaking down the range of informal relationships into five categories that are separable by the observed behaviour of the individuals exercising them. These categories were given special terms in the model and include:

1. *Close Friendship*. This relationship consists of a durable bond that transcends the military environment and includes a large measure of trust and respect between the parties and few barriers to discussion of highly personal matters. It is a rare and special relationship. In the words of one warrant officer from a particular infantry battalion: "I've maybe made only two or three close friends in my career, though I've had plenty of military friends." This rarity is an important feature. It is sufficient to recognize the existence of the relationship, but we must also acknowl-

edge that it is sufficiently scarce that it is not a regular feature of regimental life for many individuals.

2. *Friendship.* The term *friendship* is used specifically in the model to refer to a less intense relationship that is frequently found to exist between soldiers within the *informal structure*. It can have all the appearance of *close friendship*, in that individuals constantly seek each other's company, will help each other if they are in trouble, and will be prepared to share almost anything if the need arises, but it falls short of the depth and intensity of the other relationship. Bonds of *friendship* are usually formed within narrow bands of rank. Although there are no formally stated regulations that proscribe *friendships* developing between people of widely diverse ranks, such relationships are frowned upon because they are held to be potentially compromising in terms of discipline.

3. *Association.* It is often found that when two soldiers greatly separated by rank – a difference wide enough to preclude *friendship* – frequently come into regular contact with one another, they will, over time, form an informal bond of mutual trust and respect that falls short of *friendship* as defined above, but which is nevertheless an important bonding feature. Such a relationship will probably arise, for example, between an infantry platoon sergeant and his platoon commander, and an adjutant and his or her chief clerk, or between an artillery Battery Sergeant-Major and his or her battery commander.

4. *Informal Access.* It is recognized, though not officially laid down, that each individual has the right to speak informally and without a formal appointment with certain other people who are at a certain degree of structural distance (superiors in his or her chain of command, for instance), even though a link of *association* does not exist between them. Thus, a recently joined junior officer can expect to have *informal access* to his sub-unit commander from the beginning, as can a private soldier to his platoon or troop commander. Similarly, any member of a sergeants' mess can expect to have opportunities to approach the Regimental Sergeant-Major informally.

5. *Nodding Acquaintance.* The term *nodding acquaintance* encompasses all the informal relationships that are not encompassed by the other terms. In essence, it is a relationship where the parties know each other by sight, but not necessarily by name, and they acknowledge each other's existence and common participation in the same segment of the *formal command structure*. The relationship may remain as it is or it may grow into any one of the others listed above.

These five relationships are depicted in Figure 9.1:

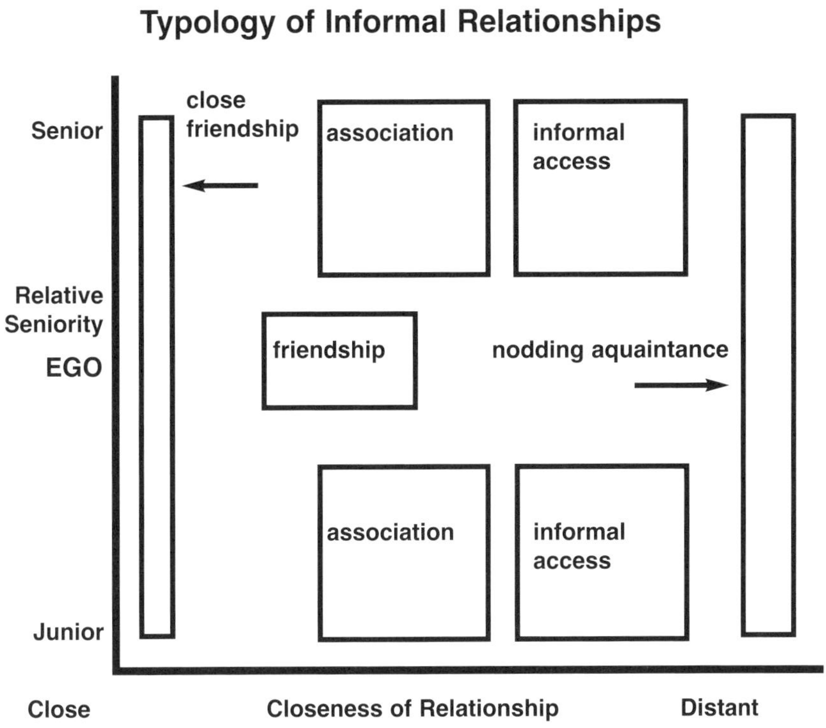

CHAPTER 9

Typology of Informal Relationships

```
                    close
Senior          friendship    association      informal
                                                access
                    ←

Relative
Seniority       friendship              nodding aquaintance
  EGO                                            →


                              association      informal
                                                access

Junior

        Close          Closeness of Relationship        Distant
```

Figure 9.1: Informal Relationships.[22]

Obeying, Bending or Breaking the Rules

The second extension to the model seeks to capture the logic of the practice of obeying, bending or breaking formal rules. This area of the model develops an original idea by Erving Goffman in his work on mental hospitals and other closed institutions.[23] Goffman noted that, although patients could secure their release by convincing the hospital authorities that they were well adjusted, conforming members of society, the mental patients whom he observed tended to obey some rules and to disobey others. He therefore made a distinction between the strict observance and bending of rules, and extended this distinction to his consideration of disciplined organizations in general. He coined phrases with which to talk about the subtleties involved using a concept that he called "adjustments." The present model builds on his work. The following terms distinguish rule-following, rule-bending and rule-breaking behaviour:

1. *Primary adjustments* are actions taken by individuals strictly in accordance with the rules. In a military context, an example would be coming to attention when ordered to do so on parade or wearing the correct

order of dress in the condition expected, that is, clean, tidy and pressed, for instance.

2. *Secondary adjustments* are actions taken by individuals that bend or break the rules, usually to make those involved more comfortable or to aid in the smooth running of the organization.

I have extended Goffman's useful distinction by further dividing *secondary adjustments* according to whether or not the person carrying them out believes that he or she will be punished if discovered. These additional terms include:

3. *Legitimate secondary adjustments* are actions that the individual knows are strictly against the rules, but which he or she does not expect will lead to punishment, even if the action is discovered.

4. *Illegitimate secondary adjustments* are actions that the individual knows are against the rules and will attract disciplinary or administrative action if found out.

In general, *secondary adjustments* are considered "legitimate" when they seem to be harmless or when they actually appear to contribute to the smooth running of the group. An example might be the trade in "buckshees" (surplus military items) between those in charge of military stores. It is against the rules to keep buckshees, but it is generally tolerated as it helps people make up deficiencies without formal write-off action. However, if *secondary adjustments* tend to be for the benefit of particular individuals, they are more likely to be "illegitimate." Examples might be skiving, bullying or selling buckshees for personal profit. This element of the model gives us a means to talk about a grey area – the observance or bending / breaking of rules – with a neutral vocabulary, and to analyze real events impartially. A small number of cases that contain an element of resistance, in light of the main model and its two extensions, will now be examined.

Case Studies of *Informal Revenge* in the British Army at Unit Level

Rather than offering a global consideration of resistance in the British Army, this chapter is interested primarily in the type of small-scale action typified by the case of the captain's pistol. Such action falls into Scott's classification of "everyday resistance." This is not to say that more serious forms of resistance do not take place, or when they do, they are not important, but rather to acknowledge that such other forms of resistance are not encountered as often. In essence, attention will be concentrated on a relatively common area of military behaviour that is well known and well practiced by soldiers, but which has not previously been formally studied or located in the wider literature on resistance. This behaviour, called here "informal revenge," consists of low-key acts of resistance that are not designed to upset the smooth running of life in the unit. In most cases, the action is reversible, causes no permanent damage to the victim and leaves the perpetrators unpunished in spite of appearing to be in the category of *illegitimate secondary adjustment*. The following cases provide more explicit examples through which this area can be explored.

Didn't you hear that Sir?

An individual in the Army Air Corps reported this case to the author in an interview that was conducted some time ago. During one particular operation, an officer in an aviation regiment headquarters (HQ), who was acting as a watchkeeper and who was also an augmentee brought in to increase the numbers of the unit from another regiment in the same corps, thought that he was much better than he actually was.[24] In short, he was "full of himself." He was formally demanding of his soldiers and had poor informal relationships with them. In the battle group command post, at those moments in which he seemed to feel important, the signallers would covertly unplug his headset so that he did not receive the relevant messages. The soldiers did not do this at times when the battle group was involved in a battle, but rather restricted their actions to times of routine. Everyone in that part of the HQ knew what the soldiers were doing and took no action because the officer was unpopular. His peers had told him that he was treating his subordinates badly, but he had not changed his behaviour.

Like the case of the captain's pistol, this situation appears to be a simple example of resistance: the soldiers felt that too much was being demanded of them and they resorted to low-key sabotage in order to embarrass the person oppressing them. This analysis, however, does not explain why the other people in the HQ did nothing about the soldiers' behaviour. At least some of them were NCOs with a duty to ensure the smooth running of the command post; officers were present as well. As none of them took any action, they tacitly accepted the signallers' activity as a *legitimate secondary adjustment*. A more culturally sensitive analysis goes far beyond the simple label of "resistance." As an augmentee, the watchkeeper was an outsider who did not fully belong to the regiment's *loyalty / identity structure*. In being "demanding," he may have felt that he was enforcing sound operational standards (*functional structure*), but his lack of informal relationships downwards in the hierarchy (*association* and *informal access*) isolated him from informal contact and support from the HQ NCOs and private soldiers. Similarly, in ignoring his peers' advice, he was rejecting the help offered through *friendship*. All these circumstances served to set him apart from the cooperative relationships and activities that might be expected in a HQ team. It is also interesting to note that the signallers reserved their actions (unplugging the headset) for those occasions that provided a high degree of embar-

CHAPTER 9

rassment for the victim, but that did not affect the operation in which they were currently engaged, thus preserving the soldierly ethos expressed in the *functional structure*.

Missing Equipment

During an interview, a member of an artillery regiment remembered a particular incident in which a group of soldiers made life uncomfortable for their sergeant during a snowy exercise in the North of England. He recalled:

> We had a sergeant who was a gun Number One [commander of an artillery piece and its detachment] ... He was of the old school ... [and] he was absolutely detested. On one particular exercise on Otterburn ... a couple of thousand pounds worth of kit disappeared off the back of the truck. He had signed for it. He spent three days looking for it. He got the message. ... He found it three days later, after the snow [had] melted.

The description of this sergeant as belonging to the "old school" implies that he was a firm, if not a harsh, disciplinarian, and insisted on using the authority conveyed by his rank. It would not be unreasonable, therefore, to see in this case a simple example of resistance in the face of oppression. However, there are some aspects which are culturally resonant and which deserve to be noted. The first is the particular form of the "informal revenge," which in itself is a product of the Army's organizational culture. It hinged on the responsibility of the individual for the equipment for which they have "signed." A soldier who loses equipment for which he or she is responsible has offended against both the conventions of the *functional structure* (by not looking after it properly) and the regulations in the *formal command structure* (by failing in his or her formal responsibility) and therefore must face formal sanctions and a loss of reputation. Second, the phrase, "He got the message," is interesting. The soldiers who took the equipment off of his vehicle and buried it in the snow were doing more than just taking revenge. They were, at least in the eyes of the interviewee, transmitting a message. This aspect will be revisited later.

A Lost Platoon Commander

Lieutenant Parsons, a platoon commander, was deeply unpopular with his men. One evening, he allowed himself to become beastly drunk when he went out with them. Once he had become disoriented, some of his men drove him to the camp of a different unit a few miles away and dropped him outside, alone and incapable. The next day, the company commander investigated this embarrassing incident by informally questioning Sergeant Merryweather, the platoon sergeant, by asking him how this incident had happened and why he had not stopped it. The sergeant replied in his defence, "Sir, you know what he is like." No disciplinary action was taken against the perpetrators.

Far from being a simple case of opportunistic resistance by subordinates against their officer, this case possesses a number of different aspects that are only understandable in the light of the models of British organizational culture that have been set out above. To begin, it seems clear that the incident had its roots in a poor relationship between Lieutenant Parsons and his soldiers. Recall that he was "deeply unpopular," which implies that he had failed to develop effective links of *association* or *informal access* with them. He certainly had not developed a strong link of *association* with Sergeant Merryweather, as can be inferred from the sergeant's reply to his company commander's question. The mutual loyalty and respect that normally characterizes platoon commander / sergeant relationships was entirely absent in the reply, "Sir, you know what he's like." It can also be seen from this exchange that Sergeant Merryweather and his company commander had an existing relationship of *association*. The company commander knew he could approach the sergeant informally and he, in turn, did not dissemble or excuse himself. The sergeant trusted his commander to understand the situation and to sympathize with him. The mode of "informal revenge" that the soldiers resorted to was embarrassing but harmless, which implies that they were unwilling to cross a line which they could be sure would get them into trouble. It seems that they were correct in their assessment, since no disciplinary action was taken against either them or Sergeant Merryweather. In essence, the special situation converted an *illegitimate secondary adjustment* into one that was by default treated as *legitimate* because of the circumstances.

The Vanishing Pilchards

During an interview, Del, an infantry soldier, recounted an incident that occurred on an exercise. He recalled:

> The platoon sergeant was lazy. He'd been in the Army a long time and he was lazy. And he wouldn't make no brews [hot drinks], no scoff [food], nothing. His radio ops [operators] had to make it all. And there were these tankies with us. ... And they had a lot of buckshee scoff and they give [sic] it to us. He [the sergeant] was asleep at the time and so me and the other lad, the runner, we ate that scoff just out of sheer spite. We felt "Sod it!" We were nearly sick. We tabbed [marched] off in the middle of the night and the next day was the last day, live firing. ... And he always used to take his webbing off, this sergeant, used to sit on it and rub his hands together ... "Right, get the old pilchards out!" – because the old tankies had given us loads of pilchards – and the bloke replied,

CHAPTER 9

> "Del's ate them Sarge!" ... When we got back we laughed about that. We'd sort of pissed him off so to speak because he used to piss us off.

The soldiers' objection to the sergeant was not that he was oppressing them, but rather that he was not performing his share of the labour. In addition, he still expected to share in the proceeds of the cooking that his two soldiers had undertaken. He was also "lazy," thus violating the expectations and the conventions of the *functional structure*. Further, in being so, he was compromising his identity as a member of that particular regiment, whose self-image is that of a tough, aggressive group with a proactive attitude toward life. The problem between them was therefore deeply seated in the organizational culture rather than in their asymmetry of rank.

Sorry Sir, did I hurt you?

During yet another interview, an infantry officer spoke of a friend of his who was at the time the commander of a battalion reconnaissance platoon with the rank of captain. On one exercise, this friend had been particularly cross and demanding toward his armoured vehicle crew of two junior NCOs. Everything seemed to be going well until an occasion when the vehicle stopped suddenly for no apparent reason, with the predictable result that the captain was projected violently forward. This movement caused him to strike his face on the edge of the hatch out of which he was looking in order to command the vehicle. His injuries were slight, but he realised that this was not a random act on the part of his driver and that it had been a deliberate attempt to hurt him. His reaction was to stop the vehicle, get the crew out of it and spend about five minutes talking to them and allowing them to air their grievances. After this, they resumed their journey with no further incident.

The officer had correctly identified this incident as what might be called a "staged accident," an *illegitimate secondary adjustment* that is impossible to take formal action against because it has all the appearance of being unintentional. Although it was in fact deliberate, the driver could not have been held to blame. In stopping the vehicle and talking to his soldiers, the officer used his existing relationship of *association* with them to provide a forum for straight talking and listening. His actions apparently defused the situation.

The Missing Cannon Balls

A soldier remembering a tour of duty overseas when he was a junior NCO clerk, recalled:

> Not many people in our [sub-unit] liked the ... Commander of the British Forces in the [overseas base]. And outside of his office he

CHAPTER 9

> had eight cannon balls [in two piles] – three on the base, outside of his door, one on the top. And to get from our accommodation you had to go across the square, past his office to our [sub-unit] bar. ... I used to do Duty Clerks [a 24 hour duty] in the headquarters building. And one day, the Commander's cannon balls went missing. And he guessed it was [us] that did it. I was on duty the night that they went missing. So he called me in [and] he said, "Find my cannon balls." So he used me to get his cannon balls back ... and I did. I didn't personally find them. Right, I got the word 'round the [sub-unit] that "you'd better have the cannon balls back p.d.q. [pretty damned quick] otherwise we're in deep shit." ... I didn't know who had taken them. ... I was the vehicle to say "Get those cannon balls back or we're in deep shit. We're in deep shit – the OC [officer commanding, sub-unit commander] downwards." And they came back. So I was the vehicle but I never knew who... you see at the time I was also the [sub-unit] barman, so I knew a lot of the people. I knew what was going on.

This incident is another example of resistance because the soldiers were taking action against a superior with whom they did not get along. However, it is far more complex than a simple act of anonymous rebellion, as can be observed when it is examined in light of the model of British Army organizational culture that has been advanced above. There are no means of knowing what had caused the difficulties between the Commander and the sub-unit to which the interviewee belonged. Whatever it was, the relationship was so bad that there was no doubt about who had taken the cannon balls. Such a reality implies that the members of the sub-unit were united in their dislike of the Commander, which further implies that their attitude toward him had become associated with ideas that could be modelled as part of the *loyalty / identity structure*. It was them against him. There are also cultural resonances in the way in which the Commander chose to deal with the incident and get his cannon balls back. Instead of taking formal action and thus making the *formal command structure* the *operating structure*, he used his relationship of *association* or *informal access* with the interviewee, whom he would have met in the course of the latter's clerical duties. He used this relationship to get a message to the soldiers who had taken his cannon balls. The clerk was a particularly appropriate choice because he was also the sub-unit barman and would thus have had an excellent network and therefore the means to transmit the message. The Commander reinforced these indirect and informal means by communicating a further message that formal action would be taken if the cannon balls did not turn up again. In the terms of the model, he would treat it as a *legitimate secondary adjustment* if they returned the cannon balls and an *illegitimate secondary adjustment* if they did not. The fact that he was successful indicates that he had judged the situation well.

CHAPTER 9

On their own, these cases do not, of course, provide enough material to create a typology of "informal revenge." Such an analysis must unfortunately wait for a future opportunity. Indeed, it may be reasonably assumed that "informal revenge" may take many more forms than those exemplified above. For instance, soldiers may decide to take revenge by obeying an irritating superior's orders to the letter so that if any task is not minutely described, they can do it badly. Such actions might be called, "wilful obedience," perhaps. Or, as another example, soldiers might adopt a process called "accept and evade," a process whereby an order is taken but somehow is never actually carried out. Historian Richard Holmes has observed such a phenomenon in the context of the British Army in the First World War.[25]

Nevertheless, with or without a typology, the analysis of these cases has demonstrated that it would be too simplistic to label acts of "informal revenge" simply as examples of "resistance" without embedding them within a cultural context. Indeed, as has been seen, significant insights are to be gained by examining the behaviour of all participants –victims, perpetrators and bystanders alike – in the light of the model of British Army organizational culture at the unit level. For instance, whilst the case of the missing pilchards might appear to be no more than a simple case of resistance (two private soldiers taking revenge on a sergeant that they did not like by eating the food that he was looking forward to), many cultural resonances that illuminate the analysis much further can also be found. As has been observed, two things from Del's statement stand out: the sergeant was lazy because he had been in the Army a long time and he had refused to share in the task of making hot drinks or cooking food. This means that his motivation to take a full and energetic part in soldierly activity (*functional structure*) was in question and he was not abiding by the conventions of the *informal structure* by sharing the burden of some of the routine tasks. He was also, by inference, using his formal power to insist that his juniors carry out these tasks for him (*formal command structure*).

If attention is now shifted to the case of the captain's pistol with which this chapter began, it can be acknowledged that this was a classic act of "resistance," in Scott's terms, but much more can be seen in it by using the above model. This example also illuminates Hockey's use of the concept of "negotiated order." This concept describes the use of resistance as a means to powerfully project a message – usually something along the lines of "You are irritating us, Sir" – and the use of that message as a negotiating tool in amending the behaviour of the offending senior individual. It also helps any observer to be sensitive to the fact that these acts are not resistance for its own sake, but rather have a wider purpose (negotiation). Hockey's concept, however, does not go far enough because it is based on an assumption of a binary opposite, an "us" and "them," in which the "us" is the category of private soldiers and the "them" comprises everyone else (all NCOs and all officers). As has been

CHAPTER 9

observed, the interplay and cooperation between ranks in the case of the watchkeeper and his unplugged headset, for example, does not fit Hockey's model at all. Furthermore, there is no room in Hockey's polarized view for the cross-rank informal relationships (*association* and *informal access*) that are expressed in this model and illustrated in the cases of the missing cannon balls, the lost subaltern and the chastised reconnaissance platoon commander.

Using the model of "social structures" and its extensions, these acts of "informal revenge" can be described in a way that goes further than Scott and Hockey in the context of the British Army. First, all cases of "informal revenge" are clearly instances of *secondary adjustment* as they are acts carried out against the formal rules to the advantage of those carrying them out. However, in spite of their obvious formal illegitimacy, they are not necessarily treated as *illegitimate secondary adjustments*. Should the authorities in the unit be in sympathy with the perpetrators, as in the case of the signallers who unplugged the watchkeeper's headset, they may informally legitimise the action by turning a blind eye to it.

Second, these acts of resistance are usually constructed to communicate a message, rather than to do damage or to provide satisfaction *per se*, although damage may result, as might have occurred in the case of the chastised reconnaissance platoon commander who was at real risk of injury when his driver braked so suddenly. The statement by the artillery soldier that his sergeant had "got the message" when his equipment disappeared is highly significant. Indeed, the transmission of a message in all the cases described can be clearly observed. For instance, the captain's crew were expressing their exasperation with him when they hid his pistol, Del and his colleagues were telling their sergeant that they did not like his behaviour, and so on and so forth.

Third, the victims of "informal revenge" tend to be individuals who have lost the support of their juniors and their peers, usually by failing to engage fully with the organizational culture, and in virtually all cases there is a lack of communication between the victim and more junior personnel. In terms of the model, victims have usually failed to develop relationships of *association* and *informal access* with their soldiers. We can see this aspect obviously played out, for example, in the cases of the sabotaged watchkeeper and the drunken platoon commander. In essence, where messages have failed to be sent and received through the communications system enabled by the informal relationships, soldiers oftentimes opt to send an even louder message by engaging in some form of "informal revenge."

In summary, then, each of the above cases, in light of the model, demonstrates that units of the British Army are not simple power / subordination social systems. There are shared ideas, rules and conventions of behaviour to which all fully integrated members subscribe and by which they can be

CHAPTER 9

judged, whatever their position and rank; there are also internal networks of relationships and communications that cut across ranks. To gain a proper understanding of "resistance," as exemplified here, it is vital to address the cultural contexts and nuances in which such activity occurs and in which it is embedded. The same can probably be said for any other aspect of life in the British Army as well.

"Informal Revenge" and the Canadian Army

Moving on, can any relevant similarities be demonstrated between the behaviour of Canadian and British soldiers? It is clear from occasional discussions with Canadian Army personnel that all the main elements that have been encapsulated in the model described above and used in the preceding analysis would also provide analytical insights into the behaviour of Canadian soldiers. Essentially, all of the Canadian soldiers that have been interviewed on occasions spanning the past ten years have embraced the model with much the same enthusiasm as British soldiers have. However, there is, *prima facie*, a potential for mismatches arising from differences in national culture, and particularly the existence in Canada of the major francophone influence that does not exist in Britain. A researcher using the model and its extensions in Canadian military contexts should therefore proceed with caution and remain on the *qui vive* for cultural differences.

Apart from the relevance of the overall model to the Canadian case, it is also clear that "informal revenge" is as much a recourse for Canadian soldiers as it is for British. Three incidents recounted by Canadian interviewees will illustrate the point and they could easily have formed three of the cases examined earlier in the context of the British Army. Again, these three cases on their own cannot prove that "informal revenge" is in any way part of the normal pattern of life in the Canadian Army. However, together with the positive recognition of the model expressed by Canadian soldiers, they give a strong indication that it may be, and that its causes may be similar. These incidents are therefore worth discussing in the context of leadership in the Canadian Army.

Load the stores, Sir? What stores?

A Canadian interviewee once described how an officer that he knew had promised his commander that certain pieces of equipment would be shipped for a particular exercise; he unfortunately forgot, however, to tell his soldiers to pack and load it. He gave his men the task at the last minute, just as they were about to stop working, having hung around all day doing nothing. This behaviour was typical of the man who seemed to behave as if only his time was important and that of his men was not. On this occasion, the soldiers somehow managed to miss the shipping time, thereby causing the stores to be left behind, much to the embarrassment of the officer. In this case, the officer appeared to treat his men as if they were not important, which implies strongly that he did not listen to their concerns and that he communicated poorly with them. On this occasion, the soldiers took the opportunity to take "informal revenge" by accepting the order but not carrying it out.

Careful with that Shovel!

A Canadian junior officer saw himself as a hard disciplinarian and habitually drove his men to work harder than they felt was justified by the circumstances. Because of his poor communications with them, he did not detect the unease that he was causing. He had not listened to his peers who had warned him that he was making a mistake. On a particular exercise, a fellow officer was forced to intervene, as one of the junior officer's soldiers was on the point of staging "an accident" with a shovel. This example, as is clear, maps directly onto the model described above. The self-styled "hard" officer had limited or no relationships of *association* or *informal access* with his soldiers and concentrated on the *functional* and *formal command structures* at the expense of the *informal structure*. His peers had seen a bad situation developing and attempted to use their relationship of *friendship* as a vehicle for telling him that he was making an error. He did not listen and carried on as before. The situation then became so bad in the eyes of his soldiers that one of them was prepared to take "informal revenge" by staging an accident with a shovel.

Poison Ivy! Oh, that's bad luck, Sir!

A team consisting of an officer and a small number of NCOs from the Canadian Battle School was conducting what should have been a standard Combat Leaders' Course. The students were all private soldiers and junior NCOs, undergoing the course as part of their career progression. This type of course was expected to be tough, but the officer in charge seemed to be taking pleasure in making it unusually so. He did not "connect" [interviewee's word] with either the students or his own staff and worked them both mercilessly. One night during the course, somebody smeared the wax from a poison ivy plant on his bedding and heavy facial swelling resulted. No culprit was ever discovered and no disciplinary action was taken. However, the interviewee related that it was not one of the students. In not connecting with either his staff or his students, this officer showed that he had found it difficult to establish informal relationships of *association* and *informal access*. In driving them harder than was considered fair and reasonable, he was violating what they saw as the conventions of the *functional structure*. The situation was sufficiently severe for a member of his own team to take "informal revenge."

One should not be surprised to learn that soldiers of any nationality find ways of resisting individuals in their chain of command who they feel are irritating or oppressing them. In the case of the British Army, a relatively common form of resistance has been described in this chapter as "informal revenge" and located in a model of British Army organizational culture. It seems clear that this model (including "informal revenge") has the potential for useful application to the Canadian Army as well, provided that the researcher applying it is sensitive to any influences from cultural differences. In describing "informal revenge," we are entering an area of military organizational culture that has not so far been described in any systematic detail, although it is easily recognised by soldiers. The perpetrators are clearly "unwilling" and "reluctant" and the victims of the revenge tend to be out of touch with their soldiers and unwilling to listen to them.

This behaviour falls far short of the sort of high profile dramatic and defiant disobedience that is a defining element of mutiny. The above cases are situated in a hinterland between obedience and rebellion, the key element of which appears to be the desire by junior personnel to communicate a message to a more senior victim who has been reluctant so far to receive it through normal channels. There is no intention to challenge or rupture the disciplinary system of the unit. The message is "We don't like you," but at this stage, the statement is tacitly completed with a term of address that acknowledges the legitimacy of formally defined differences in rank. It is not so much, "We don't like you" on its own, but rather "We don't like you, Sir."

ENDNOTES

[1] The current edition is Great Britain, Ministry of Defence [MOD], *Manual of Military Law*, Part I, 12th ed. (London: HMSO, 1972, as amended to 1 May 2001), which is similar in all relevant respects to the one that was in force at the time of the incident.

[2] MOD, *Manual of Military Law*, 311.

[3] Ibid., 350.

[4] A full bibliography would be impossible. The following titles give a flavour of the types of works that are to be found in the field: Jean Comaroff, *Body of Power, Spirit of Resistance: The Culture and History of a South African People* (Chicago: University of Chicago Press, 1985); Irene Diamond and Lee Quinby, eds., *Feminism and Foucault: Reflections on Resistance* (Boston: Northeastern University Press, 1988); Aihwa Ong, *Spirits of Resistance and Capitalist Discipline: Factory Women in Malaysia* (Albany: State University of New York Press, 1987); James C. Scott, *Domination and the Arts of Resistance: Hidden Transcripts* (New Haven: Yale University Press [YUP], 1990); Lila Abu-Lughod, "The Romance of Resistance: Tracing Transformations of Power through Bedouin Women," *American Ethnologist*, Vol. 17, No. 1 (1990), 41-55; Martha Kaplan, "Meaning, Agency and Colonial History: Navosavakadua and the *Tuka* Movement in Fiji," *American Ethnologist*, Vol. 17, No. 1 (1990), 3-22; Jo-Anne Fiske and Patty J. Ginn,

"Discourse and Defiance: Law, Healing, and the Implications of Communities in Resistance," *Journal of Legal Pluralism and Unofficial Law*, Vol. 45 (2000), 115-35; Michael Given, "Maps, Fields, and Boundary Cairns: Demarcation and Resistance in Colonial Cyprus," *International Journal of Historical Archaeology*, Vol. 4, No. 1 (2000), 1-22; Tanya Korovkin, "Weak Weapons, Strong Weapons? Hidden Resistance and Political Protest in Rural Ecuador," *Journal of Peasant Studies*, Vol. 27, No. 3 (2000), 1-29; Sabine Marschall, "Sites of Identity and Resistance: Urban Community Murals and Rural Wall Decoration in South Africa," *African Arts*, Vol. 35, No. 3 (2002), 41-53 & 91; and Patricia Ewick and Susan Silbey, "Narrating Social Structure: Stories of Resistance to Legal Authority," *American Journal of Sociology*, Vol. 108, No. 6 (2003), 1292-1327.

5   In the subject area of exposing power and oppression, Michael Foucault was one of the most influential writers of the late-20th century. See, for example, Michael Foucault, *Discipline and Punish: the Birth of the Prison* (London: Penguin Books, 1977).

6   Sherry Ortner, "Resistance and the Problem of Ethnographic Refusal," *Comparative Studies in Society and History*, Vol. 37 (1995), 173-93.

7   Michael F. Brown, "On Resisting Resistance," *American Anthropologist*, Vol. 89, No. 4 (1996), 729-36.

8   James C. Scott, *Weapons of the Weak: Everyday Forms of Peasant Resistance* (New Haven: YUP, 1985).

9   Ibid., xvi.

10 Ibid., 281-282.

11 MOD, *Manual of Military Law*.

12 John Hockey, *Squaddies: Portrait of a Subculture* (Exeter: University of Exeter, 1986).

13 Since *Squaddies*, there have been only five comparable studies. These analyses include part of a wider study on the position of officers from different regiments in the hierarchy of the British Army (Reginald von Zugbach, *Power and Prestige in the British Army* (Aldershot: Avebury, 1988)), an attempt to capture British Army culture during the Falklands War (Norah Stewart, *Mates and Muchachos: Unit Cohesion in the Falklands / Malvinas War* (New York: Brassey's, 1991)), a research project which the author undertook for MOD (Charles Kirke, *Social Structures in the Combat Arms Units of the British Army*, (MOD Defence Fellowship, 17 October 1994)), a Ph.D. thesis on culture and power in the British Army at the infantry platoon level (Paul Killworth, *Culture and Power in the British Army: Hierarchies, Boundaries and Construction* (Cambridge University, 1997)), and the author's Ph.D. thesis on social structures in the British Army at the unit level (Charles Kirke, *Social Structures in the Regular Combat Arms Units of the British Army: a Model* (Cranfield University, 2002)). In sum, the present author has made an extensive study of the organizational culture of the British Army using social anthropological techniques over the past thirty years and has developed a model of social structure and process at the unit level, part of which forms the basis of the analysis given in this chapter.

CHAPTER 9

[14] Anselm Strauss *et al.*, "The Hospital and its Negotiated Order," in Graeme Salaman and Kenneth Thompson, eds., *People and Organizations* (Milton Keynes: Open University Press, 1974), 303-20.
[15] Hockey, *Squaddies*, 158-59.
[16] This model has been developed through the following studies: Charles Kirke, *The Anthropological Analysis of Leadership*, Staff College Project (1981); Kirke, *Social Structures* (1994); and Kirke, *Social Structures* (2002).
[17] Charles Kirke, "The Organizational Cultural Approach to Leadership: 'Social Structures' – A Tool for Analysis and a Way Ahead." Canadian Forces Leadership Institute Contract Number 04/0058.
[18] See, for example, Emile Durkheim, *The Rules of Sociological Method*, George Catlin, ed., Sarah Solovay and John Mueller, trans. (Chicago: University of Chicago Press, 1938).
[19] See, for example, Anthony Giddens, *The Constitution of Society: Outline of the Theory of Structuration* (Cambridge: Polity Press, 1984), 1-40 & 163-64.
[20] Anthony Giddens, *New Rules of Sociological Method* (London: Hutchinson, 1976), 75.
[21] Words in *italics* are specific to the model and have specific meanings, all of which are defined on their first use.
[22] Explanatory Notes for Figure 9.1. 1) "EGO" is an individual of no particular rank, who has superiors and subordinates. He or she might be, for example, a sergeant or a lieutenant. This particular case was chosen because it illustrates relationships with peers, subordinates and superiors. For someone at the top or bottom of the rank structure (lieutenant colonel or private soldier) the diagram would be redrawn to show peers and **only** subordinates or superiors; 2) The boxes show the areas (rank / closeness) where relationships are expected to fall; 3) The gaps between the boxes are voids to separate the boxes for clarity only; 4) An important variable is the strength of the relationship. This is captured in the figure by the horizontal dimension of each box. On the principle that a line has an infinite number of points, each horizontal line represents a very large range of possible degrees of warmth or intensity in the relationship; and 5) This model does not seek to capture romantic or sexual relationships. This is a separate area that deserves further study.
[23] Erving Goffman, *Asylums: Essays on the Social Situation of Mental Patients and Other Inmates* (Harmondsworth: Penguin Books, 1968), especially 54-60.
[24] HQ watchkeepers are officers who work in command posts but have no executive authority to make operational decisions. Essentially, they assist the permanently established management of the HQ to carry out their duties and responsibilities. Watchkeeper posts tend to be on war establishment only and officers are brought in from outside the HQ to fill these positions as augmentees.
[25] Richard Holmes, "Red Tabs and Dugouts: British Generalship in the First World War," unpublished lecture script given to the Royal Military College of Science Military Society, Shrivenham, 1995.

CONTRIBUTORS

Lieutenant-Colonel (ret'd), Dr. **Peter Bradley** is on the faculty of the Military Psychology and Leadership Department at the Royal Military College of Canada. During his military career, he served in The Royal Canadian Regiment, the Canadian Airborne Regiment and the Personnel Selection Branch.

Craig Leslie Mantle graduated from Queen's University in 2002 with his Master of Arts degree in Canadian military history and has been employed by the Canadian Forces Leadership Institute as an historian ever since.

Dr. **Christopher M. Bell** is an Associate Professor of History at Dalhousie University. He is the author of *The Royal Navy, Seapower and Strategy between the Wars* (2000) and co-editor of *Naval Mutinies of the Twentieth Century: An International Perspective* (2003).

Christopher Ankersen's research interests include civil-military relations, civil-military cooperation in post-conflict scenarios and Canadian defence policy. Since 2001, he has acted as a consultant to government, the military, the United Nations, and firms in the private sector on policy, management and security in Canada, the United States and the United Kingdom. He was a member of the CF for 12 years, serving as an officer in the Princess Patricia's Canadian Light Infantry. He held a number of appointments within the First and Third Battalions and deployed to Croatia in 1992-1993 and Kosovo in 1999.

Colonel, Dr. **Bernd Horn** is the Director of the Canadian Forces Leadership Institute. He was the Commanding Officer, 1 RCR (2001-2003); the Officer Commanding, 3 Commando, the Canadian Airborne Regiment (1993-1995); and the Officer Commanding, B Company, 1 RCR (1992-1993). He is also an Adjunct-Associate Professor of History at the Royal Military College of Canada.

Brigadier-General (ret'd) **Gordon (Joe) Sharpe** joined the Royal Canadian Air Force in 1965. He attended Royal Roads Military College and graduated from the Royal Military College of Canada in 1969. For the next 32 years, he served in various operational, instructional and staff positions throughout the CF. He chaired both the Croatia Board of Inquiry and the Special Review Group that was established to examine CF leadership during the many deployments to Croatia. He is currently serving as a Special Advisor to the CF/DND Ombudsman on Post Traumatic Stress Disorder.

Chief Petty Officer 1st Class (ret'd) **George Dowler** joined the Royal Canadian Navy in 1966. He served in the CF for the next 36 years in a range of operational, instructional and staff positions, both at sea and ashore. He is currently acting as a Special Advisor to the CF/DND Ombudsman and

CONTRIBUTORS

working with Brigadier-General (ret'd) Sharpe on a variety of projects concerning command and control, leadership and military culture.

Lieutenant-Commander **George Shorey** holds a Master of Arts degree in Psychology and has served in the CF for more than 23 years. He is a former MARS officer who served as a United Nations Military Observer Riverine Patrol Team leader in Cambodia in 1992-1993. He served as the Task Force Personnel Selection Officer for ROTO 0 Afghanistan in 2003-2004 and has also taught for 5 years at the Royal Military College of Canada in the Military Psychology and Leadership Department. He currently works in the Professional Development section of the Directorate of Army Training – Land Force Doctrine and Training System.

Lieutenant-Colonel (ret'd), Dr. **Charles Kirke** is one of a very small number of military anthropologists working in the United Kingdom. He retired from the British Army in 2004 and is currently a Lecturer in Human Factors Integration at Cranfield University (Defence Academy Campus) at Shrivenham, Wiltshire.

GLOSSARY

AOR	Area of Responsibility
APC	Armoured Personnel Carrier
BG	Battle Group
CAR	Competency, Authority, Responsibility
CBOI	Croatia Board of Inquiry
CDA	Canadian Defence Academy
Cdn AB Regt	Canadian Airborne Regiment
CDS	Chief of the Defence Staff
CEF	Canadian Expeditionary Force
CF	Canadian Forces
CFB	Canadian Forces Base
CFLI	Canadian Forces Leadership Institute
CFNIS	Canadian Forces National Investigation Service
CLIP	Canadian Letters and Images Project
CO	Commanding Officer
CSR	Combat Stress Reaction
DHH	Directorate of History and Heritage
DND	Department of National Defence
GSG-9	Grenzschutzgruppe-9
GWS	Gulf War Syndrome
HMCS	Her (His) Majesty's Canadian Ship
HMS	Her (His) Majesty's Ship
HMSO	Her (His) Majesty's Stationery Office
HQ	Headquarters

GLOSSARY

IDF	Israeli Defense Forces
IUS	Inter-University Seminar on Armed Forces and Society
JTF-2	Joint Task Force-2
LAC	Library and Archives Canada
LRDG	Long Range Desert Group
MG	Manuscript Group
MOD	Ministry of Defence
MQUP	McGill-Queen's University Press
NATO	North Atlantic Treaty Organization
NCO	Non-Commissioned Officer
NDHQ	National Defence Headquarters
OC	Officer Commanding
OP	Observation Post
ORAE	Operational Research and Analysis Establishment
OSS	Office of Strategic Services
PDR	Performance Development Report
PER	Personnel Evaluation Report
PPCLI	Princess Patricia's Canadian Light Infantry
PUP	Princeton University Press
PW	Prisoner of War
QR&O	Queen's Regulations and Orders
RCAF	Royal Canadian Air Force
RCMP	Royal Canadian Mounted Police

GLOSSARY

RCN	Royal Canadian Navy
RCNVR	Royal Canadian Navy Volunteer Reserve
RCR	Royal Canadian Regiment
RG	Record Group
RMC	Royal Military College of Canada
RN	Royal Navy
SAS	Special Air Service
SASR	Special Air Service Regiment
SOF	Special Operations Forces
TNA	The National Archives of the United Kingdom
UAP	University of Alberta Press
UBC	University of British Columbia
UCMJ	Uniform Code of Military Justice
UN	United Nations
UNAMIR	United Nations Assistance Mission for Rwanda
UNHQ	United Nations Headquarters
UNITAF	Unified Task Force
UNPROFOR	United Nations Protection Force
US	United States
USMC	United States Marine Corps
UTP	University of Toronto Press
WO	Warrant Officer
YUP	Yale University Press

INDEX

Acapulco 98
accountability **78** *endnotes*, 152, 163, 194, 206
Acts of War 35, **40, 41, 72, 73, 76, 84, 190, 192** *endnotes*
Adams, Thomas 127, **137** *endnotes*
Adamson, Agar 48, 52, 53, 61, 63, 76, **77, 78, 81, 82, 83** *endnotes*
adjustments 221, 222, 229
    illegitimate 222, 223, 225, 226, 227, 229
    legitimate 222, 223, 225, 227
    primary 221
    secondary 222, 223, 225, 226, 227, 229
Admiralty 95, 96, 97, 98, 99, 100, 109, **110, 111** *endnotes*
adventure training 181
Afghanistan 28, 30, 33, 183, 236
Agnew, John 184
Air Force, United States **39** *endnotes*
Ajzen, Icek 17, 32, **39** *endnotes*
American Soldier 41, 132, 173, 188, 190, 191, 192
Amiens 50
Anderson, Sergeant Andy 186, **192** *endnotes*
Ankersen, Christopher 5, 113, 235
anomie 122
Appel, Lieutenant-Colonel J.W. 178
Arieli River 48
Army, British 7, **11** *endnotes*, 55, 65, **78** *endnotes*, 135, **189** *endnotes*, 213, 214, 215, 217, 222, 227, 228, 229, 230, 232, **233** *endnotes*, 236
    1st Battalion, Essex Regiment 176
    Army Air Corps 223
    Brabant's Horse 68
    East Lancashire Regiment 43
    Long Range Desert Group (LRDG) 135, **238** *endnotes*
    Parachute School 180
    Royal Marines 27, 99
    Scottish Highlanders 173
    Special Air Service (SAS) 135, 137, 139, 141, 142, 143, 170, 171, **174, 181, 187, 188** *endnotes,* **239** *gloss*
Army, Canadian 5, **9** *endnotes*, 24, 36, 43, 45, 46, 69, **77, 140, 189, 194** *endnotes*, 230, 232
    1st Canadian Parachute Battalion 47, **76, 79, 189** *endnotes*
    5th Canadian Armoured Division 48
    Battle School 231
    Canadian Airborne Regiment (Cdn AB Regt) 19, 33, 35, **39** *endnotes, 44*, **73, 75** *endnotes*, 130, 132, **140, 141, 142** *endnotes*, 143, 193, 194, 198, 210, 211, 235, **237** *gloss*
    Canadian Expeditionary Force (CEF) **8, 9** *endnotes*, 48, **81, 237** *gloss*
        4th Division 61

INDEX

    11th Brigade 61
    22nd Battalion 60
    31st Battalion 48
    42nd Battalion 50
    116th Battalion 64
    180th Battalion 60
    CANBAT 1 150, 151, 152, 153, 154, 155, 156, 157, 158, 160, 162, 164, **167** *endnotes*
    CANBAT 2 159
    French's Scouts 57
    Midland Battalion 58
    Perth Regiment 48, 51, 59
    Princess Patricia's Canadian Light Infantry (PPCLI) 25, 26, 48, 52, **76, 82** *endnotes*, 145, 147, 150, 153, 154, 155, 158, 165, **166** *endnotes*, 235, **238** *gloss*
    Queen's Own Rifles 69, **74** *endnotes*
    Royal Canadian Regiment (RCR) 37, **41** *endnotes*, 49, **84** *endnotes*, 235, **239** *gloss*
    Special Service Force 44, **73** *endnotes*, 136
    Strathcona's Horse 58
    Yukon Field Force 62, 67
Army, Croatian 164
Army, French 1, 13, 14, **78** *endnotes*, 122, 155
Army, German **140** *endnotes*
    90th Infantry Division 183
Army, United States **83** *endnotes*, 115, 127, 148
    36th Infantry Division 176
    101st Airborne Division 183
    343rd Quartermaster Company 115, 121
    517th Parachute Infantry Regiment 182
    Delta Force 135, 136, 137, **139, 141, 142** *endnotes*
    Merrill's Marauders 176
    Peacekeeping Institute 127
    Rangers 131, 135, **139, 142** *endnotes*
    SEAL Team Six 137
    Special Forces (Green Berets) 135, **137, 139, 140, 141, 142, 143** *endnotes*
Army Act (British) 213
Army Culture-Climate Survey 24, **40, 126** *endnotes*
Arone, Shidane 7, 193, 195, 196, 197, 198, 200, 202, 203, 204, **211, 212** *endnotes*
ATHENA, Operation 28
authority 1, 2, 4, 7, **10** *endnotes*, 13, 14, 19, 20, 22, 31, 32, 33, 35, 37, **39** *endnotes*, 43, 54, 63, 67, 68, **75, 84** *endnotes*, 87, 88, 89, 90, 91, 92, 93, 96, 97, 103, 107, 115, 122, 124, 127, 134, 136, 137, 150, 151, 152, 155, 162, 163, 164, 169, 175, 182, 193, 194, 195, 198, 200, 205, 206, 207, 216, 224, **233, 234** *endnotes*
authorization 22, 195, 200, 201, 202, 203, 204

INDEX

Bacovici 1, **9** *endnotes*
Balkans 113, 147, 153, **166** *endnotes*
Barris, Ted 184, **192** *endnotes*
Bartlett, F.C. 174
Bartone, Paul 30, **40** *endnotes*
Bass, Bernard **182, 191** *endnotes*
Battleford 69
Beaumont, Roger 130, 134, **139, 141** *endnotes*
Beckwith, Colonel Charlie 136, **139** *endnotes*
Beebe, Captain G.W. 178
Belet Huen 198
Belfast Gaol 101
Bell, Alan 137, **143** *endnotes*, 170, **187** *endnotes*
Bell, Christopher M. **11, 73, 74, 85** *endnotes*, 87, 88, **91, 92, 108, 109** *endnotes*, 235
Benn, Carl 179, **191** *endnotes*
Bercuson, David 35, **39** *endnotes*, 44, 49, **72, 75, 77, 84** *endnotes*, 105, **112, 210, 211** *endnotes*
Bevan, Rear-Admiral R.H.L. 101
Bird, Will 50, 54, 56, 63, **78, 79, 80, 82, 84** *endnotes*
Black Hawk Down 136, **191** *endnotes*
Black Sea 91
Blake, J.A. 24, 40
Bolshevik 90
Bosnia 29, 30, 34, 36, 136
Braddock, Major-General Edward 173, **188, 189** *endnotes*
Bradley, Peter 4, 5, 13, **40, 142, 235** *endnotes*
Brooke, Field-Marshal Sir Alan 133
Brown, Michael 215, **233** *endnotes*
Burma 176
Burns, E.L.M. 61, **79, 82** *endnotes*
Butcher, Arlo 183
Butler, S. 24, **40** *endnotes*
bystander effect 7, 195, 196, 197, 200, 202

Calvert, Lieutenant-Colonel Michael 174
Calvert, Mike 135
Calvin, Lieutenant-Colonel Jim **166** *endnotes*
Camp Julien 28
Canada's Soldiers: Military Ethos and Canadian Values in the 21st Century 36, **41** *endnotes*
Canadian Airborne Regiment (see Army, Canadian)
    2 Commando 194, 196, 197, 201, 202
    Service Commando 196
Canadian Charter of Rights and Freedoms 207

INDEX

Canadian Defence Academy (CDA) 8, **10, 11, 39, 40, 71, 126, 210** *endnotes*, **237** *gloss*
Canadian Forces (CF) 8, **9** *endnotes*, 10, 16, 18, **37** *endnotes*, 46, **57, 71, 76** *endnotes*, 84, 113, **118, 126, 140** *endnotes*, 145, **166, 187, 190** *endnotes*, 193, **210** *endnotes*, 214, **234** *endnotes*, 235, **237** *gloss*
Canadian Forces College 151
Canadian Forces Grievance Board 118
Canadian Forces Leadership Institute (CFLI) 3, 10, 39, 71, 126, 210, 217, 234, 235, **237** *gloss*
Canadian Forces National Investigation Service (CFNIS) 145, **237** *gloss*
Canadian Forces Provost Marshal 145
Canadian Press 146, **165** *endnotes*
Caputo, Philip 177, **190** *endnotes*
careerism 194
Cassels, Lieutenant Richard 58, 59, **73, 74, 81, 84** *endnotes*
Carignan, Private Sid 47
categories of discontent 121, 122
    existential 122, 123, 124
    material 122, 123, 124
chain of command 13, 14, 23, 24, 45, 65, 71, **83** *endnotes*, 116, 118, 119, 127, 134, 136, 137, 150, 152, 161, 162, 163, 164, 203, 205, 206, 208, 220, 231
character 31, 36, 37, 43, 197, 208, **210, 212** *endnotes*
Charbonneau, Leo 122, **126** *endnotes*
Chief of Army Staff 34
Chief of the Defence Staff (CDS) **9** *endnotes*, 118, 194, **237** *gloss*
Chief of the Imperial General Staff 133
Chief of the Naval Staff 105
Chindit 174, 181
Churchill, Winston i, 133, **142** *endnotes*
Clancy, Tom 127, 130, 131, 134, **137, 140, 141** *endnotes*
Claxton, Brooke 104, 105, **112** *endnotes*
Code of Service Discipline 31, 88, **109, 125** *endnotes*
Cohen, Eliot 130, 131, 134, **139, 141, 142** *endnotes*
cohesion 19, 35, 36, 37, **40** *endnotes*, 41, 66, 132, 134, **136** *endnotes*, 141, 148, 180, 182, 184, 185, 186, 203, 204, 209, **212, 233** *endnotes*
    horizontal 20, 35, 92, **234** *endnotes*
    vertical 35, 91, 92, **129, 138** *endnotes*
Cole, Lieutenant-Colonel Robert 174
Colmar Pocket 176
Combat Leaders' Course 231
Combat Motivation 21, **39, 72, 76, 83, 141, 190, 192** *endnotes*
combat refusal 115, 150
Combat Stress Reaction (CSR) 145, 147, 148, **237** *gloss*
Command and Control 6, **40** *endnotes*, 150, 151, 153, **161** *endnotes*, 166, 236
    authority

INDEX

legal 14, 29, 55, 56, 60, 65, 87, 88, 92, 115, 151, 152, 162, 163, 164, 180, **233** *endnotes*

personal 2, 17, 18, 25, 28, 30, 31, 32, 36, 37, 38, 43, 55, 56, 57, 68, **74, 76, 78, 79, 80, 83** *endnotes*, 96, 97, 148, 151, 152, 155, 162, 164, 171, 179, 193, 194, 195, 198, 201, 202, 204, 205, 206, 207, 208, 213, 219, 222

    competency 151, 152, 161, 162, 163, 164

        emotional 20, 83, 122, 151, 152, 161, 162, 163, 164, 170, 177, 178, 182

        intellectual 1, 128, 151, 152, 161, 163, 164

        interpersonal 151, 152, 161, 162, 163, 164

        physical 61, 68, 69, 70, 130, 132, **140** *endnotes*, 147, 148, 151, 152, 154, 161, 163, 164, 172, 174, 175, 177, 181, 185, 195, 201, 202, 207, **211** *endnotes*

    responsibility 7, **10, 39, 44** *endnotes*, 49, 63, 70, 77, 78, **94** *endnotes*, 95, 100, 151, 152, 153, 154, 162, 163, 164, 184, 193, 194, 195, 196, 197, 203, 204, 205, 206, 208, 209, 210, 218, 224, 237

        extrinsic 151, 162, 163, 164

        intrinsic 151, 152, 163, 164

commander's intent **11** *endnotes*, 28, 29, 34, 206

    explicit 24, 34, 35, 46, 121, 202, 207, 210, 223

    implicit 16, 21, 34, 35, 38, 43, **83** *endnotes*, 106, 119, 209

Commonwealth 2, **10, 72, 73, 77, 84, 110** *endnotes*

communication 7, 19, 34, 36, 54, 67, 202, 219, 229

conformity 5, 13, 19, 26, 34, 36, 137

Congress 116

Coroy, Sergeant First Class James 179

Cot, General Jean 155, 156, 157

Cottingham, Sergeant Peter 173, **188** *endnotes*

Cotton, Charles 134, **141** *endnotes*

court-martial 116, 201

Crawford, Major Reg 181, **191** *endnotes*

Crisp, Robert 184

Croatia 6, 25, 49, **77** *endnotes*, 145, 147, 150, 151, 152, 153, 154, 156, 160, 161, **165, 166** *endnotes*, 235

Croatia Board of Inquiry (CBOI) 49, **77** *endnotes*, 145, 146, 154, 155, 156, 157, 159, 160, 161, 163, **165, 166** *endnotes*, 235, **237** *gloss*

Croatians (Croats) 154, 155, 156, 157, 158, 159, 160

Cru, Jean Norton 13, **38** *endnotes*

cult of the elite 6, 127, 134

culture 6, 7, **9** *endnotes*, 13, 19, 24, 38, **39** *endnotes*, 40, 46, 66, **68, 74** *endnotes*, 75, 126, 134, 137, 147, 174, 180, 194, 198, 209, 214, 215, 216, 217, 224, 225, 226, 227, 228, 229, 230, **232, 233, 236** *endnotes*

Cyprus 56, **233** *endnotes*

D-Day (Normandy Invasion) 175, 191, **192** *endnotes*

Dallaire, Romeo 29

Darby, William 135, **142** *endnotes*

INDEX

Davis, Sergeant James 49, 60, **77, 80, 81** *endnotes*
Day, Adam 28, **40** *endnotes*
De La Billiere, General 135, **141, 142** *endnotes*
de Vries, Jan 173
Debrief the Leaders Project **77** *endnotes*, 116, 117, **125** *endnotes*
dehumanization 199
deontological 24, 29
Dieppe 26, 28, **40** *endnotes*, 183, 191, **192** *endnotes*
diffusion of responsibility 7, 195, 196, 197
Dinter, Elmar 136, 141, **142, 171** *endnotes*, 178, **188, 190, 192** *endnotes*
Director of Intelligence and Special Operations 127
Director of Medical Services 184
Director of Personal Services 96
discipline 1, 3, 7, 8, **9, 10, 11** *endnotes*, 14, 15, 19, 30, 31, 35, **38, 39** *endnotes*, 43, 44, 45, 46, 48, 51, 53, 55, 56, 57, 59, 63, 65, 67, 70, 71, **72, 73, 74, 75, 76, 78, 79** *endnotes*, 87, 88, 90, 94, 95, 96, 97, 101, 103, 104, 105, 106, 107, **108, 109, 110** *endnotes*, 113, 115, 121, 122, **125** *endnotes*, 130, 134, 135, 136, 137, 160, 169, 180, 182, **190, 191** *endnotes*, 207, 213, 218, 220, **232, 233** *endnotes*
disobedience 1, 2, 3, 4, 5, 6, 7, 8, **9, 10** *endnotes*, 13, 17, 18, 21, 22, 23, 24, 26, 28, 29, 36, 38, **40** *endnotes*, 43, 44, 45, 46, 47, 53, 54, 56, 58, 65, 66, 67, 69, 71, **72, 73, 74, 75, 79, 83, 85** *endnotes*, 94, 96, 98, 104, 107, 115, 117, 122, 127, 128, 134, 136, 137, 145, 147, 161, 164, 169, 171, 175, 178, 179, 180, 182, 185, 186, 187, 193, 206, 232
Divine, David 97, 98, **110** *endnotes*
divisional system 117
Dollard, John 170, 176, 177, 178, 181, 184, 185, **187, 190, 191, 192** *endnotes*
double-cropping 215
Dowler, George 6, 74, 145, 235
Drew, Major Dan 155, **166** *endnotes*
Ducournau, General 129
Dunbar, Colonel 176
Dunham, Fredrick 63, **82** *endnotes*
Durkheim, Emile 122, **126** *endnotes*, 217, **234** *endnotes*
Duty with Honour - The Profession of Arms in Canada **10** *endnotes*, 194, 207, **210, 212** *endnotes*

Eastern (Russian) Front 173
elite 6, 127, 128, 129, 130, 131, 132, 133, 134, 135, 136, 137, **138, 139, 140, 141, 142** *endnotes*
Elleman, Bruce 88, 91, 92, **108, 109** *endnotes*
English, Allan **9, 82** *endnotes*, 147, **165** *endnotes*
Erdut Ceasefire Agreement 156
esprit de corps **41** *endnotes*
ethnic cleansing 25, 27, 159, 164
ethos 7, 31, 36, **41, 74** *endnotes*, 124, **126** *endnotes*, 193, 194, 204, 206, 207,

INDEX

208, 209, 210, 224
Etzioni-Halevy, Eva 130, **138** *endnotes*
Eversmann, Specialist Matthew 181
everyday resistance 7, 215, 222
Exhibition Camp 60
exit 118, 119, 120, 121, **122, 126** *endnotes*

Farley, Lieutenant-Colonel Kelly 36, **41** *endnotes*
fear 6, 7, 8, 51, 106, 148, 149, 151, 169, 170, 171, 172, 173, 174, 175, 176, 177, 178, 179, 180, 181, 182, 183, 184, 185, 186, **187, 188, 189, 190, 191** *endnotes*, 192, 203
First World War **9, 11, 14** *endnotes*, 21, 24, 30, 48, 50, 61, 64, 69, 71, **72, 73, 78, 81, 82** *endnotes*, 122, 172, 173, 178, 228, **234** *endnotes*
Flanagan, John 185
followership 35
Fort Duquesne 173
Fort Hunter Ligget 154
Fort Ord 154
Foucault, Michel 1, **232, 233** *endnotes*
fragging 3, **11**, 149, 150, **166** *endnotes*
France 26, **76, 83** *endnotes*, 91, 114, **138** *endnotes*
Fraser, Donald 48, 59, 76, **77, 81, 187, 188** *endnotes*
Frederick the Great 169
French Foreign Legion 129, **138, 139** *endnotes*
Fritz, Stephen G. 177, **187, 188, 189, 190, 191** *endnotes*

Gallabat 176
Genert, Major William 19, **39** *endnotes*
Geneva Conventions 200, **211** *endnotes*
Genovese, Catherine 195, 196, 197, 204
Ghosts of Medak Pocket 26, **40, 166** *endnotes*
Giddens, Anthony 217, **234** *endnotes*
Gimblett, Richard **74** *endnotes*, 105, **108, 110, 111, 112, 125** *endnotes*
Goffman, Erving 221, 222, **234** *endnotes*
Gosse, Captain D.R. 158, **166** *endnotes*
Grabb, Inspector Russ 146, **165** *endnotes*
Granatstein, Jack 53, **77, 78** *endnotes*
Grant, Major 173
Grant, Vice-Admiral Harold 105
Gray, Colin 130, **139** *endnotes*
Gray, Glenn 209
Gray, Jeffrey Alan 171, **187** *endnotes*
Great Britain 2, 3, 5, **84** *endnotes*, 94, **108, 232** *endnotes*
Greer, Lieutenant-Colonel 60
Groos, Lieutenant-Commander D.W. 103

INDEX

Grossman, Lieutenant-Colonel Dave 178, **189, 190, 192** *endnotes*, 209, **211, 212** *endnotes*
grousing 60, 62
Guanabara Bay, Rio de Janeiro 90
Gulf War 116, 147
Gulf War Syndrome (GWS) 147, **237** *gloss*
Guttridge, Leonard 2, **10, 11, 108** *endnotes*

Halifax 1, **9, 81** *endnotes*, 98
Hamby, Joel 45, **73, 74, 76, 78, 79, 80, 84** *endnotes*, 114, 122, **125, 126** *endnotes*
Hamilton, V. Lee **10** *endnotes*, 15, 16, **39, 188, 189, 210, 211, 212** *endnotes*
HARMONY, Operation 52, **78** *endnotes*, 147, 152, 153, **165** *endnotes*
Hart, Major-General T.S. 184
Hartford, Master Warrant Officer Daniel 145, **165** *endnotes*
Hartigan, Corporal Dan **76** *endnotes*, 174
Hathaway, Jane 2, **10, 11, 108, 125** *endnotes*
Hayter, John 47
Hennessy, Vice-Admiral Ralph 99
Hewson, Major-General C.W. 44, **73, 75** *endnotes*
Hewson Report 75
Hibbert, Captain Jimmy 102
Hill 41 176
Hirschmann, Albert O. 118, 119, 120, **121, 126** *endnotes*
Hockey, John 216, 217, 228, 229, 233, **234** *endnotes*
Hoffmeister, Bert 48, **72, 77, 80** *endnotes*
Hollywood 129
Holmes, Richard 35, **40, 41** *endnotes*, 47, 68, **72, 73, 76, 84, 190, 192** *endnotes*, 228, **234** *endnotes*
Holms, Commander W.B.L. 99, 100
horizontal escalation 92
Horn, Colonel Bernd i, vii, 6, 7, **39, 40, 75, 76, 79, 82, 83, 84** *endnotes*, 127, 169, **192** *endnotes*, 235
Horne, Sergeant 177
Huntington, Samuel 14, 23, 28, **38, 39** *endnotes*

incidents 5, 87, 88, 89, 90, 91, 93, 95, 96, 97, 98, 99, 102, 104, 106, 107, 108, 111, 112, 114, 115, 147, 149, 164, 178, 196, 199, 230
indiscipline 6, 10, 43, 45, 69, 96, 109, 110, 113, 115, 125
indoctrination 13
influence 5, 15, 16, 17, 18, 19, 22, 25, 26, 30, 31, 32, 33, 35, 36, 38, **40** *endnotes*, 43, 47, 66, **74** *endnotes*, 89, 124, 128, 141, 150, 172, 179, 182, 185, 195, 197, 200, 201, 202, 206, 208, 209, 230
informal relationships 218, 219, 220, 221, 223, 229, 231
    association **76** *endnotes*, 105, **188, 189** *endnotes*, 220, 221, 223, 225, 226, 227, 229, 231

close friendship 219, 220
friendship 199, 219, 220, 221, 223, 231
informal access 220, 223, 225, 227, 229, 231
nodding acquaintance 220
informal revenge 7, 213, 214, 215, 222, 224, 225, 228, 229, 230, 231, 232
Institute of Psychiatry (London) 171, 172
insubordination **9** *endnotes*, 45, 71, 72, 88, 89, 91, 92, 95, 96, 106, **110** *endnotes*, 114, 115, 136
integrity 15, 19, 36, 37, **39** *endnotes*, 194, 207
Invergordon **10** *endnotes*, 95, 96, 97, 106, **109** *endnotes*, 110
Iraq 115, 121, **125** *endnotes*, 148, 149, **166** *endnotes*
Iroquois 179, **191** *endnotes*
Italy 48, 51, 57, **74** *endnotes*, 177

James, Lawrence 2, **10** *endnotes*, 49, 60, **73, 77, 83, 84, 110, 112** *endnotes*, 129, 131, **140, 141** *endnotes*, 179, **188** *endnotes*, 215, **232, 233** *endnotes*
Jones, James 129
Jones, Private Mervin 173, **211** *endnotes*
Junger, Ernst 173

Kalay, E. 37, **41** *endnotes*
Keene, Louis 65, **83** *endnotes*
Kellett, Anthony 21, 30, **39** *endnotes*, 66, **72, 76, 83, 190, 192** *endnotes*
Kelman, Herbert **10**, 15, 16, 30, 36, 38, 39, **210, 211, 212** *endnotes*
Kentish, Brigadier-General Reginald John 43, 44, 45, 54, 56, 59
Kenward, Colonel Peter 132
Kibeho 27
Kietel, Field-Marshall Wilhelm 14, **38** *endnotes*
Kigali 29
Kinmel Park 1
Kirke, Charles 7, 213, 233, **234** *endnotes*, 236
Kitchen, Martin 127, 131, 137, **138, 140** *endnotes*
Kite, Sergeant John 169
Kocour, Max 183
Korea **9** *endnotes*, 47, 58, 64, **76, 80, 83** *endnotes*
Korean War 56, **75** *endnotes*, 164, 175
Kosovo 116, 235
Kronstadt 90

Lammers, Cornelis 88, **108, 109** *endnotes*
Lapointe, Arthur 60, **81** *endnotes*
Lay, H. Nelson 98, 99, 100, 102, 110, 111, 154
Leaders' Manual for Combat Stress Control 148, **165** *endnotes*
leadership v, vii, 3, 5, 6, 7, **10, 11** *endnotes*, 14, 16, 18, 19, 30, 31, 33, 34, 35, 36, 37, 38, **39, 40, 41** *endnotes*, 43, 44, 45, 46, 47, 48, 49, 50, 51, 52, 53, 54,

55, 63, 67, 68, 69, 70, **71, 72, 73, 74, 75, 76, 79, 80, 83, 84, 85** *endnotes*, 90, 93, 94, 96, 100, 104, 113, 114, 116, 124, **125, 126** *endnotes*, 132, 133, 134, **138, 141, 143** *endnotes*, 145, 148, 149, 150, 160, 161, 162, 163, 164, 165, **166** *endnotes*, 169, 179, 180, 182, 185, 186, **187, 188, 190, 191** *endnotes*, 193, 194, 196, 202, 203, 204, 206, 208, 209, **210, 212** *endnotes*, 217, 230, **234** *endnotes*, 235, 236
    transactional 37, 38
    transformational 16, 36, 38, **212** *endnotes*
Leadership in Organizations 31, **39, 40** *endnotes*
Leadership in the Canadian Forces: Conceptual Foundations 16, 18, 37, **39, 71, 126, 187** *endnotes*
Lester, Edward 62, 64, 82, **83** *endnotes*
Lloyd, Mark 131, **140** *endnotes*
lock-ins 5, 101, 106, 107, 115
Loomis, Dan 47, 64
Lord Lovat 182
Lord Melgund 57
loyalty 14, 15, 19, 24, 35, 36, 37, **38, 41** *endnotes*, 54, **79** *endnotes*, 118, 119, 120, 121, 123, 124, **126** *endnotes*, 136, 194, 205, 207, 218, 223, 225, 227
Lucas, James 131, **140** *endnotes*
Ludwig, Hans-Heinrich 173

Mainguy, E.R. 104, **108** *endnotes*
Mainguy Report **74** *endnotes*, 104, 105, 108, 109, 110, 111, 112, 125
Malaysia 215, **232** *endnotes*
malingering 3, 149
manifestly unlawful 5, 23
Manning, F.P. 37, **41** *endnotes*, 163, 164
Manual of Military Law (British) 71, **84** *endnotes*, 216, **232, 233** *endnotes*
Manzanillo, Mexico 103
Marine Corps, United States (USMC) 177, 185, **188, 189** *endnotes*, **239** *gloss*
market theory 120
Marshall, S.L.A. 50, 171, 174, 175, 184, **189** *endnotes*
Maslenica Bridge 157, 158, 164
Masters, Major John 181
McAndrew, Bill 69, **84, 111** *endnotes*
McCann, Carol 6, 34, **39, 40** *endnotes*, 150, 151, 152, 153, 162, **166, 212** *endnotes*
Medak Pocket 26, **40** *endnotes*, 150, 158, 164, **166** *endnotes*
Medland, Commander M.A. 103
Merryweather, Sergeant (pseudonym) 224, 225
Middleton, Frederick 57
Mielert, Harry 177
Miles, Commodore G.R. 104
Milgram, Stanley 5, 13, 19, 20, 21, 26, 30, 31, 33, 34, 36, 39
Miller, Carman **8** *endnotes*, 66, **72, 75, 80** *endnotes*

INDEX

Miller, David 131, **140** *endnotes*
Minister of National Defence 64, 104
mission command 34, 206
Mogadishu 181
Monongahela River 173
Montgomery, Field-Marshal Bernard Law 179, 182, **190, 191** *endnotes*
morale **11** *endnotes*, 36, 37, **41** *endnotes*, 43, 45, 55, 56, 57, 59, 60, 61, 62, 63, 65, 66, 69, **72, 77** *endnotes*, 100, 102, 103, 104, 105, **110** *endnotes*, 133, 174, 177, 185, **190, 191** *endnotes*
Morale and Service Conditions Report 102, 105
Morice, Commander Reginald 99, 100
Morris, Eric 130, **135, 140, 141** *endnotes*
Morriss, Mack 170, 180
Morton, Desmond **8, 11** *endnotes*, 46, **74, 79, 80, 81** *endnotes*, 84, 178, **190** *endnotes*
motivation 18, 21, 24, 30, 36, **39** *endnotes*, 45, 64, 66, **72, 76, 83** *endnotes*, 132, **141, 190, 192** *endnotes*, 228
mutiny 1, 2, 3, 5, 6, 7, **9, 10, 11** *endnotes*, 14, 26, **38, 41** *endnotes*, 45, 48, 50, 56, 60, 62, 69, 71, **73, 74, 76, 77, 78, 79, 80, 82, 84** *endnotes*, 87, 88, 89, 90, 91, 92, 93, 94, 95, 96, 97, 98, 99, 100, 101, 102, 104, 105, 106, 107, **108, 109, 110, 111** *endnotes*, 113, 114, 115
    major 37, 46, 88, 89, 94, 95, **126** *endnotes*, 134, 153, 171, 172, 198, 213, 230
    minor 22, 47, 70, **79** *endnotes*, 88, 89, 90, 91, 92, 93, 94, 95, 96, 97, 98, 103, 106, 107, 148, 182, 198, 213
   seizure of power 88, 90, 91
   succession 103, 106
My Lai 35, 199

Nanking 103
National Defence Act (Canada) 14, 88, 93, **109** *endnotes*, 115, **125** *endnotes*
Naval Defence Act (British) 88
Naval Discipline Act (British) **108** *endnotes*
Navy, Brazilian 90
Navy, French 91, **109, 111** *endnotes*
Navy, German 90, 99, 110, 111
   High Seas Fleet 90
Navy, Royal (RN) 5, 87, 88, 89, 104, 106, 109, **110** *endnotes*, 235, **239** *gloss*
   Atlantic Fleet 89, 95, 96
   RN College Greenwich 96
   Ships
      Bounty 90
      Nabob 100, 102
      Warspite 97, **110** *endnotes*
Navy, Royal Canadian (RCN) 5, **73, 74** *endnotes*, 87, **108, 109** *endnotes*, 115,

INDEX

125 *endnotes*, 235, **239** *gloss*
    Royal Naval College of Canada 94
    Ships
        Assiniboine 99
        Athabaskan 103, 106, **108** *endnotes*
        Chebogue 100, 102
        Crescent 103, 105, 106, **108** *endnotes*
        Iroquois 99, 102, **108** *endnotes*
        Magnificent 91, 104, 106, **109** *endnotes*
        Micmac 102
        Niobe 98
        Nootka 102
        Ontario **10** *endnotes*, 58, 102, 104, 105, **111, 165, 187, 191** *endnotes*
        Reindeer 99
        Rivière-du-Loup 91, 101, 102
        Skeena 98
        Swansea 106
        TR 30 98
    Volunteer Reserve 99, 105, **239** *gloss*
NBC News 149, **166** *endnotes*
Neal, Dominic 176
negotiated order 216, 228, **234** *endnotes*
New York **10** *endnotes*, 11, **27, 39,** 72, **83, 84,** 108, **126,** 137, **138, 139, 140, 141, 142, 187, 188, 189, 190, 191** *endnotes*, 210, 211, 232, 233 *endnotes*
New York Times 195, **210** *endnotes*
Nixon, President Richard 150
Non-Commissioned Officer (NCO) 2, 17, 27, 28, 82 *endnotes*, 135, 136, 145, 149, 160, 170, 213, 226, **238** *gloss*
Norfolk, Virginia 100
normative social influence 195, 197
North Africa 171, 184, 186, **188** *endnotes*
North Atlantic Treaty Organization (NATO) 116, **238** *endnotes*
North West Rebellion 57, 58, 69, **74** *endnotes*
Noy, S. 33, **40** *endnotes*

oath of allegiance 14
obedience 4, 5, **10** *endnotes*, 13, 14, 15, 17, 18, 19, 20, 21, 23, 26, 31, 34, 35, 36, 37, **38, 39, 41** *endnotes*, 45, 52, 57, **76, 77, 82, 84** *endnotes*, 89, 116, 117, 119, 123, 137, 169, 194, 205, **210** *endnotes*, 228, 232
obligations 23, 24, 29, 37, **77** *endnotes*, 103, 194, 201, 204, 205, 207, 208
    hierarchical 14, 23, 35, 38, 127, 205
    non-hierarchical 23
Odlum, Brigadier-General Victor 61
Oehring, Colonel George 159, 160, **167** *endnotes*
Off, Carol 26, **40, 166** *endnotes*

INDEX

Omaha Beach 175
Ombudsman 113, 118, 119, **123, 126** *endnotes*, 235
On Fostering Integrity 19, **39** *endnotes*
Onasander 171
open door policies 118
Ortner, Sherry 215, **233** *endnotes*
Osiel, Mark 24, 26, **38, 40, 41, 78, 83** *endnotes*
Ottawa 9, **40, 41** *endnotes*, 57, **73, 74, 76, 78** *endnotes*, 100, 102, **109, 111, 112, 126, 138, 140, 165, 167, 190, 190, 192, 210** *endnotes*

Palmer, Colonel Ian 175, 184, 189, **190, 191, 192** *endnotes*
Panama Canal 100
Parsons, Lieutenant (pseudonym) 224, 225
Pearkes, George Randolph 64, **82** *endnotes*
Performance Development Report (PDR) 22, **238** *gloss*
Perrault, Gilles 130, **139** *endnotes*
personal consequences 195, 202
Personnel Evaluation Report (PER) 22, **238** *gloss*
Peruca Dam 156
Petawawa, Canadian Forces Base (CFB) 57, **237** *gloss*
Phillips, Colonel 27, 28, 29
Pigeau, Ross 6, 34, **39, 40** *endnotes*, 150, 151, 152, 153, 162, **166, 212** *endnotes*
Pippen, Walter 176
planned behaviour 17, 18, 31, 32
    attitudes 15, 16, 17, 18, 31, 32, 33, 35, 36, 52, 65, 87, 97, 138, **182** *endnotes*, 200, 203, 208, 209, 218, 219
        normative influences 17, 18, 33
        personal control 17, 18
Plymouth, England 99, **110** *endnotes*
Porch, Douglas 130, **138, 139** *endnotes*
Port Hope 58
Porter, John 128, **138** *endnotes*
Potemkin 91
Prisoners of War (PW) 200, **238** *gloss*
professional development v, vii, 8, 151, 207, 208, 210, 236
professionalism 131, 132, 194, 206, 210
psychic dissonance 30
psychological distance 195, 197, 198, 200, 202, **211** *endnotes*

Queen's Regulations and Orders (QR&O) 14, **39, 126** *endnotes*, **238** *gloss*

Rachman, S.J. 172, 187, 188, **189, 190, 191, 192** *endnotes*
Ramsay, Fredrick 64, **69, 83, 84, 138** *endnotes*
Ray, Dan 176
redress of grievance 113, 118

253

INDEX

Reimer, General Dennis 34, **38, 40, 41** *endnotes*
Renatus, Flavius 180
Report of the Commission of Inquiry into the Deployment of Canadian Forces to Somalia **9, 76** *endnotes*, 193, **210** *endnotes*
Rescher, Nichols 23, 24, 28, **39** *endnotes*
resistance 7, 16, 17, 21, 26, 30, 31, 33, 34, 35, 36, 38, 88, 115, 124, 134, 148, 207, 213, 214, 215, 216, 217, 219, 222, 223, 224, 225, 227, 228, 229, 230, 232, **233** *endnotes*
responsibility
    role-oriented 194, 205
    rule-oriented 205
    value-based 194, 205
responses to influence attempts
    commitment 16, 17, 30, 34, 36
    compliance 13, 15, 16, 17, 21, 29, 30, **38** *endnotes*
    resistance 16, 17, 21, 26, 30, 31, 33, 34, 35, 36, 38
Ridge, Captain William (Sammy) 51, 52
Roberts, Major-General J.H. 27, 28, 29
Robertson, Terence 26, **40** *endnotes*
Rodger, N.A.M. 88, 97, **109, 110** *endnotes*
Roosevelt, Theodore **143** *endnotes*, 183
Rose, Elihu 1, **10, 11, 73, 76, 108** *endnotes*, 114, 121, 124, **125, 126** *endnotes*, 169, 175
Roy, Reginald i, 64, **76, 82, 187, 188** *endnotes*
Royal Canadian Mounted Police (RCMP) 146, 165, **238** *gloss*
Royal Military College of Canada (RMC) **40** *endnotes*, 116, **191** *endnotes*, 235, 236, **239** *gloss*
rum **11** *endnotes*, 61, **82** *endnotes*, 183
Rumania 91
Ruppel, Howard 182
Rusden, Harold Penryn 57, 80, 81
Rwanda 27, 49

Sajer, Guy 174, 179, 184, **187, 188, 189, 192** *endnotes*
Scales, Major-General Robert 131, **140** *endnotes*, 171, 174, **188, 189** *endnotes*
Scislowski, Stanley 51, 57, 59, 67, **78, 80, 81, 83** *endnotes*
Scott, James C. 215, 216, 217, 222, 228, 229, 232, **233** *endnotes*
Searle, Glenn 173
Second World War **9** *endnotes*, 26, 36, 47, 51, 53, **73, 77, 79, 82** *endnotes*, 87, 97, 98, 99, 101, **110, 111, 112** *endnotes*, 129, 131, **142** *endnotes*, 172, 173, 174, 175, 176, 177, 178, 179, 181, 182, 184, 185, 209
Sector South 155, 156, 157, 158, 159, 160, 164
Sector West 153, 154, 155, 156, 157, 160
Serbians (Serbs) 154, 155, 156, 157, 158, 159
Shalit, Ben 175

INDEX

Sharpe, Gordon (Joe) 6, 74, 145, 235, 236
Shell Shock Committee (British, 1922) 183
Shorey, George 7, 193, 236
Showalter, Dennis 131, **140** *endnotes*
Sicily 176, **190** *endnotes*
Sidney, Sir Philip 186
Simpson, Commodore G.W.G. 101, **142** *endnotes*
sit-down strikes 107, 115
Slim, Field-Marshal Viscount 133
Slim, General W.J. 176
Smillie, Lieutenant R.N. 101
Smith, Leonard 1, **10** *endnotes*, 14, 38, **41, 76, 82, 84** *endnotes*
social power 31, 32, **39** *endnotes*
    person 15, 16, 20, 23, 31, 32, 33, 87, 153, 172, 173, 174, 178, 179, 185, 195, 196, 201, 202, 215, 222, 223
    position 31, 32, 33, 37, 44, 63, 69, 70, 88, 99, 107, 127, 146, 150, 153, 158, 159, 217, 218, 230, 233
social structure 217, 218, **219, 233** *endnotes*
    formal command 218, 219, 220, 224, 227, 228, 231
    functional 117, 119, 128, **189** *endnotes*, 219, 223, 224, 226, 228, 231
    informal 7, 15, 30, 33, 34, 35, **73** *endnotes*, 134, 202, 208, 209, 213, 214, 215, 218, 219, 220, 221, 222, 223, 224, 225, 227, 228, 229, 230, 231, 232
        loyalty / identity 218, 223, 227
socialization 13, 45, 207, 208, 209, **212** *endnotes*
Somalia 7, **9** *endnotes*, 19, 27, 29, 35, 39, 40, 54, **75, 76, 80, 140, 142, 143** *endnotes*, 193, 194, 195, 196, 197, 198, 199, 203, 206, 207, 209, **210, 211, 212** *endnotes*
Somalia Inquiry 54, 75, 80, 193, 196, 197, 198, 199, 203, 206
Somme 43
South Africa 1, 52, 58, 63, 64, 68, 69, **80, 233** *endnotes*
South African Constabulary 59, **72** *endnotes*
Soviet Union 90
Spithead 97
Squaddies: Portrait of a Subculture 216, 233, **234** *endnotes*
Stewart, David Morrison 58, **75, 81** *endnotes*
Stewart, Sergeant Walter 58, **80, 81** *endnotes*
Stirling, David 135
Stopford, Warrant Officer Matt 6, 26, 145, 146, 147, 150, 160, 161, 162, 163, 164, 165, **167** *endnotes*
Stouffer, Samuel 36, **41** *endnotes*, 132, 173, 177, 179, 181, 185, **186, 188, 190, 191, 192** *endnotes*
Strachan, Hew 178
Strauss, Anselm 216, **234** *endnotes*
systems view of organization effectiveness
    group 18, 19, 28, 30, 34, 35, 46, 47, 52, 55, 56, 60, 65, 66, **72, 78, 80,**

255

INDEX

82 *endnotes*, 87, 88, 94, 98, 103, 107, **111** *endnotes*, 114, 122, 127, 128, 129, 130, 132, 133, 134, 135, 136, 137, 140, 141, 149, 150, 153, 160, 166, 172, 176, 179, 180, 184, 185, 186, **189** *endnotes*, 194, 195, 198, 199, 201, 203, 209, **211** *endnotes*, 217, 219, 222, 223, 224, 226, **235, 237, 238**
    individual 3, 17, 18, 19, 31, 48, 53, 54, 55, 70, **74, 75** *endnotes*, 87, 89, 93, 95, 102, 103, 113, 115, 119, 123, **142** *endnotes*, 149, 150, 151, 152, 162, 163, 164, 165, 169, 170, 171, 178, 179, 181, 193, 194, 195, 198, 200, 203, 204, 207, 215, 217, 219, 220, 222, 223, 224, 228, **234** *endnotes*
        institutional 19, **39** *endnotes*, 113, 124, 136, 217
Szafranski, Richard 130, **139** *endnotes*

Thomas, Will 127, **137, 139** *endnotes*, 175, 177, **192** *endnotes*
three-process model of social influence 15, 16
    compliance **10** *endnotes*, 13, 15, 16, 17, 21, 29, 30, **38** *endnotes*, 47, 52, 54, 65, 68, **126** *endnotes*, 197, 205, 215
        identification 4, 15, 16, 24, 30, **39** *endnotes*, 148
        internalization 15, 16, 30, 36, **39** *endnotes*
Toffler Associates 130
Toronto 9, **10, 39, 40** *endnotes*, 59, 60, 69, **74, 75, 77, 78, 79, 81, 111, 112, 138** *endnotes*, 145, **165, 166, 188, 189, 190, 191, 192, 210, 211, 212** *endnotes*
Toronto Sun 145, **165** *endnotes*
Tousignant, Major-General Guy 27, 29, **40** *endnotes*
training 7, 8, 13, 21, 22, 46, 52, 56, 60, 64, **73, 74, 75, 79** *endnotes*, 87, 94, 100, 104, 105, **110, 111** *endnotes*, 114, 116, 127, 130, 131, 132, 136, **139, 141** *endnotes*, 148, 153, 154, 160, 163, 164, 165, 177, 180, 181, 182, 185, 186, 187, **188, 189, 190, 191** *endnotes*, 194, 201, 207, 209, **211** *endnotes*, 216, 236
trust 6, 15, 31, 33, 34, 35, 36, 37, **40** *endnotes*, 47, 48, 49, 52, 55, 58, 66, 67, 70, **75, 76, 83** *endnotes*, 137, 162, 163, 173, 186, 200, 219, 220
Tunisia 172
Turner, Staff Sergeant Thomas 175

U-Boat 100
Unified Task Force (UNITAF) 194, 198, **239** *gloss*
Uniform Code of Military Justice (UCMJ) 87, **108** *endnotes*, 116, 148, **239** *gloss*
United Nations (UN) 27, 29, 147, 153, 154, 155, 156, 157, 158, 159, 164, 165, 235, 236, **239** *gloss*
United Nations Assistance Mission for Rwanda (UNAMIR) 27, **239** *gloss*
United Nations Headquarters (UNHQ) **239** *gloss*
United Nations Protection Force (UNPROFOR) 147, **239** *gloss*
United States of America (US) 3, 19, 30, 34, 35, 36, 39, 40, 45, 83, 87, **108** *endnotes*, 115, 116, 118, 148, 154, 177, **235** *endnotes*, **239** *gloss*
unlimited liability 207
utilitarianism 24

INDEX

Veitch, J.A. 36, **41** *endnotes*
vertical escalation 91
Vertical Mosaic 129, **138** *endnotes*
Victory in Europe (VE) Day 1, **9** *endnotes*
Vietnam 35, 122, 124, 148, 149, 150, 177, 183, 199, **210** *endnotes*
Villar, R.N. 184
Virgil 176
Virtue-based 29
voice 6, 62, 68, 113, 117, 118, 119, 120, 121, **126** *endnotes*, 184, 209, 215
Vokes, Major-General Chris 52, **78, 82** *endnotes*
Von Schell, Captain Adolf 172, **188** *endnotes*
von Thadden-Trieglaff, Leopold 173

Walzer, Michael 23, 24, 28, **39** *endnotes*
Warner, Philip 133, **141** *endnotes*
Washington, D.C. 100, **111, 141, 165, 212** *endnotes*
Washington, George 173
Waterloo, Battle of 183
Watson, Major-General David 61
Wavell, Field-Marshal Earl 63, **82** *endnotes*
Weapons of the Weak 215, **233** *endnotes*
Weimar Republic 90
welfare committees 103, 104
Wenker, Lieutenant-Colonel Kenneth 14, **38** *endnotes*
Wheeler, Michael 14, 15, 36, 37, **38, 41** *endnotes*
Whitby, Michael 99, **108, 111** *endnotes*
Winnipeg 69, 153, 160
Winslow, Donna **9** *endnotes*, 19, 35, **39, 41** *endnotes*, 137, **140, 142, 143** *endnotes*, 198, **210, 211** *endnotes*
Wintringham, T.H. 1, 10
Witnesses 160, 195, 196, 197, 204
Wood, John T. 62, 171, 187, **188** *endnotes*, 199
Worthington, Peter 145, **165, 211** *endnotes*

Yugoslavia 1, **9** *endnotes*, 27, 29, 49, 60
Yukl, Gary 16, 30, 31, 32, **39, 40** *endnotes*

257